BETWEEN TWO WARS

A note for the general reader

War, Peace and Social Change: Europe 1900–1955 is the latest honours-level history course to be produced by the Open University. War and Society has always been a subject of special interest and expertise in the Open University's History Department. The appeal for the general reader is that the five books in the series, taken together or singly, consist of authoritative, up-to-date discussions of the various aspects of war and society in the twentieth century.

The books provide insights into the modes of teaching and communication, including the use of audio-visual material, which have been pioneered at the Open University. Readers will find that they are encouraged to participate in a series of 'tutorials in print', an effective way to achieve a complete command of the material. As in any serious study of a historical topic, there are many suggestions for further reading, including references to a Course Reader, set book and to two collections of primary documents which accompany the series. It is possible to grasp the basic outlines of the topics discussed without turning to these books, but obviously serious students will wish to follow up what is, in effect, a very carefully designed course of guided reading, and discussion and analysis of that reading. The first unit in Book I sets out the aims and scope of the course.

Open University students are provided with supplementary material, including a *Course Guide* which gives information on student assignments, summer school, the use of video-cassettes, and so on.

War, Peace and Social Change: Europe 1900–1955

Book I Europe on the Eve of War 1900–1914

Book II World War I and Its Consequences

Book III Between Two Wars

Book IV World War II and Its Consequences

Book V War and Change in Twentieth-Century Europe

Prepared by the course team and published by the Open University Press, 1990

Other material associated with the course

Documents 1: 1900–1929, eds Arthur Marwick and Wendy Simpson,
Open University Press, 1990

Documents 2: 1925–1959, eds Arthur Marwick and Wendy Simpson,
Open University Press, 1990

War, Peace and Social Change in Twentieth-Century Europe, eds Clive Emsley, Arthur Marwick and Wendy Simpson, Open University Press, 1990 (Course Reader)

Europe 1880–1945, J. M. Roberts, Longman, 1989 (second edition) (set book)

If you are interested in studying the course, contact the Student Enquiries Office, The Open University, PO Box 71, Milton Keynes MK7 6AG.

Cover illustration: '*Komsomol – Udarnaya Brigada Pyatletki*' ('The Young Communist League is the shock battalion of the Five-Year Plan'); poster by Vladimir Lyushin, 1931 (reproduced by kind permission of Sovietsky Khudozhnik Publishers).

WAR, PEACE AND SOCIAL CHANGE: EUROPE 1900–1955
BOOK III

BETWEEN TWO WARS

*John Golby, Bernard Waites, Geoffrey Warner,
Tony Aldgate and Antony Lentin*

**OPEN
UNIVERSITY
PRESS**

Open University Press
in association with
The Open University

TheOpen
University

A318 Course team

Tony Aldgate   *Author*
Kate Clements   *Editor*
Charles Cooper   *BBC Producer*
Henry Cowper   *Author*
Ian Donnachie   *Author*
Nigel Draper   *Editor*
Clive Emsley   *Author*
David Englander   *Author*
John Golby   *Author*
John Greenwood   *Liaison Librarian*

Antony Lentin   *Author*
Arthur Marwick   *Author and Course Team Chair*
Ray Munns   *Cartographer*
Bill Purdue   *Author*
Wendy Simpson   *Course Manager*
Tag Taylor   *Designer*
Bernard Waites   *Author*
Geoffrey Warner   *Author*

Open University Press
Celtic Court
Buckingham
MK18 1XW
England

and
1900 Frost Road, Suite 101
Bristol, PA 19007, USA

First published in 1990. Reprinted 1992, 1994, 1995

British Library Cataloguing in Publication Data

War, peace and social change: Europe 1900–1955.
  Between two wars.
  1. Europe, History
  I. Open University, A318 *War, peace and Social Change Course Team*   II. Open University   III. Colby, John
  940

  ISBN 0-335-09309-4
  ISBN 0-335-09308-6 (pbk)

Library of Congress Cataloging number is available

Designed by the Graphic Design Group of the Open University

This book is set in 10/12pt Palatino by Rowland Phototypesetting Ltd
Bury St Edmunds, Suffolk

Printed and bound in Great Britain by Butler & Tanner Ltd
Frome, Somerset
1.4

CONTENTS

Acknowledgements

Grateful acknowledgement is made to the following sources for permission to reproduce material in this book

Text

Excerpt from 'The Waste Land' in *Collected Poems 1909–1962* by T. S. Eliot, copyright 1936 by Harcourt Brace Jovanovich, Inc./Faber and Faber Ltd., copyright © 1964, 1963 by T. S. Eliot reprinted by permission of the publishers; Richard Meran Barsam, *Filmguide to 'Triumph of the Will'*, Indiana University Press, 1975, reprinted by permission of the publisher; Jean Seaton and Ben Pimlott, *The Media in British Politics*, Gower Publishing Co. Ltd., 1987.

Tables

Table 15.1: C. Hakim, *Occupational Segregation*, Research Paper, No. 9, Department of Employment, 1975; Table 15.3: Ingvar Svennilson, *Growth and Stagnation in the European Economy*, United Nations Economic Commission for Europe, 1954; Table 15.4: M. P. Fogarty, *Prospects of the Industrial Areas of Great Britain*, Methuen, 1945; Table 16.2: A. Nove, *An Economic History of the USSR*, Penguin, 1969; Tables 17.1, 17.4 and 17.5: B. R. Mitchell, *European Historical Statistics 1750–1975*, 1981; Tables 17.2 and 17.3: Carlo M. Cipolla (ed.) *The Fontana Economic History of Europe*, vol. 6, William Collins, Sons & Co. Ltd., 1976; Table 17.6: Paul Bairoch, 'International industrialization levels 1750–1980', *Journal of European Economic History*, vol. 11, no. 2, Fall 1982; Tables 18.1 and 18.2: J. Noakes and G. Pridham (eds) *Nazism 1919–1945*, vol. 2, University of Exeter, 1984; Table 19.1: David Welch, *Propaganda and the German Cinema 1933–1945*, Oxford University Press, 1983; Table 19.2: M. S. Phillips, 'The Nazi control of the German film industry', *Journal of European Studies*, vol. 1, March 1971.

UNIT 14 THE WESTERN DEMOCRACIES: ECONOMIC AND POLITICAL CHANGES 1918–1929

John Golby

Open University students of this unit will need to refer to:

Set book: J. M. Roberts, *Europe 1880–1945*, Longman, 1989

Course Reader: *War, Peace and Social Change in Twentieth-Century Europe*, eds Clive Emsley, Arthur Marwick and Wendy Simpson, Open University Press, 1990

Documents 2: 1925–1959, eds Arthur Marwick and Wendy Simpson, Open University Press, 1990

Audio-cassette 3

INTRODUCTION

The aims of Unit 14 are:

● to survey the political and economic conditions of the Western democracies immediately after and in the decade following World War I, and to determine to what extent these conditions were different from those in the pre-war years, and whether the changes that occurred were a result of the war or were already discernible in the years before 1914;

● to examine the extent to which, in these years, the policies of the governments of France, Britain and Germany were constrained by the destruction caused by the war, and the ways in which the three countries coped with the problems created by the war;

● to continue the theme of historiographical controversy by looking in some detail at one particular interpretation of Europe in the years after World War I, first put forward in 1975 by the American historian, Charles S. Maier, in his book *Recasting Bourgeois Europe*.

1 POST-WAR WESTERN EUROPE

There is no doubt that despite the profound relief and euphoria felt by the ending of World War I, the peoples of Europe faced an uncertain future. A war fought on such an unprecedented scale and for such a length of time had inevitably led to the exhaustion of both populations and capital resources. In Book II, Units 8–10, we examined the extent to which the economies and social structures of the different European countries had been affected by the war. The Russian Revolution of 1917 and the very future of a defeated Germany also raised a whole range of political expectations and concerns. Yet, after looking at all the upheavals that had occurred during the course of the war and all the uncertainties that existed in 1918, what is remarkable is the degree of social stability achieved by the Western democracies in the following decade. The questions how and why this came about lie at the centre of Charles S. Maier's study of Western Europe during this period. In a political and economic climate where, so he argues, revolution or, at the least, marked internal instability might well have been expected, it is, in Maier's words, 'Continuity and stability that need explanation'.

The reasons for spending time on the thesis put forward by Maier are threefold. First, and most important, Maier raises the sort of questions which are central to the concerns of this course. Secondly, his book *Recasting Bourgeois Europe* (1975), is generally regarded as an important contribution to the study of Europe in the inter-war years. The author of the set book for this course, J. M. Roberts, wrote in *History* in 1977 that *Recasting Bourgeois Europe* was 'one of the most important works of general history to appear in the last few years'. Thirdly, Maier's book is one of the few serious comparative histories of the period we are studying. In fact, the full title of the book is *Recasting Bourgeois Europe: Stabilization in France, Germany and Italy in the Decade after World War I*. Although Maier concentrates on these three continental powers, there are occasional references and comparisons with Britain. In addition, in 1986 an article by Christopher J. Nottingham, 'Recasting Bourgeois Britain?', was published in the *International Review of Social History*. In this article

Nottingham attempted to assess whether in Britain there was also a 'recasting' of the political system, and use will be made of his work in comparing Britain with France and Germany.

1.1   The Maier thesis

Exercise   I want you now to read 'From Bourgeois to Corporatist Europe', the introduction to Charles S. Maier's book, reprinted on pages 131–57 of the Course Reader.

1   What are the virtues, as Maier sees them, of adopting a comparative approach to the study of this period, and why does he settle on France, Germany and Italy?

2   How does Maier define 'bourgeois' in this introduction?

3   What important wartime developments does Maier regard as significant in bringing about social change in the 1920s?

4   Does Maier contend that the problems facing governments at the end of 1918 were brought about by the war?

5   Outline briefly what Maier means by a change from 'bourgeois to corporatist Europe'.

6   Drawing upon your reading so far in this course, what possible criticisms, if any, can you make of Maier's thesis? ◼

Specimen answers   1   Maier points out that not all comparative history is fruitful. Merely looking at
and discussion   historical parallels in different societies is not necessarily rewarding or true comparative history. As he states, 'Flower arranging is not botany'. What comparative history can and must do is look not just at, for example, the developments of power élites in various societies, but at the fundamental areas where power is debated or contested. It is not enough to look at the external forms of party systems or particular issues, but rather it is necessary to ascertain 'what functions were served by supposedly comparative historical phenomena in establishing and contesting power and values'.

Maier chooses France, Germany and Italy because all three countries, despite quite different outcomes, participated in what he sees as the crucial developments in the post-war political cycle, in finding a new area of stability which was based not on old ideological beliefs but upon compromise at times, and at other times new forms of coercion. In addition, although there were major differences between the three countries, there were also fundamental similarities, particularly in the area that Maier is interested in, that is, the ground over which power was contested. Unlike Britain, for example, within all three countries there were deep ideological differences existing between the contending power élites, the political scene was fragmented and 'concepts of liberalism and labels for class distinction' were common to the three countries.

2   Maier defines 'bourgeois' primarily in terms of a 'bourgeois Europe', and he equates this with the supposed stability and values which existed in pre-war Europe and to which most conservative forces after the war wished to return. This was the crucial area of conflict in the years after the war. He argues that by the end of the nineteenth century the bourgeoisie had formed close associations with the old élites, and their major mutual concern was to defend their prerogatives from

those on the Left who were advocating fundamental changes in property and power relationships. Maier insists that in the 1920s the word 'bourgeois' was accepted as a word that stood for 'the basic social divisions of a market economy and industrial social order', and that for the conservative elements in the 1920s this image of a bourgeois Europe or a pre-1918 *ancien régime* was something worth striving to regain.

3   The two developments Maier regards as significant are:

(a)   The growth in power of organized labour which had accelerated during the war as a result of the need to effect massive economic mobilization in converting to a war production economy;

(b)   The needs of a war economy demanded attempts to control prices, the distribution of raw materials and the movement of labour. This was achieved by a variety of means but the overall effect was to erode 'the distinction between private and public sectors'.

4   No, not entirely. Maier acknowledges that even the growing power of organized labour as a political force and around the bargaining table was becoming a factor before the war. More important than this, however, so Maier contends, is that during the late nineteenth century there was a significant growth in pressure groups, and that there were growing connections between these groups and political parties. This was altering the nature of representative government. Consequently, domestic policies were no longer just the preserve of the ruling interest but were achieved through bureaucratic and centralized bargaining.

5   The prime aim of conservative thought in 1918 was to return to the social order of what Maier terms 'bourgeois Europe'. In fact, a social order was attained but it was not the restoration of a pre-1914 order. For one thing, as we have already discussed in answer 4, major transformations were already taking place before the war. In addition, there was the factor mentioned in answer 3, namely the need for a wartime large-scale concentrated industrial production which necessitated as much industrial harmony as possible, and which had resulted in the growth in power of both businessmen and organized unions. Also, after the war the notable failure of liberal parliamentary leaders to solve the post-war economic and social problems by traditional methods inevitably meant a relocation of power. So what evolved was not a return to bourgeois Europe but an eventual transformation to what Maier calls a 'corporatist' Europe. What he means by this is that major political, economic and social problems became increasingly difficult to handle in unwieldy parliamentary assemblies, and decision making was gradually relocated outside parliament to individual ministries, coalition caucuses and corporate bodies such as business corporations or trade unions. Consensus, therefore, was achieved not so much through parliaments which depended from time to time on the approval of the electorate, but through continued bargaining between the state and the major organized interests.

The word 'corporatism' will be used quite often during the remainder of this course, and a good definition appears in Abercrombie, et al., *Penguin Dictionary of Sociology*, 1984, p.55.

> A form of social organization in which the key economic, political and social decisions are made by corporate groups, or these groups and the state jointly. Individuals have influence only through their membership of corporate bodies. These include trade unions, professions, business

corporations, political pressure groups and lobbies and voluntary associations.

Maier argues that this development did not take place at a uniform pace in the three countries under examination. Although he contends corporatism was apparent in Germany and emerging in Italy by the mid 1920s, in France it was in an extremely rudimentary stage.

6   This is a difficult question considering you have only just started looking at Maier's work, but it is worth referring back to Bill Purdue's remarks in Book II, Units 8–10, section 2.3, when he discussed briefly Maier's thesis, and compared it with that of Arno J. Mayer's, *The Persistence of the Old Regime*. First, Purdue points out that Mayer and Maier cannot both be right in their analyses of pre-war Europe. Certainly, the whole of Maier's thesis is based on the assumptions that pre-war Europe was bourgeois and that post-war conservative thought was intent on returning to a bourgeois Europe. These are critical assumptions because within the Marxist tradition to which both Maier and Mayer belong, as Purdue states, 'whether a society can be termed "bourgeois" or aristocratic/old regime is the most vital of all questions, for almost all else follows from it'.

It could also be argued that defining a society in class terms is reductionist and obscures other important elements which cut across class boundaries. To be fair to Maier he does state later on in his book that, 'The defence of bourgeois Europe must be mapped in three dimensions – in terms of class, élite and interest groups' (p.19). Also, in the introduction he disclaims that 'bourgeois defence was the stake of all political conflict in the 1920s' (p.7), and he goes on to cite disputes between Catholics and anti-clerical liberals, and the roles of Italian Fascists and the 'new' European Right. Nevertheless, Maier's thesis is based primarily on the belief that the prime motivating forces for change were economic and class conflict. The questions we must keep in the forefront of our minds as we examine the Maier thesis are whether these claims can be sustained and whether or not other important elements are given due weight and consideration in his analysis of European society. □

Exercise   Before we start examining Maier's thesis in any detail, it is perhaps necessary to remind ourselves of some of the fundamental economic, political and social problems which were facing the Western governments in the years immediately after the ending of the war. To do this we need to refer back to sections 2.1, 2.2 and 2.3 of Units 8–10, and to read J. M. Roberts, *Europe 1880–1945* (1989, set book), from page 359 to the end of the first paragraph on page 362. When you have done that list briefly the major problems confronting Britain, France and Germany. ■

Specimen answers and discussion   1   The growth of organized labour during the war, which is discussed on pp. 80–1 of Units 8–10. There it is stated that in both France and Italy there was evidence of both greater trade-union power and working-class militancy by 1918. This is also reflected in Britain where trade-union membership had increased from 4.1 million in 1913 to 7.93 million in 1919 and when, in the latter year, nearly 35 million working days were lost in stoppages because of strikes. In Germany, on the other hand, there was a fall in trade-union membership during the war years as more and more men were called into the army. However, immediately after the war, in the wake of the Kaiser's departure, an enormous increase took place and in the space of two years trade-union membership rose from 2.2 million in 1918 to 9.1 million in 1920.

2   The physical damage of the war, not just in loss of lives and the damage to property and resources but in the loss of production and the shortage of goods and working capital. Europe's manufacturing production in 1920 was only three-quarters that of 1913 (Roberts, p.361).

3   'The fragmentation of the old economic system' (Roberts, p.359). The hopes that with the ending of the war would come a return to pre-war economic conditions were soon shattered. The conversion of European self-sufficient wartime economies back to peacetime international trading economies could not be achieved overnight. In the meantime, export markets had been lost, many permanently, and overall Europe's financial and trading pre-eminence was gone.

4   In any case, with regard to international trade, the war had brought about a change of mood. Mutual distrust and an understandable concern for their own particular interests led to a 'new wave of protectionist thinking' (Roberts, p.360), and however much Europeans may have 'wished to return to the prewar economic system, they were psychologically inhibited from doing so, even if the possibility had existed' (Roberts, p.362).

5   The international monetary system had altered markedly since the start of the war in 1914. The huge financial costs of the war on Britain, France and Germany had been borne by heavy borrowing and the sale of foreign assets, and this had resulted in the United States becoming the world's creditor. As Roberts points out, because of the vast manufacturing potential of the United States, the European countries were unable to repay their debts through the export of goods or raw materials to the United States. Consequently debts were paid in gold and the resulting movement of gold from Europe to the United States had the effect of undermining the stability of the European currencies.

6   Other problems which affected adversely the economy of Europe and were caused, not by war itself, but by the post-war settlements, were the reparations issue and, especially in relation to Central and Eastern Europe, the geopolitical changes made to the map of Europe. □

One other immediate matter of concern for most European countries was the demobilization of their armed forces and the release and resettling of millions of servicemen into the domestic labour market.

It is essential that you bear these points in mind when examining the political, social and economic events of the 1920s.

2 BRITAIN, FRANCE AND GERMANY IN THE 1920s

In *Europe 1880–1945* J. M. Roberts divides the years between the ending of World War I and the Depression of 1929 into two distinct periods in respect to both the economic and foreign affairs of Europe. He describes the years 1918 to 1925 as ones in which relations between the European powers were turbulent, if not dangerous, and in which the various European countries were attempting to effect their economic recoveries. By 1925, so Roberts argues, most of the problems relating to the wartime destruction of parts of Europe had mostly been overcome, economic production had been restored to pre-war levels and European currencies had been largely stabilized. The period 1925 to 1929, therefore, saw years of some prosperity and also, in relation to foreign affairs, years of growing security and optimism.

While not disagreeing fundamentally with this analysis, it is possible in following Maier's thesis of a transformation from a 'bourgeois' to a 'corporatist' Europe, to break down the period 1918 to 1925 into four key sections.

1   1918 to the end of 1919: a period of great turmoil during which industrial discontent and the threat of possible revolutions were stifled and contained by the élites and the middle classes uniting and combining against the claims of the militant Left.

2   1920 to 1921: a period in which the Left was largely defeated and which resulted in crises within the ranks of socialist parties. This in turn produced schisms and the formation of communist parties. Meanwhile, governments were unable to maintain stability primarily because of both domestic and international economic problems. The problems of reparations, inflation and revaluation seemed at times insurmountable.

3   1922 to 1923: years which Maier interprets as ones where nationalist or, on occasions, authoritarian remedies were attempted and which replaced the efforts of the Left.

4   Finally, the middle years of the 1920s to 1929 are, in Maier's term, ones of 'corporatist settlement', when the hopes of returning to a pre-1914 system had to be jettisoned, and when social and economic stability was achieved by governments but only as a result of considerable influence and power being transferred to various interest groups.

Exercise   I want you now to look at Britain, France and Germany in this period in some detail. Start by reading Roberts, the section on France, from the bottom of page 397 to the top of page 401, the United Kingdom, page 406 to the top of page 414, and Germany, page 460 to the top of page 466. Also consult document I.1 in *Documents 2*, which details figures relating to industrial disputes in the three countries in the inter-war years. While reading, keep in mind and attempt to answer the following questions:

1   What country was faced with the greatest threat to its internal stability immediately after the ending of the war and why?

2   How did the governments of the three countries deal with their internal problems?

3   Why do you think there were not greater threats to the stability of Britain, France and Germany in this period?

4   Which country underwent the greatest political changes between the start of the war and 1919? ■

Specimen answers and discussion   1   Germany. With the abdication of the Kaiser a provisional government took over and for a few months it seemed as if there might be violent revolution in Germany. Mutinies in the navy, disillusionment within the army, the setting up of councils of workers and soldiers in Berlin, and widespread industrial discontent, all contributed to making the position of the caretaker government far from secure. In addition, the economy was run down, there were grave shortages of food and fuel, and the Allies were demanding the immediate return and demobilization of troops to Germany. The Allies also continued their blockade, and the blockade could well have turned into invasion if there had been signs of the government losing control to the forces of revolution. The birth of the new republic in Germany came at a time of real crisis. It was, in Roberts's words, 'born of defeat, mutiny and revolution, and almost its first act was the acceptance of a humiliating armistice' (p.460).

So tenuous was the political power of the government, that when the newly elected National Assembly met in February 1919, it convened not in the capital, Berlin, where there were fears of uprisings, but in the Thuringian capital of Weimar.

The government's task of maintaining order was a difficult one. It was challenged on all sides:

● It was challenged by those who looked towards the Bolshevik revolution for inspiration and who criticized the provisional government for being more concerned with obtaining internal stability than with effecting major socialist changes. A German Communist Party (KPD) was formed in December 1918 but it refused to take part in the elections to the National Assembly in January 1919. However, before the elections could take place, there was an 'uprising' in Berlin. The extent to which this was a real threat to the new government has been argued over by historians. Roberts calls it a 'minor civil war' while Martin Kitchen has recently claimed that 'Far from being a determined effort by unscrupulous bolsheviks to overthrow the regime, it was an ill-considered and chaotic demonstration' organized by those who were concerned by the apparent right-wing course that the provisional government was taking (*Europe Between the Wars*, 1988, p.162). Whatever the intention, the insurrection was crushed by the army and the newly formed *Freikorps*. The government, by approving the actions of the army, was condemned by many people on the Left for betraying the cause of socialism, but its supporters argued that the prime need of government at this time was to preserve law and order. Further uprisings and strikes in other urban areas of Germany followed, and there were continuous attempts by the Communist Party to challenge the Republic, from the setting up of a Soviet Republic in Bavaria in April 1919 to the abortive *coup* in Thuringia in 1923.

● It was also challenged by those on the Right of the political spectrum who distrusted the socialist leaders, feared that the communists would gain power and who opposed the peace terms. Within this grouping Roberts refers to the 'middle classes', white-collar workers and professional men who, although relieved that it was a parliamentary system which was eventually set up rather than the Soviet model republic of councils, nevertheless disliked and continually attacked the constitution of the Weimar Republic. Many of their beliefs were based on old conservative ideas of German nationalism and a desire for the restoration of the old Bismarckian era, and also the conviction that Germany had not so much lost the war, but rather had been stabbed in the back. Consequently, Versailles to them, in Roberts's words, 'was not only brutal and unjust, it was the fruit of treason' (p.463).

In many ways, the adherents of the Right were just as much, if not more, a threat to the stability of Germany as those on the extreme Left. In 1920 Kapp attempted to set up a rival government in Berlin which, for at least a few days, was successful. The nationalists were also involved in a number of political assassinations including those of Erzberger and Rathenau, and in 1923 there was the attempted putsch in Bavaria by the National Socialist Workers' Party.

Compared with France and Germany, Britain's war losses in terms of men killed were not so great. Britain did not undergo the physical destruction that occurred in France, nor did it experience the traumatic political changes that took place in Germany in 1918. Yet while, in these terms, Britain emerged from the war relatively unscathed, from the point of view of industrial discontent and the maintenance of law and order, the period immediately after the war was one of great anxiety for the British government.

With regard to industrial discontent, one interesting point that emerges from document I.1 in *Documents 2* is that the number of strikes, the numbers of workers involved in strikes and the days lost in strikes are high for all three countries in the two years after the ending of World War I. In 1921 the figures for France drop drastically, but they remain high in both Britain and Germany. Certainly in Britain, by the end of the war, the position of trade unions had never been stronger and membership virtually doubled between 1913 and 1919. Real wages and expectations had risen, and there were increasing demands not just for greater controls in the workplace but also for wider social legislation involving employment, housing and health. These expectations had been partly fuelled by the events in Russia in 1917 and, in common with most other European countries, the shock waves of the Russian revolutions were felt and reflected in a militancy of feeling among certain sections of industrial workers. There is little doubt that the beliefs, held by at least some members of the British government, that there were close connections between Bolsheviks in Russia and industrial militants in Britain, were vastly exaggerated. Nevertheless, there were many working men and women who were not only critical of their employers and the government, but who attacked their own trade-union leaders on the grounds that they had been too accommodating in entering into agreements with the government during the war, while at the same time neglecting local and shop-floor problems. As a result a powerful local shop-steward movement had grown up, especially in the mining, engineering and railway industries. In fact, what worried the government was not so much the growth of trade unions as the seeming inability of some unions to control their members. Churchill reflected this concern in February 1919 when he complained that 'the curse of trade unionism was that *there was not enough of it*, and it was not highly enough developed to make its branch secretaries (let alone its rank and file) fall into line with the head office' (Middlemas, *The Politics of Industrial Society*, 1979, pp.143–4).

In these circumstances perhaps it is not surprising that the government was extremely fearful of direct action from groups of industrial workers within the country. A government report called, significantly, 'Revolutionary feeling during the year 1919', listed a number of the workers' grievances which included: profiteering and high prices, bad housing, 'Class hatred, aggravated by the foolish and dangerous ostentation of the rich, the publication of large dividends and distrust of a "Government of profiteers"'. Interestingly, one of the factors recorded as offsetting the possibility of revolution was the popularity of the royal family (cited in James Cronin, *Labour and Society in Britain, 1918–1979*, 1984 p. 21).

The years from 1919 to 1921 proved to be the worst for industrial disturbances in Britain this century. But the unrest was not just confined to industrial workers. At the end of 1918 there were demobilization riots and mutinies by soldiers protesting against a system which required that those most needed in industry should be released first. Eventually, most of the heat was taken out of the situation when the government changed its policy to 'first in – first out'. Potentially the most worrying of all the threatened strikes in 1919 was that by the police, which came to a head with police strikes in Liverpool and London in August of that year. The strikes were in protest against legislation recently passed forbidding policemen to belong to a trade union. This legislation had been hurriedly enacted after a strike for higher wages had taken place in August 1918 by members of the Metropolitan and City of London police forces. The government's reaction was to grant the wage rise, appoint a new police commissioner, and pass legislation with the intention that this should not occur again. As it was, in August 1919 some 1,100 out of 19,000 policemen took action in London and nearly half the police force came out in Liverpool. The government's response was firm. The army was called in to put down riots in Liverpool and all the strikers were sacked.

A loyal police force was an essential prerequisite for a government expecting major industrial unrest especially in the coal-mining industry and the railways, which had been taken over by the government during the war period. At some point decisions had to be made as to whether the government should return these industries to private ownership. Any decentralization was bound to meet with resistance from large sections of the workforce, especially the coal miners who were anxious to preserve the gains they had made and who were actively campaigning for the mines to be nationalized. So there was, in Roberts's words, much 'talk of industrial action for political purposes' (p. 389) and the threat of a general strike was one which held some weight, especially as the pre-war 'triple alliance' of railwaymen, miners and transport workers was renewed immediately after the ending of the war.

An economic boom in the months immediately following the ending of the war provided the right conditions for workers to express their grievances. The year 1919 started with talk of a general strike and the 'battle of George Square' in Glasgow, during which the red flag was raised on the roof of the town hall. Despite the red flag the strike by engineers had limited economic and not political objectives, but the reaction of the government was one of great alarm. Troops with tanks and machine guns were called in and the leaders of the strike were arrested. A potentially damaging threatened strike in the coal industry in January 1919 was averted by the setting up of a Coal Mines Commission to investigate the industry, but there was a major national railway strike in the autumn of 1919. In all, nearly 35 million days were lost in strikes in 1919.

In France there were fewer trade unionists (2 million) than in Britain and, as we can see from document I.1 in *Documents 2*, although there were fewer days lost in strikes in France than in Britain during 1919 and 1920, there were, in fact, more individual industrial disputes. The *Confédération Générale du Travail* (CGT), like many unions in Britain, had worked closely with its government during the war, and many of the gains that unionists had made during these years had come through co-operation rather than conflict. Nevertheless, just as in Britain, some French trade unionists felt this co-operation had been too close and, as Roberts states, they found their leaders 'far too moderate' (p.381). Again, as in Britain, the threat of a general strike was freely talked about but French trade unions were not as well organized as those in Britain. Although the CGT, the membership of which had risen by over a million during and immediately following the war, was reluctantly forced into calling a strike in May 1920 in support of the French railway union, who were in dispute with the government and the railway owners, the strike was a failure.

2   In Britain, France and Germany the governments acted with various mixtures of repression, compromise and conciliation, and specific social legislation. (With reference to this legislation, see table 8–10.2 in Book II, pp. 98–100.) Understandably, perhaps, in Germany, where there was the greatest threat to internal stability, so too the forces of law and order were applied most forcibly. Increasingly the major role of the socialist caretaker government in Germany in 1919 seemed to be the re-establishment of stability, in order to safeguard what had already been achieved and to ensure fair elections for the setting up of a national constituent assembly. To effect this the government relied increasingly and heavily on the army and the *Freikorps* to put down the rebellions and risings of 1919 and 1920. The decision to rely on this branch of the old order which had supported the anti-democratic and anti-reformist 1914 regime was calculated and perhaps unavoidable. There is no doubt that the use of the *Freikorps* was successful in that insurrections were contained, but the often brutal manner in which the *Freikorps* acted helped to fuel working-class resentment and created bitter hatred of the government. For example, it has been estimated that some 1,200 people were killed in the reprisals carried out by the *Freikorps* following the breaking up of the Bavarian Soviet Republic in 1919.

In France, one indication of the strength and growth of organized labour resulting from the war was the winning of the eight-hour day in 1919. However, as Roberts stated, the French workers 'had to wait until 1930 for the next instalment of social reform – national insurance against sickness and old age' (p.400). Roberts does not go on to discuss the question of law and order in France, but he gives one hint that the government would take an extremely tough and unsympathetic line towards widespread political and industrial action when he comments that the French parliament in 1919 was the most right-wing parliament since 1871. In fact the Chamber of Deputies was given the name the 'Horizon Bleu' Chamber because of the number of ex-servicemen elected to it. From the breaking up of street demonstrations in Paris in March 1919, called to protest against the release from prison of the assassin of the socialist leader, Jean Jaurès, in 1914, to the abortive general strike in 1920, the police acted vigorously and often very brutally. Government action was both direct and indirect. During the rail strike the government gave money towards the formation of volunteer militias and strike-breakers. It also applied to the law courts to dissolve the CGT and union leaders were arrested on conspiracy charges. In 1921 the government took further precautions to ensure internal stability by setting up a special police force, the *garde mobile*, to deal with demonstrations and other unrest.

In Britain a Ministry of Reconstruction had been set up in 1917 partly, so A. J. P. Taylor has argued, to 'allay Labour discontent' (*English History, 1914–1945*, 1965, p.93). Certainly, many of the reports which it issued, including one involving the reorganization of government departments, came to little. But implicit in most of the work of the Ministry was the idea that, when the war ended, the government would continue to some extent in its wartime involvement in industry and industrial relations. In respect to the latter, a proposal from one of the committees responsible to the Ministry and headed by J. H. Whitley involved the setting up of national industrial councils for individual industries, which would include both employers and trade unionists and would discuss all aspects of industrial relations including wages and hours. The idea was welcomed especially by unskilled unions and often by the smaller unions where collective bargaining was virtually unknown. By 1920 there were fifty-six 'Whitley Councils' in existence. However, most of the industries involved in the scheme were small and it was only within the civil service that the Whitley Councils played any significant role. Interest in the scheme faded and many of the fifty-six Whitley Councils gradually disappeared. This lack of enthusiasm was mirrored in the events relating to the National Industrial Conference which was set up by the government in 1919. Intended as a forum for employers and employees to discuss industrial relations, wages and hours, as well as ways to reduce unemployment, all the major unions and the Federation of British Industries were represented. The Conference made a number of proposals but eventually, in 1921, despairing of any real decisions ever being made, the trade-union members resigned from the organization.

During this period the government passed some extremely important social legislation, including a Housing Act in 1919 and two National Insurance Acts in 1920 and 1921, but with regard to improving industrial relations the government at times appeared to promise much but did little. In this respect Roberts refers to the 'conciliatory skills' of the Prime Minister, Lloyd George. Roberts argues that the setting up of the Sankey Commission and the government's acceptance of the recommendation that 'some other system' of ownership of the coal industry 'must be substituted' gave hope to the miners, and initially took the heat out of a potentially inflammatory situation with the coal miners in 1919. The fact that the government then did nothing might, in the long run, have aggravated the ill-feeling that existed in the industry, but it certainly prevented a major strike in the coal industry in 1919.

Delaying tactics were by no means the only ones used in Britain. The police force was used not only to control demonstrations but the regional special branches were co-ordinated to maintain a political surveillance of potential dissident groupings. In addition, the government set up a Committee on Industrial Unrest which was intended to deal specifically with large-scale strikes. For this purpose the country was divided into twelve departments, each with a commissioner and its own staff, so that quick action could be taken whenever any disturbance took place. During the months after the Armistice use was also made of existing wartime legislation. The Defence of the Realm Act was deployed in 1919 so that a state of emergency could be declared at the time of the rail strike. Again, in October 1920, at a time when it seemed likely that the Triple Alliance would strike in support of the miners, an Emergency Powers Act was rushed through parliament. This Act empowered the government to impose emergency regulations whenever industrial actions were threatened and might result in the disruption of essential services. The Act was again used at the time of the threatened Triple Alliance strike in 1921 when the government moved troops to the outskirts of a number of key towns, prepared for the call-up of the army reserve and approved the setting up of a special defence force of 'loyal ex-servicemen and loyal citizens'. By the time of 'Black Friday' the government's actions closely resembled, so Kenneth Morgan has argued, that 'of an anti-labour front' (Consensus and Disunity, 1979, p.280).

In Germany, as a result of the war and the conditions immediately after it, this was a period when German workers were in a strong negotiating position. In a recent article Wolfgang J. Mommsen has stated, 'during the revolutionary period neither the government nor the employers risked antagonising the workers if at all possible. Demands for higher wages were frequently conceded without much hesitation . . . government and employers alike considered relatively high wage levels and full employment politically essential, and financial policies were conducted accordingly' ('The social consequences of World War I', 1988, pp.39–40).

The government tried hard to distinguish between political and industrial disruption. Whereas most attempts to challenge the state were met with force, both the government and employers went to great lengths to conciliate and seek agreements with workers claiming better wages and working conditions. Indeed, German manufacturers were prepared to make fundamental and substantial concessions in order to ensure their continued control of their industries. In November 1918 representatives of employers and trade unions met and produced the Stinnes-Legien Agreement whereby, in return for their recognition of many trade-union bargaining rights and an acceptance of the eight-hour day, manufacturers were assured that their leadership of the various industries would not be challenged, and that there would not be a radical restructuring of industry. In Richard Bessel's words, this pact, signed on 15 November 1918, was 'one of the most important compromises on which the economic and, ultimately, political order of Weimar Germany was based' (Open University, 1987, A323 *Weimar Germany*, Study Guide, pp.22–3).

There were other compromises made in Germany. We have already mentioned the alliance between the socialist government and the old order in the form of the army. But this was not all. Despite the hopes of some that the Weimar Republic would be a much more unitary centralized state, this was not the case. Like its predecessor it was essentially federal in structure and the *Länder* remained and retained many of their executive powers. Within this structure, it was the same civil servants and judiciary who now had to cope with the problems of administering Germany in the difficult years following the ending of the war. So although the government may have been in the hands of new men, many within the ranks of the old ruling groups were still in vital and important positions. It was this series of compromises – with the army, judiciary, industrialists, trade unionists and civil servants – made in the belief that it was essential to obtain and then secure stability, that the new Weimar Republic was based, and although the new liberal constitution adhered to the principles of universal adult suffrage and proportional representation, much of the real power remained in the hands of the old order.

3   The points made in answer to the previous question will have helped to explain why there was not a greater threat to stability during this period. However, there are two important factors which we have not mentioned and which need discussing. The first is highlighted well by Roberts, namely the lack of unity or agreement among the disaffected within the three countries. In relation to Germany, Roberts mentions the split within the SPD and the emergence of the German Communist Party (KPD) in December 1918, but within this division there were further splits and disagreements. The second factor has been highlighted in an article written by Wolfgang Mommsen and first published in 1978, in which he pointed out that in many respects the political parties of the Left did not reflect the feelings of much of the working-class discontent during this period. From his research in the industrial Ruhr, Mommsen concluded that the major desire of most working men was not to embrace a political ideology which demanded revolution, but rather they wanted immediate improvements in their working

conditions and they desired nationalization, especially of the coal industry. These demands were not necessarily in line with the political programmes of the left-wing parties. So theirs was much more a social protest movement than a wish to achieve major political and other structural changes (Mommsen, 'The German Revolution 1918–1920', 1981).

In addition, although this is not touched on by Roberts, it is noticeable that the insurrections and major discontent took place in the urban areas and were not supported by workers in the rural areas. Although the period saw a great development in trade unionism among agricultural workers in Germany, there were no uprisings on any large scale.

On reflection, it is clear that belief in the existence of popular support for further radical changes, let alone further revolution in Germany, was exaggerated by the government and also by later commentators. After the ending of the worst and most damaging war imaginable, it is questionable whether vast sections of the population had the appetite for renewed strife and civil war. Perhaps it is understandable that the government, when faced with having to demobilize some 6 million servicemen rapidly in late 1918 and early 1919, was anxious about how these men would react after the defeat of Germany. But, in fact, most of those who had been on active service only wished to return to their homes. Indeed, research has shown that comparatively few German soldiers who had fought on the Western or Eastern fronts were involved in the revolutionary unrest immediately after the war, and that the leaders of the revolts came from sections of the navy and workers who had spent most of their war years in Germany itself.

Undoubtedly, the German government's fear of social upheaval and its reaction to it exacerbated its own problems. Richard Bessel has argued that by authorizing the activities of the *Freikorps* in putting down revolts, and thereby tacitly approving of the brutal manner in which the *Freikorps* went about its business, it helped

> to create that very radicalism which its leaders had been determined to combat . . . Seen in this light, the radicalism of the workers in 1918–1920 appears largely defensive – motivated by a growing distrust of the new government, and fear and hatred of the *Freikorps* and the Reichswehr. It was not necessarily a movement of workers striving consciously for a particular (Marxist or otherwise) party-political programme of working-class emancipation. (Open University, 1987, A323 *Weimar Germany*, Study Guide, p.26)

If, with the luxury of the hindsight of seventy years, we can conclude that the threat of a socialist revolution largely reflected the fears of the government rather than the intentions of the vast majority of the governed in Germany, the same can certainly be said for Britain and France. In Britain, despite the shop-stewards' movement and much talk and writing about the need to achieve a democratic control of industry, there was very little revolutionary fervour among the trade-union leaders or the Labour Party, which acquired a new constitution in 1918. Although the leaders of labour often expressed sympathy with the aims of socialism and occasionally took stands to support their fellow workers, such as when the dockers refused to load boats taking arms which might have been used against Bolsheviks in the Russo-Polish war, they more often distanced themselves from any commitment to world socialism. The Labour Party did not accept the conditions of affiliation laid down by the Third International which met in

Moscow in 1920 and only a few small Marxist groups agreed to do so. They formed themselves into the Communist Party of Great Britain and immediately sought and were refused affiliation with the Labour Party. In 1921 the CP's membership was around 5,000 and, as Martin Kitchen has written, it 'was no more a threat to the established order than were the Jehovah's Witnesses to the established church or the Mormons to the institution of marriage' (*Europe Between the Wars*, 1988, p.187).

In France the split within the French socialist party (that took place around the same time as in Britain), which resulted in the formation of the French Communist Party, was almost the reverse of the outcome in Britain. In France it was the Communist Party membership in 1921 that was larger than the socialists (140,000 to 30,000) and it was the communist newspaper *L'Humanité* which sold many more copies than the socialist daily *Populaire* (200,000 to 5,000). In 1921 there was also a marked lack of unity within the ranks of the trade-union movement when the CGT, weakened after its disastrous attempt at a general strike, was itself split and the communists formed a rival, the CGTU. Again, it was the communist branch which contained the highest membership (500,000 to 370,000).

Although the communists had a greater following in France than in Britain, the militant Left in France was never really strong or united enough to pose a serious threat to the established order. Although, as in Britain, the *Parti Communiste Française* was essentially a parliamentary party, just the mention of a 'Red Peril' was enough to bring together those groups who were being particularly hard hit by the escalating inflation in the country and who united under the political banner of slogans such as the protection of private property, a return to normality and law and order.

4   Germany underwent a political revolution with the abdication of the kaiser and the replacement of an emperor with, at first, a provisional revolutionary government (composed of Majority Social Democrats led by Ebert and Independent Social Democrats), followed by elections (based on universal suffrage) to a National Assembly in January 1919 and the inauguration of the Weimar Republic in August 1919. Although (as Clive Emsley rightly points out in Book I, Unit 3, p.101) the power of the *Reichstag* was increasing in the years before 1914, nevertheless the *Reichstag* of the Weimar Republic (now elected by universal suffrage and membership of which was decided upon by proportional representation) was a more powerful forum than its predecessor. Still, it is important not to over-emphasize the changes. The popularly elected Reich President was independent of the *Reichstag*. He was head of the armed forces, he possessed the power to appoint and dismiss ministries and, in the event of national emergency, he could rule by decree. The *Länder*, with slight changes, remained, and it is important to remember that 'institutional changes had not led to a change of personnel' (Roberts, p.462). In many ways this is the key point. The bureaucratic and judicial structure was maintained by the old order and, in one sense, the form that the constitution took was of less importance. As the head of the Junker-dominated Agrarian League had written only two days after the resignation of the kaiser, the essential factor was to ensure the continuation of 'the bourgeois social order. Whether we wish to adopt republican or monarchial forms is not an issue for today' (Maier, *Recasting Bourgeois Europe*, 1975, p.54).

Also, despite the various constitutional and electoral changes, there was remarkably little change in the composition of the political parties or even political voting habits. The political parties existing in 1918 were very much the same parties as those who contested the elections in 1912, and the 1919 election to the National Assembly was essentially a fight between those parties which had been prominent before the war. (I have already referred to the split on the Left and the appearance of the Communist Party. However, the Communists refused to take part in the elections in January 1919.) The Majority Social Democratic Party won 163 seats in the Assembly in 1919 and this reflected the pre-war trend in its favour. It also adds substance to the conclusion that overall the German electorate was much more in favour of continuity than radical changes.

In Britain, important changes to the franchise had also taken place so that 2 million men and 6 million women had been added to the electoral register. The Representation of the People Act, 1918, had widened the franchise to nearly all men and extended the vote to women for the first time, albeit that thirty, not twenty-one as in the case of men, was the qualifying age. In addition, since the last election in 1910 there had been important changes in the relative strengths of the political parties. The Liberal Party had been split when Lloyd George took over from Asquith as Prime Minister in December 1916, and the events before the election of 1918 only made the split even wider. Although Lloyd George had much popular support in the country, his direct following in parliament was small, and he was dependent on Conservative support for the continuation of his Coalition government. Although for a while Britain was a country of three major parties, it was the comparatively new Labour Party which was gradually ousting the Liberals and was, after 1923, the only credible alternative to a Conservative government. Just as trade-union membership had grown in the war period and immediately after, so too did allegiance towards the Labour Party. In the elections of December 1910, 370,000 votes were cast for fifty-six Labour candidates and forty-two were returned to parliament. By 1922, Labour received over 4 million votes for its 411 candidates (nearly 30 per cent of the votes cast) and 142 Labour MPs were returned. Nevertheless, although it had grown in size and popular appeal, the Labour Party, at least in Ross McKibbin's view, had not changed markedly from the party which had existed before 1914. 'Everything points to Labour's enduring *ante-bellum* character: continuity of leadership and person-nel at all levels, effective continuity of policy and, above all, continuity of organization' (McKibbin, *The Evolution of the Labour Party, 1910–1924*, 1974, p. 240).

In France there were very few changes between 1914 and 1919. The franchise already included universal male suffrage but French women had to wait until 1944 before they eventually received the vote, and generally the parties which had dominated the political scene before 1914 were prominent in 1919. One seemingly minor electoral change made in 1919 did, in fact, have an important effect in the first election after the war. The creation of large multi-member districts, rather than the previous single-member constituency system, meant that those parties which were prepared to form electoral coalitions had a clear advantage. The socialist parties, who had agreed to a political truce during the war and had helped form the *union sacrée*, were no longer prepared to co-operate either with non-socialist parties or among themselves. Consequently, although the left-wing parties polled more votes than in 1914, their refusal to combine together, unlike the Right and Centre parties who formed themselves into the Bloc National, meant that the Bloc won over two-thirds of the seats in the Chamber. □

Exercise   Study documents I.2 and I.3 in *Documents 2*. What electoral differences existed within the three countries and how stable do you think political life was in Britain, France and Germany during the inter-war years? ■

Specimen answer   The first point to make is that in Germany and France there was a multiplicity of
and discussion   parties and no one party ever achieved much more than 33 per cent of the popular vote. In Britain this was not the case. There were far fewer parties which attained representation in parliament and, apart from 1923 and 1929–31, the Conservative Party dominated every inter-war government, even though from 1919–1922 the government was nominally a Coalition under the leadership of the Liberal leader Lloyd George and again from 1931 to 1939, when there was a National Government which in the period 1931 to 1935 was headed by the Labour politician J. Ramsay MacDonald. Just why the Conservatives were content to be part of a National Government rather than forming a government entirely on their own will be discussed in Unit 15.

In Germany up until 1933 and in France throughout the inter-war years, no one political party achieved a clear majority of seats in the *Reichstag* or Chamber of Deputies. The problem this caused can be seen in Germany where seventeen administrations in thirteen years clearly indicates a confused political scene. Government depended on coalitions and at times up to six separate parties were involved in these coalitions. Obviously this state of affairs did not make it easy for governments to make decisive and unhindered policy decisions. One reason for the multiplicity of parties in the *Reichstag* was the system of proportional representation which was adopted, but nevertheless the large number of parties clearly reflects the fragmentation of German political life in this period. The most popular party up until 1932 was the Social Democrats (SDP), but note the figures for the Centre Party which invariably won around sixty seats in the *Reichstag* in the 1920s. The Centre was prominent in all seventeen administrations, and unlike many of the other parties it claimed not to have a socio-economic base. It attracted support mostly from the Catholic electorate, although by 1912 only 55 per cent of eligible Catholics voted for the Centre Party. Although, as you can see, the Centre Party did enter into alliance from time to time with the Social Democrats, it was a moderate conservative party espousing the existing order and opposed to socialism and communism.

In France, too, the large number of political parties and the manner in which the electoral system worked meant that 'coalitions' or electoral pacts had to be made so that governments could be formed. In one sense this was even more difficult to accomplish than in Germany for, at least in the early part of this period, French political parties (as Clive Emsley pointed out in Book I, Unit 3) did not have the clear affiliations and disciplined organization possessed by most British and German political parties. As in Germany, there were no new popular political parties and throughout the period, again as in Germany, religion was to play an important part in politics. I have already mentioned the formation and success of the Bloc National at the 1919 election (a coalition of right-wing parties, nationalists and anti-socialists), but this was an uneasy alliance and there were many disagreements, particularly between the Catholics and anti-clericals within the alliance. The Bloc was succeeded in 1924 by another electoral alliance, this time formed between the radicals, socialists and socialist republicans and named the *Cartel des Gauches*. Again, the differences between the various groupings were not far from the surface. Indeed, at times the only belief they seemed to hold in common was a dislike and distrust of the Catholic Church and Catholic politicians. In fact, the difficulties of pursuing agreed policies were so great that within the space of nine months in 1924 there were six Cabinet crises. The stalemate in French politics can perhaps best be illustrated by the figures which show that between 1920 and 1940 the average life expectancy of a French government was seven months. □

Exercise We will relate Maier's thesis to the events of the 1920s in more detail later on. Meanwhile, very briefly, say in what ways the issues we have discussed so far confirm or question Maier's arguments? ■

Specimen answer and discussion Certainly the years immediately following the ending of World War I were ones of much political and industrial unrest and undoubtedly governments acted forcefully in stifling and containing this discontent. Maier contends, at least in the cases of France and Germany, that this was done with the approval of a combination of various élites and the middle classes. However, we have seen that there is considerable evidence to suggest that the fear of revolution was much exaggerated and that the possibility of revolution was remote in all three countries. If this was the case, then Maier is making too sharp a distinction between the working populations within France and Germany (and the same could be said for Britain) and other sections of society. We should question whether he is polarizing these societies too sharply in class terms and whether he gives due weight, for example, to the influence of Catholicism among the various classes within France and Germany and its important influence in the political, economic and social life of these two countries.

This last point, in relation to France and Germany, is partly borne out in documents I.2 and I.3 in *Documents 2*, which clearly show the multiplicity of parties which existed and which represented electorates divided on a host of religious, social and economic issues. However, this particular evidence does help to support another strand of Maier's thesis in which he argues that one reason for a transition towards corporatism in Germany, as he sees it, was the inability of successive German governments to deal competently with an increasing number of issues, and that the interest of influential groups became more powerful at the expense of parliament. The Stinnes-Legien agreement made in November 1918 between union and industrial leaders before the elections to the National Assembly is a clear example of a move towards a corporatist structure within Germany. The various short-lived coalition governments, and the growing unlikelihood of political parties actually being able to carry out their electoral promises when they attained office, meant that there was an inevitable loss of faith and an inability of parliaments to tackle complex economic and other problems, and so the climate was favourable for a move away from the traditional authority of parliament to a number of 'corporatist' settlements. □

So far we have discussed the immediate problems facing governments after the ending of World War I and we have concentrated on the discontent existing within the three countries. Now I want to examine in some detail other major problems that we have already touched on earlier in this unit.

2.1 Inflation and reparations

The dominating issue, which tended to obscure many other political and economic problems, particularly in France and Germany in the 1920s, was that of inflation. Governments in all three countries had to face this problem, which was primarily an inheritance from the war. The war had brought shortages of many goods and a corresponding rise in prices so that, for example, by 1918 price levels in Britain were more than twice as high as in 1914, and in France they were three times as high. In addition, France and Germany in particular had made little attempt to finance the war through internal taxation, which would have reduced spending power and thus reduced price rises, but had raised money by borrowing, either internally through war bonds or from abroad. Consequently, by the end of the war both countries faced huge repayment problems which were far too large to be paid off through trade. In any case, in France during the course of the war income from exports only covered about 29 per cent of expenditure spent on imports, and so France's foreign debts in 1918 amounted to some 19 billion francs.

In Germany the financial problems were even worse. The war had been fought in the expectation that Germany would win and would then automatically solve all its financial problems by presenting bills to the losers. November 1918 shattered this dream, and what is interesting is that the peace settlements then transferred this dream to the French nation who became convinced that their financial problems could be solved by the enforcement of reparations from Germany. The consequences of this thinking were highly damaging to both countries.

In France successive governments refused to grapple with their financial problems by introducing unpopular austerity measures because they had been voted into power on the election claim that 'the Boche must pay'. Even when allied credits were withdrawn in March 1919, and the franc fell on the international exchange markets so that within a year its value had fallen by 50 per cent, only various 'temporary' measures were employed. Very soon these measures merely aggravated the situation. In order to pay off bondholders the government raised money by borrowing at even higher rates of interest and borrowing still further from the Bank of France. This in turn put more currency into circulation, adding even more to inflation, and this, in its turn, undermined international confidence in the franc further. By 1920 price levels were five times higher than they had been in 1914.

In an attempt to accelerate the collection of reparations 40,000 French troops were ordered, much against world opinion, to occupy the Ruhr. The move was unsuccessful in that the reparations collected in 1923 were not significantly higher than in the previous year, and the government had been forced to raise taxes by 20 per cent to cover the costs of sending the army into the Ruhr. The failure of the occupation and the success of the left-wing in the elections of 1924 only led to further uncertainties and a flight of capital out of the country, which contributed to a further decline of the franc from 70 to the pound in 1924 to 250 to the pound in July 1926.

It was only when Poincaré returned as head of a government of National Union, armed with powers to govern by decree if necessary, that firm steps were taken to restore confidence within the country and especially among businessmen. Taxes were raised sharply, severe cuts were made in government expenditure and, most importantly, the drift of capital out of the country was not only stopped but reversed. In 1928 the government was able to stabilize the currency, albeit at 20 per cent of its pre-war value, but the French investor at least had not been hit as badly as his German counterpart. Gordon Wright concluded: 'The French solution to the war's financial burden – an inflation that was checked short of disaster – fell midway between that of the Germans and the British and was probably healthier than either. It was, however, a solution that was more empirical than planned' (*France in Modern Times*, 1987 edn, p.351).

Exercise   Roberts mentions the enormous inflation which took place in the defeated countries in the period after the war. Have a look at document I.4 in *Documents 2* and then answer the following questions:

1   When do prices and the exchange rate start increasing at an enormously rapid rate?

2   Is there any period when prices and/or the exchange rate do not rise?

3   What reasons does Roberts give for the inflation in Germany?

4   From your reading of this unit so far, can you think of any additional reasons for the inflation in Germany, especially in the years immediately following the war? ■

Specimen answers   1   The first enormous change in the exchange rate takes place between July and
and discussion   August 1922, and this is reflected in the almost doubling of the cost of living index between August and September 1922.

2   Apart from a few months in 1920 there is a continuous upward turn in the cost of living index. However, in the same months there is a marked improvement in the exchange rate and overall from January 1920 to June 1921, with monthly variations, the mark does hold steady.

3   On page 363 Roberts mentions 'the prolongation of scarcity and the government's too-ready resort to the printing press. Its climax was only reached with the French occupation of the Ruhr in 1923'. He then goes on to mention that the German government continued 'to print money almost unrestrainedly in order to support the Ruhr strikers against the French'.

4   Faced with severe internal unrest, there were high pay settlements. Remember Mommsen's statement, 'government and employers alike considered high wage levels and full employment politically essential, and financial policies were conducted accordingly'. □

This last point must not be underestimated. It is almost inconceivable to appreciate the figures quoted in the inflation of 1923 (and it must be noted that because of the collapse of the currency, the figures are not as precise as those quoted for the earlier years). But even by April 1920 the cost of living was ten times more than it had been in 1914.

Although there is a levelling off in the cost of living and an improvement in the exchange rate for part of 1920 and 1921, remember that this was a period of world recession. In Britain and France, rather than a levelling off, prices in 1921 fell by some 30 to 40 per cent.

The major reason for the massive inflation in 1923 was the attempt by the French to solve the reparations question once and for all by occupying the industrial area of the Ruhr. The response of the German government was to call on the workers in the area not to co-operate. The response to the call for passive resistance was impressive but extremely damaging. The price for the virtual shutdown of industries in the area was that the government had to print more and more money to pay those who had ceased work.

Exercise Again from your reading of this unit so far, and any basic knowledge you may have of economics, can you think of any advantages Germany may have gained from inflation as opposed to the hyperinflation of 1923? ■

Specimen answer Some commentators would argue that the wage increases in the period after the war, and the opportunities given for full employment, staved off a great deal of internal unrest and, indeed, went much of the way to prevent revolution. Also inflation enabled the government 'to pay off war debts . . . cheaply, permitted industrial and agricultural debtors to liquidate their debt, helped Germany recapture world markets, and provided the basis for full employment during the early 1920s' (Open University, 1987, A323 *Weimar Germany*, Study Guide, p.47). □

For those people unable to work, or who were dependent on fixed incomes, inflation had been a disaster from the very start. However, the hyperinflation of 1923 not only adversely affected most sections of the German population, but it also threatened a worldwide financial crisis. Something had to be done to stabilize the German currency. In August 1924 yet another coalition government was formed, this time under Stresemann. While acknowledging that the German actions in the Ruhr demonstrated national unity, he also realized its disastrous consequences. He called for an end to the passive resistance and changed the direction of the government's economic policy by putting tight controls on borrowing and government expenditure. The currency was stabilized with the introduction of the Rentenmark which replaced the Reichsmark. Most important of all, Stresemann worked towards obtaining a settlement of the reparations argument. This was accomplished in co-operation with the United States. The Dawes Plan was devised in 1924 and the Young Plan, which followed five years later, ensured that Germany's payments were considerably reduced and a time limit was placed on the repayments. The Dawes Plan also paved the way for the setting up of large American loans and investments in the country which did much to stimulate the country's economic recovery.

In one sense, by the end of the war the financial position in Britain had altered more markedly than in France and Germany. As Roberts points out on page 361, 'Even before 1914, there had been signs that a slowing of industrial growth and exports might make it hard for Great Britain to go on being banker to the world.' But in 1914 Britain had been the world's banker; by 1918 the United States was the leading international banker. Britain was yet another of the nations in debt to the United States, and as a result of the war Britain had lost about a quarter of its overseas investments and the National Debt was around fourteen times greater than it had been in 1913.

Apart from the period up to April 1920, Britain did not undergo the inflation experienced by the other two countries. A brief post-war boom, following the inflation which had taken place during the war, meant that by early 1920 prices were about three times the 1914 figure. But this was followed by a recession with a corresponding drop in prices and an increase in unemployment. A government committee was set up to enquire into the causes of the slump and the recommendations that there should be drastic cuts in public spending were acted upon. Whereas Germany and France more or less deliberately implemented inflationary policies in the early 1920s, the British government pursued an opposite policy of deflation.

In his book, *Recasting Bourgeois Europe*, Maier writes that the major aim of conservative thought after 1918 was that of returning to the social order of the pre-war years. Whether this was the case or not, in Britain, at least with regard to financial thinking, there was a strong desire to return to pre-1914 when Britain was the financial centre of the world. Much of British economic thinking was devoted to realizing this aim. Deflation, it was hoped, would not only reduce unemployment but would also bring back confidence to the City. It was partly as a result of this reasoning that the British government decided to return to the gold standard in 1925 at the pre-war parity of £1 to 4.86 dollars. This was an overvaluation of the pound by some 10 per cent, but it was hoped that such an action would bring stability and confidence and raise Britain once again to the position of financial centre of the world. Also, although the overvaluation would make exports more expensive, it was hoped that these higher prices would be 'offset by lower wages, greater efficiency and the consequent reduction of unit costs' (Kitchen, *Europe Between the Wars*, 1988, p.195). Unfortunately the return of the gold standard did not bring the results that were hoped for and, at least in the short run, it was to have an adverse effect on British industry.

2.2   The return of industry to peacetime conditions and its consequences

In 1913, Britain, France and Germany had been responsible for roughly 60 per cent of the exported manufactured goods throughout the world. The war had interrupted this trade and these three Western countries were never again to dominate the world market to such an extent. Peter Fearon has written:

> Nowhere was Europe more severely hit by the war than in agriculture, a sector which employed more labour than all other industries together. Throughout the conflict cereal output, the main European crop, declined in spite of desperate attempts to increase it. A shortage of labour, horsepower and fertiliser explains why Europe could not feed itself in 1919 and had to import food on credit from the United States. The withdrawal of Russia, traditionally the granary of the continent, from world trade in 1917 increased Europe's dependence on other continents; countries overseas responded by raising the output of their primary products, financing the expansion by borrowing from the United States. However, by 1925 European agriculture was back to its 1913 levels of production and seemed set to increase output even more. At the same time, production in the rest of the world, encouraged by the golden years of high prices between 1914 and 1920, was at a much higher level than in 1913.
>
> W. A. Lewis has calculated that, if the trend of output established between 1881 and 1913 in European manufacturing had been maintained, the level of output that Europe eventually reached in 1929 would have been achieved in 1921. If Lewis is correct, the war set back Europe's industrial growth by eight years. It would be a grave mistake to assume, however, that all economic events of the 1920s can be traced back to the war. The economic expansion of France in this decade, for example, is a continuation of a pre-1914 trend; the overseas trade of both Britain and Germany showed a similar structure in the post-war era to that before 1914; and Britain's staple industries would have posed a problem even if there had been no war. A further example of continuity can be found in the pattern of cyclical fluctuations in the inter-war period. In 1914, most major industrial countries were poised on the edge of a recession which the war delayed until 1920–1. The next major downturn began in 1929 and can be

seen as a return to the normal pattern of the trade cycle. Throughout the world many countries were strengthened by the war, as their economies became more diversified and more committed to manufacturing. In Europe, however, the picture was bleak, for even by the late 1920s agriculture was not prosperous, trade was relatively depressed and in most industrial nations unemployment was high. These problems were not caused by the war but were intensified by it, and while they offer no explanation as to why the depression began in 1929, we can accept the view that structural problems can lessen resistance to depression and make recovery more difficult. (Peter Fearon, *The Origins and Nature of the Great Slump, 1929–32*, 1979, pp. 14–15)

Exercise   1   To what extent does Fearon think the economic events of the 1920s in Europe were decisively influenced by the war?

2   In what area does Fearon seemingly disagree with Roberts?

3   On what topics do Roberts and Fearon agree? ■

Specimen answers   1   Fearon sees a great deal of continuity before and after the war, especially with
and discussion   regard to the manufacturing industries and finance. It was agriculture which was most severely hit by the war and the Russian revolutions.

2   On page 398 Roberts refers to the 'lack of important growth in the economy' of France. Perhaps Roberts is referring here to the inter-war years as a whole because, in fact, in the 1920s the French industrial growth rate was higher than that of any other European country. Indeed, by 1929, all production and trade figures had reached record levels. Fearon states that this economic expansion was apparent before 1914 and the French economic historian François Caron agrees with him. Caron states that in this period industrial growth was 'more marked in France than in the rest of Europe. It was as much a continuation of the growth of the immediate prewar years as of the industrialist spirit of the First World War' (*An Economic History of Modern France*, 1979, p.182).

Both Caron and Fearon are correct to point to the pre-war years as the basis for this expansion but the effects of the war on French industry must be emphasized. In the first place, the recovery of Alsace and Lorraine was important in the contribution towards the production of textiles, iron and steel. Also, the acquisition of further colonies ensured export markets for French products. The necessary rebuilding of much of the industrial areas of north-west France devastated during the war also meant the replacement of nineteenth-century industrial units with more efficient modern ones. But the war had also done much to alter the attitudes of many French industrialists and this, together with the acute shortage of labour, made French industrialists more receptive to 'Taylorism' (the application of scientific methods in management and the organization of labour, named after the American F. W. Taylor) and assembly-line production methods, than most other European industrialists. (See Maier, 'Between Taylorism and technocracy', 1970.)

Also, as we have mentioned before, the inflation which worried so many French governments played its part in this expansion. The depreciation of the franc on the foreign exchanges gave a great boost to French exports and a relatively new industry, tourism, expanded enormously as foreigners benefited from the cheap French currency. This in its turn encouraged a great deal of investment in hotels, casinos and the development of holiday resorts. However, the major areas of investment, which had started before World War I and which carried on through the 1920s, were concentrated on plant and machinery in the productive sectors of industry. It is in the engineering, metallurgical and chemical industries that this increase can best be seen.

3   Both Roberts and Fearon agree that there was a slowing down of industrial growth in Britain and in its export markets before the war. Fearon argues that there would have been problems with Britain's staple industries regardless of the war and it was these industries which were particularly hard hit in the recession in 1920. From around 1923 there was a gradual recovery, so that by 1925 production in British industries was back to pre-war levels, but unemployment was still around the one million mark. However, all the staple industries were still producing well below capacity, partly because of the loss of export markets and partly because, as we have mentioned already, the return to the gold standard had overvalued the pound. The only way to counter this overvaluation was to attempt to make Britain more competitive by reducing production costs. Unfortunately, in such labour intensive industries as, for example, coal, it was difficult to see where these reductions could be made other than in wages, and further wage reductions in the coal industry were bound to meet with opposition from the unions. □

German industrial production had also declined during the war. By 1919 the index of industrial production was only about 38 per cent of what it had been in 1913. The drop was partly because of the loss of industrial areas as a result of the peace settlement, partly because of the rundown of machinery and industrial units during the war, but also there was a marked drop in productivity figures. The industrial discontent, as seen in document I.1 in *Documents 2*, with the vast numbers of days lost by strikes in the early days after the ending of the war, was an important factor here. Another factor was that, as we have seen, many concessions were made to German workers in 1918 and 1919, with wage increases and an eight-hour day, so in fact what had happened was that there had been both a decrease in hours and an increase in wages which resulted in labour costs being higher and labour productivity being lower. One of the consequences of the German economies in 1924 was that many of the gains that German workers had obtained in the period following the war, such as the eight-hour day, were lost, wages also fell and, as unemployment increased, so the membership of trade unions fell. It was only by the end of the decade that industrial production reached the level at which it had been in 1913. But one particularly important development had taken place during this time. This was a move towards the development of larger units of production through amalgamation and rationalization, so that by the end of the decade, for example, IG Farben dominated the chemical industry and the United Steel Works controlled over half of Germany's coal production and nearly a half of the country's steel production.

Whereas German industrial production became increasingly concentrated in this period, German agriculture moved in the reverse direction. This was partly a result of Germany losing her eastern territories in the peace settlements, the areas where the vast majority of large estates were situated. In any case, as Fearon points out, this was a bad period for agriculture in all three countries. Increased agricultural production in other parts of the world kept agricultural prices low and land prices dropped. Although in Book II, Units 8–10, section 2.1, Bill Purdue states, quite rightly, that agriculture remained France's largest industry, even here there was a transfer of the population in this period away from agriculture towards the highly industrialized sector. Between 1906 and 1931 the number of male workers in agriculture fell from 5.4 to 4.4 million while the number of wage earners in industry rose from 3.7 to 5.4 million, an increase of 47 per cent.

Exercise   Look at documents I.1 and I.5 in *Documents 2*.

1   Which country suffers least from industrial discontent from the period 1925 onwards?

2   Where and when was there the greatest amount of industrial discontent in this period? ■

Specimen answers   1   From these sets of figures it appears that the industrial disruption caused by
and discussion   strikes was greater in Britain and Germany than in France. Although there are often more industrial disputes in France in certain years than the other two countries, they do not last so long and very often fewer days are lost per strike. Again, unemployment figures are much lower in France than in Britain and Germany. For France the figure of 2.7 per cent in 1921 is high, whereas in Germany from 1923 onwards the figure is never below 3.4 per cent. Britain suffered the greatest unemployment of all three countries and it was never less than 9 per cent of the workforce after 1921.

2   Clearly the key dates are 1926 in Britain, when 162 million working days are lost and some 2.73 million workers involved, and 1928 in Germany when over 20 million days are lost. □

Exercise   From what you have read in this unit and Book II, Units 8–10, list the reasons why France had less unemployment and fewer industrial disturbances than Britain and Germany between 1925 and 1929. ■

Specimen answer   1   The loss of large numbers of men killed in the war and the stagnation in
and discussion   population growth in the 1920s meant that there was a scarcity of labour, or at least French-born labour.

2   The greater growth in industrial production in France obviously helped to maintain full employment.

3   Unlike in Britain, there was little attempt until the mid-1920s to maintain the level of the currency, and the fall of the franc on the foreign exchanges was an aid to French exporting industries. □

One could well draw the conclusion from what has been said so far that at least the French industrial workers should have benefited from these conditions. But the rise in the wages of French workers in this period does not reflect this as much as one might expect. First, French trade unions were weaker in organizational structure than those in Britain and Germany. Second, and more important, there was a large-scale immigration of foreign workers, especially Italians, Belgians, Poles and Spaniards, into France in the 1920s. These men went into, particularly, the mines of northern France, the steel and iron mills and the construction industries. This was a largely unorganized labour force and, as is so often the case with immigrant workers, could be employed for comparatively low wages. So, although unemployment was not high, neither was there a great scarcity in the labour market.

It was partly because of this cheap labour force that, although there were changes within French society itself, French governments were never unduly pressed to make social reforms. Roberts mentions the social stagnation in France and certainly from the point of view of social legislation, France lagged well behind the other two countries. Although the eight-hour day had been legalized in 1919, there were few major social reforms other than secondary education acts in 1927 and 1930, an act allowing for the provision of subsidized housing in 1928, and a social insurance act in 1930 which was by no means as comprehensive as that existing in Britain.

The figures in document I.5 in *Documents 2* for Britain show that unemployment never falls below one million after 1921, but that is only part of the story. Unemployment was markedly regional and high in particular industries, especially the old staple industries. For example, in 1927 unemployment stood at 11.3 per cent but in the five industries of coal, metal manufacture, engineering, shipbuilding, cotton and woollens, it was 15.8 per cent. It was in these industries, and especially as we have already seen, in the coal industry, which was under-mechanized and in need of reorganization and modernization, that the major industrial problems and troubles lay.

The General Strike of 1926 developed because of yet another attempt by the coal owners to make their prices more competitive by reducing wages and lengthening working hours. Roberts on pages 412–4 discusses the General Strike itself as well as the events leading up to the TUC giving its support to the miners and agreeing to the strike. So all I wish to do here is add a number of points for consideration not covered by Roberts.

Firstly it is important to appreciate the deep sense of injustice that most miners felt at this time, and although the speeches of their leaders, Herbert Smith and A. J. Cook, were often inflammatory, in the last resort they regarded the strike as basically a defensive action. As Cook wrote later, and rather grandiosely, it was 'the greatest struggle ever undertaken by a section of the workers for the right to live' (*The Nine Days*, 1926).

Secondly, although Roberts correctly states that the TUC was only half-hearted in its support of the strike, there is evidence that within the trade-union movement at this time there was a swing to the Left, and that if this had not taken place, some sort of compromise may have been made earlier. Many trades councils at this time were connected to the National Federation of Trades Councils whose president was Harry Pollitt, secretary of the British Communist Party. Membership of the Communist Party, although comparatively small, doubled during 1926, and in certain areas the shop-steward movement which had been prominent immediately after the war reappeared.

Thirdly, Roberts mentions 'careful preparations' on the part of the government. In September 1925 the Organisation for the Maintenance of Supplies was set up under the direction of the Home Office, and in the following month twelve prominent Communists were arrested and imprisoned. Five remained in prison during the period of the General Strike. Special Constables were recruited and totalled some 130,000 by the time of the General Strike. The government also sponsored its own newspaper, *The British Gazette*, which put the government's arguments starkly before the public. On 6 May it proclaimed, 'there can be no question of compromise of any kind. Either the country will break the General Strike or the General Strike will break the country'.

Exercise Listen to item 1 on audio-cassette 3, 'The General Strike of 1926'. What can we learn from this? ■

Specimen answer and discussion

The government, to say the least, would not be unhappy to hear this sort of news item. The Cardinal takes the government line and represents the General Strike as both immoral and unconstitutional. Obviously, until you have listened to more bulletins it is difficult for you to comment on whether the other side of the argument had been aired. But, in fact, this item was broadcast on 9 May, and two days earlier the Archbishop of Canterbury had been refused permission to broadcast an appeal for a settlement of the dispute which had been drawn up by church leaders. The role of the BBC during this period will be discussed in Unit 19, so it is sufficient to say here that it was not the government but the director-general of the BBC, Sir John Reith, who refused to broadcast the appeal on the 7 May. (The Archbishop was permitted to broadcast later.) It was a strange action for the head of a body supposedly independent of government to make, and a possible reason for the action was that Reith wanted to keep the BBC independent and feared that if he alienated the government too much it might be taken over completely.

What I find most interesting about the news item is that it is a report of a sermon by the Cardinal of Westminster to all Roman Catholics in the country. Roberts mentions that the General Strike 'should have been the greatest demonstration of the reality of class war', but then goes on to state that the behaviour of trade unions during the General Strike showed that 'violent class warfare was a thing of the past'. The Cardinal's sermon, which was addressed to all Catholics of all classes, demonstrates that there were factors other than class which have to be taken into account in order to understand the positions taken up by the population *vis à vis* this major industrial dispute. □

The defeat of the General Strike followed by the anti-trade-union legislation of 1927 resulted in an enormous drop in industrial militancy. As you can see from document I.1 in *Documents 2*, the number of days lost between 1927 and the outbreak of World War II only slightly exceeded those lost in just the one year of 1919. Yet, at the same time, the government, unlike that in France, was involved in a whole series of social legislation, especially through the Minister of Health, Neville Chamberlain. In fact, the record of the Baldwin government of 1924–29 in this respect 'was greater than that of any of the interwar governments save Lloyd George's coalition of 1918–22' (Mowat, *Britain Between the Wars*, 1955, p.238). Twenty-one bills, planned by Chamberlain, including the Widows', Orphans' and Old Age Contributory Pensions Bill and the Local Government Act of 1929, were enacted during this period.

Roberts makes no mention of the cause for the high number of days lost in Germany in 1928, but the main reason was not so much a strike on the part of the workers as a lock-out of some 250,000 workers in the iron and steel industries by their employers. V. R. Berghahn states that this was a 'deliberately escalated confrontation' on the part of the employers (*Modern Germany*, 1982, p.107). The reasons for this, according to Berghahn, were that the particularly conservative industrialists in the heavy industries, which had undergone cartelization (agreements whereby they divided the market up between themselves, devised production quotas, and fixed prices) and rationalization and which were experiencing boom conditions, were unhappy with many of the concessions that had been made in the period immediately following the war and which were affecting their industries. They were also generally unhappy with the political liberalism of the Weimar Republic and, in particular, they resented the system of compulsory arbitration whereby wage settlements could be imposed by an arbitrator representing the state. In 1928 they deliberately challenged this procedure and refused to accept a decision for a small wage increase.

The final outcome of this lock-out resulted in a compromise whereby the wage increase was lessened but the system of state arbitration was retained. Nevertheless, the significant fact was that these industrialists were now prepared to challenge the trade unions and the state itself. Indeed, there was growing criticism of the Republic from many quarters. The ambitious Act of Labour Exchanges and Unemployment Insurance, which covered more workers than anywhere else in Europe, soon ran into problems and was condemned by many industrialists as being too costly. Although the period 1925 to 1929 in Germany appeared to be one of relative prosperity, bear in mind that much of the funding which brought about the industrial expansion came from the United States. The American stock market crash of 1929 was therefore to have more of an effect on Germany than Britain and France, and it was to heighten sharply any social and political discontent that existed within the country. This will be discussed in Unit 18.

Exercise   Read the section 'The structure and limits of stability' from Maier's book, *Recasting Bourgeois Europe*, which is reprinted in the Course Reader, pp.141–53.

1   Which country, France or Germany, does Maier believe had advanced more towards corporatism by the end of the decade?

2   What are the major changes that Maier sees within the 'corporatist' state of Germany in the 1920s?

3   Is there any evidence in what you have read in this unit or in the extracts from Maier's book which suggests that Britain had become closer to a corporatist state in this period?

4   Using the definition on pages 11–12 of this unit together with material within this unit and your reading of Roberts, what criticisms could you make of Maier's thesis?

5   Maier argues that despite all the problems some sort of stability was achieved around the middle of the decade. What was the major factor, according to Maier, on which this stability rested? ■

Specimen answers and discussion

1   Germany.

2   The early 1920s saw factory representation and trade unions as being influential participants in the making of economic and political decisions. By the end of the decade, the position of the Left had been markedly weakened and it was the cartels of industrialists, with their theories of rationalization and scientific management, who possessed most influence. This does not mean that the representation of labour had been eliminated altogether. Maier points out (Course Reader, p.145) that collective bargaining was still recognized, whereas in France this was still not the case.

3   On page 143 Maier states that an important aspect of the corporatist system was 'the blurring of the distinction between political and economic power . . . economic bargaining became too crucial to be left to the private market, and state agencies stepped in as active mediators'. In Britain, during and immediately after the war, with the setting up of the Ministry of Reconstruction, the National Industrial Conference and Whitley Councils, it appeared that ideas of collective

bargaining were becoming firmly established and that there was a move towards at least a degree of corporatism. However, by the early 1920s, with the break-up of the National Industrial Conference, the comparative failure of Whitleyism and the decision of the Coalition government to extricate itself from its commitments to the coal-mining industry, it became clear that this was not the case. The attitude of the Conservative government towards trade unions certainly showed little inclination towards a desire for collective bargaining. Christopher J. Nottingham in his article 'Recasting bourgeois Britain?' (1986) argues that

> To sustain the corporatist-tendency thesis it is not necessary to demonstrate that the government afforded the trade unions an equal share with employers in the bargaining process, but it is essential to show that they were allowed a role which was permanent and relatively constant . . . Yet the history of the post-war period, even after the immediate post-war crisis, is one of almost permanent Conservative hostility to trade unions. Moreover, it was not only the activities of unions which came under attack, but their whole legal and political identity.

4   Maier's book is nearly 600 pages in length. He drew on a vast range of sources and his arguments are complex and detailed. Clearly, by just studying the preface and conclusion we are doing Maier a disservice, and by merely outlining his arguments we are open to the criticism of oversimplifying them. However, there are a series of points that need questioning.

(a)   The first stage of Maier's thesis is his contention that the period following the ending of World War I was one of great turmoil and that a revolution in Western Europe was a real possibility. Certainly, in Germany there were attempted political insurrections, and in all three countries there was a great deal of industrial discontent, but there is little evidence to conclude from this that revolutionary fervour extended beyond all but a few small groups and there are few signs that what Maier calls 'the unparalleled violence, costs and passions occasioned by World War I' (p.142) should necessarily have been followed by revolution. If anything the threat of revolution reflected the fears of the governments in Britain, France and Germany rather than the intentions of the vast majority of the governed. So it is important to question whether the basic premise of Maier's thesis is sound or whether he is constructing an explanation for what was in any case a non-event (that is, a proletarian revolution).

(b)   Maier's next point is that any revolution that possibly would have taken place was contained by a combination of the middle classes and élites uniting against the working-class militant Left. This raises two questions. The first, which we have already discussed on pages 12 and 24–5, is: does Maier obscure the complexity of the societies in Western Europe by discussing these events in specifically class terms? (Or, to put it another way, does he have a too inflexible notion of class?) Secondly, does he over-exaggerate the strength and unity of socialist feeling in Western Europe during this period? With regard to the latter, it was not just that there were often marked and debilitating differences of opinion among leftist parties which very often prevented united action, but also the elections of 1918–19 do not show a preponderance of feeling for militancy. Indeed, the work of Mommsen and others has shown that there was a wide variety of interests, often conflicting, among different sections of the workforce, very often depending as much on job, region and religion as on socialist sympathies. Maier attempts, on page 145, to answer this point by arguing that during the 1920s, as the Left was gradually defeated, 'Class consciousness was undergoing a double evolution. In the world of work, identification as proletarian or bourgeois was becoming less compelling than interest-group affiliation, less a principle of common action in the economic arena.' What you have to consider is whether even in 1918 it was 'interest-group affiliations' which were the dominating considerations among working men and women rather than the causes of the proletariat.

(c)   The final strand of Maier's thesis is that during the middle years of the 1920s, when hopes of returning to a pre-1914 Europe had finally been abandoned, some level of social and economic stability was achieved by governments, but only as a result of some of their power being transferred to various interest groups. Consequently, Germany and Italy, and to a lesser extent France, become corporatist in tendency. Maier did not include Britain in his study and, as we have seen, apart from a brief flirtation with corporatist ideas at the end of and immediately after the war, there is nothing to suggest that corporatism was prevalent in Britain in the 1920s. Certainly, within Britain there are no signs of the political stalemate which characterized French and German politics for much of the 1920s. It was these conditions that provided ideal circumstances for the trend towards corporatism. Nevertheless, in one important respect we need to question at least part of Maier's conclusion. One aspect of the definition of corporatism (on p.11 of this unit) maintains that individuals retain an influence within the state, not so much through being enfranchised but through their membership of corporate bodies. Maier argues that the 'corporatist settlement' which was achieved in Germany in the second part of the decade, and was just beginning in France, occurred partly as a result of influence and power being transferred to various interest groups during this period. But it could well be argued that the power and influence working organizations achieved in the early 1920s was not maintained. From the point of view of trades organization there was a more corporatist element in Germany at the time of the Stinnes-Legien agreement in 1918 than during the Ruhr lock-out in 1928.

5   Maier states that stability was achieved mainly because of America's involvement in Europe. 'The equilibrium was certainly hostage to continuing American prosperity and the control of German national resentments' (p.579). □

Unit 18 examines the growth of German resentments and the sudden ending of American prosperity; its effect on Europe is one of the topics to be discussed in the next unit.

Bibliography

Abercrombie, N., et al. (1984) *Penguin Dictionary of Sociology*, Penguin.

Berghahn, V. R. (1982) *Modern Germany*, Cambridge University Press (reissued paperback 1987).

Bessel, R. and Feuchtwanger, E. J. (eds) (1981) *Social Change and Political Development in Weimar Germany*, Croom Helm.

Caron, F. (1979) *An Economic History of Modern France*, Methuen.

Cook, A. J. (1926) *The Nine Days*, Cooperative Printing Society.

Cronin, J. E. (1984) *Labour and Society in Britain, 1918–1979*, Batsford.

Fearon, P. (1979) *The Origins and Nature of the Great Slump, 1929–32*, Macmillan.

Halevy, E. (1919) 'The policy of social peace in England: the Whitley Councils', *Revue d'economique politique*. Reprinted in Halevy, E. (1967) *The Era of Tyrannies* (trans. R. K. Webb), Allen Lane.

Kitchen, M. (1988) *Europe Between the Wars: a Political History*, Longman.

Lowe, R. (1987) 'The government and industrial relations, 1919–39' in Wrigley, C. (ed.) *A History of British Industrial Relations*, vol.II, Harvester.

McKibbin, R. (1974) *The Evolution of the Labour Party, 1910–1924*, Oxford University Press.

Maier, C. S. (1970) 'Between Taylorism and technocracy', *Journal of Contemporary History*, vol.5, no.2, pp.54–9.

Maier, C.S. (1975) *Recasting Bourgeois Europe: Stabilization in France, Germany and Italy in the Decade after World War I*, Princeton University Press. (Extracts reprinted in the Course Reader.)

Marwick, A. (ed.) (1988) *Total War and Social Change*, Macmillan.

Mayer, A. J. (1981) *The Persistence of the Old Regime*, Croom Helm. (Extracts reprinted in the Course Reader.)

Middlemas, K. (1979) *The Politics of Industrial Society*, Deutsch.

Mommsen, W. J. (1981) 'The German Revolution 1918–1920: political revolution and social protest movement' in Bessel, R. and Feuchtwanger, E. J. (eds) (1981).

Mommsen, W. J. (1988) 'The social consequences of World War I' in Marwick, A. (ed.) (1988).

Morgan, K. (1979) *Consensus and Disunity*, Oxford University Press.

Mowat, C. L. (1955) *Britain Between the Wars*, Methuen.

Nottingham, C. J. (1986) 'Recasting bourgeois Britain?', *International Review of Social History*, vol.XXXI.

Open University (1987) A323 *Weimar Germany: the Crisis of Industrial Society, 1918–1933*, Study Guide, Milton Keynes, The Open University.

Taylor, A. J. P. (1965) *English History, 1914–1945*, Oxford University Press.

Wright, G. (1987) *France in Modern Times*, fourth edition, Norton.

Wrigley, C. (1987) 'The First World War and state intervention in industrial relations' in *A History of British Industrial Relations*, vol.II, Harvester.

UNIT 15 THE WESTERN DEMOCRACIES: SOCIAL CHANGES IN THE INTER-WAR YEARS

John Golby

Open University students of this unit will need to refer to:

Set book: J. M. Roberts, *Europe 1880–1945*, Longman, 1989

Documents 2: 1925–1959, eds Arthur Marwick and Wendy Simpson, Open University Press, 1990

Offprints Booklet

Audio-cassette 3

Video-cassette 1

INTRODUCTION

The aims of Unit 15 are:

●   to compare and contrast the social developments in France and Britain between the two world wars and in Germany between 1918 and the start of the Nazi regime in 1933;

●   to examine the extent of the social changes during these years and to assess how far these changes were due to the war, how far to economic circumstances and how far to parliamentary processes.

Most of the previous unit was devoted to examining the economic and political changes that took place in the Western democracies in the period between the ending of World War I and the onset of the Depression in 1929. Now I want to look at some of the major social changes that took place within the Western democracies during the inter-war years and attempt to evaluate the role of World War I in relation to these changes. I shall also continue to examine the political and economic developments in Britain and France in the 1930s.

Exercise   Start by reading Roberts, chapter 14 'Social and cultural change, 1918–1939'. (You will be referred to this chapter again in Unit 19.) Jot down in the form of headings what Roberts sees as the important developments taking place during the inter-war years in what he calls the 'rich' countries. ■

Specimen answer
and discussion

1   Changing attitudes to women

2   Changing attitudes to the family

3   Growth of new industries: urbanization

4   Social reforms: welfare and insurance schemes

5   Changes in material conditions

6   Mass communications: leisure

7   Social cohesion

You may have listed many more points than this including developments in the arts, philosophy and the sciences. You will have noticed also that I have not grouped my answers in the chronological order in which they are raised by Roberts. Rather, I have arranged them in the order in which I intend to discuss them, the reasons for which I hope will become apparent as the unit progresses. I hope you will have spotted that there is no subject in the above list that has not already been mentioned by both Arthur Marwick and Bill Purdue in their discussion of the impact and consequences of World War I in Book II, Units 8–10. What I want to do is take their discussions a stage further and trace these changes in Germany until 1932 and in Britain and France through to the eve of World War II. I shall explore whether the changes are continuations of processes already discussed in Units 8–10, or whether they are partly or wholly a result of specific economic and political developments which arise in the 1920s and 1930s. □

1 WOMEN

In section 2.8 of Units 8–10, in the course of his consideration of the changing roles and status of women as a result of the Great War, Arthur Marwick writes that there was a 'new assertiveness and self-confidence which women showed in the post-war years, but which was derived from the new experiences of war'. To a contemporary, this 'assertiveness' and 'self-confidence' was transmitted most obviously in the ways that many of the younger women in particular dressed, looked and behaved. By the mid-1920s skirts had risen to above the knees. Developments in artificial fibres had resulted in less heavy clothing, particularly underwear. There was an emphasis on a slim, boyish look with hair cut short in an 'Eton', 'bob' or 'shingle' style. There was an increasing use of cosmetics, especially lipstick, and more women were seen smoking cigarettes in public and participating in entertainments outside the home, at cinemas and dance halls. All these fashions and habits did much to make many feel that this was the era of the new 'liberated' woman. But were women liberated in other respects, for example, in employment and career opportunities?

Exercise I want you to listen to audio-cassette 3, item 2, Margaret Bondfield, a Labour MP, talking on 'The Woman's Opportunity'. One interesting point is that this item is from a gramophone record and is one in a series of party political speeches made by prominent members of the Labour Party during the general election campaign of 1929. Obviously the Labour Party is attempting to take advantage of this comparatively new means of communication and, bear in mind, there were more gramophones in the country at this time than radios.

1   What do you find interesting about this speech?

2   What are 'the women's opportunities' that Bondfield is talking about? ■

Specimen answers and discussion 1   It is interesting that this speech is addressed specifically to women. It is very unlikely that this would have been the case twenty years earlier. But the process, which had started in 1918 when women over thirty had been enfranchised, was extended in 1928 and women now possessed the same voting rights as men. As a result the electorate was increased from 21.75 million to nearly 29 million, and now there was a very real obligation on the part of political parties to court the female voter.

2   Although the speech is called 'The Woman's Opportunity' there is very little about opportunities for women in the sense of their involvement outside the home and there is no real discussion of women's employment. After an opening statement in which Bondfield claims that her party had always accepted the principle of absolute equality between men and women and had worked for a 'nobler social order', she does state that her party's record has been good in its efforts to abolish half-time working, regulate the sweated trades and improve conditions in the factories and mills. However, there is nothing about employment opportunities or equal pay. The remainder of her remarks are addressed to women as wives and mothers, and the 'opportunities' for women consist of better conditions in the home, improved child and maternity welfare, a better education for their children, and a pledge to make things easier for their menfolk who are 'crushed by unemployment'. □

It is important that we do not either underestimate the changes that had already taken place, or fall into the trap of applying the values of the early 1990s to the late 1920s. We should not necessarily condemn Bondfield because she does not address the questions *we* think she should be addressing. Bondfield herself was a career woman. She had figured prominently as a leading woman trade unionist and in 1923 she became a Labour MP. After the election she had the distinction of becoming the first woman Cabinet minister and privy councillor.

Exercise Drawing upon your reading of the last unit, why do you think Bondfield concentrated on the subject of women as wives and mothers? ■

Specimen answer and discussion At this time unemployment in Britain was higher than in the other Western democracies. It had not fallen under 10 per cent since 1921 and so it would have been misleading to suggest that vast employment opportunities were open to women. In addition Bondfield was fully aware that she must not alienate working men voters. Since the ending of the war, tensions had existed concerning the employment of women at the expense of men, especially as women's wages were invariably lower (in some industries 50 to 60 per cent lower) than men's. We must not exclude the possibility that perhaps Bondfield was saying the sort of things that appealed to many voters. After the upheavals of war many felt that it was perfectly reasonable that women's main role should be that of building a stable family life, and that improved social welfare legislation and better education were higher priorities than employment opportunities for women. After all, confronted with some 7 million new voters, most of whom were women, Labour won the election, not with an overall majority, but they were, for the first time in their history, the largest party in the House of Commons. □

Nevertheless, the proportion of women working in Britain compares favourably with France and Germany, especially if figures relating to women involved in agriculture in France and Germany are discounted. As Arthur Marwick has pointed out, there was a drop in the female workforce immediately after the war, especially in the percentage of married women employed, but in the period 1921 to 1931 the number of women who worked outside the home increased by around 500,000. Overall throughout the inter-war years, the proportion of the female working force to men remained fairly constant.

Table 15.1   *Women as percentage of labour force*

1911	29.7
1921	29.5
1931	29.7
1951	30.8

(Cited in Lewis, *Women in England, 1870–1950*, 1984, p.147)

In Germany in 1925 agriculture employed nearly half the female labour force (mostly peasant wives who were categorized as 'helping dependents'), industry a third to a quarter, and service and distributive industries an eighth. In both France and Germany, as a result of the great loss of life during the war, there was a major labour shortage, which was largely solved by the employment of women. In Germany in 1925 the number of women working was 35 per cent higher than in 1907. The general trend of female employment in the inter-war years, however, was similar in Britain, France and Germany in that the fastest growing areas of female employment were in the new light industries, public administration and commerce. In Germany in 1907 some 493,000 women were regarded as white-collar employees or 5.8 per cent of the total female workforce. By 1925 the number was 1,446,000 or 12.6 per cent and by 1933 it had risen to 1,695,000 or 14.8 per cent of the workforce (cited in Bridenthal, 'Beyond *Kinder, Kuche, Kirche*', 1973).

Women's roles in these areas of employment, however, were most often subordinate ones. The office and shop work offered to women, usually as secretaries, typists or shop assistants, was low paid and prospects of promotion were small. Nor must it be thought that the opening up of these new areas of employment automatically meant a decline in numbers of women employed in more traditional work. Although the number of women in domestic work in Britain had declined by nearly half a million in the first years of World War I, the inter-war census figures reveal that there was a return to this sort of work largely because it was one of the very few areas of employment which continued to experience a labour shortage in these years. By 1931 over 1,330,000 women were employed in domestic work, but unlike those of the pre-war years, the majority of these women were 'chars' as opposed to servants living-in.

In nearly all branches of industry, commerce and public administration, women's pay remained much lower than that of men. In Germany, immediately following the ending of the war, the principle of equal pay for equal work had been written into some contracts, but these were gradually changed after 1920 and wage differentials between women and men during the 1920s were between 30 and 40 per cent. This was an improvement on the 50 to 60 per cent existing before the war and which was around the proportion existing in many British industries in the 1920s and 1930s.

Entrance into the professions was difficult for women in all three countries. In Weimar Germany there was a marked increased in the number of women doctors, dentists and lawyers in the 1920s. The number of women lawyers quintuplicated between 1925 and 1933, but this was starting from a very small base and in 1933 only 1.5 per cent of all lawyers were women and only 5 per cent of all doctors were women. In all, about 6 per cent of the female German working population was engaged in the professions. This was about the same percentage as in Britain where the Sex Disqualification (Removal) Act of 1919 had removed legal restrictions on women entering the professions. An increasing number of women did enter professional and public life, but it was not easy and numbers remained relatively small. For example, although many more women may have wished to pursue careers in politics, the number of women selected as candidates only rose from seventeen in 1918 (one was elected) to sixty-seven in 1935 (nine were elected).

Despite this the status of women in Britain and Weimar Germany was higher than that of women in France. In Germany, immediately after the war, women had been given the vote and, in theory at least, legal equality. In Britain during the inter-war period, the Matrimonial Causes Act (1923), the Guardianship of Infants Act (1924), New English Law of Property Act (1926), the Representation of the People (Equal Franchise) Act (1928) and the Law Reform Act (1935), improved women's political rights as well as their civil rights in relation to family affairs, marriage, and the possession and disposal of property. In France, however, until the end of this period, there was very little legislation passed which improved women's working conditions and, despite the Chamber of Deputies passing legislation enfranchising women over thirty in 1919, 1925, 1932 and 1935, all the bills were thrown out by the Senate, largely because the Senate feared that votes for women would be translated into votes for the Catholic Church. In nearly every respect the legal status of married women was vastly inferior to that of men. For example, until 1937 a Frenchwoman could not obtain a passport without her husband's consent. If she married a foreigner, she lost her French nationality and did not automatically recover it on the death of her husband. This was rectified in 1927, but it was not until 1938 that married women obtained some semblance of full legal capacity. But even then, as James McMillan states, 'wives were still subject to important legal constrictions, since the husband remained the head of the family and could still veto his wife's employment and benefit from the property arrangements under the different types of community' (*Housewife or Harlot*, 1981, p.129).

2 *FAMILIES*

Exercise   In Units 8–10, section 2.1, Bill Purdue discussed some of the effects of the great loss of life caused by the fighting in the Great War and how this resulted in the inter-war years in an imbalance between the sexes, especially in those aged between twenty and forty-four. I want you now to re-read Roberts, page 482 to the top of page 486, from 'Changed attitudes affected the family' to 'thanks to cheap soap powders'.

1   What factors does Roberts regard as important in affecting attitudes towards the family in the period 1918–39?

2   What factors were specifically caused by the Great War?

3   What were the effects on family life and attitudes towards the family as a result of the imbalance between the sexes? ■

Specimen answers and discussion   1(a)   Roberts sees long-term changes in the family, especially in its role as the traditional 'organizing, disciplining and educational agency of society' (p.482), largely as a result of the industrialization of Europe, changing work patterns and increased social mobility.

(b)   The family was increasingly coming to be seen in the sense of the nuclear family rather than the extended family.

(c)   Improved methods of contraception was one factor in reducing the size of families, although Roberts points out that attitudes towards contraception varied greatly from country to country depending on religious and social attitudes.

(d)   Material changes meant that, for women, gradually less time needed to be spent in the home.

2(a)   The war put a great strain upon marriages because of long separations.

(b)   A big imbalance in numbers between the sexes was brought about by the war.

(c)   Women were involved in men's work for the first time, 'so that it was impossible later to believe they could ever have been thought unable to do it' (p.485).

3   Roberts states that the effects were seen in changes in sexual behaviour,

marriage patterns and creative activity in the period 1918–39. But the effects varied very much from country to country.

For example, in France, where we have already seen that before the war the birthrate was the lowest in Europe, and where even in 1911 the female population exceeded the male population by some 684,000, the effects of the war were to magnify this imbalance even further. If you add up the figures on page 60 of Units 8–10, you will find that the number of women exceeding men in France in 1921 was nearly 2 million and in the age group twenty to forty-four the figure is 1,200,000.

The responses in France to this imbalance were twofold and, at times, contradictory. On the one hand the shortage of men, and the consequent labour shortage, militated in favour of women working. On the other hand, there was a strong view that the home, motherhood and producing children to restore the population level was the main task of French women. This was one reason, along with the strong influence of the Catholic Church, why legislation was passed in 1920 prosecuting those people who disseminated birth control information or who made available the use of contraceptives. In 1923 further legislation was passed aimed at curbing abortions.

Despite this the population of France grew more slowly than any other European country, except Ireland, and then the increase, 7 per cent between the wars (in Britain the increase was 9 per cent and Germany 18 per cent), was only achieved by the vast immigration of foreigners. By the late 1920s nearly one-tenth of all marriages were mixed and by 1936, 2.4 million, or 5.8 per cent of the total population of France consisted of foreigners (François Caron, *An Economic History of Modern France*, 1979, p.74). The government's concern at the low birthrate was demonstrated in 1932 by the introduction of tax relief and allowances to wage-earners with families. In 1938 this was extended to small farmers and in 1939 to the whole country. Family allowances were given to those women who produced a child within the first two years of marriage and further sums were given on the birth of subsequent children.

The decline in the birthrate was a factor common to all three of the Western democracies.

Table 15.2   *Births per thousand population*

France	Germany	England & Wales	Scotland
1910–14 18.8	1913 27.5	1911–15 23.6	25.4
1920–24 19.9	1921–25 22.1	1921–25 19.9	23.0
1925–29 18.5	1926–30 18.4	1926–30 16.7	20.0
1930–34 17.3	1931–35 16.5	1931–35 15.0	18.2
1935–39 14.7		1936–40 14.7	17.6

(Statistics cited in Caron, *An Economic History of Modern France*, 1983, p.184; The Open University, 1987 A323 *Weimar Germany*, Study Guide p.15; Stevenson, *British Society, 1914–45*, 1984, p.148)

The reasons for this general decline are complex. Roberts suggests some in his discussion of the attitudes towards family life. An important factor in Britain was, as Arthur Marwick has pointed out (Units 8–10, pp.110–11), the growing awareness of various methods of contraception. Stevenson (p.150) quotes a survey carried out in 1949 where a comparison was made of birth-control habits of women married between 1910–19 and those married between 1935–39. In the first group 40 per cent used some form of birth control, although only one quarter of them used any method other than withdrawal whereas, of those married between 1935 and 1939, 66 per cent used some form of birth control and over half of this 66 per cent used some form other than withdrawal. Certainly, the inter-war years saw both the growing availability of improved methods of contraception and its gradual acceptance. In 1930 the National Birth Control Council was formed and it was renamed the Family Planning Association in 1939. But these changes must be put into perspective: there were only sixty-six branches of the FPA existing in 1939 and just how many working-class women took advantage of their advice is unknown. (The French Family Planning Movement was not founded until 1956.) What is clear, however, especially in relation to Britain, is that whereas before the war the decline in the birthrate was most marked among the upper and middle classes, in the inter-war years there is a marked lowering in the birthrate in working-class families and the idea of smaller families was becoming common to all classes.

3 GROWTH OF NEW INDUSTRIES AND URBANIZATION

As well as a marked drop in the birthrate, another important demographic change taking place in Britain during the inter-war years was the migration of population away from the old industrial areas in Scotland, Wales and the north-west and the north-east to the centres of the light and service industries in the Midlands, the south-east and London and its suburbs. The decline of the heavy staple industries was reflected in a drop in the population of Wales between the wars of around 450,000. The population of the London area, on the other hand, increased from 7.5 million to nearly 8.5 and, overall, of the total population increase in the country, 60 per cent of it was recorded in the south-east of England.

Whereas in Britain there was a great deal of internal migration between the wars, this was not the case in Germany during the period of the Weimar Republic. The large movement of population from east to west had largely subsided by the 1920s. Also there was not a substantial amount of urban growth. Although numbers in agriculture were declining, they were still substantial and, as we have seen, the growth areas in Germany in the 1920s were not industry so much as trade and transport.

In France, the trend apparent before the war of a drift of the population out of agriculture and mining into new and service industries and transport continued. The Midi and south-west became more thinly populated while the north and north-east were the areas of dense population and industry. By 1936 there were twenty towns in France with populations of over 100,000 compared with seventeen in 1920, and the remarkable growth of Paris, or rather its suburbs, continued. The growth of the capital had been accelerated further during the war when munition factories were built in the suburbs and other industries were transferred from the German-occupied areas to Paris and its surrounding area. This expansion continued throughout the 1920s and, in addition, many Parisians moved out to the suburbs as the Metro was extended and transport became easier. Between 1921 and 1931 the population of the department of Seine-et-Oise increased by 444,000, an expansion of 50 per cent. Paris, in 1936, contained a population of 2.5 million, but together with its rapidly developing suburbs, the total was 6 million.

With this burgeoning population came slums and the notorious 'la zone', which circled Paris, the conditions of which, so the French historians Bernard and Dubief claim, were far worse than those in Poplar or Whitechapel (*The Decline of the Third Republic*, 1975, p.244).

One of the important industries in both France and Britain in the inter-war years was that of vehicle production. The opportunities for work afforded on the assembly lines of these new mass-production industries meant that, in Britain, towns like Oxford, Luton and Coventry attracted workers from economically depressed regions.

Table 15.3   *Motor vehicles 000s*

	France	UK
1926	192	198
1927	191	212
1928	223	212
1929	253	239
1930	230	237
1931	201	226
1932	163	233
1933	189	286
1934	181	343
1935	165	404
1936	204	462
1937	201	508

(Cited in Kemp, *The French Economy*, 1972, p.106)

Exercise   Study the figures in Table 15.3 for vehicle production in Britain and France for the period 1926 to 1937. Why do you think there is a contraction in production in both countries in the early 1930s? ■

Specimen answer and discussion   Vehicle production, like most other industries, was hit, although not as badly as many, by the Great Depression. The Depression which started in 1929 brought about a collapse of international trade, a fall in the price of raw materials, a market reduction in the production of manufactured goods, a drop in money incomes and sharp rises in unemployment in many countries, and in so doing inevitably, to a greater or lesser extent, affected the social changes taking place in Britain, France and Germany in the inter-war years. So, before we can go on to discuss the other important changes in the list that we made at the start of this unit, it is necessary to take into consideration the effects of the Great Depression on the Western democracies. □

4 THE GREAT DEPRESSION

In Unit 14 we spent a considerable time looking at the economies of the three Western democracies in the 1920s and concluded that during the second half of the decade, generally speaking, economic production finally returned to pre-war levels, European currencies were stabilized, and as well as growing prosperity there was a new optimism in foreign relations. The 'Great Depression' was to hamper this progress seriously. Bill Purdue, in Book II, Units 8–10, raised the question of whether this depression was at least partly caused by the economic consequences of the Great War. A key text in exploring this point is the Introduction to Derek H. Aldcroft's book, *From Versailles to Wall Street, 1919–1929*, which is reprinted in the *Offprints Booklet*. If you have time, refresh your memory by re-reading this extract.

Almost all the countries of Europe were affected to a greater or lesser extent by the Depression. It was regarded by some as a catastrophe almost on the scale of that of the Great War. William E. Leuchtenburg, in an article called 'The New Deal and the Analogue of War', first published in 1964, argues that many politicians in the early 1930s used the imagery of the war when describing the Depression and, more importantly, they looked back to the experiences of the war, especially in regard to the economic mobilization which took place in these years, as the most suitable means of combating the Depression. Leuchtenburg illustrates his thesis with specific reference to the New Deal and the United States. He concludes that using the imagery of war was invaluable because it provided a feeling of national solidarity, but that in the last resort the New Deal would have been more successful if the economists and politicians had dealt with the basic economic and social problems rather than looking towards the 'analogue of war', that is, the economic expedients which were used in the war. Although Leuchtenburg illustrates his thesis with specific reference to the United States, it is one that is worthy of consideration in relation to events in Europe, and we should bear it in mind as we discuss the impact and after-effects of the Depression.

Exercise Read Roberts, pages 364–7, in which he outlines the reasons for the world slump.

1 Which of the three countries does Roberts believe was hardest hit and why?

2 Which of the three countries does Roberts state was least affected and why?

3 From your study of the figures for vehicle production in Table 15.3, documents I.5 (unemployment figures) and I.6 (industrial production indices) in *Documents 2*, do you think these statistics go some way to confirming Roberts's view? (Once again I should emphasize the difficulty of obtaining accurate figures for unemployment. Invariably, official figures are understatements of the actual numbers unemployed. However, they do illustrate trends.) ∎

Specimen answers and discussion

1 Roberts believes that Germany was hit hardest by the world slump, largely because of its heavy dependence on international credit, especially credit from the USA.

2 Roberts believes that Britain was the least affected by the world slump. The reason for this, so Roberts states, was that British industry had 'benefited less from the boom of the 1920s and lost less ground comparatively'.

3 Generally speaking, I think both the unemployment figures and industrial production indices do correlate with the statements of Roberts. In Germany unemployment rose more sharply than in Britain and by 1932 nearly 6 million people, or almost one in three of the working population, was unemployed. Nevertheless, although the percentage of people unemployed in Britain was higher before the slump than in Germany, there was still a very marked rise in unemployment and it was not until 1937 that the figures returned to the pre-1930

level. Right up until the outbreak of World War II unemployment in Britain was over 1.5 million. ☐

Again from the indices of industrial production it is clear that Germany was very seriously affected by the world slump, and that in 1932 industrial production was only 53 per cent of the output produced in 1929. In Britain, industrial production was hit less severely but it was not until 1935 that production was back to the 1929 level.

Roberts does not mention France specifically but France was affected in a different way from the other two countries. From the unemployment statistics we can see that while unemployment increased rapidly in Britain and Germany in 1930, there was only a very small rise in France in that year. In fact it was not until 1932 that the unemployment figures in France became relatively high. However, the same sort of pattern is produced in the industrial production table. Unlike Britain and Germany, industrial production did not decline in 1930 and it was only in 1932 that there was a marked drop. From all these figures it is clear that the Depression hit France later than most of the other industrialized countries of the world. The reasons for this are complex and varied but basically France was not a producer of raw materials, it was less heavily industrialized than Britain and Germany and was not so dependent on the world economy as those two countries. Also, unlike Germany, France was not irrevocably dependent on loans from the USA. In addition, as we have already seen, France was underpopulated so that unemployment was not the problem it became in Britain and Germany. Nevertheless, what is interesting from the figures is that while in Britain one can see signs of a drop in unemployment from 1932 onwards, and it is a significant drop by 1935–36, in France unemployment goes up and remains at a relatively high level right up until the outbreak of war. Also, the vehicle production figures in Table 15.3 reveal that while production is on the upturn in 1932 and exceeds all previous figures in 1933, in France there is a much slower recovery and the 1929 levels of production have not been reached in 1937. This is confirmed by the overall industrial production indices which show that whereas by 1935 Britain had returned to its 1929 level of industrial production, France's production was at its nadir and it was not until 1938 that France showed visible signs of recovering from the Depression. So, while the effects of the Great Depression were initially less harsh on France than on many other countries, in the long-run France suffered severely and recovery came slower and later than in Britain.

In our discussion of Maier's thesis in Unit 14 (that during the 1920s there was a trend towards corporatism in Europe), we noted that Maier argued that it was from around the mid-1920s that the hopes of returning to a pre-1914 economic system were jettisoned. This may well have been the case, but if any hopes still lingered the Great Depression finally ended them. Roberts quotes Harold Macmillan who, writing in 1938, was able to reflect that the slump 'liberated men's minds from a continued subservience to the economic orthodoxy of the prewar world' (p.367). However, it is impossible to exaggerate the effect, especially during the bleak years of 1930–32, that the Depression had on contemporaries. John Maynard Keynes, in a lecture in the United States in 1931, declared that:

> We are today in the middle of the greatest economic catastrophe – the
> greatest catastrophe due almost entirely to economic causes – of the
> modern world . . . the view is held in Moscow that this is the last, the

culminating crisis of capitalism and that our existing order of society will not survive it . . . there is a possibility that when this crisis is looked back upon by the economic historian of the future it will be seen to mark one of the major turning points . . . (cited in Fearon, *The Origins and Nature of the Great Slump, 1929–32,* 1979, p.9)

The devastating effects of the Great Slump on Germany have led some historians to contend that it was the major factor in breaking up the Weimar Republic and bringing Hitler to power. This is an issue that will be discussed by Bernard Waites in Unit 18. For France the 1930s were, so Douglas and Madeleine Johnson contend, a 'time of troubles' and a period of 'apprehension and protest' (*The Age of Illusion,* 1987, pp.97 and 103). In Britain the 1930s had variously been called 'the Devil's Decade', the decade of mass unemployment, and the 'hungry thirties'. Yet if this is the case, how do these verdicts square with the views of Roberts that we read at the start of this unit, and which we still have to examine, concerning the improvement in material conditions, social reforms and increased leisure activities?

Exercise I want you to spend time now looking at and listening to a number of primary sources, all of which originated in October or November 1936. It would be useful if you used them in the following order: first watch video-cassette 1, item 10 'The Prime Minister Speaks Out', 23 November 1936; item 11 'Jarrow unemployed march to London', 8 October 1936; item 12 'Jarrow marchers reach London', 2 November 1936; item 13 'Demonstration – police kept busy by street clashes in a tale of two cities', 8 October 1936. Then listen to audio-cassette 3, item 9 'Radio Gazette No. 1 – review of events at home and abroad'.

1 How does Baldwin sum up the state of Britain in 1936?

2 Does he suggest there are any problems in Britain at all?

3 How does he compare Britain with other European countries?

4 What reasons does he give for Britain's recovery?

5 In what ways do the other items confirm or contradict Baldwin's remarks? ■

Specimen answers and discussion 1 Baldwin declares that there has never been a time when the people of Britain have been more prosperous, better cared for and more contented. Industry has been on the road to recovery for five years and some industries are now breaking all previous records; for the past two years wage levels have been rising and unemployment is falling. (Note Baldwin does not mention unemployment; he states *employment* has been *increased*.)

2 The only reference Baldwin makes in this direction is that he acknowledges there are 'difficulties in some districts'.

3 We should be thankful we are British. Abroad there is economic and industrial depression; conscription; violence; withdrawal of liberties; and in Spain there is civil war.

4 There is a confidence in industry, finance and, above all, a confidence within the country between all sections of the community. At the time of crisis, instead of engaging in conflict, the country united under a National government and the men from all the political parties who formed this government took the right steps. So, unlike other European countries, Britain avoided extremes and the country has 'steered clear of fascism, communism and dictatorship'.

5   The Jarrow marchers and their petition for work are evidence that unemployment is a problem, although this could fall into Baldwin's category of 'difficulties in some districts'. Also, although Baldwin states that the country has steered clear of violence, disturbances, fascism and communism, the reports on the demonstrations in the East End indicate that the country is not totally peaceable. □

The depiction of events in France seems to confirm Baldwin's assertion that matters are worse abroad. The report concerning the devaluation of the franc clearly reveals that there are major disagreements within the French Senate and the Chamber of Deputies and that the devaluation is taking place because of a crisis in the French economy. Also, the street riots 'seem' worse than those in Britain. This does bring us to an interesting point with regard to the nature of historical evidence concerning how the media depicted these particular events. It is a topic that will be discussed in some detail by Tony Aldgate in Unit 19.

Exercise   Before discussing these events any further, I want you to read a secondary source covering the same issues. It is an extract from Stevenson and Cook's book, *The Slump,* which has been described by Arthur Marwick in a review in *History* as 'One of the most relentlessly brilliant studies of twentieth-century Britain yet published'. The extract 'The Revolution that Never Was' is the last chapter from the book and it is reprinted in the *Offprints Booklet.*

1   In what respects do Stevenson and Cook agree with Baldwin's assessment of the condition of Britain in the second half of the 1930s?

2   In what respects do they disagree with Baldwin?

3   What reasons do they give for explaining why there was no breakdown of democratic processes as in Germany, or why extremist parties did not obtain a foothold as in France? Why, in fact, was Britain, compared with France and Germany, so stable in the 1930s? ■

Specimen answers   1   Stevenson and Cook agree that the average family was wealthier, healthier,
and discussion   better housed and had a wider range of consumer goods to choose from than ever before. Britain had been making an economic recovery from 1933 to 1934 and, as we have already noted, the number of unemployed was falling.

Stevenson and Cook also acknowledged the ability of the Conservative Party, in the guise of the National government, in maintaining a stable administration during this period, and they agree to some extent with the implication in Baldwin's speech that there is an essential harmony or 'confidence in each other' within the country. As they state on page 31, 'Britain remained a relatively cohesive and insular society in which there were still a large number of shared assumptions'. Despite the inequalities that did exist there were considerable agreements between, in Orwell's words, 'the leaders and the led'. If you look back at the newsreel of the Jarrow marchers, you will notice that the commentator states, with justification, that Jarrow was 'probably the hardest hit town in Britain'. The level of unemployment in the town was around 70 per cent, yet 46.9 per cent of the electorate in the Jarrow constituency voted for the government in the 1935 election. Many working men voted Conservative and saw them as 'the saviours of the country' (p.28).

2   Within areas of the country there were very high levels of unemployment and the figures below show that Baldwin's reference to 'difficulties in some districts' was something of an understatement.

Table 15.4   *Unemployed as a percentage of insured workers in regions of Great Britain*

	1929	1932	1937
London & SE England	5.6	13.7	6.4
SW England	8.1	17.1	7.8
Midlands	9.3	20.1	13.8
Northern England	13.5	27.1	13.6
Wales	19.3	36.5	22.3
Scotland	12.1	27.7	15.9
Northern Ireland	15.1	27.2	23.6

(Cited in Stevenson, *British Society 1914–45*, 1984, p.271)

Stevenson and Cook point out that there was ill-feeling within the depressed areas of the country, especially in relation to the administration of the dole. But this anger tended to be directed against those people who administered the means test locally, namely councillors and community leaders who made up the local Public Assistance Committees, rather than towards the members of parliament who had passed the means test legislation.

3   Here there is agreement with the point made by Roberts that the onset of the Depression in Britain was not so sudden and traumatic as in Germany, nor so long lasting as in France. Unemployment in Germany was more evenly spread throughout the country, and France throughout the 1920s had been more politically unstable than Britain.

Stevenson and Cook also refer to the sense of apathy and fatalism that seemed to exist within the ranks of the unemployed, and which was reflected in a lack of interest in political activism. This is explained in a variety of ways. For example, the relative cohesiveness within the country, already discussed in answer 1. Again, the influence of religion should not be ignored and within some Roman Catholic communities, especially in the North East, unemployment was regarded as 'a cross to be borne'. Also, the trade unions which had taken a battering after the failure of the General Strike were not in a position to adopt a militant stance and they devoted most of their resources to consolidating their position and attempting to improve rates of pay and conditions of work through negotiation. Finally, Stevenson and Cook argue that a major reason why extremist parties did not gain a foothold was because of the confidence held in the National government itself and also because the major opposition party, the Labour Party, itself a major factor for stability, retained a solid body of support through-out the 1930s. ☐

Exercise   Refer back to document I.2 in *Documents 2* and study the figures relating to 1929 onwards.

1   Do the figures for Britain confirm or contradict the point made by Stevenson and Cook that support for the Labour Party remained fairly constant throughout the 1930s?

2   What evidence is there to show from these documents that France and Germany were politically more unstable and more inclined to extremism than Britain? ■

Specimen answers and discussion   1   This part of the exercise reinforces the point made by Arthur Marwick in Book I, Unit 1 when he discussed the use of statistics. 'Be sensitive to what statistics cannot do, as well as to what they can do. Be aware of their limitations . . .' (p.40). If you had merely concentrated on the table giving the number of seats won by political parties in the House of Commons, you probably would have disagreed with Cook and Stevenson's conclusion, for the number of Labour MPs was reduced from 287 to 46 at the 1931 general election. However, the table of percentages of votes cast reveals that the swing against Labour was under 8 per cent, much less than the loss of seats would seem to suggest. The explanation why the loss of seats exaggerates and obscures the percentage swing against Labour is relatively straightforward. Labour had, in one sense, been over-represented in the Commons as a result of the previous election. Then they had won more seats than the Conservatives but obtained fewer votes. They won a fair number of seats with very slim majorities and 41 per cent of their seats had been won on a minority vote in three-cornered contests. With the formation of the National government and the uniting of so many of the Labour Party's opponents, in the 1931 election over 400 Labour candidates found themselves in straight fights with only one other candidate, and in the vast majority of these contests they were unsuccessful.

At the 1935 election, there was a swing back to Labour and, although only 154 MPs were returned to the Commons, the percentage of votes cast for Labour was higher than it had been in 1929. Indeed there was just one percentage difference in the votes cast for Labour in 1929 compared with 1935, so that overall the figures do confirm the point, made by Stevenson and Cook, that support for the Labour Party remained fairly constant throughout the 1930s.

The loser in the 1930s was the Liberal Party. The percentage of votes cast for them dropped sharply in 1931 when they fielded just 118 candidates compared with 513 in 1929. Conservative support for those who now called themselves National Liberals left the remainder of the party disillusioned, and their representation in parliament was to decline even further as a result of the 1935 election.

2   In Germany the rapid success of the National Socialist party after 1928 eventually led to the break-up of the Weimar Republic. In France the political instability which was clearly present in the 1920s is even more marked in the years during the Great Depression. Seventeen different ministries were formed in the six years between July 1929 and June 1935, roughly a change of ministry every eighteen weeks.

Neither in the figures showing representation in parliament nor in the voting figures is there much sign of extremist parties being at all influential in Britain. There was no British Union of Fascist MPs and only one Communist MP from 1935 onwards. Parliament in the 1930s was dominated by the Conservative Party who formed by far the greater part of the National government. The formation of the National government had come about very swiftly at the height of the Depression in the summer of 1931 when the Labour government, which had been in power since 1929, with the support of the Liberals, was unable to agree on the extent to which government expenditure should be cut in order to obtain foreign loans and secure the confidence of foreign investors. Faced with deadlock in the Cabinet, the Prime Minister, Ramsay MacDonald, handed in his resignation to the king, but was persuaded to stay on and lead a National government composed primarily of Conservatives, some Liberals and the few members of the Labour Cabinet who still supported him. The government was formed, the cuts were made, and a general election was called for November 1931. □

Just why Britain was such a cohesive society compared with France and Germany is something to which thought should be given. Clearly there were long-term structural and ideological differences. Referring back to Unit 14, it is worth bearing in mind the reasons why Charles Maier did not include Britain in his study of *Recasting Bourgeois Europe*. His major reasons were that in Britain the political arena was not so fragmented and there were not the deep ideological differences existing between the contending power élites which could be detected in France, Italy and Germany. With regard to the power élites in France, Arthur Marwick has argued that, compared with Britain, 'France in the 1930s was characterized by an even tighter control of the positions of real power, particularly in finance and industry, by a distinctive upper class, though mediated by the strong influence over the National Assembly exercised by the provincial upper-middle class; in all areas the working class appears considerably weaker than its British counterpart' (*CLASS*, 1981, p.183).

Yet another factor we must take into account is the effects of the war on these countries, for as Bill Purdue has pointed out in Book II, Units 8–10, section 2.1, although Britain lost some 0.75 million men in the war, the war in terms of death, destruction and emotion had less impact on Britain than it had on both France and Germany. On the next few pages we shall discuss why the communist parties, which were founded in France and Germany following the Russian Revolution and the ending of the war, attracted much more support than the Communist Party of Great Britain. The same can be said for the various fascist parties which grew up on the continent after the war and attracted many war veterans to their ranks. Finally we must take into account economic factors and, as we have just seen, the Great Depression hit Germany (immediately) and France (in the long run) harder than Britain.

Exercise Listen to the 1931 election speeches of Lloyd George and Ramsay MacDonald which are items 3 and 4 on audio-cassette 3. What do we learn about attitudes in Britain in 1931 from these two speeches? ■

Specimen answer and discussion I find Lloyd George's speech particularly interesting. On page 49 I mentioned Leuchtenburg's notion of the 'Analogue of War' and how politicians used the Great War, and very often the imagery of war, to describe the Depression. Here Lloyd George does just this and harks back to the sacrifices made in the 1914–18 war. I feel that on this occasion Lloyd George already realizes that his battle is lost; although he asserts that the electorate will, in reality, be electing a Conservative government rather than a truly national one, he is aware that the Conservatives, by agreeing to serve under MacDonald under a National label, have fully appreciated the feeling within the country which is one of a desire for political unity at this particular time during the Depression.

One further interesting point is Lloyd George's plea to oppose proposals for tariffs, something to which, in the depths of the Depression, most countries were resorting. Protectionism was anathema to all who believed in the principles of Liberalism and to those who still dreamed of returning to a pre-1914 Europe. But the battle was lost. Tariffs were imposed on virtually all imports and in 1932 imperial preference agreements were drawn up and signed.

Most of MacDonald's speech is spent explaining why he is now heading a government largely composed of Conservatives. The fault lay with the previous Labour government who 'could not make up its collective mind'. The new government had to take drastic actions. 'It was a hard thing to do but it could not have been avoided.' This speech surely reveals that pragmatism rather than principle dominated British politics at this time. It would be impossible to envisage a French socialist making a similar speech and agreeing to head a government largely composed of the Right. Yet this appears to be what the British electorate wanted, for this government received greater support from an electorate than any other this century with over 60 per cent of the votes being cast in its favour. □

Parliamentary statistics, however, do not present a complete picture and there were groups who, unable to secure satisfaction within parliament, expressed their disapproval of the government by taking to the streets. The National Unemployed Workers' Movement which had been formed in 1921 attracted considerable support during the early years of the National government. Its campaign for the abolition of the means test and increased unemployment relief brought about an increase in membership from 10,000 in 1929 to 37,000 by the end of 1931. As well as arranging demonstrations and meetings, in 1932 the NUWM organized a huge hunger march and a petition protesting against the means test. But the NUWM, partly because of its strong links with the Communist Party, never received support from the bulk of the Labour Party or the TUC and, despite its efforts, it failed to obtain mass support.

The same is true of the Communist Party itself. Its membership was never higher than 10,000 in the first half of the 1930s. In the second half of the decade, with the growth of Fascist movements in Italy and Germany, and the Civil War in Spain, membership grew to just under 18,000 on the eve of World War II.

Fascist politics too did not attract much support. The British Union of Fascists formed by Sir Oswald Mosley in 1932 held many marches and demonstrations, especially in London. It has been estimated that in 1934 there were 146 BUF branches throughout the country of which 34 were in and around London. Membership figures are hard to come by but it is very unlikely that the movement contained more than 35,000 members at any one time.

Despite the failure of these movements to attract substantial memberships, the government, mainly through the Special Branch, maintained a close watch on their activities, and demonstrations and marches organized by these bodies were policed very heavily. For the entry into London of the NUWM Hunger March in 1932 some 2,000 police were on duty and 600 special constables were held in reserve (see video-cassette 1, item 14 'Hunger trek ends', which is discussed by Tony Aldgate in Unit 19). In addition, with the growth of clashes between communists and the British Union of Fascists, further restrictive legislation was introduced with the Incitement of Disaffection Act, 1934, and the Public Order Act, 1936.

Although overall the British political scene may have been one of consensus, this was certainly not true of France in the 1930s. The 1932 election brought successes for both the radicals and the socialists, but they were unable to agree on what financial policies should be adopted to cope with the effects of the Depression. Five different Cabinets were formed in 1932 and four in 1933, during which time very little progress was made. This political instability, together with the growing economic crisis in France and the collapse of the Weimar Republic in neighbouring Germany, led many commentators to argue that France itself was on the verge of collapse and that the Republic was in danger of being replaced by some form of totalitarian government.

During the early 1930s there grew up, alongside the old traditional nationalist parties like the *Action Française*, a number of right-wing groups, some of which could be designated fascist or quasi-fascist. The largest of these was the *Croix de Feu*, founded in 1928 as an organization of veterans decorated for valour, but converted into a political movement in 1931 under the leadership of Colonel de la Rocque. By 1935 the organization claimed a membership of several hundred thousand. Very little unity existed between these various right-wing groups but in 1933 they were presented with an ideal opportunity to vent their collective opposition to the government over the Stavisky affair. (For an account of this affair see Roberts, p.402.) The rioting and street-fighting that followed in Paris on 6 February 1934 resulted in the deaths of fourteen demonstrators and one policeman and over 1,500 demonstrators and policemen were wounded.

Although there were claims that the main intention of the demonstrators on 6 February was to accomplish a *coup d'état*, the disunity among the parties of the Right has led a number of historians to doubt the claim. What these events certainly did do was to rouse the Left to take some action. On 12 February the CGTU and the communists held a successful one-day General Strike. But no real progress could be made until the radicals, socialists and communists put behind them their traditional animosity and agreed to work together. After complex negotiations, eventually a Popular Front composed of radicals, socialists and communists was formed and was in a position to put forward a joint programme for the 1936 election.

Exercise   Using document I.2 in *Documents 2*, compare the number of seats won and the percentage of votes cast in the French elections of 1932–36. Are there any significant differences? ■

Specimen answer and discussion   There was a marked increase in the percentage of votes cast for communist candidates and a sixfold increase in their representation in the Chamber. It was a tremendous victory for the Popular Front in that 382 radicals, socialists and communists were returned with a majority of 160 over the other parties. However, if you compare the percentage of votes cast for these parties in the two elections, the increase is only 3.8 per cent. This is considerable but not startling. What is important is that for the first time socialists, radicals and communists were prepared to act together (although the communists refused to take positions in the government), and as a result France had its first socialist Prime Minister in Léon Blum. □

Exercise   In 1935, the year before the success of the Popular Front in France, there was a general election in Britain. Look at video-cassette 1, item 15 'General Election Section' (in which speeches are made by Clement Attlee, the leader of the Labour Party, and the Prime Minister, Stanley Baldwin, 31 October 1935) and item 16 'National Government Returned'.

1   What are the significant features of the two speeches?

2   After consulting the election statistics for Britain in document I.2 in *Documents 2*, is there anything interesting to say about the General Election Special newsreel? ■

Specimen answers and discussion   1   The 1931 speech of Lloyd George dwelt on the heroism and patriotism engendered by World War I, but between 1931 and 1935 the international climate had changed to the extent that both Attlee and Baldwin are looking towards an uncertain future and the question of rearmament is becoming a major issue. Attlee argues that money should be spent on social reforms in preference to defence. Baldwin, who had taken over the premiership when MacDonald resigned in the summer of 1935, is careful not to overcommit the country to rearmament. His main warning, however, and here again it is worth bearing in mind Leuchtenburg's warning that politicians continually employed metaphors of war in reference to the problems of the Depression, is that it would be foolish for the electorate to rock the well-balanced boat at this time of great uncertainty. He argues, in the same vein as politicians in time of war, that above all experience is needed and that confidence and unity will be shattered by political upheaval.

2   The newsreel gives the verdict that the election resulted in an overwhelming victory for the National government and, indeed, it was. However, the newsreel makes no reference to the fact that there was a clear swing of over 7 per cent away from the National government and towards the Labour opposition and that eighty-five Conservative MPs lost their seats. □

5 *SOCIAL REFORM*

In their speeches at the 1935 election both Attlee and Baldwin mention social reforms. Attlee points out the urgent need for more; Baldwin argues that more housing and slum clearance schemes have been introduced than ever before. This brings us back to the start of the unit when we made a list of the significant areas of social change in the inter-war years. Education, welfare and insurance schemes are all mentioned by Roberts. What were the extent of these reforms? Were they extensions of the social legislation introduced during or immediately following the ending of the war, or were they introduced to deal with specific problems thrown up by the Depression with its resulting unemployment?

In Book II, Units 8–10, Table 8–10.2 shows important social reforms enacted in Europe during the war and in the 1920s. Arthur Marwick has already pointed out that during the war the extent of the welfare legislation in Britain exceeded that of the other European countries.

Exercise   From your reading of both this and Unit 14, what would you regard as the major area of social concern in Britain during both the 1920s and 1930s? ■

Specimen answer   The major area of social concern in Britain during the 1920s and 1930s was
and discussion   unemployment. Remember that for most of the inter-war years unemployment levels were much higher in Britain than in France or Germany. In Unit 14 I mentioned that in the social unrest following the ending of the war, the government acted with varying mixtures of repression, compromise, conciliation and specific social legislation, and that British governments were more prepared to conciliate and legislate than French governments. The National Insurance Acts of 1920 and 1921 were aimed specifically at coping with the problem of the unemployed, and this legislation provided the basis of the system of unemployment insurance which was administered during the inter-war years. The problem was, however, that no one had envisaged a state where unemployment after 1921 never fell below 1.5 million. Consequently, in an attempt to cope with the

particular problems caused by unemployment which was both high and persistent (the 1920 Act was based on the premise of unemployment benefit being given for fifteen weeks in a year), further piecemeal Acts were passed. It was not until 1934 that an overall attempt at the rationalization of unemployment benefit was made with the setting up of the Unemployment Assistance Board. This became responsible for unemployment payments which were now funded by the Treasury out of general taxation.

In 1931, when unemployment was well over 2.5 million in the country, the cost of unemployment benefits was around £120 million of which only about a third was covered by contributions. As we have seen, it was this particular issue of the escalating costs of employment benefits and the demand that, if Britain was to receive overseas loans, retrenchment on the part of the government was essential, that led to the break-up of the Labour government in 1931. If we go back to the radio broadcast made by Ramsay MacDonald during the election of 1931 (audio-cassette 3, item 4), the drastic actions that he speaks of ('it was a hard thing to do but it could not have been avoided') refers to the new National government's decision to cut unemployment benefits and the introduction of a means test. Nevertheless, Stevenson and Cook argue 'Although the dole was often desperately near the margin of adequacy and sometimes below, it was usually sufficient to keep people from desperation and the political consequences that might have resulted' (*Offprints Booklet*, p.29). As early as 1922 a report had pointed out that a major factor for the comparative lack of political unrest after the war, compared with that during the depressions of pre-1914, was the relief measures handed out to the unemployed.

Indeed, much of the energies of successive governments in this area of social welfare between the wars was devoted to responding to particularly pressing problems rather than introducing a planned series of reforms. For example, with regard to unemployment, despite the various unemployment benefit Acts, many of the unemployed, around 400,000 in the 1920s, were not covered by various provisions and were having to apply to their local poor law guardians for relief. In areas of high unemployment this put a great strain on the local rates and different boroughs gave different levels of relief. In 1921 some of the poor law guardians in Poplar, mostly Labour councillors, were sent to prison for refusing to contribute towards the upkeep of the LCC. Their reasons for not doing so were that all their moneys were needed to provide relief. On the other hand, the government accused the Poplar guardians of distributing relief at rates higher than those recommended by the Ministry of Health. In order to rationalize these problems arising from unemployment it became necessary to restructure the poor law system, which was done by the passing of the Local Government Act 1929 and the Poor Law Act of 1930. □

Exercise   Read Roberts, pages 416–7, from 'Economic depression did little to halt . . .' to '. . . the expressed will of the electorate'. As a student of 'War, Peace and Social Change', do you find anything remarkable about Roberts's discussion of the social welfare legislation of the period? ■

Specimen answer and discussion   Roberts does not have the space to go into any detail or discuss fully the extent of the social legislation in this period, but much of the legislation that he does discuss stems from the period of the war or the period of reconstruction immediately following the war. Rent controls were introduced in 1914 and the first of the six

Housing Acts was passed in 1919. Roberts also dates the origins of the National Health Service to 1918 when free treatment for VD was provided. Also in that year, as well as an Education Act local authorities were permitted to set up maternity clinics. Again, if you glance back over the last few pages of this unit dealing with social reform, you will see that I mention the Ministry of Health, a department which was created in 1919 in response to a recommendation made by the Ministry of Reconstruction, and I also refer to unemployment insurance which was introduced on a small scale before the war, but made available to a much wider section of the workforce during it.

Roberts clearly shows that much more was being spent on housing, pensions and education than ever before, and that expenditure on the social services increased over fivefold between 1913 and 1935. One of the most visible signs of advance in Britain, especially in the 1930s, was the rapid growth in housing. Remember, in his election speech Baldwin stressed housing and slum clearance as two important features of the government's programme. Overall, between the wars 4 million houses were built, of which 1.5 million were built by local authorities for renting. In addition, as John Stevenson points out in his book *British Society, 1914–45*, 'Social welfare expenditure at both national and local level, as a proportion of national income, increased from 5.5% in 1913 to 10.3% in 1924 and to 13.0% in 1938' (1984, pp.306–7). □

In Unit 14 I stated that social welfare legislation in France in the 1920s was conspicuous by its absence, but with the formation of the Popular Front and the publication of its programme in early 1936, one section of which was devoted to 'Economic Demands', there were high hopes among supporters of the Left that radical reforms would be forthcoming. In fact, the successful election of the Popular Front was accompanied by an enormous wave of sit-in strikes throughout France involving around 2 million people. The distinguishing aspect of these strikes was, in the words of Arthur Marwick, 'the lack of political or ideological motivation and direction in these strikes – strike activity was greatest where union organisation and communist or socialist party influence was weakest' (*CLASS*, 1981, p.139). Compared with most strikes in Britain, the sit-in strikes demonstrated very little unity or identity of feeling between the workers and their trade-union leaders. Nevertheless, to those who had not voted for the Popular Front, the strikes appeared as yet another reminder of the growing power of the Left.

Exercise Once in office one of the first actions of the new Prime Minister, Léon Blum, was to call together a meeting of the representatives of employers and unions to his official residence, the Hotel Matignon. Read document I.7 in *Documents 2*, 'The Matignon Agreement' (1936). What are the major agreements and, if Charles Maier had extended his study into the 1930s, how would he have interpreted these events? ■

Specimen answer and discussion The employers agree: to collective bargaining; that they must not discriminate against trade unionists; that they must recognize shop stewards; and that they must not take reprisals against those out on strike. In return the unions will request their workers to return to work as soon as the agreements start being put into operation. In addition, there is to be an immediate wage increase averaging 12 per cent.

Maier could well argue that this was a clear example of the trend towards corporatism in which major interest groups, together with the state, make major economic, political and social decisions. On the other hand, The Matignon Agreement can be interpreted merely as a sensible act on the part of a new Prime Minister who is anxious to introduce legislation which would satisfy his impatient supporters. □

In addition to this agreement many other reforms were passed through the French parliament in the next few weeks, including a forty-hour week in industry, holidays with pay, the raising of the school leaving age to fourteen, the institution of compulsory arbitration in industrial disputes and the bringing of the Bank of France under a degree of state control. Unfortunately, these reforms brought adverse economic consequences. The various welfare measures had to be paid for and many of the employers offset the 12 per cent rise in wages by increasing prices. Gold reserves fell drastically as fear of an economic collapse grew and despite promises the government was forced to devalue the franc in October 1936 (audio-cassette 3, item 9). Nevertheless, it was not enough, and in March 1937 Blum was pushed into the position of trying to restore confidence both abroad and at home by announcing a 'pause' in the programme of social reform. This statement, in addition to failing to satisfy business interests and overseas governments, caused dissatisfaction from the Left and there was a renewed wave of strikes. Blum was forced to resign in 1937 and although he attempted to form further ministries in the following year, they were unsuccessful. By the time of the outbreak of World War II, the government contained ministers who had been outright opponents of the Popular Front.

6 *MATERIAL CHANGE*

Exercise   Although we have on a number of occasions mentioned improvements in the standard of living in Britain and France during the inter-war years, all the comments have, in fact, been very general. Even Roberts presents very little evidence to support his conclusion of a rise in standards. So look at document I.8 in *Documents 2*, a table of wages, prices and real earnings in Britain, and give your answers to the following questions.

1   What significant trends can be drawn from these figures?

2   What is the major weakness of these sorts of tables? ◼

Specimen answers and discussion   1   As we have already discussed in Book II, Units 8–10, there was an enormous increase in wages during World War I, but with the slump in 1920–21 wage rates fell markedly in the next two years. They then remained fairly constant until 1930 when they fell during the worst years of the Depression. From 1933 there was a slow but steady rise.

A similar movement can be seen with regard to retail prices in that there is a large increase during and immediately after the war. However, after 1920 prices fall more or less continuously, apart from 1924–25, until 1934. After 1935 there is a gradual rise in prices.

The important point is that for the most part during the inter-war years real wages rose and, during the Depression, prices fell faster than wages, so that average real wages increased during the worst years of the Depression.

2   Neither average wage rates nor average real wage earnings convey the problems confronting those people whose earnings were either below the average or who were unemployed. Agricultural workers, for example, earned on average £1.70 per week in 1938, well below the average industrial wage of around £3 per week and, as we have already seen, a vast number of women workers' wages were well below the average. Again, the amount coming into the house of the unemployed family varied, but a survey of families in Stockton-on-Tees during the early years of the Depression revealed that the average income of families where the wage earner was unemployed was £1.01 per week. However, as Norman McCord has pointed out in his study of *North East England*, 'in health, housing, diet, education, recreation and opportunity the situation in 1939 was appreciably better than it had been in 1920, despite the enormous economic adversity which afflicted the region during this period' (1974, p.242). ☐

As we have seen, although the new engineering industries in Britain were hit by the Depression, the disruption was comparatively light compared with those areas in which the old heavy exporting industries prevailed. In 1933, J. B. Priestley travelled around England and was particularly struck by the difference in the living standards and environment of particular regions. In fact he saw not one England but three, and in at least one of the three, Priestley describes what he saw as the important influence of the USA on British social life during these years. This is a factor which we have not touched on explicitly so far. It is also a controversial issue which will crop up again throughout the remainder of the course.

> I had seen a lot of Englands. How many? At once three disengaged themselves from the shifting mass. There was, first, Old England, the country of the cathedrals and minsters and manor houses and inns, of Parson and Squire: guide-books and quaint highways and byways England . . .
> Then, I decided, there is the nineteenth-century England, the industrial England of coal, iron, steel, cotton, wool, railways: of thousands of rows of little houses all alike, sham Gothic churches, square-faced chapels, Town Halls, Mechanics' Institutes, mills, foundries, warehouses, refined watering-places. Pier Pavilions, Family and Commercial Hotels, Literary and Philosophical Societies, back to back houses, detached villas with monkey-trees, Grill Rooms, railway stations, slag-heaps and 'tips', dock roads, Refreshment Rooms, doss-houses, Unionist or Liberal Clubs, cindery waste ground, mill chimneys, slums, fried-fish shops, public houses with red blinds, bethels in corrugated iron, good-class drapers' and confectioners' shops, a cynically devastated countryside, sooty dismal little towns, and still sootier grim fortress-like cities. This England makes up the large part of the Midlands and the North and exists everywhere; but it is not being added to and has no new life poured into it . . .
> The third England, I concluded, was the new post-war England, belonging far more to the age itself than to this particular island. America, I supposed, was its real birth-place. This is the England of arterial and by-pass roads, of filling stations and factories that look like exhibition buildings, of giant cinemas and dance halls and cafes, bungalows with tiny garages, cocktail bars, Woolworths, motor-coaches, wireless, hiking, factory girls looking like actresses, greyhound racing and dirt tracks, swimming pools and everything given away for cigarette coupons . . .
> (Priestley, *English Journey*, 1934, pp.397, 398–9, 401)

Exercise   In chapter 14, 'Social and cultural change, 1918–1939', Roberts implies that material improvements were not so marked in France as in Britain. Why? ■

Specimen answer and discussion   On page 481 Roberts states that 'in rich and poor societies alike, the countryside lagged behind in the rise of standards'. In France, although the rural population was declining in numbers, in 1931 it still amounted to almost half the population of the country and provided a third of the country's workforce. But although agriculture played a major role in the French economy, much more so than in Britain, or any other industrialized country for that matter, agriculture only produced a quarter of the country's revenue. It was not the large farmers who were hardest hit by the Depression but the small peasant farmers. Prices for farm produce fell much more sharply than prices for fertilizers and farm machinery. Overall, it has been estimated that between 1931 and 1935 peasant income fell by about a third. In addition, another factor, almost a chance occurrence, or what Arthur Marwick has called 'contingency' (see Book I, Unit 1, p.17), affected all French farmers. In 1930 a Colorado beetle epidemic covered eighteen departments, and by 1939 it had spread to the whole of France.

Although the average income rose by nearly 40 per cent between 1913 and 1929, the deep and sustained Depression of the 1930s hindered this advance. However, during this latter period the fall in prices exceeded that of the fall in money wages for many French industrial workers. The average earnings of industrial workers fell by about 15 per cent between 1930 and 1935, but as unemployment was reduced in the following five years, so average earnings returned to around their 1930 level. Compared with a similar family in Britain, the budget of a family in Paris was probably lower. Nevertheless similar developments can be discerned and there was a growth in consumer spending. Wages were being spent on a wider range of goods than before the war. The percentage of wages spent on the essentials of food fell, although in France the drop was less than in Britain and the other industrialized countries of Europe. There was also a wider range of foods available from a growing number of retail outlets, the significant feature of which was the growth of chain and department stores, the origins of which can be traced back to before the war. As more foods became available, diets improved and meat, milk, vegetable and fruit consumption all increased. In Britain by 1934 there was some 88 per cent more fruit, 64 per cent more vegetables, 50 per cent more margarine and 46 per cent more eggs being consumed than before the war. Whereas before 1914 the range of canned foods was limited, by 1939 most consumables were available either in cans or in new processed forms such as instant coffee. New methods of packaging and advertising were important factors in attracting consumers to new eating habits including breakfast cereals and potato crisps. □

Exercise   In addition to a rise in real wages, what factor, which we have already discussed in this unit, is important to our understanding of why there was more income to spend on non-essential goods? ■

Specimen answer   The average size of families was smaller, so there were fewer mouths to feed. □

The advance in technology, the chemical industry and communications, all contributed towards a wider range of consumer products being placed on the market. We have already mentioned the increasing use of rayon and other artificial fibres which enabled a wider and cheaper range of clothing. There was also an increase in the use of electrical gadgets as electricity came more and more into people's homes. The setting up of the Central Electricity Board in Britain in 1926 started the process of a national electricity grid which, by the end of our period, was virtually complete. In 1920 one house in seventeen was wired for electricity, by 1939 two houses in every three were also wired.

As we have already seen, one of the important industrial developments in the inter-war years was the development of a motor vehicle industry. Mass production meant that by 1936 a small family car could be bought for about £100, half the price it would have cost ten years earlier.

Exercise   Below are the official Wembley Stadium car park figures for the FA Cup Final between Sunderland and Preston in 1937. The attendance at this Cup Final was 100,000.

Cars: 1,540

Motor cycles: 26

Coaches: 513

What do you find interesting about these figures? ■

Specimen answer and discussion   If we assume there were, on average, three people to every car and each coach held thirty-five people, then something like 4,500 came by car and 18,000 by coach, leaving a vast majority to arrive by train, tube and local buses. However, considering that the supporters of the two teams travelled long distances, from the north-west and north-east of England, the fact that one in five or six who attended the match came by coach is significant. Although the possession of a motor car may have figured only in the dreams of the average football supporter, nevertheless in 1939 there were 3 million motor vehicles in Britain of which 2 million were private vehicles. □

7 LEISURE

Exercise   Look back at sections 2.7 and 2.9 of Units 8–10 where Arthur Marwick discusses customs and behaviour and popular culture. Also re-read Roberts from page 479 'Cultural communications also became easier . . .' to page 482 '. . . to attract attention after 1918'.

1   Does Roberts discuss any activities not mentioned by Marwick?

2   Does Roberts give any reasons for the spread of leisure activities in the period 1918–39 which are not mentioned by Marwick in his discussion of the expansion of popular culture *before* 1914?

3   Would you say there are any differences at all in the nature of leisure activities between 1918 and 1939 and, if so, what? ■

Specimen answers and discussion   1   The only activities I can find are professional sportsmanship and a preoccupation with speed and 'records'.

2   Nearly all the reasons are the same. The only difference I can discover is that Roberts writes of people 'coming to expect more of life'.

3   Yes, although there is no great change in the types of activities – going to the cinema, listening to the radio or reading the newspaper – all these leisure activities

or means of communication reach mass audiences during the inter-war years. They all become big businesses; need large amounts of capital investment; are improved by the application of new but expensive technological developments and have influence which is international not just national. The same could be said, although not quite on the same scale, for the activities not mentioned by Marwick – sport, speed and records. Again in this period the audiences become larger, more money is invested in them and many sports become international. □

The implications of all this are enormous. Roberts writes of the cinema being 'an educational force', of 'the political use of broadcasting' and so on. These are all critical issues and will be discussed in detail by Tony Aldgate in Unit 19. All I want to do here is to give you some idea of the extent of the expansion, and also touch on some other important leisure activities not mentioned by either Roberts or Marwick.

The biggest expansion in leisure activities was undoubtedly the growth of a cinema-going public. In the 1920s it was Germany that led the way with more cinemas than the other two countries and the production of more films than the rest of Europe put together. Alfred Hugenberg, leader of the German National People's Party and already a press baron, also controlled both large film production and film distribution companies. In Britain by 1939 there were a few major film distribution networks and around 5,000 cinemas throughout the country, with more opening at the rate of three per week. Cinema attendances totalled approximately 20 million per week, and a survey in Liverpool concluded that 40 per cent of the population in that city attended the cinema at least once a week and 25 per cent went twice a week or more. The advantages of the cinema, in addition to the films being shown, were that they were cheap, warm and one's stay was unrestricted: an important consideration in times of high unemployment.

Radio became the centre of home entertainment. In Germany by 1932 one house in four possessed a radio. In France before the outbreak of World War II there were around 5 million sets, and in that country three years earlier radio advertising was launched. In Britain, as Roberts points out, the BBC held a monopoly of radio broadcasting. Radio licences cost ten shillings, and this was one reason why 3.5 million, or a quarter of all households, still had no radios in 1939.

With regard to newspapers, the trend of an expansion of readership and a concentration of ownership, which was apparent in Britain before the 1914–18 war, continued. From a figure of under 5.5 million in 1920, the circulation of national daily newspapers rose to 10.5 million by 1939. It was estimated, in a survey carried out in 1939, that 69 per cent of the population over sixteen read a national daily newspaper and 82 per cent a national Sunday paper. In France, the press reflected the dominance of Paris. *Paris-Soir* had by far the largest circulation in 1939 of 1,750,000, and the Paris newspapers had a slightly larger print number than all the provincial papers put together.

Exercise From your own experience and knowledge and from what you have read so far in this unit, what other important leisure activities should be taken into consideration which I have not already mentioned? ■

Specimen answer and discussion Holidays. When holidays with pay were introduced in France in 1936, many French families went, often to the seaside, for the first time. It was in the inter-war years that the idea that sunbathing was 'good for you' and that tanned bodies were attractive took a hold, so that those who could afford it started to go to the beaches in the south of France rather than in the north and west.

In Britain around 1.5 million people had holidays with pay in the early 1920s; by 1938 this had risen to 3 million, but in that year a Holidays with Pay Act was passed which extended the right to 11 million. Once again trips to the seaside were an extension of a trend which can clearly be seen taking place before World War I. The major difference now was that as more people went on holiday, more money was invested in hotels, funfares and other seaside entertainments. On August Bank Holiday Monday in 1937, Blackpool had over half a million visitors of which 50,000 had arrived in motor vehicles. Traffic jams had become a reality.

Gambling, which had always been a love of the British, increased as more outlets became available. Horse-race betting had always been popular, although off-course betting was illegal. But the government, appreciating that vast amounts went to bookmakers on the courses, passed the Racecourse Betting Act in 1928 which legalized the tote which had been introduced in that year. Greyhound racing was introduced for the first time on any scale in the 1920s, and by 1931 attendances at meetings had reached 18 million.

The big development in gambling in the 1930s was the growing popularity of football pools. Littlewoods and Vernons built premises in Liverpool and employed large staffs to check some 5 to 7 million entries which, by 1936, were sent in each week. About £30 million a year was taken by the pools firms in forecasts. □

The leisure activities mentioned above involved the participation of all classes but some were directed specifically at a working-class audience which, in the inter-war years, had more money to spend on leisure than ever before.

8 *SOCIAL COHESION*

Exercise

Drawing upon what you have read in this unit so far and referring back to document I.1 in *Documents 2*, which country, France or Britain, would you regard as more stable in 1938 and why? ■

Specimen answer and discussion

We have seen that although the break-up of the government of the Popular Front restored some confidence in the money markets, it was also accompanied by industrial discontent. Document I.1 reveals more strikes and more workers involved in strikes in France than in Britain from 1936 onwards. In addition, during this period two new right-wing parties were created, the Popular Party and the Social Party, the latter being a revamping of the *Croix-de-Feu*. The Social Party rapidly became the largest political party in France with over 800,000 members. The rifts in French politics now were not just over domestic affairs but increasingly concerned foreign policy, especially the stance which should be taken towards Germany. However, when the Prime Minister, Daladier, proposed in November 1938 the abolition of the forty-hour week, increasing taxes, reducing government expenditure and devaluing the franc once again, the CGT organized a one-day general strike for 30 November. Before the official strike took place there were a number of unofficial ones. The government's response was to order 10,000 members of the *gardes mobile* into the Renault works to evict strikers there, and on the day of the general strike, which was not well supported, Paris, in particular, was very heavily policed. □

When we looked at the film of the street clashes in Paris in October 1936 (video-cassette 1, item 13), we concluded that they 'appeared' worse than in Britain, but we were hesitant to draw definite conclusions because of the untrustworthy nature of the film evidence. However, we must bear in mind that, unlike the British police, the French police were armed and in general they were more brutal in dealing with strikes and marches. Although it is difficult to obtain exact figures, somewhere around 200 workers were killed during strikes and demonstrations during the inter-war years in France, the bulk of them in the later 1930s.

Exercise   In our discussion of Stevenson and Cook's chapter 'The Revolution That Never Was' we mentioned a whole range of factors which were influential in making Britain a relatively cohesive society. There was one reason which Stevenson and Cook touched on but which we have not yet discussed. What was it? ∎

Specimen answer and discussion   Stevenson and Cook mention the continued regard that all classes held for the monarchy, and they singled out the great display of pomp and ceremony which celebrated George V's Silver Jubilee, and the deep regard which was held in some parts of the country for the new king, Edward VIII. If you remember, in Unit 14 I quoted a government report of 1919, 'Revolutionary Feeling during the Year 1919', in which one factor regarded as weighing in favour of stability was the popularity of the royal family. It could well be argued that this report was only echoing the exaggerated fears of the time and that rather than the monarchy 'weighing in favour of stability', there was a basic unity within the country and the popularity of the monarchy was a symbol of this unity. Nevertheless, the role of the monarchy in this period and the way it was presented to the public is important in any discussion of social cohesion. □

Exercise   Look at video-cassette 1, items 17, 18 and 19. These extracts are from newsreels concerning the abdication of Edward VIII. Are there any signs of public disquiet over this major constitutional crisis? ∎

Specimen answer and discussion   All I could spot is a shot of a car driving past with a poster proclaiming 'support the King'. Most of the footage depicts grave and serious scenes in which everyone is concerned from the Prime Minister down to the woman kneeling outside the gates. At the same time, it really is a case of 'The King is dead, long live the King', and in the same newsreels much footage is given to the new king and queen and their two daughters. □

As newspapers only print what editors want to print, and Acts of Parliament enact what parliamentarians want to deal with, clearly you would be justified here in pointing out that the newsreel editor is only including what he wants to show. This is something that Tony Aldgate will go into in some detail in Unit 19. Why I have touched on this issue is that here is an unprecedented event: the abdication of a monarch because he wished to marry a twice-divorced, American commoner. In fact, unknown to the British public because of a 'gentleman's agreement' on the part of the media not to mention the crisis, discussions had been going on for months as to whether Edward could marry Mrs Wallis Simpson and remain king. The government, most of the Labour opposition, the archbishops and the Prime Ministers of the Dominions were determinedly against it, and Edward was eventually confronted with three alternative lines of action. Either he renounce Mrs Simpson, or he marry her contrary to the advice of his Ministers who would then resign. This latter course would cause a serious and unprecedented constitutional crisis, as the leaders of both the Liberal and Labour parties had pledged to Stanley Baldwin that they would not form an alternative government in such an event. The third alternative remaining to Edward was abdication.

The matter was handled so secretly, and when it did become public so swiftly, that any public objections and support for Edward were virtually stifled before they could be uttered. Indeed, you will have noticed that one of the newsreels was so anxious to introduce the new king and queen that it did so before a title was given to the new king, and so the commentator speaks of King Albert.

So, despite the deep regard in which Edward was held, the matter was dealt with so capably that there was no public outcry. In fact, the coronation of George VI and Queen Elizabeth in 1937 was deliberately built up into a splendid and sumptuous affair, in which the king and queen with their two beautiful daughters were depicted not only as the titular head of a large empire at a time of increasing international tension, but also as a family which although royal, shared the typical hopes, fears and concerns of respectable families throughout the nation. It is worth bearing in mind when reading Units 16, 17 and 18 in what ways the packaging and presentation of the royal family in Britain compare with the ways in which Hitler, Mussolini and Stalin are presented as focal points for national unity.

The idea of the nation as a family was one which the monarchy and the Prime Minister were at pains to depict. Nevertheless, by 1939 some members of the family were doing much better than others. Although the heavy increase in taxation which had taken place during World War I (which was especially heavy on those with higher income levels) and the social benefit legislation enacted during and after the war, had brought about some redistribution of wealth, the changes were not great. For example, by 1939, 55 per cent of all wealth (land, stocks, shares and other assets) was owned by 1 per cent of the population. In 1924 the figure had been 60 per cent, whereas eight million families, or 75 per cent of the population in the late 1930s possessed personal property of no more than £100. Those who did benefit most during these years were the middle or lower middle classes who were earning between £250 and £1000 per annum. It was this group who paid the lowest percentage of their incomes in direct or indirect taxation, and those above them on the social scale who were still able to participate in certain of the more leisured aspects of the pre-1914 life style. As I have mentioned already, in 1931 there were some 1,330,000 female domestic servants and one household in nearly every five still had at least one domestic living in, and many more families retained chars who came in to do the cleaning and cooking.

In comparing France with Britain in the inter-war years we can conclude that Britain emerged from the Depression earlier; social welfare was more advanced in Britain, although this had been the case even in 1918; governments were more stable; demonstrations and strikes passed off more peaceably and there were no major confrontations between extremists on the Left and Right. The sense of unity, demonstrated partly in Britain by a popular monarchy and a National government, was lacking in France where disillusionment with politicians and political institutions had grown since the ending of World War I. All these factors go some way to explaining why Britain was more socially cohesive than France by the late 1930s, and why, in 1939, France 'failed, not merely because of the deep psychological wounds of the Great War, of a falling population, of the conduct of the British at Munich, or because of faulty military doctrine, but also because none of her governments between the wars generated the respect which leadership commands even from its opponents . . . The political institutions of France had long before lost touch with the changing realities of society and this was the politicians' fault' (Roberts, p.405).

Bibliography

Aldcroft, D. H. (1970) *From Versailles to Wall Street, 1919–1929*, Allen Lane. (Chapter 1 is reproduced in the *Offprints Booklet*.)

Berghahn, V. R. (1987) *Modern Germany*, Cambridge University Press.

Bernard, P. and Dubief, H. (1975) *The Decline of the Third Republic, 1914–1938*, Cambridge University Press (reissued paperback, 1988).

Bridenthal, R. (1973) 'Beyond *Kinder, Kuche, Kirche*, Weimar women at work', *Central European History*, March. Reprinted in Open University (1987) A323 *Weimar Germany: the Crisis of Industrial Society, 1918–1933*, Offprints, Milton Keynes, The Open University.

Caron, F. (1979) *An Economic History of Modern France*, Methuen.

Dyer, C. (1978) *Population and Society in Twentieth-Century France*, Hodder and Stoughton.

Fearon, P. (1979) *The Origins and Nature of the Great Slump, 1929–32*, Macmillan.

Fraser, D. (1973) *The Evolution of the British Welfare State*, Macmillan.

Johnson, D. and M. (1987) *The Age of Illusion*, Thames and Hudson.

Kemp, T. (1972) *The French Economy*, Longman.

Leuchtenburg, W. F. (1964) 'The New Deal and the Analogue of War' in Braeman, J., et al. (eds) *Change and Continuity in Twentieth Century America*, Ohio State University Press.

Lewis, J. (1984) *Women in England, 1870–1950*, Wheatsheaf.

McCord, N. (1974) *North East England*, Batsford.

McMillan, J. (1981) *Housewife or Harlot*, Harvester.

Marwick, A. (1981) *CLASS: Image and Reality in Britain, France and the USA since 1930*, Fontana/Collins.

Open University (1987) A323 *Weimar Germany: the Crisis of Industrial Society, 1918–1933*, Study Guide, Milton Keynes, The Open University.

Priestley, J. B. (1934) *English Journey*, Heinemann.

Stevenson, J. (1984) *British Society 1914–45*, Penguin.

Stevenson, J. and Cook, C. (1979) *The Slump*, Quartet. (Chapter XIV is reproduced in the *Offprints Booklet*.)

UNIT 16 INTERNAL WAR AND THE DEVELOPMENT OF THE SOVIET UNION

Bernard Waites

With grateful acknowledgement to Paul Lewis

Open University students of this unit will need to refer to:

Documents 2: 1925–1959, eds Arthur Marwick and Wendy Simpson, Open University Press, 1990

INTRODUCTION

The aims of this unit are to analyse the role of 'internal war' in Soviet development between 1921 and 1941, and to evaluate the 'totalitarian model' as a descriptive and explanatory account of the developed Soviet state. These aims are couched in the rather forbidding language of political science and require glossing. By 'internal war' I mean large-scale collective violence within a society, such as has often been associated with periods of revolutionary change. Civil wars, fought between conventional armies, have frequently accompanied revolutionary upheaval and, until the defeat of General Wrangel in November 1920, the Soviet state was confronted with a civil war, as well as with peasant guerrilla war in Tambov province and the Ukraine. The concept of internal war includes such conflicts, but refers also to other forms of mass violence such as the terrorization of groups identified as enemies of the revolution or the state.

Internal war in the form of political terror made an early entry into Soviet history. After the attempted assassination of Lenin in August 1918 the Soviet government gave the All-Russian Extraordinary Commission (the *Cheka*) sweeping powers of arrest and summary execution. The original rationale of securing the revolution against its active opponents was soon obscured. Peasants were terrorized for resisting grain requisitions and the sole crime of other victims was their social origins. The chairman of the Eastern front *Cheka* told his officers in November 1918: 'We are not waging war against individual persons. We are exterminating the bourgeoisie as a class . . . The first questions you ought to put [during an investigation] are: To what class does he belong? What is his education or profession? And it is these questions which ought to determine the fate of the accused' (cited in Hosking, *A History of the Soviet Union*, 1985, p.70). Political terror escalated partly because White forces were equally indiscriminate in executing those suspected of Bolshevik sympathies.

Although the *Cheka* was superseded by the OGPU (United State Political Administration) at the end of the civil war, Soviet political life was permanently brutalized by the internal class war which the *Chekists* had waged against the civilian population. The period of 'war communism' had further long-term effects on the Soviet regime in that it militarized the ruling Communist Party and provided a model and methods for the regimentation of economic and social life to which Soviet leaders could revert after 1928. These methods involved the centralization of both production and distribution by state bureaucracies (*glavki*) and by the military or militarized administration. Even tiny enterprises were nationalized by the end of 1920 and rationing (of factors of production as well as goods) was universal. Workers were forcibly mobilized into 'labour armies'; grain requisitioned from the peasants by armed squads; regular markets abolished; and money eliminated from dealings between the state and its employees whose salaries were mostly paid in kind and free services. Though the system of 'war communism' resulted in a catastrophic loss of production and inflation, and the mass desertion of the cities as starving workers returned to the countryside, it nevertheless inspired an egalitarian utopianism. Many believed that its measures embodied an irreversible leap into socialist freedom. (Lewin, *Political Undercurrents in Soviet Economic Debates*, 1975, pp.77–9 provides an incisive summary of the period.)

'Totalitarianism' has, since the 1950s, been a key concept for the political analysis of one-party dictatorships; although the term itself dates back to the official doctrine of Mussolini's Italy, by 1940 commentators were regularly using it to categorize Germany, Russia and Italy within a single political phenomenon. The essential meaning of totalitarianism is conveyed in the word itself; a totalitarian political system is one that seeks total control over society and the citizenry. Total control presupposes the development of modern technology, especially of rapid mass communication and transportation, and most would agree that totalitarianism is a twentieth-century phenomenon. During the Cold War, the definition of totalitarianism was made more extensive and precise by the political scientists, Carl Friedrich and Zbigniew Brzezinski, who identified its six institutional features as:

1   The existence of an official ideology covering all aspects of social existence which envisaged the society as moving towards a final state of man. This chiliastic doctrine legitimized the means to achieve that end and involved a radical rejection of the existing order.

2   A single, hierarchically organized mass party, led by one man, that was either superior to or intertwined with the government bureaucracy.

3   A system of terroristic police control, directed against 'enemies' of the regime and arbitrarily selected groups, that exploited scientific psychology in dominating the population.

4   A technologically conditioned monopoly of the means of mass communications.

5   A monopoly of force.

6   The central control and direction of the entire economy through the state bureaucracy.

This six-point model greatly influenced Merle Fainsod in his pathmarking survey *How Russia is Ruled* (first published in 1953) and in his research into the Smolensk Communist Party archives which resulted in *Smolensk under Soviet Rule* (1958). (The Smolensk records fell into German hands in 1941 and were captured by the Americans in 1945. They are the only unpublished sources generated by the Soviet regime accessible to Western scholars.) Some historians still regard the model as fruitful; Geoffrey Hosking has written that 'In most respects [it] seems . . . convincing' when applied to Stalinist society. However, he adds two important reservations: the model wrongly assumed that workers, peasants and the intelligentsia were passive objects of the terror and mobilization by the regime; and the model did not examine at all closely the kind of ruling stratum the leader would need to exercise his power (Hosking, *A History of the Soviet Union*, 1985, pp.204–5). Other commentators have gone further in questioning the validity of the totalitarian model and as we work through this unit we will consider their objections.

A final word of introductory clarification: we will be concerned with the *development* of the Soviet Union between the ending of 'war communism' in March 1921 and June 1941, when Hitler's invasion began 'The Great Patriotic War', and by this I am referring to the momentous social changes associated with industrialization, the collectivization of agriculture and urbanization. These laid the basis for, among other things, Soviet military might (*before* Hitler's attack Russia had the world's largest tank park) and could scarcely be ignored in any course dealing with war, peace and social change in twentieth-century Europe. It might be objected, however, that the capacious concept of 'internal war' has been introduced to establish a bogus relevance with the main course theme of examining the role of war in bringing about social change.

Those brought up in Britain will, understandably, tend to think of war as armed conflict between sovereign states, officially declared and, in twentieth-century Europe, fought until military defeat brought about a change of regime for the vanquished. The arena for wars of this type is the system of nation states and, arguably, it is in the international system that such wars have had their most profound consequences. People from other societies can perhaps more readily appreciate that war is a highly differentiated phenomenon: not only may the arena of war differ (with conflicts erupting within a society and assuming a bitter struggle over its political form and social system – as in Spain or Greece) but the modes of warfare have varied greatly too. 'Irregular' warfare has been a feature of peasant societies undergoing revolutionary upheavals, as in much of Russia between 1918 and 1921. From the perspective afforded by international war there is a clear demarcation between war and peace. Diplomatic and legal conventions recognize belligerent status and define, in theory, the conduct of belligerent powers towards neutrals and enemy prisoners. There is no such clear demarcation between internal war and social peace, for internal wars arise from conflicts endemic to the society and their modes of warfare are frequently intensified forms of chronic violence. 'Irregular' warfare, for example, is often barely distinguishable from banditry and other forms of lawlessness. Furthermore, the relationship between internal war and social change is not always a straightforward one of cause and effect. Many Soviet leaders in the late 1920s and early 1930s, for example, saw the massive violence inflicted on the Russian peasantry as a *necessary precondition* for the rapid industrialization of the country and the inauguration of socialism. Interestingly, Western historians have echoed this view by debating whether Stalin's violent coercion of the peasantry was really 'necessary' to provide the economic surplus needed for capital investment (Millar and Nove, 'Was Stalin really necessary?', 1976). There is a not dissimilar question as to whether the purges of the Soviet Communist Party in the 1930s were 'necessary' in order to renew the ruling élite. What these arguments are implying is a functional rather than a causal relationship between internal war and social change. We will return to these important questions, but it is worth stressing here that in arguing that Stalin was 'necessary' no one is attempting to justify or apologize for the crimes against humanity for which he was largely responsible.

1   THE NEW ECONOMIC POLICY

The change of economic course forced upon the Soviet regime in February/March 1921 came 'surreptitiously' with few at the time appreciating the enormity of what was happening (Cohen, *Bukharin and the Bolshevik Revolution*, 1980, p.106). After lengthy debate in the Politburo, the Soviet Central Executive Committee decreed on 16 March the replacement of grain requisitioning by a fixed and fair tax in kind, leaving all the surplus to the individual peasant to dispose of in 'the local market'. Internal war precipitated the measure, for it was taken in response to peasant uprisings and wildcat strikes in major cities, as well as the prospect of total economic paralysis. The revolt of the Kronstadt sailors (many peasants by origin) in March during the Tenth Communist Party Congress may have convinced many of the need for major economic concessions to the peasantry, although the change was initiated before the revolt began.

No comprehensive policy reversal was intended by the abolition of requisitioning. Lenin did not anticipate the restoration of a national private market in grain, which was to become a key feature of the New Economic Policy (NEP). He expected peasants' surpluses not sold locally to be bartered directly with state industries. The sheer impracticality of this, and the desperate need to shift grain to famine regions during 1921–22, forced the regime to tolerate merchants and entrepreneurs. The need for free exchange of goods was such that 'once trade of any kind was legalized . . . it grew like a snowball and swept away restrictions' (Nove, *An Economic History of the USSR*, 1969, p.84). The number of traders (known as NEPmen) increased rapidly; by 1922–23 75 per cent of all retail trade was in private hands. Though most NEPmen were very small-scale entrepreneurs, a few made fortunes which scandalized the Bolshevik rank and file.

In May and July 1921, the regime liberalized small-scale production. Handicraft industry largely returned to independent proprietors, though comparatively few employed more than one or two workers. Larger enterprises were mainly leased by the Supreme Council of National Economy (VSNKh) to entrepreneurs and outright de-nationalizations were rare. The 'commanding heights' of the economy – banking, foreign trade, large-scale industry – were retained in the hands of the state, for whom the vast majority of those engaged in manufacturing and mining continued to work (Nove, 1969, pp.85–6).

During 1921–22 the bureaucratic control of industrial production by *glavki* (see above p.73) under which enterprises had simply produced to order, regardless of cost, was dismantled. Many factories were closed because of fuel shortages and state industry as a whole was rebuilt on a commercial basis, with enterprises (now organized under autonomous trusts) having to pay money wages and meet economic criteria of efficiency. One consequence was considerable industrial unemployment as state firms shed surplus labour. (This proved a protracted problem for throughout the later 1920s unemployment in the industrial labour force averaged about 13 per cent.) Another consequence was a sharp twist to the existing inflationary spiral as the abolition of rationing and price control unleashed a pent-up demand for goods which industry could not possibly satisfy. As in the Weimar Republic, the economy was bloated by a huge increase in paper money during 1921–23. However, in early 1924 the Commissariat of Finance managed to achieve relative monetary stability by enforcing budgetary and financial orthodoxy. The regime was able to commute the agricultural tax in kind to a money payment.

The considerable degree of economic liberalization introduced under NEP did not mean that Soviet Marxists had relinquished the ambition to subject the economy to political co-ordination and planning, which all took to be a basic institutional feature of socialism. Planning under NEP, however, had a quite different character from that adopted in 1928. There was no 'command economy' with production targets; rather a novel and sophisticated attempt at national accounting and the forecasting of economic growth in order to guide strategic investment decisions and determine priorities (Nove, 1969, p.101). It is an interesting indicator of the comparative political liberalism of the NEP period that much of the planning was done by non-party, even 'bourgeois', economists, just as within industries 'bourgeois' technicians and specialists were employed to manage factories.

1.1 Strengthening the Bolshevik Party's internal discipline: the ban on factions and the rise of Stalin

On the last day of the Tenth Party Congress, Lenin suddenly produced two new resolutions, on 'Party Unity' and on 'The Syndicalist and Anarchist Deviation in our Party'. The first drew attention to the formation within the party of 'groups with separate platforms and with the determination to a certain extent to become self-contained and to create their own group discipline', and it called for the immediate dissolution of all such groups, on pain of expulsion from the party. One target of this resolution was the 'Workers' Opposition' – a rank-and-file movement of communist trade unionists – who had demanded more party democracy in such matters as the election of local union committees and greater autonomy for the unions both as genuine representatives of organized labour and agents of workers' control of industry. The second resolution condemned these ideas as 'a complete rupture with Marxism and communism', and its passage by a large majority demonstrated that the one-party state would not tolerate the development of an independent labour movement. The Party Unity resolution, which called on 'All class-conscious workers' to realize 'the perniciousness and impermissibility of factionalism of any kind', was even more significant for the future for it concentrated power within the hands of the party's Central Committee. One protocol of the resolution (not published until January 1924) authorized the Committee to expel those deemed guilty of factionalism, provided a two-thirds majority existed within it for such an extreme measure. Hitherto, the power of expulsion had been wielded only by the party congress and the Tenth Congress' decision to keep this protocol secret 'revealed an understandable reluctance to document the growing power of the central party machine' (Hough and Fainsod, *How the Soviet Union is Governed*, 1979, p.101).

The strengthening of the party's machine is intimately connected with the rise to supreme power of Joseph Stalin, the Georgian who served as People's Commissar of Nationality Affairs in Lenin's government and became General Secretary in April 1922, shortly before Lenin's first stroke. In this position Stalin built his image as 'a hard-working, accessible servant of the party' which was to prove a major weapon in his rivalry with other Bolsheviks during the next few years (McNeal, *Stalin: Man and Ruler*, 1988, p.67). Probably because of his party position, Stalin was made Lenin's virtual legal guardian during his protracted terminal illness and so the General Secretary was able to isolate Lenin from rivals for the succession, as well as assume some of the prestige of the stricken leader. In a secret testament of December 1922 in which Lenin assessed his colleagues, he warned of the concentration of 'boundless power' in Stalin's hands since his becoming General Secretary, and in a later postscript suggested his demotion because of 'intolerable' rudeness. But Lenin's assessment of Stalin (who had been one of his most able and energetic lieutenants during the civil war) was in other respects highly favourable. He and Trotsky were declared the 'two outstanding leaders of the present Central Committee', and the shortcomings attributed to Stalin were less likely to damage his reputation with the party rank and file than those ascribed to Trotsky, who had a non-Bolshevik political past to live down and was disadvantaged by being born a Jew.

In the autumn of 1922 Trotsky isolated himself from other leading Bolsheviks in the Politburo by his apparently arrogant refusal to accept the position of Deputy Chairman of Sovnarkom (the Council of Commissars). His behaviour suggested he regarded himself as so indispensable as to make exertion unnecessary in the succession contest. In early 1923 Stalin struck up a loose anti-Trotsky alliance with Zinoviev, Kamenev and other Politburo members which helped ensure his main rival's exclusion from the leadership (although Trotsky remained Commissar for Defence until January 1925). The ban on 'factionalism' now proved an insuperable barrier to Trotsky's efforts to widen his support within the party, for these were adeptly condemned by Stalin at the January 1924 Conference as a violation of Lenin's policy on party unity. Furthermore, Stalin had exploited his own institutional base to secure the appointment of full-time party officials who were his supporters or sympathizers, and Trotsky's frequent attacks on 'bureaucratism' merely consolidated the *apparatchiki* behind the General Secretary. Whatever slim chance Trotsky had of remaining in the highest leadership was dashed by his absence from Lenin's funeral in January 1924: politically this was extraordinarily insensitive for the apotheosis of Lenin had already begun and Stalin used the occasion to define, and identify himself with orthodox 'Leninism' (a term just gaining currency). Stalin did not play a major role in the cult of Lenin (although this later served as a model for the veneration of his own personality) but he quickly established himself as the pre-eminent authority on Leninist ideology. In a party that prided itself on the 'scientific' rigour of its doctrines, this was of no small consequence in the consolidation of Stalin's power.

Whether the political conceptions that Stalin put forward in the mid-1920s were consistent with Lenin's is a matter of debate. One which certainly appears so is Stalin's insistence that the Leninist party 'represents unity of will, which precludes all factionalism and division of authority in the party'. But Stalin elaborated on this doctrine in a way that may have distorted Lenin's views, for he argued

> Petit-bourgeois groups penetrate the party and introduce into it the spirit of hesitancy and opportunism . . . To fight imperialism with such 'allies' in one's rear means to put oneself in the position of being caught between two fires, from the front and from the rear. Therefore ruthless struggle against such elements, their expulsion from the Party, is a prerequisite for the successful struggle against imperialism. ('The Foundations of Leninism', 1926, quoted in McNeal, *Stalin*, 1988, p.92)

Stalin added that the notion that such enemies could be defeated by ideological struggle within the party – what you and I might call internal debate – was 'a rotten and dangerous theory'. During the purges of the late 1930s, 'rotten theory' was to be the reiterated catchphrase of Stalin's main justification for the bloodletting, although we must be careful about allowing this hindsight to colour our view of the Soviet Communist Party during the 1920s when there *was* considerable internal debate.

Stalin did more to shape twentieth-century Europe than any other single individual, yet the career of no other comparable figure is so difficult to explain or assess. His emergence as the most powerful Soviet leader in 1923/24, ahead of rivals who were more intellectually impressive and personally attractive, will remain somewhat enigmatic until archival research into such key matters as the relations between the party's central leadership and its rank and file becomes possible. Our present knowledge suggests that his rise to power was built on the trust he enjoyed among the great majority of Bolsheviks as a dedicated, selfless revolutionary whose moderation in the major issues preoccupying the party during the 1920s, and whose 'colourlessness', were guarantees against personal dictatorship.

1.2 Recovery and growth under NEP

In 1921–22 all indices showed the devastating effect on the Russian economy of war, revolution and famine. Estimated deaths attributable to the multi-faceted seven-year crisis were 7 million. The population (within the Soviet Union's current borders) was 159 millions in 1913. Population statistics are available for 1924 and subsequent years and show a great fall, but they refer to the area within the September 1939 borders and are not directly comparable with 1913.

One legacy of the seven-year crisis which needs emphasizing is the 'ruralization' of Russia as people fled the starving towns; in 1922 the number of industrial workers – who were the revolution's social base – was a mere 42 per cent of what it had been in 1917 (Filtzer, *Soviet Workers and Stalinist Industrialisation*, 1986, p.16). Despite considerable recovery from the nadir of 1921, the urban population was still, in 1926, over 2 million less than it had been in 1913. Another legacy was the particularly grave losses of young men who were the most productive part of the labour force; and a third the creation of a wave of homeless children – the first of a number of such waves which constituted one of the Soviet Union's gravest social problems during its first forty years (Stolee, 'Homeless children in the USSR, 1917–1957', 1988).

Agriculture recovered more rapidly than industry after 1922, although under NEP neither the total sown area nor the total grain yield reached those of 1913 – admittedly a year of exceptional agricultural prosperity. The peasants were so famished in early 1922 that the total sown area was only half what it had been before World War I; fortuitously the grain yield was relatively good. In 1925 and 1926 bumper harvests, almost equal to 1913, were produced from a sown area still significantly smaller. Industry recovered more slowly because it had fallen much further. The total value of factory production, at constant prices, in 1921 was only a fifth of the 1913 figure and the outputs of coal, iron and steel, and electricity were far below those of pre-1914. From the mid-1920s, Soviet industrial production

Table 16.1

	Total population	Proletarians	Peasants	Others*
1924–25	140.8m	25.3m	105.7m	9.8m
1925–26	144.0m	30.0m	103.4m	10.6m
1926–27	147.4m	32.5m	104.0m	10.9m

		Urban	%	Rural	%
1929	153.0m	28.7m	19	124.7m	81
1939	170.3m	—		—	
1940†	194.1m	63.1m	33	131.0m	67

*Principally artisans, craftsmen and professionals.
†Within the Soviet Union's current borders.

(Sources: Carr, *Foundations of a Planned Economy 1926–1929*, 1971, p.491; Lane, *Politics and Society in the USSR*, 1979, p.560; Rosefielde, 'Excess mortality in the Soviet Union', 1983, p.388)

Table 16.2

	1913	1921	1925	1926
Industrial production				
(million 1926–27 roubles)	10251	2004	7739	11083
Coal (million tons)	29.0	8.9	18.1	27.6
Electricity				
(million kwts)	1945	520	2925	3508
Pig iron (000 tons)	4216	116	1535	2441
Steel (000 tons)	4231	183	2135	3141

(Source: Nove, *An Economic History of the USSR*, 1969, p.94)

accelerated sharply and by 1926 was approximately equal to that of late tsarist times.

The gradual recovery of industry brought with it a growth in the number of workers, but they did not reach their 1917 level until 1928–29.

1.3   Economic debates and political schisms under NEP

The very success of NEP in bringing about economic recovery confronted Soviet leaders with grave ideological dilemmas and (despite the ban on factions) sharpened controversy within the Communist Party to the point where it threatened to tear itself apart. Lenin had at first painted the concessions to market forces of 1921 as a 'temporary retreat' but before he died he adapted the theory to the new realities. He became convinced that NEP policies provided a method for reaching socialism in a society where the great mass of the population were small proprietors and 'petit bourgeois' in outlook (Lewin, *Political Undercurrents in Soviet Economic Debates*, 1975, p.87). Commentators have read his last dictated articles as evidence that he died believing that the Soviet Union could 'go it alone' by a gradual transformation to socialism. His final directives to the party urged that the emphasis of its activities should shift from the (violent) political struggle 'to peaceful organizational "cultural" work' (quoted in Cohen, *Bukharin and the Bolshevik Revolution*, 1974, p.138). This conversion to political gradualism created an incipient division with the Trotskyist Left whose slogan 'Permanent Revolution' embodied the idea that the realization of socialism (and the security of the Bolshevik regime) depended on successful revolutions in advanced capitalist societies. Trotsky had been a powerful advocate of the coercive measures of 'war communism' (such as the militarization of labour), was deeply committed to planning and favoured the rapid expansion of heavy industry. He and his followers distrusted the 'pro-peasant' policy of NEP and feared that the party's revolutionary edge was being blunted by 'bureaucratic degeneration'.

As I mentioned before, during 1923 Trotsky's astonishing political ineptitude led to his exclusion from real power by the triumvirate of Stalin, Zinoviev and Kamenev. The most significant theoretical opponent of NEP proved to be E. A. Preobrazhensky. He argued that the fate of socialism in Russia depended on her rapid industrialization and this could only occur after the accumulation of vast investment capital. The socialized state sector could not, he believed, generate this surplus from its own exiguous resources; given the failure to attract foreign investment the only alternative source of investment capital was the peasantry. Preobrazhensky drew an analogy between the plundering and exploitation of colonies during the early stages of 'capitalist accumulation' and the extraction by the socialist state of surplus value from the peasantry. He did not, in fact, advocate violence and the confiscation of property but argued that 'socialist accumulation' could be achieved by keeping the price of agricultural goods artificially low and industrial goods high, and by taxation. Nevertheless, his proposals struck at the compromise between the state and the peasantry – and the market relationship between town and country – on which NEP rested.

The Soviet leader who did most to justify theoretically NEP's combination of state action and market forces was Nikolai Bukharin. In an outstanding biography, Stephen Cohen has argued that – whatever Bukharin's failures as a political tactician – his economic programme was a viable alternative to the Stalinist form of modernization which Russia actually experienced. The starting point of his programme was the *smychka* (link or union) with the peasantry, for Bukharin took the indispensability of the peasants' support to be the cardinal lesson of Russia's revolutionary history (Cohen, *Bukharin and the Bolshevik Revolution*, 1974, p.166). Like all Bolsheviks, he accepted industrialization as the party's foremost goal but believed that the key to growth was an expanding consumer market of prosperous peasants. It was in this light that Bukharin justified the controversial agrarian reforms of 1925 which removed the legal restrictions on the hiring of labour by richer peasants and their long-term leasing of land from poorer neighbours. Bukharin advised the peasantry to 'enrich' itself and advocated expanding the market by private enterprise and trade. The state sector, he argued, required competition to increase its efficiency and cheapen its costs. Bukharin's programme (unlike the Left opposition's) gave priority to the consumption industries over the capital goods industries and because it conceded an important role to market forces he rejected the 'command economy' planning advocated by the Left.

Economic debates during the 1920s interlaced with factional disputes about the character of party life. The Left accused the Politburo majority (led from the summer of 1925 by Stalin and Bukharin) of subordinating party democracy to bureaucracy, as well as needless concessions to the 'petit-bourgeois' peasants. It was in the context of these factional disputes that Stalin's doctrine of 'Socialism in One Country' acquired signal importance as an ideological cement binding together a majority in the party. In its origin, the doctrine was a blow struck in the struggle against Trotsky and propounded as a counterblast to his theory of 'permanent revolution' (Carr, *Socialism in One Country, 1924–1926*, 1959, p.45). But from the summer of 1925 it served to reinforce the political legitimacy of NEP by emphasizing the national character of the revolution and so 'reawakened a vague sentiment of . . . patriotism which had been temporarily silenced, but not destroyed . . .' (Carr, 1959, p.57). For much of their history, Russians (and not least the Bolsheviks) had sensed an inferiority with respect to the more advanced industrial societies. 'Socialism in One Country' asserted that Russia would lead the world not only in carrying out a socialist revolution, but in building a socialist economy; it was 'a declaration of independence of the west' (Carr, 1959, p.57).

1.4   Intellectual and cultural life under NEP

The Soviet state under NEP was a relatively liberal dictatorship which tolerated considerable cultural and social pluralism. The Communist Party monopolized political power but was itself a forum of lively debate, not only about industrialization, but over cultural and intellectual matters as well. Radical literary critics, grouped in the All-Russian Association of Proletarian Writers, wanted a complete break with existing literary traditions and the censorship of 'fellow-travelling' writers. Trotsky, in 1923, argued (against the radicals): 'It is fundamentally incorrect to set in opposition to bourgeois culture and bourgeois art a proletarian culture and proletarian art' (*Literature and Revolution*, quoted in Carr, 1959, p.89). At that time, mere association with Trotsky's name did not yet suffice to damn any policy and his ideas on culture carried great weight in the party. Lenin and most of the Old Bolsheviks shared Trotsky's position; Bukharin was a particularly notable patron of the non-party intelligentsia.

This openness to cultural and intellectual diversity made the 1920s a decade of memorable variety and achievement, both in the party's own intellectual life and outside. The combination of the revolutionary experience and freedom from official cultural dogma created a context in which artistic and cultural experiment thrived: '. . . the modernism of the cultural avant-garde flourished spectacularly if briefly under the lenient reign of the political avant-garde' (Cohen, *Bukharin and the Bolshevik Revolution*, 1974, p.272). Novelists and poets, such as Pasternak, Mandelstam and Akhmatova, produced their major works; Eisenstein, Pudovkin and others pioneered the modern cinema; experimental producers like Meyerhold and Tairov revolutionized the theatre; artists like Tatlin, Rodchenko and Lissitzky placed the Soviet Union at the forefront of modernist painting, architecture and design (Cohen, 1974).

Exercise   Go back to the 'totalitarian model' and consider to what extent the Soviet Union under NEP conformed to the model, and whether there were identifiable *tendencies* to totalitarianism during this period. ∎

Specimen answer   Even proponents of the totalitarian thesis would, I believe, concede that Soviet
and discussion   society under NEP did not conform at all closely to the model. True, this was a one-party dictatorship wedded to an official ideology, but it tolerated political diversity within the party and intellectual and cultural diversity without. Furthermore, the state staffed its bureaucracy with (in the majority) non-party personnel and conceded considerable economic and social autonomy to the most numerous class in society, the peasantry. A much more difficult question concerns the identifiable *tendencies* within NEP for they can be 'read' as quite divergent. If we personalize matters and identify NEP with Bukharin, then the fundamental tendency of the period seems to be towards economic liberalization and social pluralism. But NEP was also the period of the consolidation of Stalin's power, the expulsion of Trotsky from the party (in 1927) and the routing of the joint opposition led by him and Zinoviev. □

1.5   The state and the peasantry in the 1920s

On the eve of the collectivization of agriculture, the Soviet state was like a string of urban islands in an unfriendly rural sea. Only a tiny fraction of the rural population worked on state and collective farms; its great mass lived in autonomous, patriarchal peasant households that were literally and metaphorically remote from the urban milieux of Bolshevism. The party was grievously weak in the countryside. In October 1928, out of 1.36 million party members or candidate members, only 198,000 (14.5 per cent) were peasants or agricultural workers by present occupation. There was only one rural party member for every 420 rural inhabitants (as compared with one in twenty-five for urban inhabitants) (Davies, *The Socialist Offensive*, 1980, pp.51–2). As E. H. Carr remarked, 'many villages can never have seen a communist except in the guise of an occasional visiting official' (quoted in Davies, 1980). The rural soviets were unpopular and only a small proportion of peasants voted in elections to them. By contrast, the traditional organization of village government, the *Mir*, took on a new lease of life after 1917. The nationalization of land during the revolution had resulted in equal distributions which assimilated rich and poor peasants to the middle stratum of rural society. By 1927, 95.5 per cent of holdings were communally owned and managed by the *Mir* which guaranteed the individual peasant household a holding in perpetuity. The system was egalitarian, but tended to reinforce the technical backwardness of Russian agriculture because the periodic re-allocation of land hampered efforts to improve farming.

The cultural level of the peasantry restricted the influence of the Soviet regime in the countryside, as well as hampering efforts to make agriculture more efficient. On the eve of collectivization, more than half the peasantry was illiterate, and therefore oblivious to the printed propaganda which poured off Soviet presses. For the same reason many were impervious to technical advice on such matters as multiple crop rotation. Peasant life had been brutalized by civil war and famine. Drunkenness, wife-beating and savage brawling were so commonplace as to make the countryside 'a mass killer' (Lewin, *The Making of the Soviet System*, 1985, p.54). A more endearing trait of the village was its solidarity in the face of the outside world. Popular religion, which blended orthodoxy with magic and paganism, still had a strong hold on the peasant mentality (Lewin, 1985, ch.2). The educated stratum in rural society – to whom one would have looked for a civilizing leaven – was wafer thin; there were, for example, 7,000 doctors for 120 million rural inhabitants in 1926.

Technical backwardness meant that agricultural yields in the Soviet Union (in terms both of acres tilled and numbers employed) were lower than in any other major European country (lower, even, than in fourteenth-century French estates). The historic problems of low productivity had been compounded by the revolutionary land settlement which brought about the dissolution of the great estates (responsible for most pre-1914 agricultural exports) and the downfall of the prosperous *kulak* farmers created by the Stolypin land reforms. Though total harvests during NEP's last years were only slightly less than before 1914, the proportion *marketed* by the peasants was considerably less. Post-revolutionary peasant society was more oriented to subsistence farming, more inclined to feed its surpluses to animals and directly improve its own way of life. This made the provisioning of the towns and the Red Army a chronically precarious matter; and meant, too, that no surplus was available for export to pay for the capital goods needed for industrialization.

Severe though the technical and economic deficiencies of agriculture were, it is a moot point whether the political unreliability of the peasantry was not, for the Bolsheviks, at the heart of the agrarian question. Lenin had described the typical 'middle' peasant as 'partly a property owner, partly a worker . . . the problem of our attitude towards this vacillating class is one of enormous difficulty'. To many, the fundamental tendencies of NEP appeared to be strengthening the property-owning characteristics of peasant society and establishing the social basis for counter-revolution. It is difficult to distinguish between the irrational fears of radicals, excluded from power, aghast at the revival of private profit-making and the presence of so many non-Bolsheviks in the state bureaucracy and management, and the real social trends. The 1926 census provided evidence for those who wanted to believe that NEP was accentuating social stratification in the countryside and engendering a new capitalist class. Over three-quarters of a million peasant households were found to be hiring permanent wage labour; but these employers included a substantial number of women, with large young families and without adult males, who were more exploited than exploiting (Danilov, *Rural Russia under the New Regime*, 1988, p.66). In addition, there were about 66,000 rural craft enterprises employing two to three workers on average. The 'capitalist' group (including dependents and working family members) enumerated by the census was nearly 4 million or about 3.5 per cent of the rural population. In fact this included many (such as female-headed households) whom it was absurd to designate 'capitalist' and excluded many richer peasants who had prospered through commercial transactions. When *kulaks* were identified by other criteria, such as the number of animals, money-lending and the hiring of tools, then it was found that only about half employed wage labour on a permanent basis. The great majority of the *kulaks* were poor by Western European standards and there was no clear distinction between them and the great mass of *serednyaks*, or middle peasants, many of whom employed labour occasionally. *Kulaks* were often merely the ablest and hardest-working farmers in the village and agricultural aid to the middle peasants simply had the politically 'negative' effect of producing *kulaks*. At the bottom of rural society lay the day-labourers (*batraks*), though very few had no plot of land at all. They numbered about a million, and about the same number gave waged employment as a secondary occupation. Conditions for *batraks* were often servile; many were paid in kind and virtual slave-labour, in the guise of education, fictitious marriage or blood relationship, was a common occurrence. There was 'no domain of Soviet life in which the gulf between doctrine and reality was more blatantly obvious, and more compromising for the socialist idea . . .' (Lewin, *Russian Peasants and Soviet Power*, 1968, p.52).

Exercise Were the problems of agriculture so intractable that a socialist regime bent on industrialization had to resort to the drastic solution of 'internal war' to solve them? ■

Specimen answer and discussion Those who believe that forced collectivization was not 'necessary' argue that technical improvements (such as the substitution of the steel for the wooden plough) did, in fact, take place under NEP, that considerable strides were made in rural education, that the failure of peasants to market their produce was due principally to low state grain prices, that peasant society was basically homogeneous and engendering its own socialist forms (such as rural co-operatives). Against this we can pose the arguments of a Soviet scholar (otherwise fiercely critical of Stalinist collectivization as it actually occurred) that 'the lag of agricultural growth behind industrial growth, and the widening gulf between increasing urban demands for food and raw materials and the limited potential of smallholding peasant production, made the need for socialist reconstruction in the countryside critical'. He adds 'Ending poverty and exploitation was impossible on the traditional basis of peasant economy. Peasant participation in national economic development necessitated a colossal improvement in productivity, the transfer of millions of peasants into industry and enormous advances in technology and culture.' The countryside was chronically over-populated and peasant labour under-employed. 'This vicious circle could not be broken on the basis of the smallholding peasant economy' (Danilov, *Rural Russia under the New Regime*, 1988, p.304). □

2 *INTERNAL WAR*

2.1 Internal war on the peasantry: the grain crisis of 1927–28

The immediate origins of forced collectivization lay in the procurement crisis which confronted the Soviet authorities towards the end of 1927. A war scare had led to a run on the shops, aggravating a grain shortage the main causes of which were the peasants' refusal to sell because of the low state price and speculative hoarding in expectation of a price rise. Faced with discontent among troops and industrial workers, the regime authorized the seizure of grain by administrative fiat. The operations were similar to those of the civil war and military in method: the procurement campaign was looked on as a 'front' to which 30,000 party activists were drafted to supplement the militia. Stalin singled out Siberia (the country's richest source of grain) as 'his personal battle-ground' (Lewin, *Russian Peasants and Soviet Power*, 1968, p.218). There he berated local party officials for their tenderness towards the *kulaks* and demanded the drastic enforcement of article 107 of the penal code, which prescribed stiff prison sentences and the confiscation of property for speculation. The regime's tactic was to divide the peasantry among itself by painting the crisis as a 'strike of the *kulaks*' and by fomenting the class hostility of the poorer peasants against their richer neighbours. Whether this succeeded is doubtful, but it had the important side-effect of inspiring the party cadres with the blind devotion which had seen the regime through the civil war. The party spoke of 'the battle for grain', and 'the term was not entirely figurative . . . in the regions affected by the procurements [events] very often assumed the lineaments of a real battle' (Lewin, 1968, pp.219, 222).

The emergency measures of early 1928 brought to an end the free market in grain and restricted ancillary private trades, like flour milling. In June Stalin ordered the markets to re-open, but the order was ineffective, possibly because the punitive levies being imposed on *kulaks* discouraged any peasant from marketing his surplus. Under pressure from Moscow, local authorities organized illegal house-to-house searches and grain confiscations. In places, committees of poor peasants were incited to seize the *kulaks'* implements and animals – the first inklings of 'dekulakization'. Generally villagers of all strata in the grain-producing regions 'lived through a reign of terror, characterized by arbitrary procedures, extortion, injustice and arrests at every turn . . .' (Lewin, 1968, pp.229–30).

2.2 Internal war as cultural revolution

Simultaneously with the rural campaign against *kulaks* and hoarders, class warfare was being whipped up in the cities. In May 1928 the heavily publicized trial of the Shakhty 'saboteurs' opened, with the regime drumming up 'its "social-political significance" as an element in the class struggle against the implacable hostility of the bourgeoisie at home and abroad . . . [The trial] riveted attention on the bourgeois affiliations and sympathies of the accused rather than their specific acts' (Carr and Davies, *Foundations of a Planned Economy, 1926–1929*, 1969, pp.622, 624). In a social ferment that was partly spontaneous, the revolution's supporters began to root out its internal enemies. Throughout industry 'bourgeois specialists' in management were baited by the workers. The 'fellow-travelling' non-party intelligentsia came under attack from radicals demanding 'proletarian hegemony' in cultural and intellectual life. Students harangued their professors for their social origins and forced them to undergo 're-election' to their positions. Private traders – NEPmen – were squeezed out of business and, together with those of bourgeois origin, stripped of their civil rights. An anti-religious campaign was started in the summer of 1928: monasteries were closed, monks exiled, and an all-Union congress of the 'militant godless' called in June 1929.

This social ferment of 1928–31 was called at the time a 'cultural revolution', and Western scholars have seen in it several parallels with the Maoist cultural revolution of the 1960s. One of its dynamics was certainly the state's need to mobilize society for the great industrialization drive of the First Five-Year Plan (operative from October 1928) by creating a siege mentality. The people were to be goaded by a demonology of external and internal enemies and inspired by the cult of Stalin's personality. Open political trials, modelled on the Shakhty affair, were staged between 1929 and 1931 in which 'bourgeois specialists' were arraigned for plotting with Poland to promote Ukrainian separatism, sabotaging the food-supply system, organizing counter-revolutionary political parties, espionage and industrial wrecking. But there was an important dynamic to the 'cultural revolution' that welled up 'from below'. It was associated with the influx of great numbers of communist workers into the professions and an antibureaucratic and iconoclastic youth movement in higher education. These young militants were inspired by a new sense of revolutionary purpose and were an important source of societal support for the regime. In some ways, they embarrassed the regime with their radicalism for they propounded theories of the withering away of the state, school and the law which threatened the institutional framework of Soviet life (Fitzpatrick, *Cultural Revolution in Russia, 1928–1931*, 1978, pp.1–7).

2.3   Internal war and forced collectivization

The mass collectivization of agriculture had not been part of the original Five-Year Plan, but in January 1928 Stalin demanded, in response to the grain crisis, a rapid development of the existing state and collective farms so that by 1932 they would supply at least one-third of all the state's grain requirements. Collective farm membership grew from a mere 286,000 households to over one million by June 1929 (nevertheless, only one household in twenty-five) (Davies, *The Socialist Offensive*, 1980, p.109). Though the collective farms were far more mechanized than individual holdings, their land was often unconsolidated and their members usually *batraks* and poor peasants who lacked capital. To the better-off peasants, most collectives seemed unattractive and poverty stricken. During 1929, following renewed difficulties with grain collection and in the face of growing industrial problems, the regime formulated ambitious plans for giant mechanized collective farms, although it was still assumed that collectivization was voluntary and three-quarters of the peasantry would be in individual households at the end of the Five-Year Plan. During the summer the pace of collectivization quickened, with local and regional party organizations taking the initiative in organizing collectives; by the autumn, the central authorities 'were confronted "from below" with plans which exceeded their own expectations' (Davies, 1980, p.133). Faced with the stubborn refusal of the better-off to join collectives, zealous party officials began to threaten them with arrest and deportation, heavy fines and expulsion from the *Mir*. Resistance was particularly fierce among women and often blended with the peasants' religious beliefs: there were rumours that the anti-christ had arrived and the end of the world was at hand. Simultaneously with the acceleration of collectivization came the first public attacks (after months of bitter in-fighting) on Bukharin and the 'Right' opposition, which swelled into a systematic campaign of political defamation unsurpassed in party history (Cohen, *Bukharin and the Bolshevik Revolution*, 1974, p.332).

The publication on 7 November of Stalin's *Pravda* article, 'The Year of the Great Breakthrough', was the decisive signal for all-out collectivization. The article strongly emphasized the voluntary movement of the peasants to the collectives and its confident tone formed part of a concerted campaign to encourage the enthusiasm of party cadres. At the plenum of the Central Committee later in the month, Stalin's call for collectivization was endorsed (though with some reservations, for the party was not yet his utterly pliant instrument) and Bukharin, the chief ideologue of NEP and the *smychka* with the peasantry, expelled from the Politburo. A collectivization commission was set up under the All-Union Commissar for Agriculture, with the party secretaries of the principal grain regions among its members. In the localities party officials tempted the middle peasants into the collectives with unfillable promises of tractors and credits, and branded all who refused as enemies of the Soviet regime. On 27 December, Stalin announced the 'liquidation of the *kulaks* as a class', probably because he wanted to demonstrate to the middle peasants that the individualist path to betterment was irrevocably closed to them. During the locally driven collectivizations of the previous months, many districts had refused admission to *kulaks* because it was thought they would undermine the collectives from within; others would only admit them after they had contributed all property to the common fund. Henceforth, 'dekulakization' and collectivization were inseparable strands of the agrarian revolution. Since any peasant opposed to collectivization could be branded as 'objectively' a *kulak*, expropriations of property, arrests and deportations affected a stratum far wider than those designated *kulaks* in 1926.

The Smolensk archives are particularly illuminating on the military and brutal character of collectivization. Before November the region experienced an escalation of violence because *kulaks* responded to the forced requisitioning of 1928–29 by 'terrorist acts' against party and soviet workers who were mostly special emissaries from the towns. Local officials could not be trusted to enforce collectivization for they frequently identified with the peasants, and even shielded the *kulaks*. The urban emissaries had no such tender feelings; one responded to a local secretary who asked that *kulaks* be left enough grain for sowing and feeding the children: 'When you are attacking, there is no place for mercy; don't think of the *kulak*'s hungry children; in the class struggle philanthropy is evil' (Fainsod, *Smolensk under Soviet Rule*, 1958, p.241). There was a revival of banditry and reports of killings and arson (usually the burning of collective farm property) multiplied, to the point where the emissaries had to beg the OGPU for reinforcements.

At the signal for all-out collectivization, militia forces were released from other duties for deployment in 'dekulakization' and arms supplied to all party personnel participating. The OGPU arrested all *kulak* households listed as 'counter-revolutionary', while a second group were rounded up for deportation to distant parts of the Soviet Union. Remaining *kulaks* were not deported but removed to swamps and other poor land within the region where they were expected to perform serf-duties for the state *and* fulfil production and delivery quotas. The archives make clear that the *kulak* category was interpreted to embrace anyone opposed to collectivization. It was found necessary to address a top-secret letter of February 1930 'unconditionally' prohibiting deportation or resettlement of poor and middle peasants:

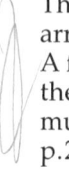

> This warning is issued because in many cases emissaries dekulakize and arrest poor peasants on the ground that the latter are ideologically *kulaks*. A firm class line must here be prepared. A wedge must be driven between the *kulaks* – the class enemy – and the rest of the peasants, and the latter must be mobilized to help in annihilating the class enemy. (Fainsod, 1958, p.243)

'Dekulakization' at this point had no legislative basis, and was unplanned and unsystematic (Davies, *The Socialist Offensive*, 1980, p.231). Its local details testify to the barbarization of social life: women and children were stripped of their clothing and footwear in mid-winter. The slogan of many of the dekulakization brigades seizing *kulak* property was: 'drink, eat – it's all ours'. This lawlessness induced a terrible despair among the well-to-do peasants: a wave of suicides swept the richer households; *kulaks* were killing their wives and children and then taking their own lives. Others entered fictitious divorces in the hope that some property would be saved and the lives of their women and children spared (Fainsod, 1958, pp.245–8).

The high-handed tactics of indiscriminate and arbitrary confiscation and deportation turned many poor and middle peasants into bitter opponents of the regime. They themselves were often bullied into collectives at gunpoint. Among peasants' letters to the local newspaper (most of them unpublished) several refer to the Red Army brigades detailed to the villages to persuade the peasants to sign up for the collective farms. One letter-writer remarked: 'Say something against collectivization, and you're put in prison . . .' (Fainsod, 1958, p.253).

It would be a misunderstanding of the collectivization drive if the extraordinary commitment of the quarter of a million urban emissaries to building a new society was ignored. Their mission was compared at the time to the populist movement 'to the people' of the 1870s and a recent Western scholar has called it 'a crusade as much as a revolution' (Davies, *The Socialist Offensive*, 1980, p.205). An enormous effort was made to educate the peasants to the complex tasks of collectivization by providing thousands of short courses and training programmes in early 1930. Committed communists from the Red Army and the industrial workforce voluntarily settled, after crash training programmes, in the collective farms as directive and technical personnel. As with the industrialization drive, much of this missionary and educative effort was a massive waste of energy and zeal. Activists in the brigades left their training programmes not knowing wheat from stinkweed or a young cow from a heifer, and incapable of allaying the immense suspicion country people had for the towns and the state. In the longer term, however, this settlement of activists brought the regime the benefit of greatly strengthening its presence in the countryside. The autonomous government of the *Mir* and its assembly played no part in collectivization and their existence was formally ended in 1930.

The bogus character of 'voluntary' collectivization was displayed when in March 1930 the central state decided to restrain the abuses it had done so much to encourage. Stalin condemned the cadres as 'dizzy with success' in a *Pravda* article of 2 March 1930. The retreat was forced on him by very wide-scale peasant demonstrations, many of them armed, against the socialization of animals, the attacks on religion and dekulakization. One thousand 'terrorist acts' were registered in the first six months of 1930. Popular anger probably spread to the forces, for the Commissar for War reportedly told Stalin that he would not be responsible for the army if the process of ruthless and indiscriminate collectivization continued (Davies, 1980, p.260). In his article Stalin insisted that collectivization 'must not be imposed by force'. By the end of March, millions of peasants had left the collective farms, taking with them their animals, implements and seed, and demanding land (Davies, 1980, p.277). The percentage of households collectivized in the main grain regions fell from 70 per cent on 1 March to 40 per cent in May.

During the autumn and spring of 1930–31 the collectivization drive was renewed in response to serious shortcomings in the industrial economy. Rather than lower the Plan targets, the unrelenting drive for industrial expansion carried with it a determined effort to squeeze agriculture still further. Peasants were harassed into the collectives by extra taxes and delivery obligations and by being kept on inferior land if they stayed outside. The regime achieved its objective of transforming the social structure of the countryside; by 1932, over 60 per cent of households and more than three-quarters of the sown area were collectivized, and by 1935 only 5 per cent of the sown area was in private hands. Though the total harvests did not increase, state grain procurements rose sharply; in 1933, they were 22.6 million tons as compared with 10.8 million in 1928. In May 1933 Stalin – having achieved his basic objectives – ordered the end of the illegal repressions of *kulaks* and the release of half of the labour-camp inmates imprisoned during collectivization. In November 1934 much of the draconic apparatus of collectivization was dismantled: the 'political departments' set up in the countryside which had driven the peasants into the collectives and extracted their harvests at gunpoint had their activities curtailed, and the police were no longer empowered to execute without regular court procedures. Furthermore, the state, which in May 1932 passed a decree entitling collective farmers to sell surpluses at markets or bazaars, made further concessions to them in the form of private plots and, later, animals.

2.4   The human costs of collectivization

The loss of life attributable to collectivization has never been satisfactorily computed but there are good reasons for believing that it was horrendous. In 1932–33, man-made famine was the principal cause of death. Peasants had responded to collectivization by slaughtering their animals, including their draft horses. Promised tractors did not materialize so fields could not be ploughed, harrowed or manured and this was catastrophic for the 1932 harvest. Additionally, the collective farms were often grossly inefficient; a secretary of one of the Smolensk districts reported in February 1931 on the 'absence of labor discipline in them [and] "anti-moral phenomena" like drunkenness, thievery . . .' (Fainsod,

Smolensk under Soviet Rule, 1958, p.258). Discipline was generally so poor, with mass pillage of communal property, that draconic penalties (including death) were introduced in 1932 for pilfering. In spite of the very poor harvest, the state insisted that the grain would be divided among collective farmers only after appropriate norms had been delivered to feed the towns. What is more, Moscow informed localities which had failed to meet their 1931 delivery quotas that their shortfalls of undelivered grain would be reckoned as part of the grain available for local consumption and that supplies from central reserves would be substantially curtailed. Of course, delivery quotas had not been met in 1931 simply because the grain was not there. Furthermore, the state's central reserves had been depleted by very high exports. When peasants starved in southern Russia and Central Asia, militia and Red Army detachments stopped them leaving the famine areas and the state refused to seek international aid or even acknowledge the existence of the crisis. Victor Kravchenko, who as a young communist engineer was attached to one of the political departments in the Ukraine (set up to ensure that the crops were harvested), recalls: 'Despite harsh police measures to keep the victims at home, Dniepropetrovsk was overrun with starving peasants. Many of them lay listless, too weak even to beg, around railroad stations. Their children were little more than skeletons with swollen bellies.' When he told a colleague in the political department that he had seen seventeen emaciated bodies in a village square, that latter replied: 'Only seventeen? Some days there are more. What can we do but collect the bodies and bury them? You see, the government pumped all the grain out of them last fall [i.e. 1932]. What little they got for their work or managed to hide they've used up long ago' (Kravchenko, *I Chose Freedom*, 1947, pp.113, 114).

Why Stalin chose to exacerbate the famine by refusing international aid (such as Russia had accepted in 1921) and keeping the peasants in the stricken areas is a difficult question. Both Robert Conquest, in his recent history of the famine, and scholars of Ukrainian descent now based in Canada, have interpreted it as a deliberate act of genocide imposed specifically on the Ukraine to destroy its nationalist feeling and identity. The Ukraine had enjoyed a brief independence in 1920 and had put up a stubborn nationalist and anarchist resistance to Soviet rule. It was, furthermore, a region of peasant prosperity where many were classed as *kulaks*. According to the 'genocide' argument, Stalin saw the 1921–23 famine as a model and seized the occasion to liquidate both national and class enemies (Conquest, *The Harvest of Sorrow*, 1986; Serbyn and Krawchenko (eds) *Famine in Ukraine 1932–1933*, 1986). It must be said that this argument is plausible but until the Soviet archives are accessible quite unproven.

In addition to famine deaths mortality was (we may reasonably assume) high among arrested *kulaks*, who formed the largest single group in the forced labour camps of the Gulag archipelago where an unknown number (possibly millions) were worked to death. Fragmentary evidence suggests that the fate of deportees in the inhospitable regions of the Union was only a little less horrifying.

Western scholars have attempted to arrive at estimates for the total death roll by projecting forward the natural rates of increase recorded by the 1926 census and comparing a counterfactual figure with the actual population enumerated at the post-collectivization census. Unfortunately the demographers responsible for the 1937 census were purged and their results suppressed – possibly because they were damning evidence of the lethal impact of collectivization. Calculations from the available Soviet statistics of excess deaths (from all unnatural causes) during

1929 and 1939 range between 5.5 million and 9.2 million, but are based on a total for 1937 which may be fictitious (Rosefielde, 'Excess mortality in the Soviet Union', 1983, p.387). Conquest has arrived at a higher figure of 14.5 million for dekulakization and famine (which if true means that collectivization was more lethal than World War I on *all* its fronts) (Rosefielde, 1983, p.301). The most alarming calculations have been Rosefielde's, who has inferred from post-1945 census figures that excess deaths during 1929–40 were 22.1 million – greater, that is, than Soviet losses during the 1941–45 war – of which 8.5 million is attributed to collectivization and forced labour in Gulag (Conquest, 1986, p.394). Rosefielde published his calculations in the authoritative journal *Soviet Studies* and we can assume that an academic referee approved his article before publication. Unfortunately the confidence that a non-Russian reading, non-demographer like myself had in the credibility of Rosefielde's views was rather undermined by the sharp criticism of his inferences which appeared in the same journal. (For the critique of Rosefielde's calculations see Wheatcroft, 'A note on Steven Rosefielde's calculations . . .', 1984.) I am not qualified to adjudicate between them, and clearly it would be wrong to imply that the human costs of Stalin's 'revolution from above' have been quantified with any certainty. There is good reason for believing, however, that this 'internal war' had destructive consequences of the same order of magnitude as the world wars.

Whether this great social dislocation was 'necessary' or – to use the economist's term – 'optional' for the constructive purpose of industrialization is very doubtful. The value of the property confiscated from the *kulaks* was pitifully small and, rather than being squeezed of a surplus to pay for industrialization, agriculture was a net recipient of real resources between 1928 and 1933 because the state had to invest heavily in tractors to compensate for slaughtered draft animals. To give the collective farmers some incentive to produce, prices moved in favour of the agricultural sector in the early 1930s (Millar in Millar and Nove, 'Was Stalin really necessary?', 1976).

Exercise Mass collectivization has been described as 'a veritable civil war, fought by both sides with unyielding obduracy' (Lewin, *Russian Peasants and Soviet Power*, 1968, p.19). Summarize the social changes consequent on that war and say how they can be interpreted as both evincing and strengthening totalitarian tendencies in Soviet Russia. ■

Specimen answer and discussion We can begin with the severe demographic consequences which, even if they cannot be quantified with certainty, had persistent effects on Soviet population trends. Next we must consider the destruction of an independent peasantry, the end of the social pluralism of the NEP period, greater state control over agricultural resources and marketing, and the release of a vast pool of labour from the countryside which could be mobilized for industrialization. The political strengthening of the regime among the rural population and the dissolution or weakening of traditional institutions (the *Mir* and rural religion) should also be mentioned. Although we might share many reservations about the totalitarian model, we can scarcely deny that the war on the peasantry was massive evidence for the ambition of a one-party regime to secure total control of society, and the fact that it was able to implant itself much more successfully in the countryside after collectivization strongly supports the thesis that a totalitarian tendency was being realized. Furthermore, specific points of the model appear to be validated:

the terrorization of the rural population, the role of a chiliastic ideology in mobilizing party cadres, and the ambition to subordinate agriculture to bureaucratic control can be cited as empirical aspects of totalitarianism.

We must not, however, succumb to the absurdity of thinking of the totalitarian model (or indeed any hypothesis in social science) as a 'truth' which reality 'confirms' – or to which it conforms. To refer, as I have just done, to the validation of specific points in the model rather suggests that it is a checklist the items of which we tick off as we come into possession of the appropriate historical facts. Clearly this is silly. The model is primarily useful in so far as it helps us understand and explain a reality which is otherwise puzzling or inexplicable. Since, as historians, we have a special concern with change through time, we also want the model to help us explain historical development. Agreed, the model may help us refine our descriptions of the Stalinist regime and facilitate comparison with other regimes, but it is debatable whether it takes us very far in explaining why that regime acquired its most salient characteristics and why it was able to mutate with time. I return to these points in the conclusion. □

3 INDUSTRIAL GROWTH AFTER 1928

The launching of the First Five-Year Plan in 1928 (which was declared completed in 1932, ahead of target) began the transformation of Soviet Russia from an underdeveloped rural society to an industrial, urbanized superpower. That transformation was by no means complete before World War II, and, as students of this course, it will be a major question for you to decide whether the war simply pushed Russian society further along the lines laid down by Stalinist moderniz-ation, or whether it deflected development in specific ways. Between 1929 and 1940 the urban population rose from 28.7 to 63.1 million – from 19 to 33 per cent of the total. Industrial output at the onset of the Plan, in 1928, was equal to only 6.9 per cent of total US industrial output, but by 1938 total Soviet industrial output was 45.1 per cent of US output (Lane, *Politics and Society in the USSR*, 1970, p.67).

The achievements (and some of the shortfalls) of the First Five-Year Plan are summarized in the following figures:

Table 16.3

	1927–28 (actual)	1932–33 (plan)	1932 (actual)	1940 (actual)
Gross industrial production (1926–27 roubles in 100m)	18.3	43.2	43.3	138.5
Electricity (100m. kwts)	5.05	22.0	13.4	—
Hard coal (m. tons)	35.4	75	64.3	165.9
Pig iron (m. tons)	3.3	106.2	—	
Steel (m. tons)	4.0	10.4	5.9	18.3
Machinery (m. 1926–27 roubles)	1822	4688	7362	—
Total employed labour force (millions)	11.3	15.8	22.8	—

(Sources: Nove, *An Economic History of the USSR*, 1969, p.191; Filtzer, *Soviet Workers and Stalinist Industrialization*, 1986, p.7)

Two points revealed by these figures are worth dwelling on: firstly, the 137 per cent increase in industrial production by 1932 was gained with only a 103 per cent increase in the labour force. There was, therefore, some increase in labour productivity: workers worked harder for (as we shall see) lower wages. Secondly, there were very significant discrepancies in the planned and the actual outputs of such basic items in an industrial economy as steel. These should lead us to ask how the overall growth in industrial production was achieved, for without steel neither machinery nor factories can be built. In fact, Western economic historians have argued that the figure for aggregate industrial output was statistically 'inflated' by the Plan's price base. (Thus, using 1926–27 prices to value machinery production inflated the actual increase in output because in 1927 machines were rare and expensive – Nove, 1969, p.192.) The figures should also alert us to the bottlenecks and sheer chaos which characterized the implementation of the Plan. One conception of planning involves the organic co-ordination of different sectors of industry so that adjustments in the targets for one feed back into another, and the whole economy maintains its equilibrium. Soviet planning never corresponded to this conception. In the course of the first Plan, output targets for specific industries were drastically increased without considering the feedback consequences, and the regime's methods for achieving them became an ever-tighter control over resources, the mobilization of 'shock brigades' for key projects and a belief in the triumph of revolutionary political will over material conditions. Wasteful imbalances were constant features of growth: expensive imported machinery rusted because factories were not built, or was wrecked by the illiterate unskilled workers who manned it. Managers given near impossible production targets hoarded labour and materials, and so on.

Despite manifold imperfections the basic achievements of the plan are undeniable and, as the selected figures for 1940 indicate, industrial growth continued during the Second and Third Five-Year Plans. When the country was invaded in June 1941 it was industrially self-sufficient with a large-scale iron and steel industry, automobile plants, chemical industry, electric power stations and engineering works. It mined all of its own coal and drilled and refined all of its own oil. The mechanization of agriculture and transport were far advanced: only 1,150 tractors were produced in 1926–27, in 1938 49,200; output of trucks and buses rose from 1,670 to 18,400.

Exercise   I want now to turn to the ideology and rhetoric that inspired this great social effort. Please read the extracts (in document I.9 in *Documents 2*) from the speech Stalin made to a conference of industrial managers on 4 February 1931. Summarize the main points Stalin was making and say what section of the speech you find most emotionally charged; with what was Stalin identifying himself and his policy in this passage? What are the special problems of handling this kind of evidence? ■

Specimen answer   Stalin begins by referring to the pledge to meet 'control figures' (that is, targets
and discussion   laid down in the Plan) ahead of schedule. In the subsequent paragraphs he calls on communists to become the masters of industrial technique and management, and cites the Shakhty case as evidence of the 'wrecking' activities of non-party specialists. Stalin warns that 'the class enemy is seriously resisting the socialist offensive' – a constant theme of his speeches and articles at this time. A communist monopoly of industrial expertise was required for the one-man

management needed to enforce discipline in industry. Stalin alludes to those who had asked for a slackening in the tempo of industrialization, and rejects this in what I find the most emotional part of his speech where he refers to the many occasions Russia had been beaten because of its backwardness (by the Mongol khans, the Turkish beys, the Swedish feudal lords, and so on). What is so remarkable is Stalin's identification of himself and his policy with the Russian past. He warns that 'our socialist fatherland' will similarly be beaten if it does not 'put an end to its backwardness in the shortest possible time . . .' He then goes on to say that the Soviet Union's obligations to the world's proletariat require the elimination of its backwardness: '. . . in ten years we must make good the distance which separates us from the advanced capitalist countries.' In conclusion, he reiterates his demand that Bolsheviks master industrial technique.

The public addresses of Stalin are difficult to assess as evidence because they frequently use 'coded' language to allude to conflicts within the party hierarchy. (Who are the people pressing for a slackening of the tempo? What arguments in the Politburo are being hinted at here?) Moreover, one can't be sure how the speaker took his own propaganda: Did Stalin and his audience believe the chiliastic rhetoric ('We must march forward in such a way that the working class of the whole world . . . may say: This is my vanguard . . .')? Or was it the sort of incantation of faith, equally evident in other political cultures, which leaders make and audiences expect on certain public occasions, although they know that policy will be conducted by the light of more practical calculations? (General Eisenhower once told a presidential campaign audience: 'Without God there could be no American form of government, nor an American way of life. Recognition of the Supreme Being is the first and most basic expression of Americanism.' The General and the General Secretary may have been equally sincere in their basic values.) □

3.1   The social consequences of industrialization: internal war on the working class

Stalin's speech gives us a feeling for that sense of international isolation and an inevitable international class war which contributed to the breakneck speed of Soviet industrialization. Western scholars – who have only recently begun to write the social history of the 1930s – have argued that mobilizing politically for the industrialization was made possible only by 'internalizing' this class war. In the three years following the Shakhty trial, 1.6 million employees in the state apparatus were investigated and 11 per cent purged. Of those purged, 23,000 were classified as 'enemies of Soviet power'; they and their families were stigmatized and many were imprisoned (Kuromiya, *Stalin's Industrial Revolution*, 1988, pp.32, 47). Engineers and technical workers were similarly caught up in this rooting out of the enemy within, and the mentality of internal war became so pervasive as to lead one American journalist to write in the early 1930s: 'The Soviet Union is a land at war. This is a first and a last impression . . . [One senses] an atmosphere of militant struggle, a nation under arms living figuratively but effectively under martial law and subsisting on the short rations of a beleagured state' (H. R. Knickerbocker, quoted in Kuromiya, *Stalin's Industrial Revolution*, 1988, p.108).

The mobilization of labour for the industrial drive was a central task of the regime after 1928, one made particularly difficult by the fact that it could offer the

workers no material incentives. In fact, their standard of living fell catastrophi-
cally during the First Five-Year Plan. Western estimates are that average real
wages in 1932 were half or less their 1928 level, but these estimates fail to convey
the real extent of the destitution. Because of the failures of collectivization,
workers had to rely more on privately marketed food, the price of which shot up
and, at the same time, face higher deductions from their wages in the forms of
compulsory subscriptions to state loans and trade-union dues. The rationing of
bread (introduced in 1929/30) and public catering in works' canteens did something to protect nutritional levels, but everyday life for consumers was a miserable
round of shortages: of accommodation, foodstuffs, clothing and such basic
commodities as matches and salt (Filtzer, *Soviet Workers and Stalinist Industrialisation*, 1986, pp. 91–2). The desperate housing crisis was such that, in 1931, workers
were sleeping on factory floors and at railway stations, and even faced the
prospect of spending the winter homeless.

Because of the dearth of material incentives, coercion and exhortation played
large parts in the mobilization of labour. A significant, though as yet unquan-
tified, contribution to industrial growth was made by forced labour, particularly
on giant construction projects, such as the White Sea canal, undertaken in
extreme conditions. Less extreme forms of coercion for the industrial rank and file
were introduced in response to the appalling breakdown of labour discipline.
Most of the recruits to the factory workforce were peasants, many illiterate or
barely literate, for whom the shift to industrial labour would in any circumstances
have meant a difficult adjustment to a new social and cultural pattern. But these
recruits had the experiences of collectivization, famine and state brutality fresh on
them; their industrial attitudes and behaviour suggest a 'demoralization' or,
perhaps more aptly, anomie in the face of the recent past. Labour turnover was
extraordinarily rapid: by 1930 the average worker was changing jobs every eight
months (in coal mining every four months) in search of better wages or accommodation. This instability of the workforce undermined industrial authority and
was compounded by absenteeism, drunkenness at work, hooliganism and
machine breaking. The regime responded with 'a volley of draconian measures'
(Lewin, *The Making of the Soviet System*, 1985, p.242). The dearth of housing and
supplies was turned into a weapon against truculent workers who faced not only
dismissal but deprivation of bread-rationing cards and eviction from lodgings,
irrespective of the season. A law of November 1932 aimed to strengthen the
power of management by making factory administrators responsible for issuing
workers' ration books and coupons, and therefore able to withdraw ration
privileges.

Coercion of the labour force was easier to achieve because of the trade unions'
servility under NEP and, from 1928, their complete subordination to the party and
the state. All collective organizations of workers were broken up by the regime
(even those formed in support of the industrialization drive) and the workforce
was atomized by piece-work, other incentive schemes and the formation of
groups of 'shock workers' who were entitled to better rations, special tables in
factory dining rooms, special access to footwear and clothing in short supply, and
numerous other privileges. The factory workforce became highly differentiated in
its wages and standard of life and the regime deliberately fostered inegalitarian-
ism throughout society.

However, there were limitations to the control over the working class achieved
by the regime. Workers used a variety of effective means to mitigate the harshness

of labour legislation and the enforced speed-up of production. Because of the labour shortage they were able to extract concessions from managers anxious to retain their workforce, and well aware of the unrealistic nature of the demands coming from above. So breaches of discipline were often ignored, wages illegally inflated, production norms kept lower than planned, and poor quality work tolerated.

During 1934 and 1935 workers enjoyed some respite from the pressures of industrialization and an improvement in living standards, but in August 1935 a new spur to increased productivity was devised when the miner Aleksei Stakhanov hewed a record amount of coal in one shift. This and other highly publicized achievements of 'heroes' of Soviet labour were orchestrated into an industrial strategy – 'Stakhanovism' – which led to a widening differential between the rank and file and an élite of politically loyal record breakers, with renewed downward pressure on the earnings of the majority, and very high rewards, with privileged access to housing and consumer goods, as well as opportunities for promotion to management, for the minority. The record outputs achieved by the heroic few – often with special equipment and in highly favourable conditions – were used to set new norms for the many, who enjoyed no such benefits, and had to produce 25 to 50 per cent more simply to retain their original earnings. It is no wonder that the Stakhanovites were widely detested and their labours sometimes deliberately sabotaged. The strategy was also 'part of a general attempt by the élite to exercise increasingly authoritarian control over society' (Filtzer, *Soviet Workers and Stalinist Industrialisation*, 1986, p.177). The peak of Stakhanovism in 1936 came simultaneously with the Great Purges (whose victims included many Red Directors in industry) and with highly conservative social and cultural policies, such as the outlawing of abortion.

Exercise   The internecine conflicts caused by Stakhanovism, the increasing political control and purging of industrial managers, and the frequent disruptions of production because of labour and material bottlenecks led (according to Kravchenko) to 'an era of anarchy and civil strife in industry' (*I Chose Freedom*, 1947, p.188). Assuming that this is an accurate summary, how in your view does it affect the applicability of the totalitarian model to the analysis of Soviet society during the 1930s? ■

Specimen answer   In my view it undermines the general thesis behind the totalitarian model which,
and discussion   as you will recall, argued that totalitarian regimes achieved total control over society, and I think it contradicts the sixth point of the model which portrayed the economy as subordinate to the state bureaucracy. To elaborate slightly, many of the measures which the regime took to achieve control over, for example, industrial labour were actually *dysfunctional* to that purpose because of the countervailing social pressures and forces they generated. However, we should not treat the model as a straw person; its proponents could rightly argue that many of the points raised in this section (such as the smashing of all rank-and-file organizations and the atomization of the workforce) were manifestations of the totalitarian tendencies of the regime. □

3.2   Women and the industrial workforce

Not the least of the social consequences of industrialization was a veritable revolution in the position of women in the workforce. The Soviet regime shared none of the fascist scruples about the mobilization of women's labour, and it recognized that if it was to attract them into production then it would have to provide crèche and childcare facilities, and public amenities (such as laundries, public catering) which would lessen the burden of housework. Although women's share in industrial labour as a whole rose by only about a quarter, they entered industries and trades that before intense industrialization had been virtually closed to them. In January 1929 women were 28.5 per cent of workers in large-scale industry, but they predominated in trades (such as textiles and clothing) where women's work was well established. By July 1935 women were 39.8 per cent of workers in large-scale industry, and it is clear that the huge expansion of the extractive and capital goods industries could not have taken place without their labour. They had risen from under 8 per cent to 24.1 per cent of those in coal mining and from 8.9 per cent to 26.2 per cent of the engineering and metalworking labour force. Clerical employment had witnessed a great influx of women workers; they rose from 12.4 per cent to 44.3 per cent of the clerical labour force. Despite concerted efforts to attract women into factory training schools, they were generally confined to the lowest-skilled and worst-paid jobs, where they had little prospects for promotion. Those who tried to improve their industrial status often encountered considerable male resistance and harassment. (The source for this section is Filtzer, *Soviet Workers and Stalinist Industrialisation*, 1986, pp.63–7.)

3.3   The social consequences of industrialization: the making of the Stalinist élite

Exercise So far we have concentrated on social aspects of industrialization which alienated many from the regime, even if their disaffection did not take articulate political form. What aspect of industrialization would have bound others to the regime and extended its popular support? ∎

Specimen answer and discussion I hope you thought of the enormous social mobility created by industrial expansion. The shortage of skilled technicians, industrial managers, and low-level supervisory personnel led to the rapid promotion of workers to responsible positions. These 'promotees' became the major base of support for the Stalinist élite, if not actually joining it. Between 1930 and 1933, some 660,000 'worker communists' rose into the administrative and educational apparatus. Their movement into positions of authority was accelerated after the Great Purges of 1937 removed much of the older industrial managerial stratum and allowed a new wave of upwardly mobile ex-workers to take their place.

In addition to the direct promotion of workers into technical and supervisory grades, the regime created a new élite political stratum by directing, during the First Five-Year Plan, hundreds of thousands of worker communists into the higher technical institutes which trained them as the managers and political executives of the new industrial society. By the beginning of 1933, 233,000 communists (about 25 per cent of party membership at the end of 1927) were full-time students (Fitzpatrick, 'Stalin and the making of a new élite, 1928–1939', 1979). Many of the new young graduates received dramatic promotions and rich material rewards. After graduating as a twenty-nine-year-old engineer, Kravchenko found himself 'overnight, transformed into one of the élite . . . one of the million or so top Party officials, industrial managers and police functionaries who were, taken together, the new aristocracy of Russia'. He was installed in a commodious five-room house with a car in the garage and a couple of fine horses at his disposal, and earned at least 1,500 roubles a month though with bonuses his income was often more than 2,000. Foremen and skilled men at his factory rarely earned more than 400 roubles, while the unskilled and women earned only 120 to 175. Though he wanted to establish friendly relations with the workers, he found that 'for an engineer in my position to mix with [them] might offend their pride; it smacked of patronage. In theory we represented the "workers' power", but in practice we were a class apart' (Kravchenko, *I Chose Freedom*, 1947, pp.174–5). ☐

This process of élite formation through technical education meant that henceforth expertise was a monopoly of the Communist Party and it led to profound changes in the character of the party. Previously the party intelligentsia was trained in Marxism and social science, but after the creation of the Stalinist cadres the typical highly educated party member was an engineer. While the traditional intelligentsia (party and non-party alike) was savagely purged, the new technical élite created by the Stalinist regime survived and prospered during the 1930s. The trial of G. Piatakov (Deputy Commissar for Heavy Industry) in January 1937 was the signal for mass demotions and arrests among the Soviet political and managerial élite, and the young workers who had been plucked from the bench and sent through technical education stepped into the vacated positions. It has been estimated that 89 per cent of all First Five-Year Plan graduates were in the leading cadres in 1941, and the percentage surviving and holding responsible jobs was actually much higher (Fitzpatrick (ed.) *Cultural Revolution in Russia, 1928–1931,* 1978, p.63).

This process of élite formation was a crucial aspect of Stalinist modernization because through it the regime acquired a stable social structure appropriate to a modern industrial society. It helped ensure the continuity and evolution of the Soviet state after Stalin's death because it enabled most of the succeeding generation of political leaders to rise to power. Paradoxically this 'Class of 1938' who gained most from the political terror of that period were to prove a deeply conservative group in their taste and cultural outlook, with a yearning for status and what to Western eyes seems terribly like middle-class respectability (Hough in Fitzpatrick (ed.) 1978). Though comparisons are fraught with difficulty, it could be argued that a fundamental difference between Stalinism, and Nazism and Fascism, was that while the social and institutional foundations of a state which would outlive Stalin were being laid down, the German and Italian regimes were intimately tied with the personal fortunes of their dictators. The odious glorification of Stalin in his lifetime, and the pejorative term 'Stalinism', may equally have misled by identifying the Soviet state that developed in the 1930s too closely with the personality of its master.

4 INTERNAL WAR ON THE PARTY: THE COURSE AND CAUSES OF THE 'GREAT PURGE'

4.1   Purging, terror and totalitarianism

Accounts of the political terror which engulfed the Soviet Union in the autumn of 1936 are central to the totalitarian 'image' of the regime, an image we derive as much from two brilliant works of fiction, Koestler's *Darkness at Noon* and Orwell's *1984*, as from political science and history. What differentiated this period of terror from others is that it was directed against the party (and industrial and military élites staffed by party members) as much as against the rest of society. It is worth emphasizing that party membership protected individuals from the severest punishment for political 'crimes' until 1935. When a middle-ranking communist, Mikhail Riutin, was arraigned in 1932 for circulating a secret programme cataloguing Stalin's mistakes and abuses of power and calling for his removal (by force if necessary), the Politburo majority allegedly refused Stalin's call for his execution, a defeat of the General Secretary which 'reaffirmed the sacrosanct prohibition against shooting party members' (Cohen, *Bukharin and the Bolshevik Revolution*, 1974, p.344). (There were no scruples about the torture and execution of non-communist specialists.) Several authorities have argued that the 'Riutin affair' was a turning-point in the politics of the 1930s and date to it 'Stalin's determination to rid himself of all such restraints represented by the existing Bolshevik Party, its élite, and its political traditions' (Cohen, 1974; Schapiro, *The Communist Party of the Soviet Union*, 1960, p.393; Haslam, 'Political opposition to Stalin . . .', 1986). Stalin's mass assault on the party in 1937 has been interpreted as the extirpation of moderate opposition to his 'revolution from above' which crystallized in 1932, an interpretation given some support when Nikita Khrushchev published the secret directive of September 1936, in effect inaugurating the first great wave of arrests, which accused the OGPU of being 'four years behind' in dealing with the menace of counter-revolution (Schapiro, 1960, p.393; a more detailed attempt to relate the origins of the terror to the political opposition to Stalin is made in Haslam, 1986).

In the totalitarian image of the regime, the mass expulsion of party members is rather casually linked with the waves of arrests and executions which were at their height during the *Ezhovshchina* (the phase of terror associated with N. Ezhov, Commissar for Internal Affairs between August 1936 and December 1938). An historian who has used the Smolensk archive to study the party in the 1930s has argued that we must distinguish between apolitical purging (for which there were several precedents in the 1920s) and the political attacks of the *Ezhovshchina* when the rank and file were incited to denounce the upper and middle echelons of the party leadership for 'bureaucratism', lack of vigilance, failure to follow the correct economic line, and so on (Getty, *Origins of the Great Purges*, 1985).

This radical terrorization of local and regional officials had a more recent parallel in the destruction of entrenched officialdom by revolutionary zealots during the Chinese Cultural Revolution. It bore little resemblance to a 'purge' (*chistka*) as the CPSU understood the term, which applied only to periodic membership screenings to weed out the corrupt, idle and drunken. Undoubtedly many were attracted to the party only by the privileges of membership which included special rations, clothing and, before the mid-1930s, immunity from arrest by the civil authorities. These privileges made membership cards valuable commodities and led to large numbers of 'dead souls' on party rolls. Evidence from the Smolensk archives indicates that even leadership positions in the region were at various times filled with drunks, embezzlers, petty thieves and womanizers. Purges of such undesirables had been carried out in 1921 (when a quarter of the national membership was expelled) and 1929 by the Central Control Commission (TsKK), a screening body independent of the party's Central Committee. On both occasions, only a minority was purged for political or ideological deviations. An estimated 1 per cent of purges in 1929 was related to factional struggles in the party. Although not in the hands of TsKK, the *chistka* ordered in January 1933 (which lasted about two years) was not fundamentally different in character from previous purges. Between 1931 and 1933 there had been a 65 per cent growth in all-Union party membership and most of the 1.14 million expelled during 1933–34 (the figure given in Schapiro, *The Communist Party of the Soviet Union*, 1960, p.435) were relatively recent recruits rather than adherents of the pre-1929 opposition. The Smolensk archives do not provide evidence of terror or hysteria (as some authors have suggested), nor of a witch hunt against oppositionists.

The general re-registration of party membership and check on all records of 1935 (known as the *proverka*) was, Getty argues, of a similar, basically apolitical character. The results of this re-registration quite belie notions of the totalitarian party as exhibiting ruthless bureaucratic efficiency for they suggest that confusion, disorder and inertia were characteristics of the political network. Half of the membership cards checked in the Leningrad district in 1935 were either invalid or false, with the wrong names and false dates of membership entered, or no stamp signifying that they had been lawfully issued. The impression conveyed by the *proverka* expulsions is not of a hysterical witch hunt or rising pattern of violence, but of a bureaucracy forced to be meticulous against its very nature (Getty, *Origins of the Great Purges*, 1985, ch.3). The vast majority of expulsions were for defects in personal behaviour. However, one novel element of the *proverka*, which did make it something of a prelude for the *Ezhovshchina*, was the encouragement the Stalinist Central Committee gave the rank and file to attack the 'bureaucratism' of local leaders.

4.2   Historical interpretations of the terror

The image of the terror associated with the totalitarian thesis is usually portrayed as methodically diffusing outwards from a single centre of power – Stalin – and the purges are regarded as a single phenomenon, orchestrated by the dictator from the opening movement that followed the murder of Sergei Kirov, the Leningrad Party Secretary, in December 1934, to the crescendo of the last show trial of Bukharin, Rykov and others in March 1938. Kirov's death is attributed to Stalin who, it is argued, removed a major rival and created a pretext for mass terror at a single stroke. The best-known history of the purges written in the West, Robert Conquest's *The Great Terror* (1968), gives substance to this image and has long influenced standard accounts of the period.

This image of the Stalinist terror drew largely on the memoirs of defectors and reflected and fed back into the politics of the Cold War. Recent studies by J. Arch

Getty (1985) and R. McNeal (1988) have called both the overall shape of this image and many of its details into serious question. They do not rehabilitate morally either Stalin or his regime, but argue that the image is inconsistent with the archival evidence available in the West and with what can be established from published Soviet sources. Where the totalitarian image portrays a monolithic apparatus of terror singlemindedly and systematically deployed by Stalin against all potential opponents, they have argued for a much more chaotic situation, in which Stalin was responsive to pressures 'from below' and often acted as the mediator between 'radical' and more 'moderate' factions.

The thesis that the terror was the working-out of Stalin's long-term design rests heavily on his responsibility for Kirov's assassination, and the evidence for this has so far been tenuous. Several scholars have argued that Stalin had nothing to gain by killing Kirov, who was one of Stalin's key supporters with a central part in the Second Five-Year Plan (Ulam, *Stalin*, 1974, pp.375–88; Getty, 1985, pp.207–10). Whatever Stalin's real role, he certainly capitalized on Kirov's death to order the prompt execution as 'counter revolutionaries' of more than a hundred persons already in custody, to effect the sweeping arrest of oppositionists in Leningrad, and to re-arrest and try his old opponents, Zinoviev and Kamenev, for complicity in Kirov's murder. A secret party directive, issued immediately after Kirov's death by Stalin and only later approved by the Politburo, prescribed summary investigation and immediate execution of those accused of 'terrorist' offences. They were denied defence lawyers and no time was given either to refute charges or appeal for mercy. As Khruschchev later declared, this directive 'became the basis for mass acts of abuse against socialist legality' (quoted in Schapiro, *The Communist Party of the Soviet Union*, 1960, p.401).

Here was the instrument of terror. Was, as some authorities have argued, early 1935 the initial phase of the 'uprooting [of] all actual or potential opposition in the party . . . the first time it felt the brunt of terror' (Hough and Fainsod, *How the Soviet Union is Governed*, 1979, p.172)? Getty's examination of the Smolensk archive does not support this thesis; the attrition of party members was, in fact, negligible. The scale of the purges in January 1935 was limited; sentences imposed were lenient by later standards. (Zinoviev received a ten-year and Kamenev a five-year prison sentence. They had not been tortured and did not confess.) It was not until August 1936 that the first great public trial of opposition leaders, and the first mass arrests, took place. The intervening period was, Getty suggests, one of comparative political quiescence and saw very little of anything resembling terror. The framing and discussion of the new constitution (formally adopted in 1936), with its provisions for direct elections by universal franchise and secret voting and its guaranteed freedoms of speech, press and assembly, dominated public life in 1935 and early 1936 (Schapiro, *The Communist Party of the Soviet Union*, 1960, p.406). While the total discordance between the constitution and Soviet realities is a commonplace, few commentators have seen much discrepancy between the totalitarian image of mounting terror and the democratic and liberal rhetoric of this period. Yet this rhetoric was quite inappropriate to a premeditated strike against the party and contrasts strongly with the paranoia whipped up in late 1936, with its war and spy scares, xenophobia, and demands for constant vigilance against the traitors within.

Where the totalitarian interpretation sees a strong continuity between the purges and the *Ezhovshchina*, revisionist writers see a distinct break. This new phenomenon (as the latter see it) opened with the circulation of a top-secret letter

to the party apparatus warning them of the 'Terrorist Activities of the Trotskyite-Zinoviev Counter-revolutionary Bloc' and anticipating the trial of Zinoviev and Kamenev in August. The letter concluded that 'the inalienable quality of every Bolshevik must be the ability to detect the enemy of the party, however well he may be masked'. This invocation of the cunningly disguised enemy within became the hallmark of the terror. It inspired mutual suspicions and denunciations, and justified the vast network of informers who degraded everyday life, making it a routine of constant dread.

The trial and execution of old leaders of Zinoviev's and Kamenev's stature 'came as a bombshell to the great majority of party members', who could have been left in no doubt from the nature of the evidence that this was to be the first of many trials of former oppositionists (Schapiro, 1960, p.409). Why Stalin should have made this unanticipated move at this time is not clear in any interpretation. There are no indications that he planned the *Ezhovshchina*, nor that it was undertaken with the intention of rearranging the political structure. We can point to two factors which may jointly have precipitated the onslaught. The beginning of the Spanish Civil War and the generally deteriorating international situation certainly contributed to the obsession with security, and Stalin and the Central Committee were losing patience with the failure of the party's ossified and unpopular regional apparatus to reform itself. Party officials had become bureaucrats and administrators, rather than political leaders and educators, and the party's traditions of internal democracy and self-criticism had atrophied or been stifled. Stalin persistently incited the rank and file against the local satraps as a matter of anti-bureaucratic policy and practice, and his favoured lieutenant, A. Zhdanov, frequently demanded the revival of party democracy. In the totalitarian interpretation, rank-and-file denunciations of bureaucracy during the *Ezhovshchina* are dismissed as the populist fig-leaf covering Stalin's machinations, but in the revisionist interpretation they were an integral part of the process by which the bureaucracy was destroyed from above and below in a wave of voluntarism, chaos, and even a kind of perverse revolutionary puritanism. Similarly, most authors have read Stalin's public calls, in February and March 1937, for moderation in party expulsions and an end to the arrests of former oppositionists who had severed all connection with Trotsky and genuinely ceased oppositional activity, as examples of his staggering duplicity. Yet these can be seen as real attempts to restrain dangerous forces he himself had unleashed.

Whether intentionally or not, the political structure was shaken to its foundations by the virtual destruction of the party leadership at the level of the *oblast* and *raikom* (major and lesser administrative districts). Only three, out of more than a hundred, *oblast* secretaries escaped arrest. By the middle of 1939, only seven out of 136 *raikom* secretaries in the Moscow region were still in their posts. Almost all the rest had been arrested and shot (Medvedev, *Let History Judge*, 1971, p.203). One reason for this rate of attrition may be found in the territorial organization of the Red Army, which meant that its officers worked closely with the party officials in their military districts. When the liquidation of officers began in the early summer of 1937, their civilian associates were often destroyed too.

Though it may not have been Stalin's purpose, a major result of the *Ezhovshchina* was the rejuvenation of the party. According to a report submitted to the Eighteenth Party Congress in 1939, of the 1.589 million full members at that date, only 8.3 per cent had joined earlier than 1920. Less than a fifth of the membership at the beginning of 1921 remained party members in 1939, by when over 70 per cent of members had been recruited after 1929. Delegates to the Eighteenth Congress reflected the comparative youth of the party: about half were under thirty-five, over three-quarters under forty and scarcely any over fifty (Schapiro, *The Communist Party of the Soviet Union*, 1960, pp.437–9).

This rejuvenation and the liquidation of most of Lenin's former comrades has led many to conclude, quite reasonably, that the Old Bolsheviks were specific targets for attack. Interestingly, however, where the careers of representative samples of party personnel have been traced, the analysis does not support this conclusion. Biographical data on the Moscow party élite of 1917 shows that only (*sic*) 50 per cent of members surviving into the 1930s were victims of the terror. The criteria for liquidation appear to have been one's position in the party bureaucracy and in the economic administration, rather than veteran status as such (Getty and Chase, 'The Moscow party élite of 1917 in the Great Purges', 1978).

4.3   The scale of the terror

The number of victims of the terror, which spread far beyond the confines of the party, is simply not known; estimates of arrests have ranged between 4 million and 8 million, of executions between tens of thousands and 1 million, and camp deaths have been taken to account for several million. The present (1988) period of *glasnost* has promised an impartial enquiry and until such is completed speculation is pointless. We can get an impression of the extent of the terror within the party from the facts that of the 1,966 voting and non-voting delegates to the Seventeenth Party Congress of 1934, more than half (1,108) were arrested on charges of counter-revolutionary crimes and of the full members of the Central Committee elected by the Congress, two-thirds were imprisoned or shot (Schapiro, *The Communist Party of the Soviet Union*, 1960, p.417; Getty, 'The "Great Purges" reconsidered', 1979, p.507). These were the most prominent communists and the arrest of each usually implicated rank-and-file associates, subordinate officials, relatives, even children.

Similarly, we can gauge the extent of the purges in the military élite. They began in May 1937 with the arrest of M. N. Tukhachevski, the leading soviet marshal and potential commander-in-chief, and fell equally on military and political officers. They destroyed about half the officer corps; three out of five marshals; thirteen out of fifteen army commanders; fifty-seven out of eighty-five corps commanders; 110 out of 195 division commanders; 220 out of 406 brigade commanders; all eleven Vice Commissars of War; seventy-five out of eighty members of the Supreme Military Council, including all the military district commanders (Schapiro, 1960, p.420). The naval and air forces were no less savagely purged. Those in the highest military echelons were never formally charged or tried, but the accusations brought against them included conspiring with Germany and Japan to bring about a *coup d'état* and dismember the Soviet Union. They were given some credence by documents, forged by the German Secret Service and skilfully leaked through Czechoslovakia, implicating Tukhachevski and his circle with the German General Staff. It is, however, simply incredible that Stalin and the NKVD actually believed in a conspiracy embracing the majority of the country's military officers (how could such a plot have failed?) and it is impossible to answer satisfactorily why they took a step which so grievously weakened Russia's military capacity. It is worth noting that, although there was a definite slackening in the civilian purges by the end of 1938, the military purges continued until 1941, the threat and the actual advent of war notwithstanding (Erickson, *The Road to Stalingrad*, 1975, p.19).

4.4   The enigma of the show trials

The public trial of Old Bolsheviks, including many of Lenin's closest comrades, presents us with still more enigmatic features of the terror: it has often been asked why brave and hardened revolutionaries confessed in court to such astonishing crimes as plotting the deaths of Stalin and Lenin, conniving with the exiled Trotsky and his (fictitious) underground opposition, and conspiring with foreign intelligence agencies in the same plot of which the military were accused. Prolonged physical and mental torture, and threats against the relatives of the accused, are sufficient explanation for these confessions, and the enthusiastic complicity of Radek and others in the monstrous farce which destroyed them was doubtless elicited by promises of leniency. It seems to me that the real enigma of the show trials is the attitude of Stalin (a secret observer at Bukharin's trial) and his prosecutor, A. Vyshinsky, towards them. I find it quite impossible to imagine the frame of mind and feelings of Vyshinsky as he denounced the accused, or of Stalin observing the process. Why did they require this ritual, with its extravagant denunciations of 'criminals who have sold themselves to enemy intelligence services, criminals whom even ordinary felons treat as the basest, the lowest, the most contemptible, the most depraved of the depraved'? (cited in Cohen, *Bukharin and the Bolshevik Revolution*, 1974, p.374). Stalin and Vyshinsky can scarcely have believed in the charges themselves and the evidence (apart from the confessions) adduced at the show trials was easily shown to be fabricated. Stalin was, possibly, trying to impress foreign observers with the 'legalism' of the terror and justifying to soviet citizens the all-pervasive repression. But perhaps it is a mistake to seek a 'rationalist' explanation: confession is basically a religious act, and confession and recantation have always been required of heretics. The show trials may belong to the psychopathology of religion and require the same empathetic understanding that historians bring (for example) to the witch hunts of early modern Europe.

5   *CONCLUSIONS*

5.1   State violence and social development

In this unit we have charted enormous changes which were not simply social but societal. Clearly the historical context of these changes was not 'peace', such as Britain and France were enjoying during the 1920s and 1930s. Though we might talk of these societies as experiencing 'class war', this is hyperbole. Despite profound conflicts of interest between them, the classes in these societies did not engage in armed struggle and the violence that occurred during social conflicts arose almost invariably from the attempts of the police to enforce law and order. The capitalist economy in these societies was relatively insulated from the polity. The state's monopoly of force was not placed directly at the disposal of any class or group in society and it was not brought to bear on processes of economic and social development. By contrast, internal war is not a hyperbole to describe the context of societal change in Soviet Russia. There the state's monopoly of violence was brought to bear upon development; the great mass of people were coerced into changing their ways of living by the police, the militia, party cadres and the army. To be sure, coercion was complemented by exhortation and state-directed cultural change, but even these non-coercive aspects of 'social revolution from above' were scarcely irenic for they often propagated a psychosis of internal war: *kulaks*, hoarders, NEPmen, bourgeois specialists, Trotskyists, wreckers . . . the list of internal enemies was seemingly endless. Whether state violence had a comparable role in effecting socio-economic change in fascist states is a question we will examine in later units.

5.2 Totalitarianism

This unit has been rather critical of the totalitarian model and it is important to acknowledge that the concept was a valid attempt to explain a form of authoritarian rule qualitatively different from previous dictatorships and despotisms. Whatever its defects, the model is much more analytic and persuasive than explanations of the course of Soviet history couched in terms of Stalin's 'mistakes' or his 'degeneracy'. (The most notable account of Stalinism written from within the USSR, Roy Medvedev's *Let History Judge*, adopts precisely this stance towards its subject. Though an invaluable chronicle of Stalin's repressions, the only explanation he has for them is – Stalin.)

The objections Western scholars have raised against the totalitarian model in the last fifteen years or so have been of four basic kinds:

1   Use of the model has produced a 'tunnel vision' of Soviet history which sees the party-state unerringly advancing on totalitarian lines from 1917 to 'high Stalinism'. This linear view blinds us to the sharp discontinuities in Soviet history and the significant differences in Soviet authoritarianism before and after 1929. The idea that a 'totalitarian trajectory' was determined by the nature of the party and its ideology in 1917 can easily be refuted by reference to the remarkable changes in membership, organization and ideology that the party experienced during the 1920s (Cohen, 'Bolshevism and Stalinism', 1977).

2   The model assumes that 'society' was overwhelmed by the one-party state which supposedly became the sole source of power, able simply to impose its programme and ideology on a passive people. This obscures the societal pressures the state had to contend with, as well as the social basis of its support. It obscures, too, the fact that the regime was sometimes faced with militant groups demanding *more radical* social change than it would tolerate. (The 'cultural revolutionaries' of the First Five-Year Plan are a notable example.) There were social dynamics both to the great transformation after 1928, and for that matter to the 'Great Terror', which simply do not figure in the totalitarian model.

3   The system of rule was less efficient and less effective than the totalitarian model posited. The ruling institution, the Communist Party, was subject to corruption and inertia, and included conflicting interest groups. The ability of the state to enforce its will in the remoter geographic regions during the 1930s was hampered by distance, the weakness of communism in rural areas and the presence of armed mounted bands. The state did not yet command the technological sophistication which characterizes dystopian images of totalitarianism such as *1984*.

4   The model is too static and descriptive. When formulated, it could not predict the considerable changes that were to take place in Soviet society after Stalin's death and it is difficult to account for them historically within this paradigm. This is obviously more a matter for the later part of your course.

In the subsequent units in this book we will ask how applicable the model is to Fascist Italy and Nazi Germany. What has been said here should already have given you reason to doubt that they can be lumped with the Soviet Union as 'three of a kind'.

References

Carr, E. H. (1959) *Socialism in One Country, 1924–1926*, vol.2, Penguin.

Carr, E. H. (1971) *Foundations of a Planned Economy, 1926–1929*, vol.2, Macmillan.

Carr. E. H. and Davies, R. W. (1969) *Foundations of a Planned Economy, 1926–1929*, vol.1, Penguin.

Cohen, S. (1974) *Bukharin and the Bolshevik Revolution*, Wildwood House, Oxford University Press paperback edition, 1980.

Cohen, S. (1977) 'Bolshevism and Stalinism' in Tucker, R. (ed.) (1977).

Conquest, R. (1968) *The Great Terror*, Macmillan.

Conquest, R. (1986) *The Harvest of Sorrow*, Hutchinson.

Danilov, V. P. (1988) *Rural Russia under the New Regime*, Unwin Hyman.

Davies, R. W. (1980) *The Socialist Offensive: the Collectivisation of Soviet Agriculture, 1929–1930*, Macmillan.

Erickson, J. (1975) *The Road to Stalingrad*, Weidenfeld.

Fainsod, M. (1953) *How Russia is Ruled*, Harvard University Press.

Fainsod, M. (1958) *Smolensk under Soviet Rule*, Macmillan.

Filtzer, D. (1986) *Soviet Workers and Stalinist Industrialisation*, Pluto.

Fitzpatrick, S. (ed.) (1978) *Cultural Revolution in Russia, 1928–1931*, Indiana University Press.

Fitzpatrick, S. (1979) 'Stalin and the making of a new élite, 1928–1939', *Slavic Review*, vol.xxxviii.

Getty, J. Arch (1979) 'The "Great Purges" reconsidered: the Soviet Communist Party, 1933–1939', Boston College PhD.

Getty, J. Arch (1985) *Origins of the Great Purges: the Soviet Communist Party Reconsidered, 1933–1938*, Cambridge University Press.

Getty, J. Arch and Chase, W. (1978) 'The Moscow party élite of 1917 in the Great Purges', *Russian History*, v, no.i.

Haslam, J. (1986) 'Political opposition to Stalin and the origins of the Terror in Russia, 1932–1936', *The Historical Journal*, 29, 2.

Hosking, G. (1985) *A History of the Soviet Union*, Fontana.

Hough, J. (1978) 'The Cultural Revolution and Western understanding of the Soviet system' in Fitzpatrick, S. (ed.) (1978).

Hough, J. and Fainsod, M. (1979) *How the Soviet Union is Governed*, Harvard University Press.

Kuromiya, H. (1988) *Stalin's Industrial Revolution: Politics and Workers 1928–1932*, Cambridge University Press.

Kravchenko, V. (1947) *I Chose Freedom*, Hale.

Lane, D. (1970) *Politics and Society in the USSR*, Weidenfeld.

Lewin, M. (1968) *Russian Peasants and Soviet Power*, Macmillan.

Lewin, M. (1975) *Political Undercurrents in Soviet Economic Debates*, Pluto.

Lewin, M. (1985) *The Making of the Soviet System*, Methuen.

McNeal, R. H. (ed.) (1974) *Resolutions and Decisions of the Communist Party of the Soviet Union, vol.3, The Stalin Years, 1929–1953*, University of Toronto Press.

McNeal, R. H. (1988) *Stalin: Man and Ruler*, Macmillan.

Medvedev, R. (1971) *Let History Judge*, Macmillan.

Millar, J. R. and Nove, A. (1976) 'Was Stalin really necessary?', *Problems of Communism*, xxv, no.iv.

Nove, A. (1969) *An Economic History of the USSR*, Penguin.

Pethybridge, R. (1974) *The Social Prelude to Stalinism*, Macmillan.

Rosefielde, S. (1983) 'Excess mortality in the Soviet Union: a reconsideration of the demographic consequences of forced industrialisation, 1929–1949', *Soviet Studies*, xxxv, no.3.

Schapiro, L. (1960) *The Communist Party of the Soviet Union*, Methuen University Paperbacks.

Serbyn, R. and Krawchenko, B. (eds) (1986) *Famine in Ukraine 1932–1933*, Edmonton.

Stolee, M. K. (1988) 'Homeless children in the USSR, 1917–1957', *Soviet Studies*, vol.xl, no.1, January.

Tucker, R. (ed.) (1977) *Stalinism*, Norton.

Ulam, A. B. (1974) *Stalin: the Man and His Era*, Allen Lane.

Wheatcroft, S. G. (1984) 'A note on Steven Rosefielde's calculations of excess mortality in the USSR, 1929–1949', *Soviet Studies*, xxxvi, no.2, April.

UNIT 17   ITALY 1918–1940

Geoffrey Warner

Open University students of this unit will need to refer to:

Set book: J. M. Roberts, *Europe 1880–1945*, Longman, 1989

Course Reader: *War, Peace and Social Change in Twentieth-Century Europe*, eds Clive Emsley, Arthur Marwick and Wendy Simpson, Open University Press, 1990

Documents 2: 1925–1959, eds Arthur Marwick and Wendy Simpson, Open University Press, 1990

Maps Booklet

INTRODUCTION

This unit deals with the history of Italy between 1918 and 1940. For all but the first four years of this period, of course, Italy was ruled by Benito Mussolini, the *Duce* or 'Leader', with the support of his *Partito Nazionale Fascista* or 'National Fascist Party' (PNF). For this reason, Fascism naturally bulks large in the unit. But, in accordance with the theme of the course, much attention will be given to the relationship between Fascism and war. By the end of the unit you should be able to answer the following questions:

• What were the consequences of World War I for Italian politics and society?

• What was the nature of Fascism and to what extent was it a product of World War I?

• How and why did Fascism come to power in Italy in 1922? To what extent was this 'inevitable'?

• What was the nature of the Fascist regime? How much support did it enjoy and how does it fit into the so-called 'totalitarian model'?

• How far was war basic not only to Fascist theory, but also to Fascist practice?

1 ITALIAN POLITICS AND SOCIETY AT THE END OF WORLD WAR I

Exercise   Read Roberts from the beginning of the section on Italy at the foot of page 449 as far as the sentence, 'The nature of Fascism, and the context in which it appeared, made this impossible', about a third of the way down page 452. (Don't bother with the cross-reference to Fiume on page 450 at this stage, since we shall look at that later in the unit.)

When you have finished the passage from Roberts, try to answer the following related questions:

1   Why, in Roberts's opinion, did World War I precipitate a crisis in Italian politics and society?

2   Was this crisis primarily economic or political? ■

Specimen answer   Pre-war Italy's constitutional and parliamentary foundations were weak, and World War I undermined them still further for two main reasons. The first was that Italy's economy, being less strong than those of its allies, suffered pro-portionately more from the economic consequences of the war, such as inflation and unemployment. The second reason was political. First of all the war, in Roberts's words, 'accentuated the divorce between patriotism and the left which had lain in the teachings of prewar Socialism'. This led to increasing polarization between the Left and the nationalist Right. Furthermore, successive Italian governments seemed unable to cope with either the economic or political situation. This was because the political system in which they were accustomed to operate depended upon the absence of mass parties and, unfortunately for them, the aftermath of World War I saw not only an increase in the strength of the

Socialists, but also the emergence of a second mass party, the Roman Catholic *Partito Popolare* or 'People's Party'.

Roberts does not directly address the question of whether Italy's post-war crisis was primarily economic or political, but the implication of his analysis is, surely, that political factors were more important. Even if we accept his contention that the Italian economy was more severely affected than those of other countries, his emphasis is much more upon politics than economics: the polarization between Left and Right; the threat of revolution; and the impotence of Italian governments. Of course, you could argue that it was economic developments which produced the political problems that Italian governments were unable to tackle, but I would rather not explore this particular example of the chicken and egg. □

Discussion   Since we are principally concerned with the impact of World War I, I think it is important to emphasize that Roberts makes it clear that the war did not create Italy's problems; it merely exacerbated them. Despite the rhetoric of the *Risorgimento* or 'Revival' (the process which led to Italian unification in the nineteenth century), Italy was not united by a mass movement from below, but by conquest from above. One state, Piedmont, had extended its control over the rest of the peninsula by a mixture of war, diplomacy and subversion. This left a profound legacy of alienation between rulers and ruled, made worse by regional differences (most 'Italians' did not speak Italian, but a local dialect), ignorance (as late as 1911 four-fifths of Italians were illiterate), poverty (Italy's infant mortality rate was among the highest in Western Europe), and religious antagonism (the Roman Catholic Church, which claimed the allegiance of most Italians, was at daggers drawn with the anti-clerical state which had annexed its temporal lands). The outcome was that, until the eve of World War I, Italy's political system could hardly be called democratic. It was characterized by what was known as *trasformismo* or 'transformism', a shifting pattern of loose parliamentary coalitions based upon a restricted suffrage and local patronage.

Although Italy remained a predominantly agricultural economy well into the twentieth century, there had been a rapid expansion of industry in the 1890s and 1900s and, in common with other countries, this had encouraged the growth of socialism. The *Partito Socialista Italiano* or 'Italian Socialist Party' (PSI) was formed in 1892, and the parallel trade-union movement, the *Confederazione Generale de Lavoro* or 'General Confederation of Labour' (CGL), in 1906. As Roberts indicates on page 450, the PSI had not supported the war – its official policy was summed up in the slogan, *né aderire né sabotare* or 'neither support nor sabotage' – but its antimilitarism had not been forged by the experience of World War I, but by that of an earlier conflict, the war of 1911–12 against Turkey, as a result of which Italy annexed Libya. It was, indeed, in 1912 that the so-called *massimalisti* or 'maximalists', with their intransigent and revolutionary views, won over the reformists and gained control of the PSI. Contrast the situation in Italy with that in Britain, France and Germany, where the socialist parties were controlled by reformists and supported their countries' war efforts. Although the wartime consensus had begun to break down in these countries by 1917, it had never existed in Italy.

As Roberts also points out on page 451, the PSI was one of the two mass political parties, the growth of which helped to destabilize the post-war Italian political system. What he does not mention here, however, is that its growth was greatly assisted by another pre-war development: namely, the expansion of the franchise, which took place in 1913. This almost trebled the proportion of adult males eligible to vote, from 32 per cent to 90 per cent. Women did not obtain the right to vote in Italy until after World War II.

Having looked at what Roberts has to say about the causes of the post-World War I crisis in Italian politics and society and commented on the extent to which it was rooted in developments prior to 1915, let us now examine the post-war scene in more detail.

1.1   The economy

The only effective way of ascertaining the extent to which Italy suffered economically as a result of World War I is to make comparisons with other belligerents. Unfortunately, the necessary statistics are not always available, and those that are often leave much to be desired in the way of accuracy. The comparisons which follow, therefore, should only be taken as a very rough guide.

In terms of military casualties, Italy does not appear to have come off too badly. Although a higher proportion of the male working population was killed than in the United Kingdom (6.2 per cent as opposed to 5.1 per cent) this was much lower than in France (10.5 per cent) or Germany (15.1 per cent). On the other hand, Italy suffered much more in the great influenza epidemic of 1918 than any other West European belligerent. Thus 274,000 died of the disease in Italy, compared with 188,000 in Germany, 112,000 in the United Kingdom and 91,000 in France.

The position with regard to inflation is set out in the following table, which reproduces the cost-of-living index for the same four countries between 1914 and 1922:

Table 17.1

Year	France	Germany	Italy	UK
1914	100	100	100	100
1915	118	125	109	123
1916	135	164	136	146
1917	159	245	195	175
1918	203	293	268	203
1919	259	401	273	215
1920	359	987	359	249
1921	312	1299	427	226
1922	300	14576	423	184

(Source: B. R. Mitchell, *European Historical Statistics 1750–1975*, 1981, Table 12)

Exercise   How would you compare Italy's wartime and post-wartime rate of inflation with those of the other countries in Table 17.1? ■

Specimen answer   Inflation in Italy was certainly worse than that in the United Kingdom, but nowhere near as bad as in Germany, especially in the post-war period. Although the pace varied in the two countries, the French and Italian rates ended up at exactly the same point in 1920, although inflation in France then fell back much more sharply than it did in Italy. While Italian prices continued to rise until 1921, these figures would not suggest that inflation in Italy was particularly severe in comparison with that in other countries. □

Discussion   This conclusion clearly casts some doubt upon the thesis put forward by Roberts on page 450 that 'Italy had in comparison with them [i.e. its allies] undergone *a much greater* financial and economic strain' (emphasis added). Ironically, he goes on to demolish a possible counter-argument by stating that 'Wages during the war did not lag far behind prices', for if they had, the position of the Italian wage-earner could still have been a lot worse than that of his or her opposite numbers elsewhere. It all depends, of course, on what you mean by lagging far behind. For the record, while prices in Italy rose more than one-and-a-half times between 1914 and 1918, wages only rose by three-quarters. This seems quite a large gap to me. Unfortunately there are no comparable figures for other countries.

Turning to unemployment we once again face a dearth of comparable statistics. On the face of it it would seem that the peak figure for unemployment in Italy during the period 1919–22 was only about 3 per cent of the labour force, compared with 6 per cent in Germany and 22 per cent in Britain. However, it is only fair to point out that the Italian figures are almost certainly a gross underestimate.

We are on slightly firmer ground when it comes to output. Once again, Italy does not fare at all badly in comparison with other countries. Take, for example, the index of industrial production printed below (note that 1913=100):

Table 17.2

	France	Italy	UK
1919	57	104	90
1920	62	104	98
1921	55	95	80
1922	78	107	93

(Source: Carlo M. Cipolla (ed.) *The Fontana Economic History of Europe*, 1976, Vol.6, Part 2, pp.687, 689–90, 692–3)

If we turn to agricultural production, we find a similar picture. Thus, if we take the average annual output of a country's five main grain crops over the years 1910–14 as 100, the index for 1920–24 is as follows:

Table 17.3

France	86
Germany	66
Italy	96
UK	99

(Source: Cipolla, *The Fontana Economic History of Europe*, Vol.6, p.670)

It is only when we look at foreign trade that there is a substantial deterioration in Italy's position compared with pre-war. Italy is poor in natural resources and had to import both raw materials and foodstuffs. In 1913 its exports paid for 68 per cent of its imports; in 1919 the proportion was only 36 per cent.

Despite this last statistic, the argument that Italy suffered proportionately more economically than other West European belligerents as a result of World War I does not hold water. It seems more likely, therefore, that the roots of Fascism are to be found in politics rather than in economics.

1.2   The polity

There were three main developments on the Italian political scene in the after-math of World War I. These were: the growth and increased combativeness of the socialist trade-union movement and of the PSI; the birth and rapid development of the Catholic People's Party and of the Catholic trade-union movement; and the ferment of nationalist forces, which were hostile to both socialism and the liberal parliamentary system.

The first two phenomena have already been mentioned. In the elections of November 1919, for which the last barriers to universal male suffrage were removed and proportional representation introduced, the PSI obtained 32.4 per cent of the vote and trebled its strength in comparison with the last pre-war election (1913), becoming the largest single party in the Chamber of Deputies with 156 seats out of 508. At the same time, the CGL, which had 250,000 members in 1918, saw its strength increase to 1,150,000 in 1919 and to 2,200,000 in 1920.

We have alluded (see above, p. 112) to the militancy of the Italian socialists. An indication of the way in which this manifested itself was labour unrest. Once again, this becomes clearer if we compare the situation in Italy with that in other West European countries. In the following table I have computed (very roughly!) the number of hours lost through strike action per 1,000 workers in France, Germany, Italy and the United Kingdom in the immediate post-war period:

Table 17.4

	France	Germany	Italy	UK
1918	45	45	49	303
1919	713	1034	1221	1806
1920	1064	523	1672	1372
1921	324	808	447	4436
1922	181	866	378	1025

(Source: B. R. Mitchell, *European Historical Statistics 1750–1975*, 1981, Tables C1, C3)

It will be seen from this table that labour unrest was widespread in West Europe during this period and that it peaked in the two years 1919 and 1920. These were known in Italy as the *biennio rosso* or 'red two years'. (The main reason the unrest decreased in 1921, incidentally, albeit not in Britain, was because that year saw a sharp downturn in the economic cycle.) It also emerges from the table that Italian labour was more militant than French and German labour, although less militant than labour in Britain.

There were two particular features of Italian labour unrest to which I should like to draw attention, as they were of great concern to contemporaries. The first was that the industrial unrest culminated, in September 1920, in large-scale factory occupations in such northern cities as Turin, Genoa and Milan, where Italian industry was concentrated. The prime minister at the time, Giovanni Giolitti, who was the great political manipulator of pre-war Italy, did not take the occupations too seriously, reasoning that the workers were less dangerous inside the factories than on the streets and that they would sooner or later have to come to terms. He was right, but his alleged passivity in the face of what looked like the revolutionary expropriation of private property, and his pressure upon the bosses to grant concessions to their workforce in order to bring the occupations to an end, antagonized the employers and the middle classes generally.

The second special feature of post-war Italian labour unrest was that it extended into agriculture. Indeed, during the *biennio rosso*, four out of ten Italian strikers were in the agricultural sector. Since Italy was still a predominantly agricultural economy, it is perhaps not surprising that there should have been trouble in the countryside, although agrarian unrest was not a feature of post-war discontent elsewhere in West Europe. It was accompanied, moreover, by widespread seizures of land by the poorer peasantry and landless labourers, who had been encouraged by wartime promises of the 'land fit for heroes' variety. It is estimated that the number of peasant proprietors in Italy doubled to 3.5 million between the censuses of 1911 and 1921. Although much of the land seized in this way was barren or uncultivated, landowners, like industrialists, felt that the government was not doing enough to protect their property and was even encouraging the agitation by such measures as its September 1919 instruction to its local representatives to recognize seizures of uncultivated land.

Neither the factory occupations nor the land seizures were revolutionary in intent – there are, after all, few people less revolutionary than peasant proprietors – but the rhetoric of the PSI and its allies made them appear so. The consequences were serious for the stability of the political system. As the British historian, Martin Clark, has pointed out:

> The PSI's revolutionary posturing meant that it was not 'available' to friendly politicians like Giolitti; it could not be tacitly 'absorbed' into the system by public works schemes or union concessions, as in pre-war days . . . The PSI's public Bolshevism, its support for strikes and factory occupations, frightened the respectable middle classes away from a Liberal regime that seemed incapable of dealing with overt subversion. (Clark, *Modern Italy, 1871–1982*, 1984, p.212)

The second main development in Italian politics after World War I was the emergence of a powerful Roman Catholic party and trade-union movement. Italy had been united against the opposition of the papacy. The papal lands in central Italy, including the city of Rome, had been forcibly incorporated into the new kingdom, and Piedmont's liberal, anti-clerical legislation was extended throughout the peninsula. It was not surprising, therefore, that relations between Italy and the Vatican were very bad. Indeed, in the early years after unification, the Church even tried to prevent Catholics from voting in parliamentary elections by threatening them with excommunication if they did so. By January 1919, however, Pope Benedict XV had come to the radical conclusion that 'a democratic party with an advanced political and social programme . . . [was] the surest instrument for furthering the church's interests in Italy' (Seton-Watson, *Italy from Liberalism to Fascism*, 1967, p. 514). Although the *Partito Popolare Italiano* or 'Italian People's Party' (PPI) was not formally set up by the Vatican and was careful, even in its title, to avoid too close an identification with the Church, it could never have been established without the latter's permission and its leader, Luigi Sturzo, was in fact a priest. A Catholic trade-union organization, the *Confederazione Italiana de Lavoratori* or 'Italian Workers' Confederation' (CIL), had already been formed in September 1918.

In the election of November 1919 the PPI won 20.5 per cent of the vote and 100 seats, making it the second largest party after the socialists. As for the CIL, its membership rose from 500,000 in 1919 to 1,250,000 in 1921. As indicated above, the new Catholic mass movements were socially progressive, drawing much of their inspiration from the encyclical *De Rerum Novarum*, or 'Concerning New Phenomena', promulgated in 1891 by Pope Leo XIII, which had criticized the excesses of unrestrained capitalism. Thus, Catholic organizations played their part in the post-war social unrest which affected Italy. This was particularly true in the countryside, where priests and PPI activists frequently organized the land seizures by a predominantly Catholic peasantry. One Catholic peasant leader, Guido Maglioli of Cremona, was even known as 'the white Bolshevik'.

Nevertheless, the PPI was not a 'revolutionary' party in the way that the PSI purported to be and it even took part in government. Like the PSI, however, it did represent a group which had been outside the mainstream of Italian political development since unification. In some degree, therefore, it too was an 'anti-system' party which found co-operation with Italy's traditional ruling élite none too easy. Unfortunately, it did not find co-operation with the anti-clerical and atheistic PSI any easier – and *vice-versa* – so that we have the alarming situation in which the country's two largest political parties were, to a greater or lesser extent, alienated both from the political system in which they operated and from each other.

Both the growth of the PSI and the emergence of the PPI were a direct result of World War I. One should not posit too much of a connection between death and deprivation, whether in the trenches or on the home front, and political radicalization, but it is surely significant that increased unionization of labour, greater industrial militancy, and heightened demands for political, economic and social reform were well-nigh universal phenomena in all belligerent countries. The old order had failed. Indeed, the war itself had underlined the failure. It was time for a better tomorrow and ordinary men and women seemed more inclined to organize and agitate for it.

The ferment of right-wing nationalism, which was the third major development in post-war Italian politics, also grew directly out of the war, but in a different way. Although 1918 had witnessed the disintegration of Italy's traditional enemy, the Austro-Hungarian empire, and although the subsequent peace settlement awarded Italy much additional territory at its expense (see map 6 in the *Maps Booklet*), the nationalists who had propelled the country into war in 1915 were still not satisfied. In order to find out why, you should read the relevant passage from Roberts, beginning just over half-way down page 340 with the sentence, 'It would be superficial to begin the story of Italian revisionism in 1918', and ending near the top of page 342 with the sentence, 'Giolitti hastened to come to terms and agreed that the Italians too should leave (2 August 1920)'.

Exercise   Why, in Roberts's opinion, did Italy fail to obtain all that it had been promised under the Treaty of London, and what were the consequences for post-war Italian politics? ■

Specimen answer   The chief obstacle to Italian ambitions was President Woodrow Wilson, who refused to be bound by the Treaty of London and similar inter-allied agreements to which the United States had not been a party. It was he who objected most strongly to Italy's claims upon the new state of Yugoslavia, the existence of which he supported, and to Italian aims in Albania. The French, however, were also opposed to Italian gains at the expense of Yugoslavia, a state which they saw as 'a future ally and client'. The Italo-French quarrel had repercussions upon the redistribution of non-European territory, as did the failure to partition Turkey. Nationalist rhetoric and resentment over these issues, according to Roberts, 'combined to weaken the prestige of the government and the parliamentary system'. □

Discussion Although Roberts describes the intervention of the nationalist poet Gabriele d'Annunzio in Fiume as 'almost comical', it illustrated not only the strength of nationalist feeling, but also the connivance of some sections of the armed forces – the local Italian commander allowed d'Annunzio to take over – and the relative impotence of the Italian government, which was unable to retrieve control of the situation for more than a year. This connivance in right-wing defiance of the government on the part of sections of the state apparatus, and the apparent inability of the government to deal with either the defiance or the connivance, was to be a feature of the rise of Fascism.

At a more symbolic level, d'Annunzio's occupation of Fiume provided a foretaste of Fascist theatricality. As the British historian, Christopher Seton-Watson, has written,

> The uniforms and the black shirts [originally worn by the *arditi* or 'shock troops' in World War I], the 'Roman salute', the 'oceanic' rallies, the party hymn, *Giovinezza* [or 'Youth']; the organisation of the militia into cohorts and legions, commanded by consuls; the weird [and meaningless] cries of *Eia Eia Alalà!*, the demagogic technique of 'dialogue' between orators and massed audiences; all the symbolism, mystique and 'style' with which the world was later to grow so familiar, were plagiarized from d'Annunzio . . . (Seton-Watson, *Italy from Liberalism to Fascism*, 1967, p.596)

Right-wing nationalists like d'Annunzio were, of course, bitterly opposed to the PSI, which they accused of trying to undermine the country's war effort. Yet like the PSI, they had nothing but contempt for the effete parliamentary democracy which had failed to win the peace and brought about instead what d'Annunzio called a *vittoria mutilata* or 'mutilated victory'. All three major developments on the Italian political scene after World War I, therefore, were a challenge to the existing system.

2 *THE RISE OF FASCISM*

A brief sketch of the rise of Fascism is provided on pages 452–5 of Roberts. You should read this now, from the sentence beginning, 'The first organization of Fascism . . .' about a third of the way down page 452 as far as the end of the first paragraph at the top of page 455.

Roberts glosses over the fact that, while Fascism was part of the post-war nationalist ferment in Italy, its size and influence was minimal until the end of 1920. Its leader, Mussolini, had begun his political career as a revolutionary socialist and was, in fact, the director of the PSI's newspaper, *Avanti!*, at the outbreak of World War I. Before the end of the year, however, he had broken with his erstwhile comrades over the issue of Italian participation in the war, believing that this was essential in order to create the necessary conditions for a socialist revolution. He founded his own newspaper, *Il Popolo d'Italia* or 'The Italian People', and his was undoubtedly the most powerful voice on the Left arguing for Italian intervention. It was only at the end of the war that Mussolini began to move towards the Right and the programme of the *Fasci di combattimento* or 'fighting groups' still contained many left-wing ingredients, such as the seizure of Church property, the replacement of a standing army by a short-term people's militia, and a swingeing tax upon capital.

> In this phase [writes the Italian historian, Marco Revelli] Fascism . . . was still a volatile and fluid amalgam of frustrated minorities drawn from the most varied political and cultural backgrounds . . . Their common denominator was a radical rejection of the political realities of the day and, characterised above all by the *combattentismo*, the war-veteran's cult of the fighting spirit. It was first and foremost an *urban* phenomenon, a phenomenon of the big cities in fact, almost exclusively confined to the North, and found especially in Milan, the only large-scale concentration of industry and commerce in Italy. Of the 112 'founders' of the Fascism movement at the meeting of 23 March 1919 . . . as many as 60 were Milanese and another 14 came from the immediate surroundings . . . Among these 112 there were nine lawyers, five army or navy officers, five professors, five doctors, three accountants, two parliamentary deputies and one senator. All the rest appear to have had no particular professional or academic qualification. (Mühlberger, *The Social Basis of European Fascist Movements*, 1987, p.11)

Although the movement claimed 137 *fasci* and 40,385 members in October 1919, it only succeeded in picking up about 2 per cent of the vote in Milan in the general election of 16 November, a performance which puts it roughly on a par with David ('Screaming Lord') Sutch's Monster Raving Loony Party in this country. If Fascism does indeed appear to have been a direct outgrowth of World War I, it was a very tender plant, and by the end of 1919 its strength had fallen to 31 *fasci* and 870 members.

What undoubtedly kept it alive was Mussolini and his newspaper, *Il Popolo d'Italia*. This appears to have been financed by the Perrone brothers, who controlled the giant Ansaldo armaments combine and other Milanese industrial interests. You may wonder why these people bothered to hand out cash to the equivalent of the Monster Raving Loony Party, but it should be remembered that Mussolini was a skilled and influential journalist, and that *Il Popolo d'Italia*'s fierce anti-socialism and nationalism were grist to the mill of industrialists, and especially of arms manufacturers. In any case, Mussolini and his newspaper were not the only beneficiaries of their largesse.

Three developments in the last quarter of 1920 rescued Fascism from the doldrums and transformed it from the status of an irrelevant sect to that of a mass movement contending for power. These were: (a) the factory occupations of September and the parallel agrarian unrest; (b) the local elections of September/ October, as a result of which the PSI gained control of 2,022 communal and 26 provincial governments compared with 400 and 4 in the previous elections in 1914; and (c) the Treaty of Rapallo between Italy and Yugoslavia in November, by which the former renounced its claims to Dalmatia, Fiume was declared a free city, and d'Annunzio and his supporters were subsequently driven out by the Italian armed forces. For the Right, the first two developments constituted a major challenge to the existing structure of property relations and political power, while the third was regarded as an act of treachery on the part of the government.

Doubtless defeated by the demands of compression, Roberts's account implies that Fascism had been growing steadily since its foundation in March 1919, but, as we have seen, this was not the case. Moreover, Roberts fails to bring out the crucial significance of the developments mentioned in the previous paragraph. Particularly significant for the expansion of Fascism was the reaction of land-owners in the Po Valley and Tuscany to the agrarian agitation and land seizures. Despairing of effective support from the government, they turned to private enterprise, in the shape of squads of Fascist thugs, for help in fighting the peasant unions and their political allies. From the end of 1920 a kind of civil war raged in the countryside between the Fascists and the Left. A near-contemporary account of a typical example of what took place is provided by the Italian anti-Fascist historian, Gaetano Salvemini, and you will find it reproduced as document I.12 in *Documents 2*. You should read it now.

Exercise
What impression do you get from Salvemini's account of the attitudes of the forces of law and order to the activities of the Fascists? ■

Specimen answer
To judge from Salvemini's account, their attitude was one of passivity or complic-ity. The *carabinieri*, the military police force in the countryside, made no attempt to stop the Fascists from attacking socialist property in Foiano on 12 or 17 April 1921. They did nothing to prevent the Fascist reprisals against the alleged perpetrators of the ambush on 17 April either. Indeed, they appear to have collaborated with the Fascists in hunting down the latter. Finally, while the courts handed out heavy sentences to those convicted of participation in the ambush, no Fascists received any punishment whatsoever. □

Discussion
If anything, Salvemini's account of events at Foiano underplays the complicity of the state authorities in Fascist violence. Christopher Seton-Watson sums up their involvement as follows:

> Fascism could never have prospered so rapidly without at least the tolerance of the state authorities. Many prefects, police and military commanders went far beyond tolerance. In Venezia Guilia the *squadre* [or 'squads'] enjoyed virtually official status. Elsewhere, particularly in Tuscany, they were supplied with lorries and arms, and serving officers joined the *fasci* with the approval of their superiors. Sometimes soldiers and *carabinieri* accompanied the *squadre* on punitive expeditions, fully armed and in uniform. Long-suffering policemen and state officials, after years of forced subservience to provincial socialist bosses, took little trouble to conceal their delight at the turning of the tables. (Seton-Watson, *Italy from Liberalism to Fascism*, 1967, p.576)

Seton-Watson goes on to emphasize that this complicity was local in origin, and that the central government repeatedly enjoined its local representatives to curb the activities of the squads and punish crimes of violence. This may have been true in general, but as we shall see, even Prime Minister Giolitti was prepared to turn a blind eye to Fascist thuggery during the election campaign of May 1921.

Fascism grew in leaps and bounds during this period, although its point of departure was nowhere near as high as Roberts suggests on page 452. The official Fascist figures for the end of 1920, which are unlikely to be an underestimate, were for 88 *fasci* with 20,615 members. By the end of March 1921, these had risen to 317 and 80,476, and by the end of June to 1,192 and 204,506. Originally heavily concentrated in the north of the country (75 per cent of the membership in March 1921), it did gradually extend its influence into other parts of Italy, but as late as October 1921 only a quarter of Fascists were to be found in the south compared to over one-third of the population as a whole. The reason for this was that the old political élite still retained much of its control over this backward part of the country. Like the PSI and the PPI – over four-fifths of whose parliamentary seats in 1919 had been won in north and central Italy – Fascism was essentially a northern phenomenon.

It must be stressed that the Fascist surge was a counter-revolution and not, as it was so often portrayed by apologists at the time and since, a defensive action against the threat of 'Bolshevism'. As you will recall from page 115, labour unrest in Italy had peaked in 1920 and fallen back sharply in 1921. In addition, the *Partito Communista Italiano*, or 'Italian Communist Party' (PCI), split off from the PSI in January 1921 in response to the dictates of Lenin and the Third International. Mussolini himself wrote in *Il Popolo d'Italia* on 2 July 1921, 'To maintain that the bolshevist danger still exists in Italy is to mistake fear for reality.' What was happening was that the 'victims' of the *biennio rosso* were getting their own back, with interest.

When Giolitti originally formed his government in June 1920, he had per-suaded the PPI to join it. The latter had loyally supported him, but was becoming progressively more disillusioned with his failure to implement some of the more cherished parts of its programme. Giolitti was aware of its growing disillusion-ment and, mindful also of the split in the PSI, decided to go to the country in May 1921 in order to obtain a new parliamentary majority. As Roberts says, he even offered the Fascists a place on the government ticket. Although he no doubt hoped that he could thereby trim the claws of the movement, he was perfectly prepared to make use of its organized thuggery in his election campaign, explaining to a British official, 'These Fascists are our Black and Tans'. Among the thirty-five Fascists elected was Mussolini himself. The other results, which Roberts cites, show that Giolitti had failed in his bid to create a new majority at the expense of the socialist/communist Left and the PPI. When Mussolini repaid his patron by withdrawing his support, Giolitti did not so much 'step off the stage . . . to leave others to discover they could not do without him' (Roberts, p.452) as find himself pushed over the edge. Italy seemed more ungovernable than ever.

The extent of Mussolini's own opportunism at this time is illustrated by the fact that he toyed with the idea of an alliance with the PSI and the PPI, and he actually concluded an agreement in August 1921 which promised a cessation of hostilities between the Fascists and the socialist trade unions. In doing this, however, the *Duce* had over-reached himself. The local Fascist bosses, or *ras* as they were called after Abyssinian chieftains, men like Dino Grandi of Bologna, Roberto Farinacci of Cremona, and Italo Balbo of Ferrara, were not prepared to have deals of this kind struck above their heads. Mussolini was forced to backtrack. In October 1921 the PNF was founded. Its programme, adopted a month later, was unabashedly right-wing and nationalist. As the American historian, Charles Delzell, has written:

> It is clear . . . that the tenuous 'socialism' of 1919 had given way to 'integral' nationalism. The abolition of 'demagogic' fiscal measures such as taxes on inheritance and bondholders was called for, as were strikes in the public services. The program . . . demanded complete freedom for the Catholic Church in the exercise of its spiritual office. It repudiated the League of Nations and called for a large standing army instead of the short-term militia that had been favoured in 1919. (Delzell, *Mediterranean Fascism 1919–1945*, 1971, p.27)

We are fortunate in having a picture of the social composition of the PNF in November 1921, drawn from a sample of about half the total membership. It is instructive to compare it with the composition of the Italian population as a whole, taken from the 1921 census, which was held at about the same time.

> The social structure of the party [writes Marco Revelli] was a fairly faithful reflection of the general distribution of classes and occupational groups (achieving in a sense the ambition of representing organically and faithfully the whole nation), except for some significant cases of over- and under-representation in certain categories. Industrialists, for example, accounted for 2.8 per cent of [party] members (while . . . the entire *haute bourgeoisie* numbered at the time only 1.7 per cent [of the population]). The figures tally almost perfectly for the middle classes (56.5 per cent in the party compared with 53.3 per cent in society), but there was a conspicuous imbalance in favour of the petty bourgeoisie formed by white-collar workers in the public and private sectors (15.7 per cent in the party as against 3.2 per cent in society). On the other hand workers were under-represented (a mere [4].2 per cent discrepancy). (Mühlberger, *The Social Basis of European Fascist Movements*, 1987, p.19)

Exercise   How far do you think the above figures support the traditional view of Fascism as the protest movement *par excellence* of the lower middle classes against inflation and working-class militancy? ■

Specimen answer   Although the much higher proportion of members of what Revelli calls 'the petty bourgeoisie' (which is another name for the lower middle class) in the PNF as opposed to the country as a whole gives some support to the traditional view, the figures clearly imply much more than that. As Revelli himself points out, the PNF could justifiably claim to be representative of the nation as a whole and not just of a particular class. □

Discussion   In fact, the PNF was more representative than Revelli's figures suggest. This is because even the corrected figure for workers which he gives is misleading, since it applies only to those in industry: 15.4 per cent in the party; 19.6 per cent in the country as a whole. If agricultural workers are included, the under-representation of the working class in the party virtually disappears, since the former were actually *over*-represented: 24.3 per cent in the party compared with 21.8 per cent in the country as a whole. Depending upon your point of view, this last figure either signifies a degree of resentment on the part of some agricultural labourers at the closed shop implemented by the socialist unions, or the success of the intimidatory tactics employed by the Fascist squads.

More significant than class, perhaps, was age. One scholar has estimated that no less than a quarter of the PNF's membership at this stage was under twenty-one. Certainly 13 per cent were students. And while Mussolini himself was approaching forty in 1921, the three powerful *ras* mentioned above – Grandi, Farinacci and Balbo – were still in their twenties. Youth is no doubt an asset when you are going around beating up your political opponents.

In January 1922 Pope Benedict XV died. He was succeeded by Pope Pius XI (1922–39), who was much less sympathetic to the PPI than his predecessor had been, especially as Mussolini was showing signs of withdrawing from his earlier anti-clericalism and was hinting that the Church could expect favourable treatment from a Fascist government. In a confidential circular to Italian bishops at the beginning of October, the Vatican formally dissociated itself from the PPI, a step which was bound to benefit the Fascists in their drive to power.

As for the socialists, they became even more fragmented after the unions called a general strike on 31 July in protest against Fascist excesses. Support was not strong outside the major cities, and even there, the Fascists gained credit with the public by using their own personnel to break the strike in key services such as transport. On 3 August the unions ordered their members back to work. The Fascists launched a counter-offensive by physically driving out socialist councils in such cities as Milan, Genoa and Leghorn and taking control in their place. Once again the authorities did nothing to prevent this crude exercise in brute force.

When the reformist socialist, Filippo Turati, had the temerity to suggest that the opponents of Fascism should actually form a coalition to fight it, hard-line purists in the PSI expelled him and his followers from the party in October. He formed a new, moderate socialist party, the *Partito Socialista Unitario* or 'Unitarian Socialist Party' (PSU). Italian socialism was now split three ways – PSI, PCI and PSU – at precisely the time it most needed to be united.

The feeling was growing that, sooner or later, Mussolini and the PNF would have to be taken into the government, if only to turn these rather vicious poachers into gamekeepers. Unfortunately Mussolini did not want to serve under any-one else; he wanted to be prime minister himself. Roberts has described the *dénouement* on page 453. The motive for the king's refusal to support Facta and his ministers is unclear. Some say that it was because he felt he could not rely upon the army. 'Your Majesty,' he is reported to have been advised, 'the army will do its duty. However, it would be well not to put it to the test.' Others believe it was because he feared that his pro-Fascist cousin might usurp the throne, or that he was persuaded by the equally pro-Fascist Queen Mother.

Exercise   Going back to Roberts's account of these events, why do you think I have not ended this section of the unit with 'the march on Rome' and Mussolini becoming prime minister? (Hint: concentrate on what Roberts says at the bottom of page 453 and the top of page 454.) ∎

Specimen answer   Mussolini's accession to power did not at first seem to signify a fundamental change in the governmental system. His was a coalition government; it contained only four Fascists and the special powers it took were only for a limited period. As Roberts says, 'It was clear that Italy was to have vigorous, strong government; it was not yet clear that the constitutional state had been set aside. The imposition of dictatorship was gradual.' □

Discussion   What we need to know is how and why Mussolini became a fully-fledged dictator; or how and why his government became a regime. Unfortunately, I do not think that Roberts's account (on pages 454–5) is terribly clear about this, although he does provide most of the information necessary to address the question. In particular, it seems to me, he fails to bring out the full importance of the 1924 elections, the Matteotti murder and the so-called 'Aventine secession'.

It was not just the electoral law that enabled Mussolini's supporters to win the 1924 elections, but also the widespread fraud and intimidation which accompanied its implementation. It was this that was denounced by the PSU's secretary-general, Giacomo Matteotti, in the Chamber on 30 May 1924, and it was his denunciation which led to his disappearance on 10 June. Although Matteotti's body was not discovered for some weeks, it was widely and correctly assumed that he had been murdered by the Fascists on account of his accusations.

While the 'Aventine secession' (named after an incident in the history of Ancient Rome) was an unfortunate tactic on the part of the opposition parties, it might have achieved more if they could have agreed on something else as well. As it was, the PCI soon returned to the Chamber, while Pius XI vetoed a promising initiative for an alliance between the PPI and the PSU. Even then Mussolini's position remained weak, especially as evidence of Fascist complicity in Matteotti's abduction and murder mounted. Once again, however, the king failed to act; the general and admiral serving as war and navy ministers refused to join some of their civilian colleagues in resigning, thus in effect pledging the support of the armed forces for Mussolini; and Italian business, enjoying the effects of a mini-boom and good labour relations, came out in favour of the government. Most decisively of all, perhaps, the Fascist leadership itself urged Mussolini to take the offensive. He did so in a famous speech to the Chamber on 3 January 1925 in which he took 'full political, moral, and historical responsibility for all that has happened' and warned that 'when two irreducible elements [i.e. Fascism and anti-Fascism] are locked in a struggle, the solution is force'.

This speech is usually seen as marking the inauguration of the Fascist dictatorship. Even so, this did not happen overnight. Thus it was not until December 1925 that the Decree on the Powers of the Head of the Government made Mussolini responsible only to the king and not to the Chamber, and elected local governments were abolished in two stages in February and September 1926. If the rights of opposition trade unions were effectively removed by the Palazzo Vidoni pact of October 1925, under which employers agreed to negotiate only with the Fascist trade-union confederation, it was not until 1926 that all opposition political parties were banned. This latter step took place after the latest in a succession of attempts on Mussolini's life and was accompanied by other measures, including the establishment of a Special Tribunal for the Defence of the State to try political offences.

There was nothing 'inevitable' about the course of events in Italy between 1918 and 1925. Before 1922 Fascism could have been stopped in its tracks at almost any time if its opponents had (a) got their act together and (b) displayed sufficient resolution. Even at the time of 'the march on Rome', the evidence suggests that the forces of law and order could and would have disarmed the Fascists if both king and government had not caved in before the threat of violence. The trouble was, as Roberts suggests in the concluding paragraph on page 453, that too many politicians thought they could 'use' the Fascists when the Fascists were in fact 'using' them. It was also true that too many anti-Fascists were as, if not more, suspicious of each other as they were of their common enemy. The balance became harder to redress once Mussolini was in power, especially after a hitherto largely neutral Roman Catholic Church and big business had swung into line behind him. Even then, however, the *Duce*'s position was not impregnable, as the Matteotti crisis had shown.

Going back to the principal theme of this part of the course – the impact of World War I – our analysis has, I think, clearly shown that, while Italy was not destabilized economically by the conflict, it was destabilized politically. The emergence and/or growth of the PSI, the PPI and the Fascist movement itself, all of which were attributable in large measure to the war, posed a powerful threat to the pre-war liberal regime which the latter was, in the end, incapable of surmounting. However, this is not the same thing as saying that World War I led to the accession of Fascism to power. The weakness of the Italian political system was due, not so much to the war, as to the way in which Italy had been united and the way that it had been ruled since unification. There had been neither the time nor the inclination to lay the foundations of a stable democratic tradition. Fascism proved more able to profit from this state of affairs than its rivals.

3 FASCISM AND TOTALITARIANISM

The purpose of this section of the unit is to examine the nature of the Fascist regime in Italy and, in particular, to explore the extent to which it conforms to the totalitarian model. In order to refresh your memory as to what totalitarianism is, you should go back to pages 73–4 of Unit 16 and re-read what Bernard Waites has to say about it. You will note almost immediately that the concept was Italian in origin. Indeed, Bernard Waites describes totalitarianism as 'the official doctrine of Mussolini's Italy'. You would therefore expect the Fascist regime to conform fairly closely to the model.

Exercise You should now read Roberts, from the paragraph beginning, 'To understand Fascism one must begin with Mussolini', near the top of page 455, down to the end of the section on Italy on page 460. When you have done this, write down how far you think Roberts addresses the question of whether the Fascist regime conforms to the totalitarian model and what his conclusions are. (Note: don't forget to use the description of the model set out by Bernard Waites.) ■

Specimen answer Although Roberts does not specifically refer to the model, it is clear that he draws upon it. Thus he begins with a discussion of ideology (Point 1), refers to Fascist control of the economy (Point 6), and discusses the question of terror (Point 3). On the other hand he does not examine the role of the party (Point 2), the monopoly of mass communications (Point 4), or the monopoly of force (Point 5).

As to the degree of conformity of the Fascist regime to the totalitarian model, Roberts clearly does not believe that it was very close. 'As a totalitarian system', he writes on page 456, 'Fascism was far less impressive than Bolshevism.' He seems to reach this conclusion for three main reasons:

1   The weakness of Fascist ideology. 'Fascism', he writes on page 455, 'never presented any real ideological coherence', adding a little later on that there was a 'lack of positive content in Fascism'.

2   The relative independence of certain sectors of society. In this context Roberts refers specifically to the monarchy, the Church, and the economy.

3   The inefficacy of Fascist terror. Although Roberts concedes that 'terror had been a weapon of Fascism from the start', he nevertheless argues that 'when all is said and done, it is difficult to see terror as Fascism's mainspring in Italy' (p.459). This was because the regime was never able to terrorize its opponents into total submission, and he cites the widespread evasion of the anti-Jewish racial laws of 1938 in support of his contention. □

Discussion In one sense, of course, the rest of this section of the unit is a discussion of the issues raised by this exercise, but for the moment I should merely like to draw your attention to two points. The first is a relatively simple one, although easily overlooked. Roberts says that 'as a totalitarian system Fascism was far less impressive than Bolshevism'. But this can be put another way, and is indeed by the American scholar, A. James Gregor, when he writes, 'By the commencement of World War II the Fascist government exercised more control over the lives and activities of its citizens than any other government save the Soviet Union' (Cannistraro, *Historical Dictionary of Fascist Italy*, 1982, pp.540–1). In other words, just because Fascism was less totalitarian than Stalinist communism, this does not mean that it was not very totalitarian at all. Fascist Italy should be compared, not only with the Soviet Union, but also with other contemporary regimes, and particularly with Nazi Germany.

The second point relates to the definition of totalitarianism. It seems to me that Roberts – and Gregor – are going beyond the six-point definition produced by Friedrich and Brzezinski to something which is, at one and the same time, both simpler and more profound. Roberts is very scathing about the 1932 encyclo-paedia article which, he says, was 'the main theoretical document of the [Fascist] movement' (pp. 455–6). This article was actually called 'The doctrine of Fascism' and was supposedly written by Mussolini himself, although it seems that the philosopher Giovanni Gentile had a hand in it. Repetitive and disorganized though it is, the article does emphasize one crucial element in Fascist thinking: the centrality of the state. Extracts from the article are reprinted as document I.11 in *Documents 2*, and you should read them now.

If 'outside the State there can be neither individuals nor groups (political parties, associations, syndicates, classes)', if 'the Fascist State . . . is a force . . . which takes over all the forms of the moral and intellectual life of man', and if 'it is the State alone that grows in size, and power', the definition of totalitarianism which emerges is one characterized not so much by any descriptive 'list' of its features, such as Friedrich's and Brzezinski's six points, as by its purpose: the progressive annihilation of the boundaries between state and society. Friedrich and Brzezinski recognized this themselves in a later formulation of their model in which they maintained that it was a tendency of totalitarian regimes to become more totalitarian as time went on.

Roberts clearly believes that Fascism failed more or less completely to achieve this objective. Thus he argues, on page 455, that 'Fascist rule was important in Italian foreign policy, yet effected no substantial changes at home.' Even in foreign policy, he goes on to say on page 456, Fascist theory and practice were only combined with disastrous results. The theory and practice of Fascist foreign policy are the subject of the final section of this unit. For the remainder of this section, let us take a closer look at developments on the home front.

Much of the confusion as to whether Fascist Italy was a totalitarian political system or not arises out of a consideration of the role of the Fascist Party. To begin with, it did seem as though Mussolini was building up the PNF as a rival to the state apparatus. Thus, on 1 February 1923, he turned the blackshirted Fascist squads of bully boys into the *Milizia Volontaria per la Sicurezza Nazionale* or 'Voluntary Militia for National Security' (MVSN), which superficially looked like a parallel security force. However, the real purpose of the move was to bring the squads – and, even more, the *ras* who ran them – under central control. This was clearly demonstrated when the MVSN was brought under army authority in August 1924.

Similarly, although the highest authority of the PNF, the Fascist Grand

Council, was given what looked like impressive powers in December 1928, including the right to be consulted over the succession to the throne and the royal prerogatives, international treaties involving boundary changes, and the succession to Mussolini, it rarely met after 1929 and, when it did so, merely acted as a recipient of the *Duce*'s wishes and decisions. Only in July 1943, when Italy had been defeated and invaded by the allies, did the Grand Council seize the initiative and carry the motion of no confidence which led to Mussolini's dismissal by the king.

The true nature of the relationship between party and state power was shown in the circular which Mussolini sent to all prefects – the central government's local representatives – on 7 January 1927.

> The prefect [he wrote]. . . is the highest authority of the State in the provinces. He is the direct representative of the central executive power. All citizens, and in the first instance all those who have the great privileges and the highest honour of being Fascist militants, owe respect and obedience to the highest political representatives of the Fascist regime, and must work with him under his control in order to make his task easier. Where necessary, the prefect must stimulate and harmonise the activity of the party in its various forms. But it must remain clear to all that authority cannot be exercised on a shared basis, nor can slippages of authority or responsibility be tolerated. Authority is single and uniform. If this is not so, there is a collapse into complete disorganisation and the disintegration of the State, thereby destroying one of the fundamental bases of Fascist doctrine . . . Now that the revolution has been completed, the Party and its hierarchy, from top to bottom, are merely a conscious instrument of the will of the State, both at the centre and at the periphery. (Aquarone, *L'Organizzazione dello Stato Totalitario*, 1965, p.485)

It is an interesting commentary upon the above text that between 1922 and 1929 only 20 out of 86 new prefects appointed came from outside the prefectoral corps, and that even at the end of the regime in 1943, only 37 out of a total of 117 prefects in office were political appointees. There was, therefore, no large-scale 'colonization' of this key sector of the state apparatus.

Of course, the very fact that Mussolini felt obliged to send a circular such as that of 7 January indicates there was a problem of rivalry between the PNF and the state. The *ras*, in particular, had been, and could still be, a threat to the *Duce*'s authority, and the latter took good care to see that they did not become too influential. Farinacci, for example, who had become secretary-general of the PNF in February 1925, was dismissed in March of the following year and remained in the political wilderness until 1933, while Balbo, who became an international celebrity as an aviator in the late 1920s and early 1930s, found himself exiled to the governorship of Libya at the end of 1933.

Farinacci's successor as secretary-general of the PNF, Augusto Turati, presided over a transformation of the nature of the party. In the words of the British historian, Philip Morgan,

> In a drastic reshaping of party membership, at its height before the official closing of party rolls in 1927 but continuing into 1928–29, many thousands of ex-squadrists and extremist Fascists were expelled from the party, their numbers swollen by the spontaneous defections of other disillusioned old members. There was a corresponding recruitment drive attracting to the

party an influx of opportunists and white-collar public employees in particular, a more passive membership that mirrored the consensus at the basis of Mussolini's dictatorship. (Cannistraro, *Historical Dictionary of Fascist Italy*, 1982, p.405)

Until 1932 there were never more than a million members of the PNF, or about 2.5 per cent of the population, but subsequently more and more of the opportunists described by Morgan were allowed to join, so that by June 1943 membership had reached a total of 4,770,000. No wonder that some wits alleged that the initials PNF really stood for *Per Necessità Familiari* or 'for family reasons'!

Although one can therefore agree that, in accordance with Friedrich's and Brzezinski's Point 2, Fascist Italy possessed a single, hierarchically organized mass party, led by one man, that was either superior to or (in the case of the PNF) intertwined with the government bureaucracy, its influence was not on a par with the German NSDAP or the Russian CPSU. At the same time it must be recognized that Hitler's 'night of the long knives' in June 1934 and Stalin's purges in the late 1930s are sometimes described in terms of 'victories' by the dictators concerned 'over' their parties. Indeed, one is entitled to ask: how important is a single mass party to the concept of totalitarianism? Even Friedrich, writing in 1969, conceded that the monopoly control which was at the heart of totalitarianism need not be exercised by a political party at all, but by 'whatever "élite" rules the particular society and thereby constitutes its regime' (Schapiro, *Totalitarianism*, 1972, p.19).

As for the system of terroristic police control – Point 3 in Friedrich's and Brzezinski's original list – there is no doubt that this existed at one level in Fascist Italy. It has been calculated that, in a typical week, the political police alone would conduct 20,000 visits, searches, arrests, seizures of literature, and so on. On the other hand, throughout its history the Special Tribunal for the Defence of the State imposed only twenty-six death sentences, and seventeen of these were during the war years 1940–43. The preferred penalty for political offences was imprisonment – some 5,000 individuals were sentenced to a total of 28,115 years – or the so-called *confino* or 'banishment', which gave northern anti-Fascist intellectuals their first revealing glimpse of life in Italy's backward south. While not wishing to condone Fascism's persecution of its political opponents, it has to be conceded that this was small beer compared to what went on in Nazi Germany and the Soviet Union.

Point 4 of Friedrich's and Brzezinski's list of the characteristic features of a totalitarian system refers to the technologically conditioned monopoly of the means of mass communication. The expression 'technologically conditioned' reflects the fact that the twentieth century has seen the growth of a technology which has revolutionized the ways in which governments – or others – can approach a mass audience. In the nineteenth century the press was the only genuine mass medium; today there is cinema, radio, television and video. Together with the press, cinema and radio were available to the totalitarian regimes of the inter-war period. How did Fascist Italy make use of them?

Even before the abolition of the opposition political parties in 1926 there had been close censorship of the press. Afterwards there were no opposition papers at all and detailed guidelines were issued to editors. Nevertheless, not all news-papers were owned or run by the PNF or the government, and it seems that Italians preferred to read the ones they had always read. In 1933, for example, the Milanese daily, *Corriere della Sera* or 'Evening Courier', had a circulation of over 600,000 compared with the official *Popolo d'Italia*'s 100,000.

It was the Italian radio pioneer, Guglielmo Marconi, who suggested to Mussolini in 1923 that there were advantages in setting up a national radio network in Italy. An organization was duly set up in August 1924 and taken over by the state in November 1927. The number of radio licences grew as follows:

Table 17.5

1928	63,000
1930	176,000
1931	239,000
1932	305,000
1933	373,000
1934	431,000
1935	529,000
1936	697,000
1937	826,000
1938	978,000
1939	1,142,000
1940	1,321,000

(Source: B. R. Mitchell, *European Historical Statistics 1750–1975*, 1981, Table G9)

Impressive though this expansion may appear at first sight, its importance should not be exaggerated. In 1938 there was still only one radio licence for every forty-three Italians, compared with one for every seven Germans and one for every five Britons. The problem was that radios were still too expensive for most Italians and so the government tried to attract a collective audience by distributing free sets to schools, municipal buildings and local Fascist Party headquarters. It would also be wrong to assume that the Fascist radio carried a high proportion of political propaganda. Most programmes consisted of popular entertainment, such as music, sports commentaries and comedy. Even for news it was always possible to tune in to the independent Vatican Radio or, in the north of the country, to the Swiss Italian language station.

Although Mussolini once claimed that 'the cinema is the strongest weapon', the state did not take over the entire film industry as it did radio. Its main influence was indirect: through censorship, and through the encouragement of the Italian film-makers in 1931. Finally, in 1938 the government took a decisive step in introduced specifying the proportion of Italian films which had to be shown in cinemas. This began at 10 per cent in 1926 and was raised to 25 per cent two years later. Secondly, the government began directly subsidizing independent Italian film-makers in 1931. Finally, in 1928 the government took a decisive step in eliminating the American domination of the market by taking direct control of the importation of all foreign films. This led to a reduction in the number of licences granted to American films from 163 in 1938 to only 58 in 1939, which was below the Italian output of 79 for the same year. As in the case of radio programmes, however, it would be a mistake to believe that most independently produced Italian films were overtly Fascist in content.

Purely propaganda films came mainly from the LUCE Institute, which was made a state agency in 1925 and which was responsible for newsreels and documentaries. (LUCE stands for *L'Unione Cinematografia Educativa* or 'Educational Cinematographic Union' and is also the Italian word for 'light'.) From 1926 all cinemas were required to show a LUCE film as part of each programme.

What the above analysis of the Italian mass media under Fascism shows, I believe, is that while government influence was considerable, it would be a gross exaggeration to claim that the regime possessed anything approaching a monopoly of them. Its greatest achievement probably lay not so much in propagating its own values as in preventing the expression of those of the opposition.

I do not propose to spend much time discussing Point 5 of Friedrich's and Brzezinski's list of the characteristics of a totalitarian system: the monopoly of the use of force. This is because it is generally conceded that one of the features of *any* modern state is precisely that it claims a monopoly of the use of force within its boundaries, and that when force is employed by other organizations or individuals, this is normally regarded as constituting criminal behaviour. To argue that Fascism claimed and exercised such a monopoly does not therefore take us very far.

Much more important is the sixth and final point: the central control and direction of the entire economy through the state bureaucracy. You should note straight away that 'control and direction' is not the same thing as ownership, although if the state did 'own' the entire economy – as was more or less the case in the Soviet Union under Stalin – that would clearly imply 'central control and direction'. The latter can also exist in a predominantly privately owned economy, as for example in Britain, France and Germany during World War I.

Before turning to a more detailed examination of the way in which the economy functioned in Fascist Italy, however, it is important to dispose of one red herring: corporatism or corporativism (the two terms are interchangeable). If you go back to pages 458–9 of Roberts you will see that he devotes a couple of paragraphs to this phenomenon in the context of his discussion of Fascism's lack of control over the economy. Unfortunately, he never explains what it means. For some enlightenment, let us turn to the American historian, Alexander de Grand, who defines corporatism/corporativism as:

> . . . a system of institutional arrangements by which capital and labor are integrated into obligatory, hierarchical, and functional units (corporations) recognized by the state, which become organs of self-government for issues relating to the specific category as well as the basis for participation with other corporatively organized interests in policy decisions affecting the whole society . . . The corporations may be the controlling power in the state, or they may, as in Italy, be controlled by a political authority that exists independently of and outside the corporative system. (de Grand, *Italian Fascism*, 1982, pp.79–80)

As both Roberts and de Grand indicate, Fascist Italy displayed the characteristics of a developed corporatism. Since this corporatism was inspired and organized by the state, Italy was a corporate state. If these state controlled corporations ran the economy, this could clearly imply the 'central control and direction' of the totalitarian model.

Fascist theorists tried to describe the corporate state as 'a third way' between capitalism and communism, according to which employers and employees ran their industries under the benign supervision of the state. The foundation stone of the corporative system had been laid by the trade-union law of 3 April 1926, which permitted only one officially recognized association of workers and employers for each branch of production, prohibited all strikes and lockouts, and created a system of compulsory arbitration of labour disputes. 'In essence,' the American historian Shepherd B. Clough has written, 'it created machinery to serve the government in handling all problems between employers and employees' (Clough, *The Economic History of Modern Italy*, 1964, p.233).

The supposed equality between capital and labour in the system was undermined by the decision in November 1928 to break up the Fascist trade-union confederation, which had getting on for 3 million members, into six smaller units. This was done partly in order to appease the business community, but also because Mussolini feared that the head of the single confederation, Edmondo Rossini, might otherwise become too powerful. This possibility was all the more likely since the electoral reform of May 1928 had given the Fascist unions the right to nominate candidates for the new nationally constituted Chamber of Deputies.

In March 1930 a kind of corporative parliament was set up in the shape of the National Council of Corporations, which was made up of the seven large employer and worker organizations for the main branches of agriculture, industry, services and the professions. Finally, in January 1939, the Chamber of Deputies itself was replaced by a new Chamber of *Fasci* and Corporations. These are no doubt the 'further changes . . . which, on paper at least, appeared to extend the corporative structure beyond the purely economic sphere to become a new form of political and social control' to which Roberts refers on page 459.

Roberts's scepticism about the role of corporatism in Italy's economic life is justified. The National Council of Corporations, for example, was a purely consultative body. But, as he indicates, the object of the corporate structure was not primarily economic, but political and social. Unfortunately Roberts goes on to undermine the force of his own argument by suggesting that the *Istituto per la Ricostruzione Industriale* or 'Industrial Reconstruction Institute' (IRI) was part of the corporate structure. It was not and, as we shall see, it did play an extremely important part in the 'central control and direction' of the economy.

There was little need for such control and direction in the early stages of Fascist rule, since the accession to power of Mussolini fortuitously coincided with an upturn in the economic cycle. His first finance minister, Alberto De' Stefani, who occupied his post from October 1922 to July 1925, adopted a more or less completely non-interventionist approach, abolishing the remaining wartime controls and tax surcharges. The economy grew, although whether this was due more to the international boom than to De' Stefani's policies is a moot point. In any event, the budget was balanced in 1925 for the first time since before World War I, and in the following year pre-war levels of production and consumption were regained. There had also been a remarkable improvement in the balance of payments. Whereas Italy's exports had financed only 47.6 per cent of its imports in 1921, the proportion had risen to 75.7 per cent by 1924.

The continuing deficit on the balance of payments did, however, lead to a steady depreciation of the lira. At around 90 to the pound when Mussolini came to power, it fell to 145 in 1925. In August 1926 Mussolini announced that the lira's value would be restored to 90 to the pound. This was a much higher value than Italy's economic position warranted and was only achieved as a result of harsh deflationary measures.

The government also took steps to reduce the balance of payments deficit. One of the most spectacular was the so-called 'battle for grain', launched by Mussolini in June 1925 and designed to end Italy's dependence on imports of wheat. Tariffs on imported wheat were raised and domestic producers were thereby enabled to charge more for their crop. As a result Italian wheat production rose from an annual average of 5.2 million tonnes in 1922–25 to 7.6 million tonnes in 1936–39, which was a position of self-sufficiency. Italy's overall balance of payments deficit was reduced from 19.5 billion lire in 1920–24 to 8.6 billion in 1925–29 and 165 million in 1930–34, although there were, of course, many other factors at work in this process. Moreover, it rose again in the second half of the 1930s, totalling 3.9 billion lire in 1935–39.

Two developments led to a much greater degree of state intervention in the economy in the 1930s than in the 1920s. These were the onset of the Great Depression in 1929 and Italy's increasingly belligerent foreign policy, commencing with its invasion of Abyssinia in 1935 and its involvement in the Spanish Civil War in 1936. Both gave rise to growing pressure for autarky, or self-sufficiency, a process by which Italy could become less dependent upon the outside world and particularly upon potential enemies.

IRI, to which reference has already been made, was set up in January 1933 in order to help the banks out of the difficulties caused by the depreciation during the depression of the shares they had acquired in industry and commerce. By purchasing these shares it gradually acquired a stake in many industries. Indeed, it has been estimated that, on the eve of World War II, IRI controlled 90 per cent of Italy's merchant shipping, 80 per cent of its shipbuilding, 77 per cent of its pig iron production, 75 per cent of its metal tubes, 67 per cent of its iron ore, 50 per cent of its arms and ammunition, 44 per cent of its steel, 39 per cent of its power machinery, 23 per cent of its engineering, and 22 per cent of its aircraft construction. As the Italian economic historian, Rosario Romeo, has observed,

> If one adds to the industries controlled by IRI those which the state already managed in various forms, beginning with the railways, it will become clear that from 1936 onwards the Italian state owned a proportionately larger share of industry than any other European state apart from the Soviet Union. (Romeo, *Breve Storia della Grande Industria in Italia 1861–1961*, 1982, p.173)

And Martin Clark has added that, with its new generation of managers trained in the running of state and semi-state enterprises, IRI was 'the key economic legacy of the Fascist period' (Clark, *Modern Italy 1871–1982*, 1984, p.266).

If the existence and role of IRI suggests that the state was indeed responsible for the 'central control and direction' of the economy during the 1930s, that picture must be modified by taking into account the fact that large private firms also played a significant part. Government policy did, in fact, encourage the process of industrial concentration in this period with the result that, also on the eve of World War II, the chemical giant Montecatini controlled the output of rayon and three-fifths of that of chemical fertilizers; Snia Viscosa controlled between 60 and 65 per cent of artificial fibre production; Fiat controlled 83 per cent of automobile production; Pirelli enjoyed a monopoly in the field of rubber and, in addition, controlled 60 to 70 per cent of cable production; and Edison was responsible for 45.5 per cent of the output of electric power.

Shepherd B. Clough sums up Fascist economic policy in the following words:

> It may be said with justice that Fascism helped to preserve private capitalism, although it should be added quickly that capitalists were frequently pushed around – were made to pay heavy taxes, take workers that they did not need, and to pursue policies of which they did not approve. (Clough, *The Economic History of Modern Italy*, 1964, p.238)

Together with the information contained in the previous few paragraphs, this judgement implies, I believe, that while Roberts's dismissal of the totalitarian nature of the Fascist economy is too severe, it would be equally wrong to argue that Italy did fulfil Friedrich's and Brzezinski's criterion of 'central control and direction of the entire economy through the state bureaucracy'.

The above analysis, of course, says little or nothing about the success or otherwise of the Fascist economy. Compare these two statements:

> Economic growth was slow: National income at 1938 prices went from 115.1 billion lire in 1925 to 138.2 billion in 1938 and on a per capita basis increased between the same years from 2,923 to only 3,201 lire. So far as labor was concerned the index of real wages appears to have fallen from 111.8 (1913 = 100) to 100.5 in 1938. (Clough, *The Economic History of Modern Italy*, 1964, p.238)

> Italy by 1939 was more industrialized than she had been in 1922, and rather more prosperous. Gross domestic product [another term for national income] had increased by 1.2 per cent per year on average, more than double the growth of population; manufacturing production had gone up by 3.9 per cent p.a. (Clark, *Modern Italy 1871–1982*, 1984, p.267)

Both statements are correct, and it is not simply the choice of dates which is responsible for the different – one might even say opposite – impression conveyed by them. What you need to bear in mind is the point of departure and the comparison with other countries. The Swiss economist, Paul Bairoch, has made some estimates of levels of industrialization in various countries over a period of more than 200 years. The following table selects some of these estimates in order to measure Italy's performance against those of the same countries we used at the beginning of this unit. They show the per capita level of industrialization measured against the United Kingdom level in 1900 (=100).

Table 17.6

	1913	1928	1938
France	59	82	73
Germany	85	101	128
Italy	26	39	44
UK	115	122	157

(Source: Bairoch, 'International industrialization levels from 1750 to 1980', 1982, p.302)

What this table shows is that while Italy had gained on the other three powers since 1913, it was still behind them all in 1938, and well behind Germany and the United Kingdom.

It should also be pointed out that Fascism had done nothing to narrow the gap between the more prosperous north of Italy and the backward south. Indeed, that gap had widened. On the eve of World War II, the Turin-Milan-Genoa 'industrial triangle', with only a quarter of the Italian population, had half the industrial employees, more than half the installed horsepower, and almost two-thirds of the share capital.

On page 126 I wrote of an alternative definition to totalitarianism, one that sought to encapsulate the concept in the notion of the progressive annihilation of the boundaries between state and society. That this is, perhaps, a more fruitful approach to the subject is shown by the fact that it enables us to discuss an important aspect of the Fascist regime which falls outside Friedrich's and Brzezinski's six-point syndrome, notably the question of mass socialization.

The American historian E. R. Tannenbaum has written:

> One of the most novel, yet typical, features of Italian Fascism was its effort to regiment large segments of society, particularly youth and labor, into mass organizations. By the mid-1930s Nazi Germany and the Soviet Union were equally totalitarian in this respect, but the Italian effort was the first and was all the more remarkable for having had practically nothing to build on from the nation's liberal past. (Tannenbaum, *The Fascist Experience*, 1972, p.119)

What we are concerned with here, essentially, are the regime's educational, youth and leisure policies.

Although the Fascist government's first education minister – the philosopher, Giovanni Gentile – carried out a reform of Italy's educational system as early as May 1923, it was not until the end of the decade that the 'Fascistization' of the schools began seriously. It was in February 1929 that all schoolteachers were compelled to take an oath of loyalty to the regime. University staff had to follow suit in October 1931, and after 1933 all new appointees to any post in the public educational system had to belong to the PNF. During the same period the state began publishing its own school textbooks and excluding all others from state schools. Fascist propaganda permeated the entire curriculum. Tannenbaum cites the example of the timetable of a class of eight-year-olds in 1937:

> The largest number of hours was devoted to practice in the Italian language [the use of dialect had been banned in 1934]; about half of the drill material was on Fascist topics – the regime's public works, the Ethiopian war, the Mediterranean Sea as *mare nostro* [or 'our sea']. The geography class also emphasised *mare nostro*, while the history class discussed famous naval battles and the First World War . . . In arithmetic the following problem was to be solved: 'In 1902 the salary of Mussolini the teacher was 56 lire a month. How much a day? A year?' (Tannenbaum, *The Fascist Experience*, 1972, p.164)

As students progressed through the educational system, the amount of specifically Fascist indoctrination they encountered declined, partly no doubt because of the exigencies of public examinations. If they went on to university, they found a completely different atmosphere, with no state textbooks and few compulsory courses. The regime's influence in universities was exercised through its student organization, the *Gioventù Universitaria Fascista* or 'Fascist University Youth' (GUF), but this also sponsored non-political, and popular, activities such as sport and film shows.

The GUF was only one of a number of organizations which sought to regiment the nation's youth. The most prominent was the *Opera Nazionale Balilla* or 'National Balilla Institution' (ONB), which was founded in 1926 and named after an eighteenth-century boy who became an early hero of the Italian nationalist movement. The ONB was divided into a number of sections according to age and sex: the *Figli della lupa* or 'children of the she-wolf' for boys and girls of six and seven; the *Balilla* proper for boys between eight and thirteen; the *Piccole Italiane* or 'Little Italian girls' for girls between eight and thirteen; the *Avanguardisti* or

'Vanguard' for boys between fourteen and seventeen; and the *Giovani Italiane* or 'Young Italian girls' for girls between fourteen and seventeen.

Exercise You will find reproduced as document I.10 in *Documents 2* extracts from the decree law of January 1927 setting out the functions of the *Avanguardisti* and the *Balilla*. You should read these now and then answer the following questions:

1   From these extracts, what would you say was the principal objective of the *Avanguardisti* and the *Balilla*?

2   Do you note any particular connection with Italy's past?

3   Would you say that there was anything in these extracts which casts doubt upon the totalitarian nature of the *Avanguardisti* and the *Balilla*? ■

Specimen answers 1   The principal objective of the two bodies, as it appears from these extracts, is the preparation of boys for the army. Note in particular the military organization of both the *Avanguardisti* and the *Balilla* and the emphasis upon discipline and obedience. Physical training, of course, also fits in with this objective.

2   The historical allusions in these extracts are to Ancient Rome. Almost all the sub-divisions of both bodies are named after Roman precedents: centuries, maniples, cohorts and legions.

3   Two items in the extracts which cast doubt upon the totalitarian nature of the two bodies are the fact that membership is voluntary and not compulsory (Article III) and that Roman Catholic religious beliefs be inculcated in members (Article XXXVIII). □

Discussion Membership of the ONB was made compulsory in the early 1930s, although this was difficult to enforce once children had left school, which was as early as eleven for many Italian boys and girls. In October 1937, it was amalgamated with the non-student movements for young people between the ages of eighteen and twenty-one to form the *Gioventù Italiana del Littorio* or 'Italian Youth of the Lictors' (GIL), another Roman allusion. The new organization was under direct party control, whereas the ONB had been run from the Ministry of Education. In June 1939 the GIL had a membership of around 6,700,000 which was about half the relevant age-group. This was a higher proportion than that which existed in respect of similar organizations in Nazi Germany. Membership was proportionately much higher in the north of Italy than in the south.

The third principal agent of mass socialization in Fascist Italy was the *Opera Nazionale Dopolavoro* or 'National Afterwork Institution' (OND), which was set up by a decree of 1 May 1925 and the purpose of which was 'to provide healthy and profitable leisure-time activity for the workers by means of institutions that develop their physical, intellectual, and moral qualities'. By 1939 the OND had 3.5 million members: a majority of white-collar employees, nearly 40 per cent of industrial workers, and a quarter of the eligible peasants. The secret of the OND's success, as Martin Clark points out, was that it 'was fun, not propaganda; it was recreation, not self-improvement'.

> The *Dopolavoro* clubs [he writes] had bars, billiard halls, libraries, radios and sports grounds, they put on concerts and plays; they provided virtually free summer holidays for children; they organized charabanc trips, ballroom-dancing, mountain walks, and days at the seaside. They also handed out welfare relief in poor areas; both circuses and bread. No wonder they were popular. It was the first time in Italian history that mass

leisure activities had existed, let alone been encouraged and subsidized by politicians. (Clark, *Modern Italy 1871–1982*, 1984, p.245)

There may seem little that was political in all this, but many of the OND's cultural activities, with their emphasis on Italian traditions as opposed to twentieth-century cosmopolitanism and 'Americanization', were distinctly nationalistic in tone. And at the time of the Ethiopian war in 1935–36 the OND was used, and used successfully, to help mobilize public opinion in support of the regime's objectives. It was the OND, for example, which organized the famous 'plebiscite of gold' in which, among other things, women gave their wedding rings to be melted down to help pay for the war effort.

If one thinks of a young Italian in the 1930s, being educated by Fascist teachers on the basis of Fascist textbooks, joining the ONB for out-of-school activities, beginning work as a member of a Fascist trade union and with his or her spare time organized by the OND, totalitarianism does not seem such a fanciful concept. Nevertheless, it is important to bear in mind that, as we have seen, membership of the ONB and the OND, while high, was nowhere near universal, and that since there were no free elections, let alone anything approaching modern opinion polls, it is not easy to assess the effects of all this indoctrination in the shape of the degree of support which the regime enjoyed.

It should already be clear from what has been said in this unit that Fascism was opposed by a great many Italians from Mussolini's accession to power in October 1922 down to the consolidation of the regime after the Matteotti crisis in 1924. Most historians seem to agree that its popularity peaked at the time of the Ethiopian war in 1935–36, but that it declined thereafter, especially with Italy's growing alignment with Nazi Germany and the danger of a general war. It was certainly the case that, when Mussolini did take Italy into World War II in June 1940, the prefects reported that this decision was not popular. The position is perhaps best summed up by Martin Clark:

> Did all this Fascist effort at 'social control' actually work [he asks]? The judicious historian gives a prosaic answer: yes and no. Yes, in the sense that until 1936 most people swallowed most of the propaganda most of the time, at a fairly superficial level. Italy was stable, the *Duce* was popular, open dissenters were rare. It made sense to go along with the regime, and patriotism is a natural feeling even in Italy. But there was little enthusiasm for Fascism – as opposed to patriotism and Mussolinism – and the regime's claims to 'totalitarianism' were laughable. Religion, family sentiment, individual ambition and cunning, the parish pump, the art of *arrangiarsi* [or 'fixing'] – all these traditional institutions and values survived and flourished . . . In short, there was acceptance but not devotion, consensus but not commitment, let alone 'hegemony'. Still, even the Fascist consensus was a great deal more than most Italian regimes had achieved. On balance the ideological efforts paid off. It took years for most people to see through Fascism. (Clark, *Modern Italy 1871–1982*, 1984, p.247)

There also existed, as Roberts points out on pages 456–8, important political forces that were largely independent of Fascism. He refers specifically to the monarchy and the Roman Catholic Church. Roberts refers to the concessions accorded to the latter under the terms of the Lateran treaties of 1929, and rightly maintains that these were more important than those which the Church gave in return (p.457). But they were not the only concessions to the Church by any means. We have already seen how Roman Catholicism was to be inculcated in members of the ONB (see above, p. 135). It was the same in the schools. Fascism broke with the traditions of the liberal state in instituting compulsory religious instruction in state schools, and it was taught at the secondary level not by lay teachers but by priests.

Roberts should also have mentioned the armed forces as one of the independent organizations in Fascist Italy. Although the regime made ample use of them in its propaganda, they were careful to brook no interference from Fascist busybodies in running their affairs. Even the *Duce* largely confined himself to acting as an arbitrator in conflicts between the different branches of the armed services.

Of course these organizations went along with Mussolini and Fascism for most of the time, but this was because their interests temporarily coincided. They had no particular love for Mussolini, or he for them, as we shall see in the final section of this unit. They retained a capacity for independent action and, indeed, opposition, and it is significant in this connection that it was a coalition between the king and the armed forces which was mainly responsible for the downfall of Mussolini in July 1943. It is also significant that the new political élite which eventually replaced the Fascists after World War II had mostly served their apprenticeship in the ranks of Catholic Action, a network of lay organizations controlled by the Church and set up, not in 1931 as Roberts claims (p.458), but well before World War I.

4 FASCISM AND WAR

This final section of the unit is geared specifically to the article by the American historian MacGregor Knox, 'Conquest, Foreign and Domestic, in Fascist Italy and Nazi Germany', extracts from which are printed on pages 158–89 of the Course Reader. Profoundly dissatisfied over the results so far of the historical and political debate on the nature of fascism, which purports, among other things, to draw out the common features of Italian Fascism and German Nazism, Knox makes his own comparison of the two regimes in terms of what he sees as the inseparable connection between their domestic and foreign policies. I do not propose to discuss the validity of this comparison. It is something which you will be better equipped to make up your own mind about after you have read Bernard Waites's Unit 18 on Nazi Germany, which also refers to the article. I shall confine myself to Knox's analysis of Fascist Italy. You should now read the article.

Exercise   I want you to concentrate on the second section of the article, which is entitled 'From mission to programme' (pp.160–72 of the Course Reader). Try to answer the following questions in a couple of short paragraphs:

1   What, in Knox's opinion, were the sources of Mussolini's world view and how did World War I affect it?

2   What, according to Knox, was Mussolini's vision of Fascist Italy and how did he intend to realize it? ■

Specimen answers   Mussolini's underlying assumption was that life was a perpetual struggle. This was linked with two myths: the idea of revolution, which he took partly from Marx and partly from Sorel; and the idea of the nation, which he took from Mazzini and other Italian nationalist thinkers. World War I removed the contradiction between these two myths and indeed permitted their fusion. If Italy's participation in the war was motivated by nationalist considerations, it would also lead to revolution.

Mussolini wanted, in his own words, 'to fascistize the nation, so that tomorrow Italian and Fascist, more or less like Italian and Catholic, will be the same thing'. This new Italy would reject old stereotypes – 'mandolin players' and 'exquisite manners' – in favour of a tough, ruthless image. Expansion and war would be the means of achieving this objective. ☐

Discussion   The importance of war in Fascist ideology is, of course, brought out in document I.11 in *Documents 2*, the extracts from Mussolini's article 'The doctrine of Fascism' (1932). As he stated in that article:

> Above all, Fascism . . . believes neither in the possibility nor in the utility of perpetual peace . . . War alone brings up to their highest tension all human energies and puts the stamp of nobility upon the peoples who have the courage to meet it. All other trials are substitutes, which never really put a man in front of himself in the alternative of life and death.

Knox shows how the 'battle for grain', which I discussed in section 3 in a different context, was also launched in order to create the demographic prerequisites for Italian power and expansion. Indeed, the regime adopted a whole panoply of measures in the 1930s in order to boost Italy's birth rate: family allowances, marriage loans (part of which was written off each time the happy couple produced a child), job discrimination in favour of family men (women, of course, were encouraged to stay at home and breed), and a surtax on bachelors. Despite all these incentives, the birth rate continued to decline: from 26.7 per 1,000 of the population in 1930 to 23.5 per 1,000 ten years later. On the eve of World War I the rate had exceeded 30.

If you cast your mind back to the previous section of this unit, you will no doubt recall other facets of the regime's policies which were geared to preparation for war, notably the emphasis upon military-style training in the ONB and the drive for economic autarky.

You will find a brief account of the approach to World War II in chapter 15 of Roberts and a more detailed analysis in Antony Lentin's Unit 20. I do not wish to go over this ground again, but I should like to address the question of what I see as, if not the inevitability, at any rate the strong likelihood of Italy's eventual alignment with Germany as opposed to Britain and France.

Knox states (on page 172 of the Course Reader) that Mussolini 'remained uncommitted to a specific alliance structure until 1936'. This is true, but Britain and France would have found it extremely difficult to win the *Duce*'s permanent allegiance. This was not only because of the 'humiliation' which they, together with the Americans, heaped upon Italy at the end of World War I, but also, and more importantly, because of Mussolini's geopolitical vision, which Knox outlines on pages 166–8 of the Course Reader. It was not the Germans who were the principal obstacle to Fascist Italy's Mediterranean ambitions, but the British and the French.

Mussolini himself spelled it out in a speech to the Fascist Grand Council on 4 February 1939.

> States that cannot communicate freely with the oceans and are enclosed in inland seas are semi-independent [he declared] . . . Italy . . . does not have free connection with the oceans. Italy is therefore in truth a prisoner of the Mediterranean, and the more populous and prosperous Italy becomes, the more its imprisonment will gall. The bars of this prison are Corsica [French], Tunis [French], Malta [British], Cyprus [British]. The sentinels of this prison are Gibraltar [British] and Suez [British]. Corsica is a pistol pointed at the heart of Italy; Tunisia at Sicily; while Malta and Cyprus constitute a threat to all our positions in the eastern and western Mediterranean. Greece, Turkey, Egypt have been ready to form a chain with Great Britain and to complete the politico-military encirclement of Italy . . . From this situation, whose geographical rigor leaps to one's eyes and which tormented, even before our regime, those men who saw beyond considerations of momentary political expediency, one can draw the following conclusions:
>
> 1   The task of Italian policy which cannot have and does not have continental objectives of a European territorial nature except Albania, is to first of all break the bars of the prison.
>
> 2   Once the bars are broken, Italian policy can have only one watchword – to march to the ocean. Which ocean? The Indian Ocean, joining Libya with Ethiopia through the Sudan, or the Atlantic, through French North Africa.
>
> In either case, we will find ourselves confronted with Anglo-French opposition . . . (Knox, *Mussolini Unleashed*, 1982, p.40)

If Fascist Italy's principal expansionary thrust was to be directed towards the south, Nazi Germany's was to be directed towards the east and north. As Hitler told Mussolini's son-in-law and foreign minister, Galeazzo Ciano, on 24 October 1936, 'by steering our two dynamisms in these two exactly opposing directions, there can never be a clash of interests between Germany and Italy' (Mosca, *L'Europa verso la Catastrofe*, 1964, Vol.I, p.101). Hitler's sense of direction may have been somewhat astray, and notwithstanding their joint protestations, both dictators were keenly interested in the fate of the Balkans and hence potential rivals in the peninsula, but the Axis was probably based more on this convenient division of spheres of influence than upon ideological solidarity.

Exercise   I should now like you to look again at the final section, 'Unholy War', of Knox's article (pp.172–82 of the Course Reader) and then describe briefly the attitude of the independent forces in Fascist Italy – the monarchy, the armed forces and the Roman Catholic Church – to Mussolini's expansionism from 1935 to 1939. ∎

Specimen answer   In order to launch his war against Ethiopia, Mussolini had to overcome army (though not navy and air force) opposition, and hesitancy on the part of the king. Only the Church was enthusiastically in favour of his policy. The Church, too, favoured the 'anti-communist' intervention in the Spanish Civil War, although, once again, both the monarchy and the armed forces were doubtful. By September 1939 the Church, which was upset by the regime's new racial laws and the alliance with Germany, joined forces with the king, the military, and others to restrain Mussolini from plunging into World War II at Hitler's side. □

Discussion This section of Knox's article brings out the growing antagonism between the independent forces and the regime. He even alludes to the possibility of a royal *coup* against Mussolini in March 1940, something which materialized in a slightly different form in July 1943 in the wake of Italy's comprehensive defeat in World War II. Knox's analysis shows not only the limits of Mussolini's totalitarianism, but the *Duce's* awareness of those limits and his own determination to do something about them, as for example in his plans to get rid of the monarchy.

Finally, I should like to focus upon Knox's principal conclusion: that 'foreign policy was internal policy and vice versa; internal consolidation was a precondition of foreign conquest, and foreign conquest was the decisive prerequisite for a revolution at home that would sweep away inherited institutions and values . . .' (p. 183 in the Course Reader). This is clearly of considerable importance in the context of a course that is specifically concerned with the relationship between war, peace and social change.

Some elements of Knox's proposition do not seem to take us very far. After all, there is a close connection between foreign and domestic policy in most modern states, and not only fascist regimes would attempt to consolidate their position at home before embarking upon adventures abroad, although some governments have, of course, used war as a means of rallying support. Knox, however, goes much further than this. What he appears to be saying about Fascist Italy – and, I repeat, I am not talking about Nazi Germany – is that Mussolini's totalitarian revolution had only gone off at half cock, and that it required war and foreign conquest to complete it.

This is not the same thing as saying that war and foreign conquest were an essential ingredient of Fascism. I think they were, but this could have been for other reasons; ideological conviction, a desire to strengthen the regime by constant mass mobilization in support of external objectives, or the perceived need to distract the population from problems at home. Knox, on the other hand, is arguing that the motive for war and foreign conquest was precisely to overcome the remaining obstacles to his totalitarian rule.

In order to make his case, Knox would have to show that the opposition from king, armed forces and Church prompted the wars, and that Mussolini saw no other way of neutralizing these independent forces except by means of war. I don't think he does. The *Duce* was undoubtedly hostile to what Knox sometimes calls 'the Establishment', and was exasperated by its criticisms of his policies, at home as well as abroad. But where is the evidence that Mussolini embarked upon expansion because of this hostility and these criticisms, as opposed, for example, to the geopolitical ideology, which Knox so convincingly demonstrates the Italian dictator held from the very outset?

5 *CONCLUSION*

Returning to the questions we asked at the very beginning of this unit, we can conclude that although the economic effects of World War I were no worse in Italy than in other West European countries, the conflict did have important political consequences in the form of the growth or emergence of powerful mass parties and movements which challenged the old liberal regime. Fascism itself grew out of the war as one of the currents in the ferment of nationalism which the conflict and Italy's alleged mistreatment in the peace settlement had produced, but it did not become a mass movement, let alone a major threat to the parliamentary system until the end of 1920, when it was able to take advantage of the reaction against the industrial and agrarian unrest of the *biennio rosso*. This mass Fascist movement was broadly representative of Italian society as a whole, but its accession to power was by no means inevitable. This occurred because of the failure of the liberal regime to crack down on Fascist violence, the illusion on the part of some politicians that they could 'use' Fascism for their own ends, the divisions in the ranks of the opposition, and the benevolent neutrality of organizations such as the monarchy, the armed forces, and the Roman Catholic Church.

After surmounting the Matteotti crisis of 1924, the Fascist regime managed to build a degree of consensus which was probably greater than that created by any of the liberal governments which had preceded it. The totalitarian model may legitimately be applied to it, although it was Mussolini and the state apparatus rather than the Fascist Party as such that exercised the control, and its mobiliz-ation of the populace and of the economy was by no means complete. Most important of all, important independent foci of power remained in existence, notably the monarchy, the armed forces and the Church, which, in the crisis brought about by the regime's participation in World War II, were able to move decisively against it. The fact that war brought about Fascism's collapse was in a sense paradoxical, since war and foreign conquest were essential both to Fascist theory and practice.

References

Aquarone, A. (1965) *L'Organizzazione dello Stato Totalitario*, Einaudi.

Bairoch, P. (1982) 'International industrialization levels from 1750 to 1980', *Journal of European Economic History*, vol.11, no.2, Fall, pp.269–333.

Cannistraro, P. V. (ed.) (1982) *Historical Dictionary of Fascist Italy*, Westport Greenwood Press.

Cipolla, C. M. (ed.) (1976) *The Fontana Economic History of Europe*, Volume 6, Part 2, *Contemporary Economics – 2*, Collins/Fontana.

Clark, M. (1984) *Modern Italy 1871–1982*, Longman.

Clough, S. B. (1964) *The Economic History of Modern Italy*, Columbia University Press.

de Grand, A. (1982) *Italian Fascism: Its Origins and Development*, University of Nebraska Press.

Delzell, C. F. (1971) *Mediterranean Fascism 1919–1945*, Macmillan.

Knox, M. (1982) *Mussolini Unleashed 1939–1941: Politics and Strategy in Fascist Italy's Last War*, Cambridge University Press.

Mitchell, B. R. (1981) *European Historical Statistics 1750–1975*, second revised edition, Macmillan.

Mosca, R. (ed.) (1964) *L'Europa verso la Catastrofe*, Vol.I, Il Saggiatore.

Mühlberger, D. (ed.) (1987) *The Social Basis of European Fascist Movements*, Croom Helm.

Romeo, R. (1982) *Breve Storia della Grande Industria in Italia 1861–1961*, Cappelli.

Schapiro, L. (1972) *Totalitarianism*, Pall Mall.

Seton-Watson, C. (1967) *Italy from Liberalism to Fascism*, Methuen.

Tannenbaum, E. R. (1972) *The Fascist Experience: Italian Society and Culture 1922–1945*, Basic Books.

UNIT 18 STATE, ECONOMY AND SOCIETY IN NAZI GERMANY 1933–1939

Bernard Waites

With grateful acknowledgement to Richard Bessel

Open University students of this unit will need to refer to:

Set book: J. M. Roberts, *Europe 1880–1945*, Longman, 1989

Course Reader: *War, Peace and Social Change in Twentieth-Century Europe*, eds Clive Emsley, Arthur Marwick and Wendy Simpson, Open University Press, 1990

Documents 2: 1925–1959, eds Arthur Marwick and Wendy Simpson, Open University Press, 1990

1 HISTORICAL APPROACHES TO THE THIRD REICH

Nazi Germany dedicated itself to military expansion and was the most destructive state in world history. On so much all would agree, but when we ask 'What were the sources of this destructive dynamic?' we encounter a variety of explanations. For some years after 1945 the historiography of the Nazi state reflected the Cold War and the division of Germany between East and West. In the East, orthodox Marxism-Leninism portrayed National Socialism as a variant of *fascism* which the Seventh Congress of the Comintern had defined (in 1935) as 'the open terroristic most imperialistic elements of finance capital'. Fascism, according to this interpretation, constituted the 'shock troops of the counter-revolution, chief incendiary of the imperialist revolution, instigator of a crusade against the Soviet Union' (given in Aycoberry, *The Nazi Question*, 1981, p.53). East German historians have assiduously attempted to substantiate this thesis by documenting the role of powerful capitalist interests in promoting economic autarky and an economy geared to aggression. But though they have demonstrated the importance of powerful pressure groups in implementing economic preparations for war, they have persuaded few not already wedded to the Comintern thesis that economic interests were the driving force behind German foreign policy (Carr, 'National Socialism', 1976, p.135).

The view of National Socialist Germany as the political outgrowth of monopoly-finance capital (which harks back to Lenin's analysis of imperialism) has, in fact, had few defenders in the West, even among Marxists. One of Hitler's most deeply felt convictions was 'The primacy of politics' (over economics) and in a notable essay T. W. Mason, a leading neo-Marxist historian of Nazi Germany, argued that this did, indeed, characterize the Nazi regime, but he attempted to explain this from a Marxist methodological starting point. According to Mason the increasing independence of the Nazi government, after 1936, from the influence of the economic ruling classes, and the adoption of policies contrary to their interests, could only have taken place after far-reaching structural changes both in the economy and in society. The terminal crisis of Weimar Germany was such, argues Mason, that civil society was unable to reproduce itself; economic collapse had accentuated the class struggle and led to the splintering of political blocs into rival interest groups. Only through radical political means could social disintegration be averted and only National Socialism could provide them. There were, then, specific economic and social preconditions for the emergence of a regime which practised 'pure politics', unconstrained by economic or rational calculations, and which subordinated capitalism to the state in a way quite untypical of capitalist societies. In Mason's view, this relationship of politics to economics in Nazi Germany was 'unique in the history of modern bourgeois society and its governments: it is precisely this which must be explained' (Mason, 'The primacy of politics', 1968, p.167).

We have here a boldly drawn sketch of a regime which stood outside the normal processes of history as Marxists conceive them, and the destructive irrationality of which can be explained by its singular abnormality. Other Western historians influenced by Marx have acknowledged the regime's unique destructiveness, but drawn on Marx's writings on Bonapartism to place it in a category of exceptional dictatorships that occur in moments of critical stalemate in the class struggle, when neither the bourgeoisie nor the proletariat can establish its dominance. In this situation, the 'Bonapartist' theory runs, a charismatic leader is able to seize power by portraying himself as the arbiter of contending interests, saviour of the social order and guardian of national grandeur. Nicos Poulantzas advanced a more complex version of this 'critical stalemate' theory: in his interpretation the 'ruling class' is an uneasy alliance of heterogeneous elements (big industrialists, financiers, landowners, and so on) who form an unstable power bloc. Fascism arises when a crisis within the power bloc and stalemate in the class struggle occur simultaneously: the fascist state is, in these circumstances, able to achieve an exceptional degree of autonomy from capitalist interests although it generally tends to secure the hegemony of monopolistic industrialists (Poulantzas, *Fascism and Dictatorship*, 1974). But while this is an interesting theory of the origins of fascist states, it is much less illuminating on their common tendency to external aggression.

Such, in brief, are some of the main themes of Marxist interpretations; what of the non-Marxist? It would be wrong to suggest that there is a sharp dichotomy between the two. As we have seen, the Comintern thesis took National Socialism to be a variant of fascism. During the 1960s, Western non-Marxist interpretations came to share some common ground with the thesis when historians (such as Ernst Nolte in his book *Three Faces of Fascism*, 1965) developed the generic concept of fascism to refer to the mass mobilization of anti-Marxism in the inter-war period. Hitherto, Western historiography and political science had been in the thrall of the totalitarian model which portrayed National Socialist Germany and Soviet Russia as two aspects of a single, continuing phenomenon. During the Cold War, totalitarianism had served as a complementary orthodoxy to the Comintern formulation. After the work of Nolte and others had been published, the ideology of fascism and the historical specificity of fascist movements and regimes (that is, the particular circumstances in which they flourished and came to power) received much more attention from historians.

Although totalitarianism was an orthodoxy, it was not merely an orthodoxy, and in the work of Karl Dietrich Bracher and his associates the concept helped shape accounts of the dissolution of the Weimar Republic and the Nazi seizure of power which have stood the test of time. In *The German Dictatorship*, Bracher restated the totalitarian interpretation: the Nazi regime's three fundamental characteristics, he argued, were its 'claim to the total control of man and the reshaping of his functions in the service of the new order . . . [its] omnipotent leadership dictatorship [and] its terror system' (1971, p.427). In Bracher's view, these gave the regime its revolutionary and destructive dynamic and justify placing it in a category of totalitarian ruling systems typified by a 'closed' understanding of politics, as opposed to the 'openness' of liberal democracy. Bracher acknowledges that the now amply documented administrative and institutional rivalries of the Nazi state call for a modification of the original totalitarian model, but do not basically invalidate it.

Other historians would go much further and argue that competition between rival centres of power was such an essential feature of the Nazi state that it should be called a 'polyocracy' – a designation incompatible with the monolithic totalitarian concept – and they see this anarchic contest for power within the Reich as a basic cause of its uncontrollable drive towards external aggression. Although liberal scholars – such as Martin Broszat in *The Hitler State* (1981) – have produced the most authoritative analyses in this vein, their work has much in common with the remarkable study *Behemoth* (1942) by the exile Marxist Franz Neumann. Neumann concluded that Nazi Germany had no coherent political theory and could not even be designated a state in the sense of having a recognizable sovereign entity wielding unified political power. Rather, he maintained, the regime operated by compromises between the party, the bureaucracy, the army and industry; each had totalitarian power in its own sphere and there was no integrating system of authority above them. Neumann took from Jewish myth – and Thomas Hobbes – the monstrous figure of Behemoth to represent the chaos and lawlessness of the Nazi empire.

This image of Nazi Germany and the polyocratic concept are now widely accepted, but they have not produced a consensus among historians, particularly in West Germany. On the contrary, because the polyocratic thesis refers so little to human agency in explaining the development and destructiveness of the Nazi regime, it has been accused of shifting responsibility for the regime's deeds from real people to abstractions like administrative chaos. The controversy has an interest for the discipline of history as a whole because it involves a sharp methodological disagreement as to the weight we should attach to Nazi (and more particularly Hitler's) intentions and ideology in explaining German expansionism. It leads us to ask 'What suffices for an explanation in history?' (T. W. Mason, 'Intention and explanation', 1981, is a lucid guide for the controversy.)

Some would trace the bellicose instability of the regime to a consistent political 'programme', formulated by Hitler in his years as a beer-hall rabble-rouser of the extreme Right (1919–22) and codified in *Mein Kampf* (dictated in prison in 1924). The basic points of this programme were the need to secure by force *Lebensraum*, or 'living space', in the east, and anti-Semitism. It was intellectually buttressed by a crude 'internal' and 'international' Social Darwinism (the maxims that human life within and between societies was a matter of constant struggle in which only the fittest survived) and by the *völkisch* racism current in Vienna and Munich before and after World War I. We can call the type of interpretation which emphasizes Hitler's programme 'intentionalist'. A scholar representative of this approach is Eberhard Jaeckel, who has written: 'Perhaps never in history did a ruler write down before he came to power what he was to do afterward as precisely as did Adolf Hitler. Hitler set himself two goals: a war of conquest and the elimination of the Jews' (Jaeckel, *Hitler in History*, 1984, p.23).

Though Jaeckel emphasizes Hitler's intentions in explaining Nazi destructiveness, he recognizes that Hitler often had to act in conditions he did not choose, and that his actions had all sorts of unintended consequences. These qualifications notwithstanding, there are clear differences between Jaeckel's paradigm (or explanatory framework) and that of the 'functionalist' historians who trace the destructive dynamic of Nazi Germany primarily to its anarchic institutional arrangements, the chaotic competition between centres of power, and the lack of clear lines of responsibility for formulating and executing policy. It is to these relatively impersonal factors, rather than ideological fixations, that functionalist historians have attributed the Third Reich's 'cumulative radicalization' (Mommsen, 'National Socialism', 1979, p.156). The phrase is Hans Mommsen's, one of the most trenchant exponents of the functionalist approach and a powerful critic of interpretations of Nazi destructiveness which emphasize either Hitler's personality or his ideological obsessions. According to Mommsen, Hitler was indecisive, exclusively concerned with upholding his prestige and personal authority, and in some respects 'a weak dictator'. In both domestic and foreign policy, Mommsen argues, Nazi actions were often inconsistent with Hitler's ideological programme: the Nazis' domestic achievements were, in many cases (some discussed below), the exact opposite of their original intentions, while the regime's many and varied foreign ambitions had no clear aim save 'expansion without object' (Mommsen, 1979, p.177; see also Kershaw, *The Nazi Dictatorship*, 1985, p.62).

The opposition between 'intentionalist' and 'functionalist' interpretations is no more evident than in attempts to give an historical account of the 'Final Solution': Hitler's vicious and frequent denunciations of Jews, his public demands (made both before and after his coming to power) for their removal from Germany and their destruction in the event of war, when coupled with his dictatorial position constitute a powerful case for the 'intentionalists'. Against them the 'functionalists' explain the genocide as an escalating process of bureaucratic improvizations, driven forward by *ad hoc* responses of different agencies to the problems caused by the forcible evacuation of Jews to Eastern Europe and the zeal of subordinates independently carrying out 'the Führer's will'.

It is difficult to adjudicate between 'intentionalist' and 'functionalist' paradigms either with respect to accounting for the 'Final Solution' or as more general frameworks for the study of the Third Reich. My purpose is to alert you to a major methodological dispute in contemporary scholarship and to a debate which Open University students may well have to work through in their assignments or at summer school. In the sections that follow we will be returning to some of the issues raised by this summary of historical approaches. We shall be asking: what was the relationship between Nazism and capitalist interests before and after Hitler's accession to power? How was it that a man with the declared intention of destroying the Weimar Republic came to be appointed its Chancellor? How far did he have a blueprint for aggression and to what extent were economic and social policies dictated by the purposes of foreign conquest? How are we to best explain the apparently uncontrollable dynamism of Hitler's Germany: by reference to a totalitarian dynamic or to its 'polyocratic' instability?

2 THE NATIONAL SOCIALIST MOVEMENT BEFORE THE ACCESSION TO POWER

The Nazi movement originated on the semi-legal fringe of extreme nationalist politics in Munich in 1919 and was reconstituted as the National Socialist German Workers' Party (NSDAP) at a mass meeting of February 1920, by which time Hitler was already the foremost propaganda speaker of the new organization. In the spring of 1920, NSDAP, assisted by officers from the national *Freikorps* and Defence Leagues, organized the 'Storm Detachments' (*Sturmabteilungen* – SA), and this military arm of the party made physical force or the threat of force 'an established instrument in the Nazi struggle for power' (Broszat, *The Hitler State*, 1981, p.19). The SA closely resembled Mussolini's 'Action Squads': both organizations served to protect party meetings and demonstrations, they carried out punitive forays against opponents, and with their uniforms, banners and parades they helped infuse politics with the martial, 'front-line' spirit.

The twenty-five-point programme of the new party was eclectic and essentially negative: it was anti-Marxist and anti-capitalist, anti-parliamentarian and anti-Semitic, but above all against the Versailles settlement. It called for the recreation of the national community, such as had existed after the outbreak of war in 1914, but was utterly vague as to how this *Volksgemeinschaft* was to be achieved. Some specific points – such as the demands that all income not earned by work and all war profits were to be confiscated – were 'Leftish' and conformed with the self-stylization as a socialist workers' party. (Members addressed each other as 'comrade' and party flags and posters were red.) Other demands reflected the hostility of the *Mittelstand* to big business: department stores were to be turned over to small tradesmen and land speculation outlawed to protect small farmers. Appended to the programme was a specific reference to 'breaking the shackles of finance capital', which indicates that, whatever its later evolution, the party did not originate from capitalism's most reactionary and chauvinist elements. Other points – such as the demands for living-space and for measures against the Jews – were derived from the nationalist and *völkisch* sects, notably the Pan-German Thule Society, to which many of the original members (although not Hitler) had belonged. It was these sects which had promoted the racist ideology of 'Aryanism' and which had first used the swastika as a symbol of political racism.

Hitler was later to describe this programme as 'unalterable', though many points – particularly the socially radical proposals – were tacitly abandoned, even before 1933, principally to secure the co-operation of Germany's traditional élites in industry, the army and the bureaucracy in the accession to power and the rearmament programme. But it would be unwise to dismiss it *en bloc* as mere expediency. Hitler was obsessed by the absolute truth of his basic ideas. To over-estimate his opportunism and not take the part played by ideology in National Socialist policy seriously is to repeat the mistake made by Hitler's contemporaries at home and abroad. The anti-Semitism of the programme, and its racist and expansionist ideas and formulations, were never officially rescinded or changed (Bracher, *The German Dictatorship*, 1971, pp.314–5).

Moreover, the programme had a particular functional importance in relation to the party membership and its wider constituency. Both were remarkably hetero-geneous: the old lower middle class of small producers and traders was somewhat over-represented among the membership, but the party became a genuinely 'mass' movement joined by men from all social strata. (Women were much under-represented until the later stages of World War II; in 1935 they were only 5.5 per cent of members.) Perhaps more importantly, members joined for varying, even contradictory, reasons. Many party activists saw it as egalitarian and revolutionary, and hoped that it would break the authority of the traditional élites and introduce a new and more meritocratic social order. Others were attracted to it for socially conservative reasons: they saw it as a movement reasserting traditional German values, above all national pride. Later, many came to vote for it as an act of protest against the discredited Weimar Republic. The eclecticism of the party programme, and the vagueness of its goal of national integration, 'encouraged individuals and groups to identify their own particular hopes and aspirations with the party and its leader. In other words, Nazism came to mean many things to many people' (Noakes, 'The Nazi Party and the Third Reich', 1980, p.2).

The first phase of National Socialism's history ended in fiasco in November 1923 when Hitler, Ludendorff and other extreme nationalists attempted a *coup* in

Bavaria as a preliminary to 'a March on Berlin'. The failure of the putsch persuaded Hitler that he had to adopt 'a policy of legality' and take the electoral road to power. Wider developments during his imprisonment, which ended prematurely in December 1924, indicated that this strategy required patience. In the winter of 1923–24, the central government used its emergency powers to undertake a number of measures (including monetary reform) which promoted economic and social stabilization and helped protect the Republic from insurrectionary overthrow either by the Left or the Right. The political success of these measures can be gauged from the ebbing popular support for anti-Republican forces which, for the next five years, reduced the Nazis to an electorally insignificant splinter group. (For the Weimar electoral figures, see document I.2.)

Although popular support eluded Hitler until 1929, a number of developments occurred within his movement which were to have a powerful bearing on the Nazi state. Firstly, the socially radical faction in National Socialism, led by Gregor Strasser, was subordinated by Hitler. In this process he was able to reassert his position as undisputed dictator of the party and establish a relationship with its disparate and often disputatious elements that was transferred into the Nazi power structure after 1933. The *Gauleiter* or district leaders, for example, were his personal agents: he appointed them and they reported directly to him. The Führer did not attempt to bind his party together by forbidding factions (as Lenin had attempted to do in the CPSU in 1921) or through regular control of the party machine. Rather, he made personal subordination to his unique leadership the party's cohesive element and acted as the arbiter of intra-party conflicts. 'It was as if he was "floating" above the party' (Broszat, *Hitler and the Collapse of Weimar Germany*, 1987, p.64). Both the 'leadership principle' and the arbiter's role above factions characterized the later dictatorship.

Secondly, a mythology grew up around Hitler which helped secure rank-and-file loyalty to his movement. Even before Hitler's career began, the cult of the heroic leader who would redeem Germany from squabbling petty interests was a notable feature of political discourse and imagery. Hitler and his myth-makers (notably Joseph Goebbels) both exploited and developed this existing cult in a way which skilfully set him above, and apart from, the NSDAP. Hitler was perceived as dedicated, endowed with a religious sense of mission and purpose, ascetic, incorruptible. These perceptions of him bound together his heterogeneous party following: after he became a national leader they were shared by most Germans (even those hitherto hostile to National Socialism) and acted as a crucial integratory force in the Nazi system of rule (Kershaw, *The Hitler 'Myth'*, 1987).

Thirdly, there began a process by which the conflicting interest groups of Weimar Germany came to be represented within the National Socialist movement itself. Leagues of Nazi lawyers, doctors and teachers were established, and in 1928 the NSBO, or National Socialist shop-floor organization, was set up. During the economic crisis of 1929 to 1933, this process of sectional representation accelerated: National Socialist organizations were established for farmers, civil servants, white-collar workers. Though interest-group representation obviously facilitated the growth of a mass movement, it had the dysfunctional effect of 'introducing the fragmentation of German society into the party itself' (Noakes, 'The Nazi Party and the Third Reich', 1980, p.13).

The Nazi breakthrough from electoral insignificance to mass following began with the 1929 referendum on the Young Plan for the rescheduling of reparations.

In alliance with the German National People's Party (DNVP) and the ex-servicemen's *Stahlhelm* organization, the National Socialists forced a plebiscite designed to reject the Young Plan. Their opposition was couched in such extreme terms that it won the support of only 12 per cent of the voters, but the campaign brought Hitler the great advantage of political respectability as an acknowledged spokesman of the 'National Opposition', and gave the Nazis a platform from which to outdo all others in their denunciation of Versailles. Furthermore, Alfred Hugenberg, the leader of the DNVP, was Germany's leading press magnate and henceforth Hitler and the National Socialists were sympathetically treated in his newspapers. That the Young Plan campaign brought the NSDAP greater electoral popularity was almost immediately evident from the provincial elections in Thuringia in December 1929, when the party trebled its previous share of the vote.

Exercise   Using the electoral statistics in document I.2 in *Documents 2* (and discussed in Unit 14), and the discussion in Roberts on pages 467–9, I want you to write four short paragraphs outlining the main changes in popular support for Germany's political parties between 1929 and 1933, relating these to economic developments and saying (if you can) which major groups in society were likely to be sources of resistance to Nazi rule. ■

Specimen answer and discussion   1   There is clear evidence for the radicalization of popular opinion with the extreme Right and Left both gaining ground. The communists were as hostile to Weimar as the NSDAP, and while the growth of Nazi support (up to mid-1932) is the most striking feature of the table, the large increase in communist votes is also notable. Obviously there were many first-time voters in this period, and these new voters may well have voted disproportionately for the Nazis who proclaimed themselves a party of youth. However, there is a close correlation between Nazi gains and DNVP losses, and we can infer that the NSDAP grew chiefly at the expense of its conservative ally and of the bourgeois liberal parties. The figures indicate that the Nazis attracted some disaffected socialists since the combined socialist and communist vote declined by about 4 per cent between 1928 and July 1932.

2   Although political allegiance was flowing away from the bourgeois conservative and nationalist parties to the Nazis, elsewhere it was fairly stable. The Catholic Centre's vote scarcely altered. Similarly, electoral support for the Left remained quite solid; though there was some erosion of the combined Left vote, the Nazis made relatively few gains among the industrial working-class constituencies of the SPD and the KDP.

3   It is tempting to see a straightforward connection between the growth of Nazi electoral support and the catastrophic slump which hit the German economy. However, the Nazis did not make their gains among those groups most affected by mass unemployment (chiefly the industrial working class) and the connections between Hitler's rise to power and the economic crisis were more indirect than is often assumed. Before the collapse of the industrial economy, major gains were made among the stricken farming communities of Protestant northern Germany. Because of falling prices, greater foreign competition and higher tax bills, many farmers faced bankruptcy and foreclosure; the Nazi party was able to mobilize their discontent and that of the independent artisans, shopkeepers and merchants of small-town Germany. The NSDAP thrived on the disappointments of all classes, but the most solidly pro-Nazi sector of the electorate was to be found

among Germany's large self-employed labour force, whether in agriculture or handicrafts.

4   I would have concluded that under free elections two 'sub-communities' – the Catholics and industrial workers – had largely lain outside the Nazi constituency, and we might therefore have supposed that they would have been sources of resistance to the Nazi state. In section 6 we will discuss the extent to which they actually were. □

3 THE NSDAP AND BUSINESS INTERESTS BEFORE 1933

The identification of Nazism with finance or monopoly capitalism was an element in the context of Hitler's rise to power, as well as providing a Soviet bloc historical orthodoxy. The response of the Left – particularly the German Communist Party – to Hitler's accession to the chancellorship was partly determined by the ideological dogma of the monopoly-capitalist manipulation of fascism which dated back to the early 1920s. The Left expected the new regime to fall apart under the weight of its internal contradictions, and adopted a fatal policy of waiting upon events (Broszat, *The Hitler State*, 1981, p.60). Even non-communist intellectuals subscribed to the general features of the dogma; in the summer of 1932, the influential Left-liberal historian, Eckart Kehr, privately described Hitler and his following as 'whores' to Fritz Thyssen, the Ruhr steel magnate, and other industrialists (Turner, *German Big Business and the Rise of Hitler*, 1985, p.351).

No historian now seriously contends that Hitler was the puppet of monopoly capitalism, and those (including East German scholars) arguing that the support of business interests was an important factor in his rise to power now do so in a much more nuanced way than was once the case. They stress the many divisions within the business community, particularly that between heavy industry (coal, iron and steel), which was highly dependent on the domestic market during Weimar, and the electrical and chemicals industries, the export record and profitability of which were much better. Heavy industry never worked to its full capacity even during Weimar's best years; its leaders favoured the economic autarky advocated by the nationalist parties, and were hostile to the Republic's social welfare policies, its compulsory wage arbitration and the influence of trade unionism in the state. Export-oriented industrialists, led by men such as Carl Duisberg of IG Farben, were much more supportive of the democratic system, favoured free trade and economic liberalism, and were prepared to co-operate with the unions. With the onset of the world economic crisis, the informal accord between 'progressive' industrialists and Weimar broke down, and an increasing number of industrialists were prepared to tolerate the NSDAP in a bourgeois coalition the purpose of which was to shore up capitalism and dismantle Weimar's welfare and labour legislation. (Geary, 'The industrial élite', 1983, pp.85–99 summarizes the arguments of those still attributing weight to the attitudes of business in Hitler's accession to power.)

H. A. Turner has argued forcibly against even the most nuanced interpretations of recent years; for him the role of business in Hitler's rise to power is simply a comprehensive myth, which has persisted because historians have preferred to 'theorize' about the relationship between capitalism and fascism, rather than engage in research. Many of his points appear unanswerable. Most employers were thoroughly hostile to the NSDAP before its electoral break-through in 1930 (which was achieved without their aid), and with good reason. Here was a plebeian, avowedly anti-capitalist party whose spokesmen put forward unorthodox fiscal and monetary policies which businessmen generally thought either ridiculous or dangerous. They looked to the liberal parties (the German People's Party and the State Party) to represent their interests; these parties received subventions from business and were, indeed, known as businessmen's parties. The NSDAP, by contrast, was a self-financed party in which money from subscriptions and newspaper sales flowed from the rank and file to the leadership.

According to Turner, economic power did not easily translate to political power under Weimar, and big business played only a secondary part in the disintegration of the Republic between the elections of 1930 and the winter of 1932–33. The major participants in setting up a regime based on presidential authority (discussed further below) were military officers, President Hindenburg's immediate advisers and representatives of the traditional aristocratic élite. The executives of Germany's great industrial corporations simply had no role in the effecting of the transition from parliamentary to presidential rule (Turner, *German Big Business*, 1985, p.341). It is true that after their near extinction in the 1930 elections, the 'businessmen's parties' were denied their customary subventions and business interests began 'a flirtation' (Turner's phrase) with the NSDAP. On their part, the Nazis tried to neutralize businessmen's understandable fears of the party programme's social radicalism, and Hitler muted his anti-Semitism when addressing business audiences for this prejudice was uncommon among leading industrialists.

The high-point of this flirtation was Hitler's address, at Thyssen's invitation, to a packed meeting of the Dusseldorf Industry Club on 26 January 1932. Hitler's appearance there should not in itself be taken as a sign of empathy or collusion between speaker and audience: the previous guest speaker had been a Social Democrat. Furthermore, Hitler did not attempt to win businessmen's support and funds with promises to curb the unions, or provide lucrative arms contracts if he came to power. Much of his speech was taken up with Social Darwinist generalities about the need for competition, which for him meant approval of the capitalist system, while, without denying his movement's 'indomitable aggressive spirit', he yet pledged it to law, order and authority. His audience was doubtless reassured by all these sentiments and it seems reasonable to assume that his respectability in the eyes of the industrial élite was enhanced. However, the speech did not initiate a Nazi campaign for financing from industrial backers (which would have greatly embarrassed the NSDAP in the electoral struggle in working-class districts). Hitler's purpose, Turner surmises, was 'to neutralize big business, not to bring its leaders behind the NSDAP or to exploit its financial resources for his party' (Turner, *German Big Business*, 1985, p.217). When Hitler contested the presidency in March/April 1932, of those major industrialists taking a political stance, the most prominent joined a committee to re-elect Hindenburg, while others supported the *Stahlhelm* candidate. Only two, Emil Kirdorf and Thyssen, endorsed Hitler. Thyssen was the only capitalist of note who became a loyal adherent of Nazism before 1933.

The 'flirtation' of big business with the NSDAP did not last beyond the early summer of 1932. Businessmen generally supported the authoritarian Cabinet of Franz von Papen, which the Nazis attacked vociferously, and in the later months of 1932 it seemed that the socially radical elements in National Socialism were once more coming to the fore. In November, the Nazis lost a great deal of middle-class and élite support when they allied with the communists in promoting the Berlin transport strike.

Turner argues that most of the support for the Nazis from the business community came from lesser industrialists, whose businesses were outside the cartels and price-setting arrangements of 'organized capitalism', and poorly supported by the great national business associations. Such men did not feel threatened by Nazi denunciations of the *Konzerne* and they were often attracted by the ideas of deficit spending and the corporatist organization of industry which the Nazis promoted. It was among such lesser businessmen that the Nazis made inroads before the accession to power, but they had no part in the backstairs intrigues that jobbed Hitler into office. It is an indication of the modest financial resources they afforded Hitler that by the end of 1932 his party was bankrupt from incessant electioneering. Hitler's appointment came just when relations between his movement and the most powerful sectors of the business community had reached their lowest ebb. The peak organization of German industrialists actually attempted to dissuade Hindenburg from according Hitler a prominent place in the new Cabinet formed at the end of January 1933.

4 *THE ACCESSION TO POWER*

The collapse of democracy and the slide into authoritarianism began during the chancellorship of Heinrich Brüning (March 1930 to May 1932). His Cabinet did not enjoy a *Reichstag* majority and Brüning relied on President von Hindenburg's constitutional authority to rule by emergency decree. This routine use of quasi-dictatorial powers made authoritarian solutions to the simultaneous crises in the political system and the economy more and more attractive. The elections Brüning called for September 1930 simply compounded his problems; the number of Nazi deputies increased from 12 to 107, giving Hitler, the notorious opponent of parliamentary democracy, the prospect of office. Brüning rejected all efforts to form a broadly-based administration and the *Reichstag*'s functions were reduced to tolerating his Cabinet, which grievously undermined public confidence in parliamentary processes. When confronted in November 1931 with clear evidence of Nazi plans for a terrorist regime after a *coup*, the government and the judiciary demonstrated their own inability to defend democracy by failing either to prosecute Hitler for treason, or deport him as an undesirable stateless person. (Hitler did not acquire German citizenship until February 1932, when he was appointed to the nominal position of government councillor for Brunswick by the National Socialist Ministry of the state.)

Government by decree also enabled the ultra-conservative clique around Hindenburg and the army leadership to play major roles in political intrigues. Nazi demands for rearmament and 'military preparedness' harmonized with the professional interests and ideology of the officer corps, some of whom wanted to use the SA as a border militia to supplement the limited numbers of the professional *Reichswehr*. The fact that, by 1932, the army leadership was willing to countenance Hitler's claim to office was an important, even decisive, factor in his accession to power.

After his re-election as President in April 1932, Hindenburg dismissed Brüning at the end of May. Acting on the advice of the *Reichswehr* Minister, General von Schleicher, he appointed to the chancellorship Franz von Papen, who had no popular base whatever and whose Cabinet of aristocratic 'gentlemen' was avidly anti-republican. Papen hoped to use Hindenburg's prestige to overthrow the Constitution and install an authoritarian, corporate state. He looked for Hitler's support in this, and as a concession to the Nazi leader lifted the ban on the SA which had been imposed in many states. There ensued a sharp rise in the number of political brawls and murders; in the most infamous incident seventeen people died in the mayhem caused by a Nazi march through the working-class district of Altona on 17 July. Lifting the ban on the SA did not achieve its ulterior political objective of securing Hitler's co-operation; indeed, with cool effrontery and their customary venom, the Nazis began to defend the prerogatives of parliament and to attack Papen's presidential 'Cabinet of barons'. So in a reckless attempt to break out of his political isolation by a display of authoritarian self-confidence, Papen (with the support of the President and the army) staged a *coup d'état* against the SPD-led Prussian government of Otto Braun. On the pretext that the *Land* ministry was incapable of maintaining public order, he appointed himself Reich Commissioner and thus gained control of Prussia's substantial police forces. The Prussian administration was purged and reorganized in a foretaste of the Nazi *Gleichschaltung* ('co-ordination') of the state apparatus in 1933.

Papen acted against Prussia during the political interlude that followed the dissolution of the *Reichstag* immediately after his appointment and its reconvening at the end of August. The July elections had given Hitler, as leader of the largest party, a strengthened claim to the chancellorship, although even with the nationalists he could not command a majority, and their common 'Front' had been temporarily fractured by running different candidates for the presidency.

However frightening the prospect of a Hitler government, scarcely any of the political parties would tolerate Papen who was anathema to the democrats and too insubstantial a figure to fill the power vacuum created by the deadlock of social and political forces. He suffered a massive vote of no confidence when the *Reichstag* re-assembled at the end of August, but avoided resignation by calling fresh elections. In the interim, he had attempted to incorporate the National Socialists within the government, and control their seemingly inexorable advance, by persuading Hindenburg to offer Hitler the vice-chancellorship in August. Hitler would accept nothing less than the chancellorship; indeed, in the words of the official communiqué of his conversation with Hindenburg, he 'demanded the same sort of position for himself as Mussolini had possessed after the March on Rome' (quoted in Eyck, *A History of the Weimar Republic*, 1957, p.427).

The November election results did at least suggest that the momentum of the Nazi party's vote-winning machine had been halted, but gave no reason to believe that Papen's position was any more tenable within the existing Constitution. Hindenburg regretfully dismissed him on 2 December, before the new *Reichstag* assembled, and appointed Schleicher Chancellor. As *Reichswehr* Minister, Schleicher had been an indispensable conduit of influence between the military and the government, and was responsible for securing the army's support for the *coup* against Prussia. He entertained installing a military-dominated, populist regime (such as existed in Pilsudski's Poland) by allying with the Nazi left-wing and the non-communist labour movements. So long as Hitler demanded the chancellorship in a presidential Cabinet, Schleicher's plan could be realized only after a split in the NSDAP, and that seemed quite likely: many of the rank and file were fed up with Hitler's intransigence, depressed by election losses and were leaving the party. The scheme was scotched by the fatal indecision of Gregor Strasser, the leader of the Nazi Left, whose nerve failed him when it came to promoting a mass defection from Hitler. In an extraordinary display of ferocious will, the Führer re-imposed his authority on his fragmenting party, and in the process abolished its central administrative agency, the Political Organization, which Strasser had dominated. The *Reichstag* refrained from passing an immediate vote of no confidence in Schleicher, and the Christmas recess gave him a respite in which to seek either an extra-constitutional solution to the political crisis or an accommodation with a coalition within the *Reichstag*. Even before his appointment, Schleicher had been negotiating with Hitler over the terms on which the Nazis would enter government. Hitler's patience in hanging out for the highest executive office was finally rewarded on 30 January: Schleicher had suggested to Hindenburg that the Constitution be broken, but this the President would not countenance. A constitutional alternative was made possible by the revival of the 'Front' between the Nazis and the DNVP and by Alfred Hugenberg's publicly declared willingness to serve under Hitler. Like Papen, who acted as the President's agent in the final political crisis, Hugenberg deluded himself that Hitler could be constrained within a coalition. After Schleicher's entire ministry had resigned, Hindenburg appointed Hitler Chancellor in a Cabinet numerically dominated by Nationalists and with Papen enjoying, on paper, wide powers as Vice-Chancellor. Hitler had only two National Socialist colleagues in the Cabinet, Hermann Goering and Wilhelm Frick, but since Goering was appointed to the Prussian Ministry of the Interior, formidable police powers fell into National Socialist hands throughout the greater part of Germany.

Though he had never disguised his intention of destroying the parliamentary republic, Hitler's accession to power was formally constitutional. He had calculated that his revolutionary purpose would be more effectively achieved by observing legal formalities; even when he became Chancellor he preferred to postpone a ban on the KPD until he had secured a *Reichstag* majority to enact a draconic Enabling Law. To many on the Left it appeared that the real beneficiaries of 30 January were the reactionary Nationalists who, it seemed, had made a 'prisoner' of Hitler.

4.1   The Nazi seizure of power

Hitler consolidated a one-party regime in two stages. Firstly, during February, March and April of 1933 he used the police and the SA to crush the left-wing parties and the trade unions, and then he compelled the middle-class and Nationalist parties to renounce their political independence. The Nazi consolidation of power followed the established tactic of legality; one of Hitler's first acts was to persuade his Cabinet to hold fresh elections which would provide a majority to enact the legal instruments of the National Socialist *Gleichschaltung*. After the *Reichstag* was dissolved, a presidential decree (actually drafted by a previous government) 'For the Protection of the German People' was used to suppress the left-wing press and political meetings on the grounds of 'disseminating false information' which 'endangered vital interests of the state'. The Prussian

Landtag was dissolved against the wishes of its majority, and Goering continued the purging of pro-republican civil servants, counsellors and police chiefs which Papen had begun.

The Prussian police were given *carte blanche* to use arms against the government's opponents and ordered to co-operate with the 'National' paramilitary organizations (the SA, SS and the *Stahlhelm*) whose members were, in late February, enrolled as auxiliary police volunteers. The Communist and Social Democratic parties in Prussia were quickly driven into a half-clandestine existence by police raids, newspaper bans and unchecked Nazi terrorization. There was some juridical mitigation of Goering's draconic measures by the Reich and Prussian Supreme Courts, but little to hinder the creation of extraordinarily favourable electoral advantages for the governing coalition by a combination of force and a near monopoly of the means of mass communication. The constitution of the Reich Broadcasting Corporation, in which the government had a dominant position, allowed Hitler and Goebbels to make masterly use of radio for domestic propaganda. Furthermore, Hitler was able to exploit the prestige of his office at a meeting of leading industrialists on 20 February 1933 when, in a reversal of recent experience, a substantial election fund for the Nazis was secured (Broszat, *The Hitler State*, 1981, pp.60–9).

On 27 February 1933, the Nazis' intimidation of their opponents was aided and accelerated by the burning of the *Reichstag*. The incident seemingly confirmed the existence of a communist insurrectionary conspiracy, which the Nazis had often invoked and in which they may have believed. All KPD deputies and leading officials in Prussia were immediately arrested and the party's papers banned indefinitely. On 28 February, a presidential decree introduced a far-reaching state of emergency which ended the hitherto constitutional rights of personal freedom, freedom of the press and of association, and protection of property and homes, and authorized the Reich government to exercise the powers once reserved for the *Länder* governments. This improvised decree typified the *ad hoc* process of establishing the despotism of the police state: it did not put forward any clear legal definition of changes in the law and in the powers of authority, and instead made do with the general abolition of existing basic and constitutional rights (Broszat, 1981, p.71). The decree forced Communist Party officials who had escaped capture either to emigrate or go underground and led to a wave of arrests among the intellectual and literary Left.

Given the circumstances it is unsurprising that the election of 5 March secured for the governing coalition a majority (51.8 per cent) of the votes, with the NSDAP itself receiving 43.9 per cent. Indeed, the number who resisted intimidation and were not swayed by government propaganda seems remarkable; despite its persecution, the KPD polled 4.8 million votes and the SPD's vote scarcely changed. However, the election underwrote the decisive preponderance of the NSDAP within the coalition: because of the arrest of communist deputies, the Nazis commanded a *Reichstag* majority irrespective of their coalition partners who were now treated with disdain. Up to the election, Hitler had been careful to speak of a 'National' government. The results inaugurated the process of National Socialist revolution, 'which although it was directed and legalized from above, was first made possible through pressure and terror from below' (Broszat, 1981, p.77).

The unguided revolutionary impulse coming 'from below' took the form of the occupation of town halls, newspaper and trade-union offices, banks, courts and other public buildings by SA and SS detachments who compelled the dismissal or detention of 'unreliable' or Jewish officials. A wave of enforced vacations and resignations swept through local government and speeded the 'co-ordination' of the *Länder*. On their own initiative, the auxiliary police hunted down communists and other known opponents of National Socialism and the SA organized boycotts of departmental stores and Jewish businesses. Attempts by the Nazis' Nationalist allies to persuade Hitler to restrain these excesses were rebuffed: he told Papen that he would permit nobody 'to deflect him from his mission' of 'destroying and exterminating Marxism', and this was to be the standard justification for the subversion of constitutional and legal order (Broszat, 1981, p.79). The first concentration camps for political prisoners, run by the SA and SS outside normal police and juridical control, sprang up in Dachau, Oranienburg and elsewhere.

To orchestrate the revolution, Hitler created a Reich Ministry of Information and Propaganda headed by Goebbels. He promptly stage-managed the first great state ceremony of the new regime with the convening of the *Reichstag* on 21 March at the garrison church in Potsdam where the Hohenzollerns were buried. In contrast to the uncontrolled violence on the streets, this occasion established the regime's legitimate descent from the Prussian authoritarian state. The youthful Chancellor and the eighty-five-year-old Field Marshall exchanged a handshake on the church steps which was subsequently reproduced a million-fold on postcards and posters. Inside, the Kaiser's seat was kept empty, but behind it sat the Crown Prince in full-dress uniform. The Protestant God was called on to sanctify the union of old and new (Fest, *Hitler*, 1977, pp.601–2). It was an occasion when Hitler and National Socialism represented themselves as the bearers of traditional German virtues with, apparently, great emotional effect. A host of new members – 'the March converts' – flocked into the NSDAP at this time, many no doubt climbing aboard the bandwagon, but others persuaded that the movement stood for the reassertion of national pride, Christian values, as well as recovery from economic misery.

The only task of the *Reichstag*, whose formal proceedings began on 23 March, was to enact the Enabling Law which empowered the government to take the legal measures, including constitutional changes, necessary 'to relieve the distress' of the German people. This measure required a two-thirds majority, and could not be passed without the support of the Liberal parties (already weakened by rank-and-file defections to the NSDAP) and the Centre. A majority of Catholics was persuaded to support the Law by promises to protect confessional schools, to preserve good relations with the Vatican, and by Hitler's publicly expressed regard for the Catholic and Evangelical Churches 'as among the most important factors of our nationality' (Broszat, 1981, p.83). The Centre deputies also allowed themselves to be swayed by the Law's limiting provisions: Clause 5 stated it was to lose its validity 'if the present federal cabinet is replaced by another'. This meant – or should have meant – that the Law could only be applied by the government formed in January in which the Nationalists predominated, and would lapse if the government's composition was changed.

The Law was of fundamental importance in securing the collaboration of non-party civil servants, judges and prosecutors in the National Socialist revolution. These were men of highly legalistic training and strong attachments to the status hierarchy and social order. The Law satisfied their professional commitment to the *Rechtsstaat* – the legal state – and secured for the Nazi revolution expertise in spheres where the NSDAP was weak. The legality of the seizure of power rested on these alliances and compromises with non-Nazi office and influence holders and formed a marked contrast to the Bolshevik revolution (Bracher, *The German Dictatorship*, 1971, p.342).

Since the communist deputies were either in hiding or under arrest (and their party effectively proscribed), the only opposition to the Law came from the SPD. The days of its legal existence were numbered: its combat organization, *Reichsbanner*, was banned in several states and, after the SPD had suffered dissension between those who wished to go into emigration to fight the regime and those who wished to continue within Germany, a directive of 22 June outlawed the SPD. The socialist trade unions attempted to accommodate themselves with the regime, but were repressed. Other political parties and organizations were soon wound up or banned. The Liberal parties – which had been insignificant for some time – dissolved themselves. The organizational independence of the Nationalists was ended by defections to the NSDAP, police harassment and Nazi concessions allowing former DNVP deputies to be included in the NSDAP parliamentary group and the *Stahlhelm* to merge with the SA. Hugenberg, who had grossly over-estimated his ability to 'contain' Hitler and had lost the support of Hindenburg, resigned his posts of Minister of Economics and Agriculture on 26 June. The Centre, whose membership and electoral support had been so solid up to March, was gravely weakened by the fact that the Catholic hierarchy began to negotiate directly with the government in order to preserve the position of the Church; as part of the new Reich Concordat the Vatican agreed to forbid any political activity on the part of the German clergy. Now that it was disowned at the top, large numbers deserted political Catholicism for the first time. The Nazis' call for the dissolution of the Centre party was acceded to on 5 July. On 14 July, a salvo of decrees battered the remnants of political pluralism: the NSDAP was declared the sole legal party and anyone undertaking political activity outside its ranks was liable to three years' penal servitude; the assets of the SPD, KPD and political and Jewish expatriates were confiscated. Rule by charismatic leadership became the fundamental principle of the state and dictated the formalities of everyday official life; civil servants were instructed to employ the Hitler salute. Henceforth, after taking major decisions (such as leaving the League of Nations in October) the regime used plebiscites to proclaim the popular legitimacy of its actions.

4.2   Liquidating the revolution

Simultaneously with the establishment of one-party rule Hitler was calling for the winding up of the revolution. He told a meeting of Reich Governors on 6 July: 'Revolution is not a permanent condition . . . The ideas in our programme do not commit us to behaving like fools and destroying everything, but to realising our conceptions wisely and carefully . . .' (quoted in Broszat, 1981, p.204). What 'programme' did he have in mind and why was the continuation of the revolution a threat to it? It is reasonable to assume that he was thinking of the intimately connected goals of rearmament and economic recovery, and probably too of the aggressive foreign policy for which these were the instruments. (Evidence for this is offered in section 8.) The spontaneous turbulence of the revolution 'from below', and its frequent violence, threatened these goals by arousing foreign hostility, and thus the possibility of concerted international action (such as an economic boycott) against Germany. Furthermore, the militants' demand for 'The Second (social) Revolution' to complement the seizure of political power, and their brutal indifference to law and order, profoundly disturbed the businessmen and civil servants whose co-operation was indispensable for the realization of Hitler's 'programme'. Germany's professional military establishment, too, was increasingly distrustful of the pretensions of the SA under Ernst Röhm to set itself up as the rival of the *Reichswehr*, and even to submerge the professional army in a mass revolutionary 'People's Army'. Although the officer corps generally welcomed the SA as a supplement to Germany's exiguous forces, subordination to the likes of Röhm was a thoroughly abhorrent prospect. In this dispute, Hitler – who wanted a mass army but under total professional control – sided with the generals.

In July and August 1933, a series of measures was taken to discipline the SA and dismantle its 'private' concentration camps and torture chambers. The auxiliary police were disbanded and, in Prussia, a prosecuting office set up to investigate and punish SA and SS illegalities. The Secret State Police (*Geheime Staats Polizei*), formed by Goering out of the old Prussian political police, were given a major role in suppressing SA terror, initially under the auspices of the Ministry of Justice and Central State Prosecutor's office, although the political police was to grow into an autonomous empire in a way which typified the accretion of un-coordinated nuclei of power.

At first Hitler hoped for a compromise between the SA radicals and those who wished to consolidate the Nazi regime. On 1 December a law was promulgated 'to ensure the Unity of the Party and the State' which, in theory, conciliated the radicals. The NSDAP was designated the 'bearer of the concept of the German state' and made a public corporation, and therefore was to be publicly funded. The party deputy, Rudolph Hess, and Röhm, as SA Chief of Staff, were made members of the government (although without portfolios). In practice the law was highly ambiguous and failed to define party–state relationships satisfactorily. Although the party was elevated in theory, the real effect of the law was to strengthen the central-state apparatus. At a conference of *Gauleiter* in February 1934, Hitler defined the essential tasks of the party as educating the people, supporting the government and helping it carry out its measures, and he immediately linked this definition of the party as an auxiliary of the government to a condemnation of 'those people who maintained that the revolution was not finished . . .' He then 'described what difficulty he had in filling all the posts with the right people and went on to say that we had people in the movement whose conception of revolution was nothing but a permanent state of chaos' (Noakes and Pridham, eds, *Nazism, 1919–1945*, 1984, p.236).

Soon after this meeting Hitler determined to crush the SA leadership. This was apparently linked with the allaying of foreign apprehensions about his regime for, on 21 February, he confided to Anthony Eden that he intended to reduce the SA by two-thirds and insure that the remaining formations received neither weapons nor military training (Fest, *Hitler*, 1977, p.676). Rumours of an intended SA *coup* were circulated, as well as defamations of the moral characters of Röhm (a homosexual) and his associates, in order to prepare party and public opinion for a purge. In close collaboration with the *Reichswehr*, which supplied weapons and transport, SS detachments shot Röhm and dozens of other high-ranking SA leaders on 30 June/1 July. Hitler also took the opportunity to settle political scores with old opponents: Schleicher, Gregor Strasser, and reactionaries who had deserted him during the 1923 putsch were murdered, together with an unknown number of victims of 'private' feuds.

The purge both demonstrated and ensured that Hitler exercised untrammelled power. His erstwhile conservative allies were now quite insignificant: Papen was placed under house arrest, and later relieved of the Vice-Chancellorship and given a diplomatic post in Vienna. A terse law of 3 July legalized the murders as 'justifiable acts of self-defence by the state'; on 13 July Hitler was declared 'Supreme Judge of the German people'. The death of Hindenburg on 2 August allowed Hitler to assume formally the roles of Chancellor and Head of State; shortly after this the army swore a personal oath of loyalty to the Führer. The purge also quickened the process by which Hitler's public image and popularity were dissociated from that of the Nazi Party. The Führer's personal standing in the eyes of the great majority of Germans was, all the evidence suggests, greatly enhanced by his sanctioning of the state murders. These met the traditional bourgeois demands for 'peace and quiet' and 'law and order' which the unruliness, arbitrary violence, and public outrages of the SA had threatened (Kershaw, *The Hitler 'Myth'*, 1987, p.93).

4.3   The reversion to legality and the 'dualism' of the police and SS

Despite Hitler's untrammelled power, neither the purging of party veterans nor acts of blatant, murderous illegality characterized Nazi rule between 1934 and 1939. Unlike Stalin, Hitler did not massacre old comrades with whom he disagreed and he retained their fidelity virtually to the end. After the Röhm purge, the regime preferred to pursue its internal opponents (of whom very few were from the political or social élites) by legal procedures and through the judicial system which it had inherited. The SA's terrorist violence against domestic foes ceased to be a regular part of the regime's *modus operandi*, although the notorious *Kristallnacht* (described below) was an important exception. True, the courts were now applying draconic legislation which defined treason and subversion in extraordinarily wide terms. Special Courts with streamlined procedures were created to try infringements against the *Reichstag* Fire Decree and a 'Decree on malicious gossip' which made even spoken criticism of the regime an offence punishable by penal servitude. Between 1934 and 1937, as a result of the use of judicial proceedings, the number of political prisoners detained in the regular prison system was greater than those held by administrative fiat in the concentration camps (Broszat, 1981, p.302). The camps were reduced in number, their staff even made liable to proceedings for maltreating political prisoners, but they were nevertheless firmly institutionalized and the Gestapo was able to decide for itself what constituted 'political' acts. Consequently there arose a persistent dualism in the prosecution of political 'offenders', with the coexistence of the traditional legal system, derived from the authoritarian *Reichtsstaat*, and an improvised system uncontrolled by the regular organs of state government and justice whose dubious legality came from 'emergency' decrees. There were numerous parallels to this dualism in the Nazi state, which many have discerned as its basic characteristic.

5 *THE PARTY AND THE STATE AFTER 1934*

The Nazis themselves, and later historians and political scientists, sometimes asked: What is the sovereign power in National Socialist Germany? On what theory does its sovereignty rest? These questions are important because they lead us to ask whether the regime ever established the institutional conditions for its peaceful persistence. Much of the reckless instability of Nazi Germany, it has been argued, resulted from the absence of any impersonal and rule-governed authority structure, which in the modern state is normally identified with a public office or a complex of offices and institutions. Sovereign power was invested in the Führer, who embodied the will of the people, and the legitimizing principle of this sovereignty was charisma – the idea that the leader was endowed with super-human qualities which emanated from him and pervaded the state, party and people (Neumann, *Behemoth*, 1942, p.75). Charismatic rule is an irrational and inherently unstable mode of domination. It usually originates during political crises, and is difficult to prolong and renew without recurrent crises which justify the leader's exalted position and allow him to display his exceptional qualities. One of its consequences for Hitler's Germany was that collective decision-making rapidly fell into disuse; there were seventy-two Cabinet meetings in 1933, only four in 1936. Government came to resemble a feudal court, where a minister's real power depended on his access to the Führer.

We have here a schematic and partial explanation for the 'adventurism' of Hitler's foreign policy, particularly after changes in the Foreign Office and High Command in early 1938 removed the restraining influences of conservative diplomats and generals. But we can supplement this explanatory sketch by considering how relations between the state and the party exacerbated the instability of charismatic rule.

Germany had a strong state tradition which the Nazi dictatorship could, and to a certain degree did, exploit to secure its rule. The Italian Fascist regime had developed the theory of the totalitarian state which the Nazi leadership initially appropriated as the official doctrine of the new Germany. On several occasions in 1933 Hitler spoke of establishing the 'totality' of the state and, in November, Goebbels declared: 'The goal of the revolution must be a totalitarian state pervading all spheres of public life' (quoted in Neumann, 1942, p.47). But totalitarian theory had not figured in Hitler's political conceptions before 1933; in *Mein Kampf* he rejected unconditional obedience to the state, which he described as only a means for the preservation of the racial community. He affirmed a people's 'biological' right to resist in the interests of its own self-preservation. 'The ruling power may use a thousand so-called "legal" means, yet the instinct of self-preservation of the oppressed is always the most sublime justification for their fighting with all weapons . . . Human rights break state rights' (quoted in Neumann, 1942, p.58).

Hitler is not everyone's idea of a champion of human rights, and there is a strong temptation to dismiss such utterances as mere verbiage. We must not, however, accord consistency to Hitler's foreign and racist policies and deny that quality to his other political notions. As a racist Social Darwinist he valued the 'dynamic' virtues he discerned in the *Volk* and the movement above the 'static' formalism of the state and its bureaucracy. It can be argued that Hitler espoused totalitarian theory during the seizure and consolidation of power only because it met the practical needs of the moment: the doctrine was useful in restraining the SA, and in legitimizing the co-ordination of the *Länder*, and the unification and concentration of legislative power in the Reich. After the liquidation of the revolution in June 1934 Hitler discarded totalitarian theory; at the NSDAP Congress of September 1934 he asserted the sovereignty of the movement as the authentic representative of the racial community: 'It is not the state which commands us but rather we who command the state. It was not the state which created us but rather we who created our own state' (Noakes and Pridham, eds, *Nazism 1919–1945*, 1984, p.236).

It is of course arguable that Hitler's purpose, when addressing party militants, was morale boosting. Many individuals were disgruntled by the fact that, after years of political struggle, they had not been given public office, and they had seen bureaucrats retain their positions merely by joining the NSDAP; indeed, many civil servants had not even made this nominal conversion. But evidence for consistency in Hitler's thinking is provided by his party address in 1935, when he reiterated the idea of the state merely being an instrument for the organization of the *Volk*, whose vital will was given immediate expression in the Nazi movement. He linked this 'fundamental principle of National Socialist theory' with a threat to hand over functions for which the state bureaucracy was unfitted to other institutions (Noakes and Pridham, eds, 1984, p.237).

Hitler's address belied the unity of state and party which the decree of December 1933 had theoretically established and, in practice, there was constant tension between the sovereignty claims of the NSDAP and the state apparatus. In principle, the party was, after 1934, assigned the functions of politically training and educating the people, and preparing them psychologically for war, while administration was left to the state. This division of roles foundered on a number of factors. As we have noted, the Nazi leadership was able to take over the existing machinery of the state intact and secure the co-operation of the bureaucracy. Purges of the higher administration under the Law for the Restoration of the Professional Civil Service (April 1933) mainly affected Jews and fell far short of 'Nazification'. Consequently a traditional state bureaucracy, with its legally trained personnel, coexisted with a party whose organization and collective outlook was quite different. This coexistence was made chronically antagonistic because there was no means of internally integrating the party itself, and after the seizure of power its component parts either infiltrated the state apparatus or set up quasi-official agencies which rivalled those of the state. The *Gauleiter*, for example, acquired senior state offices but at the same time shook off the last vestiges of control by the central party organization. Like feudal barons, they answered only to their liege lord Hitler. In some instances, this penetration of the state by party bodies resulted from an individual's personal union of party and state officers: Goebbels, who became Minister for Propaganda, and Walther Darré, who headed the party's agrarian organization and became Minister for Agriculture, are two examples (Noakes, 'The Nazi Party and the Third Reich', 1980, p.15). But in many instances party and state institutions existed alongside each other, with overlapping competences that gave rise to institutional confusion and a chaos of personal rivalries (Noakes and Pridham, eds, 1984, pp.203–4). We have already noted how the SS, a party organization, usurped some of the functions and powers of the police. During the war it encroached on those of the army. Mention should also be made of the rival state and party bodies influencing the conduct of foreign affairs.

Hitler may have promoted what has been called 'institutional Darwinism' (Schoenbaum, *Hitler's Social Revolution*, 1966, p.206) because he believed that only through organizational struggle could the fittest to rule survive. But it also served two distinct political purposes: firstly, it reinforced his position as the sole co-ordinating authority in the government of the Reich. Secondly, the fact that the totalitarian movement, with its hard core of committed racists, was not incorporated into the 'Establishment' meant that it could act as a goad for the civil service, and its dynamic fanaticism could be held in reserve for the more radical policies adopted in 1938 (such as the anti-Jewish pogrom on 9 November). From the point of view of our course, institutional Darwinism, and what has been called the 'shapelessness' of the Nazi state, were of fundamental importance because they were preconditions for an unrestrained will to war from 1938 and the horrific mass murders which occurred during the war. As Broszat concludes in his remarkable study of the Third Reich's internal structure: '. . . the more the organizational jungle of the National Socialist regime spread out the less chance there was of restoring any rationally organized and consistent policy-making and governmental process.' He goes on to argue that the development of Nazi policy cannot just be interpreted as 'steering towards and carrying out prefabricated long-term ideological aims in small doses . . . The disruption of the unified bureaucratic state order, the growing formlessness and arbitrariness of legislation and of decision-making, played a part in speeding up the process of radicalization which was every bit as important as any ideological fixity of purpose' (Broszat, *The Hitler State*, 1981, pp.358–9).

6 *ECONOMIC RECOVERY AND THE NAZI ECONOMY*

The economic recovery of Germany fell into two phases – 1933 to 1936, and 1936 to 1939 – distinguished by the role of rearmament in promoting revival and growth. In both phases, state expenditure and investment were basic instruments of economic policy, but during the first, spending on the military represented a relatively modest proportion of government outlays. During the second, spending on rearmament, and on projects intended to ensure Germany's strategic self-sufficiency, became the dynamo of economic expansion. (Overy, *The Nazi Economic Recovery, 1932–1938*, 1982, provides a clear summary of economic recovery.) This second phase, inaugurated by the 1936 Four-Year Plan to put the economy on a war footing, is discussed in more detail in section 8; here I will describe the overall features of German economic revival which made it a different process from recovery in Britain and elsewhere.

The Nazi Party was generally ill-prepared for power in terms of specific policies, but during 1932 it established the broad outlines of an economic programme to restore production and employment, and finance rearmament. In terms of Germany's place in the international economy, the programme's main objective was autarky (or economic self-sufficiency) within a 'large economic area' (*Grosswirtschaftsraum*), dominated by Germany and protected by tariff barriers.

The latter idea had a long pedigree in German economic nationalism and closely resembled the plans for *Mitteleuropa* which had been a key German war aim in 1914 (Noakes and Pridham, eds, 1984, p.260; see also Unit 6). The project had been given renewed vitality by the collapse of the international economy and the emergence of protected trading blocs in the British Empire, Japan and the United States of America.

With respect to the domestic economy, the Nazis planned greater state intervention and a policy of reflation by deficit-spending through a major series of public works. The Papen and Schleicher governments had, we should note, put forward similar 'work-creation' proposals and the coalition formed in January contented itself with continuing a programme launched by Schleicher. This resulted in 600 million marks being allocated to public contracts for agricultural improvement, and house and street building. While Hugenberg remained Minister of Economics, no purely National Socialist measures to deal with unemployment were implemented. His chief concern was to relieve the plight of German farmers, particularly the large estate owners, on whose behalf a ban on the foreclosure of farms for debt and increased agrarian tariffs were introduced.

One of Hitler's main purposes during the spring and summer of 1933 was to keep the economy out of the hands of the SA and to reassure financiers and industrialists that the National Socialist revolution would leave the capitalist system basically untouched. When, in early June, a programme was enacted to supplement the work-creation scheme, this was done after talks with leading industrialists, though these discussions did not allay their many reservations about the Nazi proposals for the economy. A billion marks was provided to finance public building works – including the construction of the autobahns – and to subsidize certain private sector buildings, while tax concessions were given to domestic machinery producers. Various measures reflected Nazi ideology and the government's obligations to the Nazi rank and file: women were encouraged to leave the labour market through marriage loans and, in the provision of work for the unemployed, SA and SS members enjoyed priority. From the summer of 1933, the regime turned to tackling unemployment with the frenetic energy and in the style that had brought National Socialism to power. As in other spheres, propaganda – the art of political rhetoric in mass society – was as important as the substantive content of policy. The campaign against unemployment served to divert the party rank and file from the incompleteness of the National Socialist revolution; it mobilized many non-Nazis behind the new regime and offered a kind of compensation for the destruction of civil liberties and trade unions (Broszat, *The Hitler State*, 1981, p.137).

A long-term objective of Nazi economic policies was the establishment of a *Wehrwirtschaft* or 'military economy'. On 8 February 1933, Hitler told his Cabinet that 'Every publicly sponsored measure to create unemployment had to be considered from the point of view of whether it was necessary with respect to rendering the German people again capable of bearing arms for military service. This had to be the dominant thought, always and everywhere' (Noakes and Pridham, eds, 1984, p.263). Although this certainly expressed Hitler's intentions, the circumstances of the early years of Nazi rule meant that it was impossible to pursue rearmament with such fixity of purpose. An initial political priority was the re-absorption of the unemployed for which the defence industries, being capital-intensive, were ill suited. (Besides, the army, which was enlarged after

1933 but remained a voluntary force until 1935, simply could not have coped with a huge input of weapons.)

The labour-intensive industries were building and construction, agriculture, and domestic and personal services. Between 1933 and 1936, tax concessions to farmers and businessmen to encourage them to take on labour, government investment in construction projects, and subsidies for the employment of domestic servants, were among the most important in the 'package' of measures designed to reduce unemployment. The numbers employed in construction, for example, grew from 0.666 million in 1933 to 2 million in 1936 (Overy, *The Nazi Economic recovery, 1932–1938*, 1982, p.51). Furthermore, the government promoted two measures to stimulate technological development and rapid growth in areas where the German economy had performed poorly since 1918; these were electrification and motorization. Though German engineers had pioneered both fields, during the 1920s European competitors had caught up with and outstripped their German rivals. (France, with a smaller population, had nearly twice as many motor vehicles as Germany in 1930.) In April 1933, the German government abolished motor-tax for new cars, and took several other measures to increase the production and purchase of motor vehicles. These included a savings stamp scheme for the Volkswagen, which was designed on Hitler's orders in 1934 to promote private motoring. In practice, the stagnation of working-class real incomes between 1933 and 1939 was a major barrier to mass motor-car ownership and the most important element of the *Motorisierung* policy was the construction of 3,000 kilometres of autobahn.

The policies pursued from 1933 greatly increased the powers of the state over the economy and initiated the process by which 'politics' established its primacy over economics. The regulation of the economy which the Nazis introduced, without following any preconceived plan, effectively superseded the capitalist system in several essentials by 1938. True, private property rights were guaranteed by the Nazi state which returned some state and municipal property to the private sector. But though the means of production remained legally in private hands, the freedoms of contract normally enjoyed by employers and employed in capitalist societies were severely curtailed, and the market was displaced as a key regulative institution by state agencies or private agencies endowed with new powers by the state. For example, a statute of July 1933 introduced compulsory cartelization into an already highly cartelized economy. Associations to maintain prices and, if necessary, restrict capacity and output thereby received official sanction, and many marginal independent producers were driven out of business (Neumann, *Behemoth*, 1942, pp.216–8). Obligatory labour service for young men was introduced in 1935 and the state's power to direct labour greatly extended in June 1938. Employers lost their right to sack workers – for after 1934 dismissals had to be sanctioned by the Labour Exchanges – and wage ceilings were imposed to stop employees selling their labour to the highest bidder and to control inflation. To compensate labour for wage restraint and protect living standards, the prices of consumer goods and services were decided administratively after 1936, rather than by market forces; food prices, rents, professional and school fees, transport rates, cinema charges – all now had to be authorized by a Federal Commissioner whose rulings were enforced by severe penalties (p.250). The compulsory limitation of dividends and strict foreign exchange controls were further encroachments on the freedoms normally enjoyed in a capitalist market system. Indeed, it has been argued that the state's panoply of economic controls brought the economy 'closer in character to [that] of Stalin's Russia than to those of the capitalist West' (Overy, *The Nazi Economic Recovery, 1932–1938*, 1982, p.66).

We cannot push this comparison too far, because the Nazis introduced nothing approaching the central economic planning discussed in Unit 16, and they pursued their objectives of recovery and rearmament by *ad hoc* methods and agencies. The most important of the state's powers in terms of stimulating recovery was its command of investment. The severity of Germany's economic collapse had been largely due to the outflow of foreign investments made in the 1920s, and the Nazi government was determined that the economy would not again be exposed to the vagaries of international financing. Between 1933 and 1938, 45 per cent of gross investment was paid for by government funds, and a good deal of nominally private investment was controlled and directed by the state. Firms were compelled to maintain high levels of internal investment from the undistributed profits of their businesses; the banks lost their former role as the financiers of industry and the private investment market virtually disappeared. Chiefly as a result of very high levels of public investment, state spending accounted for 33 per cent of GNP in 1938, as against only 17 per cent in 1932. The Nazis preferred to work with, rather than against, private enterprise but, where and when private corporations would not co-operate with their plans, the state set up rival institutions which were fiefs of the NSDAP. Such was the case, for example, with the Hermann Goering steel works created in 1937 to process low-grade native ores, a task the private steel trusts would not undertake because it was uneconomic. The government compelled private industry to contribute to the financing of the Goering works. Within a short time, this 'gangster organization' had acquired machine, armament, automobile and railway-car factories (many expropriated in Austria after March 1938) and was the Reich's largest industrial enterprise (Neumann, *Behemoth*, 1942, p.245).

A high level of investment is a prerequisite for initiating economic growth, but the common experience is for increasing levels of consumption and gains in labour productivity to play major roles in sustaining expansion. Neither happened in the Third Reich. The output of production goods (machines, and so on) rose much more quickly than that of consumer goods: taking 1933 as 100, the production goods index was 255.6 by 1938, but the consumer goods index only 145.1 (Noakes and Pridham, eds, 1984, p.296). Wage-earners were, to a great extent, denied the benefits of economic growth during the 1930s. Labour's share in the national income declined, real hourly wages were held below 1929 levels until 1938, and many consumer goods were in constant short supply. Because of import restrictions, working-class families had to cut back upon a whole range of imported foodstuffs and make do with inferior (but not cheaper) substitutes. The mediocre productivity record in Nazi Germany was due to several factors: manual labour, rather than machines, was used on many projects to create work (albeit poorly paid) for the unemployed; the government contracting system, and the position of the German Labour Front in industry (discussed in section 7) discouraged employers from using labour more efficiently; and workers played 'ca'canny' as a mute form of protest against the regime. In previous and later periods, German economic growth was export led, but the opprobrium attaching to the regime's violence and racism, and its tariff and credit-control policies, damaged German trading prospects.

Here we have identified some features of the Nazi economic revival which differentiate it from the rapid expansion during the Wilhelmine period and the post-1945 economic miracle. They also distinguish it from the economic recovery in Britain during the 1930s, where market forces and the growth of private consumption were far more important. In a long-term historical perspective, the performance of the German economy under the Nazis was not particularly remarkable. Though growth accelerated sharply between 1933 and 1938, there is much evidence that thereafter the weight of rearmament in the economy made further rapid expansion unsustainable. Veiled inflation, and material and labour shortages, were seriously imperilling economic performance on the eve of World War II, and internal economic difficulties may have contributed to a war psychosis in 1939. (This is a matter reverted to in the next section, and in the article by Richard Overy in the Course Reader that you will read in connection with the establishment of a 'war economy'.)

This is not to deny that Nazi economic policies enjoyed a fair measure of success which historians have been rather loath to acknowledge. Ever since Allied intelligence agencies revealed extensive under-utilization of productive resources until the later stages of World War II, the inefficiency of the Nazi economy and its unsystematic improvization have been bywords of progressive folk-wisdom. It is rather refreshing, therefore, to read one economic historian's assessment:

> Though certainly not frictionless, the German economic machine worked and worked quite well, on a narrowly economic level, compared to the other economic systems of the time . . . Contempt for the political and social doctrines of the Nazis should not interfere with a dispassionate analysis of their economic system. The Nazis subscribed neither to central planning along Soviet lines nor to the market economy of the Western world, but selectively and without dogmatic qualms used those economic tools that seemed to serve their purposes. (Hardach, *The Political Economy of Germany in the Twentieth Century*, 1980, p.66)

All the objective indices of economic performance bear this out. Total industrial production rose extremely rapidly from its nadir in late 1932 and by 1938 had more than doubled. This was twice the rate of growth in contemporary Britain, although since Germany had suffered far more during the Depression it had much more to recover (Landes, *The Unbound Prometheus*, 1969, p.391). The rate of inflation in Germany between 1933 and 1938 was about half that in Britain and America, which testifies to the effectiveness of Nazi price controls. Above all, Nazi Germany did far more than any other industrial society to restore employment. We have noted that, by 1938, Germany (with year-round average un-

Table 18.1   *Level of unemployment 1933–39*

	end of January	June	Total industrial production – index
1933	6.014 m.	4.857	100
1934	3.773	2.481	130.8
1935	2.974	1.877	149.5
1936	2.520	1.315	168.9
1937	1.853	0.648	187.2
1938	1.052	0.292	205.1
1939	0.302	0.049	?

(Source: Noakes and Pridham, eds, 1984, pp.296, 359)

employment of 1.3 per cent) was experiencing acute labour shortages; America (with 18.9 per cent of its labour force unemployed) and Britain (with 8.1 per cent) must have wished they had Germany's problem (figures in Hardach, 1980, p.61).

How did the Nazi economy compare with the Nazis' stated intentions? Nazi ideology came closest to practical fulfilment in the reorganization of agriculture. In order to foster a racially pure stock of yeoman farmers the Nazis introduced the entailment of farms (which meant they could only be passed on to a single male heir). A corporatist organization of agriculture led to the stabilization of farm prices and the elimination of middle-men. In other spheres, however, practice was discrepant with ideology. The Nazi political programme and propaganda had pledged the party to protect the small and medium-scale entrepreneur, the handicraftsman and trader, and to break up the monopolistic *Konzerne*. The actual effects of its economic policies were the reverse of these intentions. The regime promoted measures to purge industry of its less efficient, marginal producers; as a consequence, the number of handicraft businesses fell from 1.734 million in 1934 to 1.471 million in 1939. At the same time, the process of capital concentration and monopolization received an enormous stimulus from a number of factors.

One was Aryanization under anti-Semitic legislation which allowed large industrial combines to grow still bigger by buying Jewish businesses at knock-down prices. More important, however, was compulsory cartelization, for the largest producers could normally dominate the cartels under rules which allocated votes in proportion to output. Consequently, the power of the big industrial magnates was extended behind the democratic facade of the cartels. But a further, and perhaps crucial, factor in promoting monopolies was the exploitation, at the behest of the state, of scientific and technological developments where the capital costs of entry were so high that they could only be undertaken by giant firms (Neumann, *Behemoth*, 1942, pp.225–37). Synthetic fuel, rubber and fibres all required huge investments and the logic of their production dictated backward integration to secure raw materials (like coal) and forward integration to control distribution.

The impulse towards monopolization can be, and has been, cited in support of Marxist interpretations of the Third Reich. To quote one East German historian: 'The fascist state was a state of monopolies, its policy the concentrated pressure of their economic relationships, that is to say of the conditions and needs of the ruling monopolies . . . [The Second World War] was a war of monopolies for the control of Europe and the world' (D. Eichholtz, given in Milward, 'Fascism and the economy', 1976, p.412). The thesis that the regime pursued capitalist interests is much more persuasive than the dogma that business interests brought the Nazis to power, but it is not entirely convincing. All would agree that employers benefited from the destruction of trade unions, the wage freeze, the creation of a system of industrial relations heavily weighted in their favour, and the use of the Gestapo to weed out left-wing activists and malingerers. Moreover, the Nazi *Gleichschaltung* put the leading employers at the head of a system of 'industrial self-administration' which strengthened their hold over production and increased their power to regulate the economy. (Gillingham, *Industry and Politics in the Third Reich*, 1985, chapter 2 analyses both developments from the perspective of the Ruhr coal industry.) But we have to distinguish between contingent benefits that capitalists enjoyed because of Nazi rule and the actual identity of interests between industry and the regime. There is very little evidence that capitalists dictated political and strategic aims to the Nazis and while certain sectors of industry identified with the regime's macro-economic objectives, others did not. Those traditionally reliant on exports did not generally support autarky, the chief beneficiary of which was the chemicals industry. IG Farben was the 'model' Nazi corporation, totally committed to the Third Reich; its managers designed and administered the Four-Year Plan. The Ruhr mining companies, by contrast, never identified with Hitler's aims and methods and above all else wanted stability, including in foreign policy (Gillingham, 1985, pp.163–5; on IG Farben see Hayes, *Industry and Ideology*, 1987).

7 STATE AND SOCIETY

Drawing a boundary between the state and society is not easy in any circumstances. It is particularly difficult for the Third Reich – where the state was so amorphous – for the Nazis sought to obliterate all distinctions between public and private life by creating an array of institutions which would organize the major social groups (workers, youth, women) behind the leadership of the NSDAP. After 1933, nearly all voluntary organizations of a professional or social type were dissolved, and their members and functions absorbed by satellites of the Nazi party enjoying official status. For example, the Nazi Women's Group – *NS Frauenschaft* – displaced women's voluntary organizations and the regime attempted to mobilize the great mass of women through official unions of German housewives and maidens: *Deutsches Frauenwerk* and *Bund deutscher Mädel*. The task of representing women in society, which in Weimar had been undertaken by self-governing women's organizations, now fell on parts of a very complex party-cum-state apparatus. In the course of this section I will examine the deeper historical motives behind the Nazis' attempt to obliterate the distinction between state and society, and ask how far this intention was realized. By looking at three instances of state/society relationships – anti-Semitism, the regime's relationship with the working class, and the adaptation of the Catholic community to Nazi rule – we will see how the regime attempted to remake society according to the dictates of ideology, but also how social groups were able to resist (in an apolitical way) total domination by the state.

7.1   State and civil society in historical perspective

The Nazi utopia was a racial political community unified behind a single leader: *Ein Volk, Ein Reich, Ein Führer*. This ideal represented a reaction against the relative autonomy of society from the state which had resulted from the economic and political liberalization of nineteenth-century Europe. European liberalism had made a distinction between the state – a sovereign association co-ordinated by command – and 'civil society' in which freely contracting individuals voluntarily associated in pursuit of their private interests. We owe the concept of 'civil society' to the classical economists and my formulation suggests that it was simply the sphere of social life devoted to economic ends or material interests. But we can trace its origins to the spiritual claim, first made in the sixteenth and seventeenth centuries, for the individual's freedom of conscience and religious practice, and to the subsequent demand that religious dissent should not need politically disabling. By 1914, the state/civil society distinction was recognized and more or less institutionalized throughout Europe (Russia partially excepted). Although the roles undertaken by the state differed greatly between Western and Eastern Europe, all states acknowledged the core freedoms of civil society: of property, contract, exchange, association, religious belief and worship. All states had to put up with a critical intelligentsia which was an historical and logical consequence of a social sphere where thought was free.

For the historian, one measure of the liberalization of individual European states is their progress towards granting full civil, political and economic rights to Jews, and this also indicates the making of the state/civil society distinction. Christian states had traditionally placed Jews under special legislation which regulated their occupations and settlement; such special jurisdictions were incompatible with the concept of civil society, the basic doctrine of which was the equality of all individuals before a universal civil law. Jewish emancipation demonstrated that an 'alien' religious community not only enjoyed the toleration of the liberal state and the protection of its laws; its members could be included within the political nation. It was the proclamation of the Rights of Man by the French Revolution which began the process of Jewish emancipation, for these rights logically entailed a universal category of citizenship through which men participated in the state, combined with a social plurality of beliefs and private interests. They entailed, that is, the state/civil society distinction.

7.2   The interdependence of domestic and foreign conquest

Although Hitler rejected the totalitarian doctrines of Fascist Italy as setting the state above the race, he and Mussolini shared the objective of re-fusing state and civil society in new political totalities with monopolistic claims to allegiance. Hitler wrote in *Mein Kampf*: 'the [National Socialist] *Weltanschauung* is intolerant . . . and peremptorily demands its own exclusive, and complete recognition as well as the complete adaptation of public life to its ideas' (quoted in Bracher, *The German Dictatorship*, 1971, p.315). In conformity with this precept, the regime attempted to impose a 'co-ordination' of intellectual and cultural life through institutions like the Reich Cultural Chamber, set up to censor critics and inculcate the leadership principle and martial values, and the 'Strength through Joy' organization which was meant to control the private lives of workers through communal leisure and holidays.

This drive to shape society from above might be termed the creative aspect of Hitler's totalizing ambition; its negative aspect was the determination to purge society of internal foes (notably Jews and Marxists) and 'racially unhealthy' elements (such as homosexuals and the mentally ill). From the previous unit on Fascist Italy, you will already be familiar with the thesis put forward by MacGregor Knox that the common essence of Mussolini's and Hitler's regimes was the intertwining of domestic and foreign conquest. Both dictators regarded internal war against domestic enemies as inextricably linked with foreign aggression. What Knox calls their 'visionary programs' blended demography and geopolitics, but in Hitler's case, the rationale for his bellicose 'world view' lay in a racist external and internal Social Darwinism, which took foreign aggression and domestic revolution to create fitness for war to be inescapable in the struggle for survival. Hitler was quite explicit about the interdependence of foreign and domestic policy:

Domestic policy [he wrote in his unpublished 'Secondbook'] must secure the inner strength of a people so that it can assert itself in the sphere of foreign policy. Foreign policy must secure the life of a people for its domestic political development. Hence domestic policy and foreign policy are not only most closely linked, but must also mutually complement one another. (Quoted in Course Reader, p.172)

7.3   Viewing Nazi society 'from the bottom up'

Such, then, were the basic premises of the Nazis' programme for society. Understandably they have acted as powerful influences on the historical inter-pretation of Nazi Germany: in 1945 the world was confronted with horrifying evidence of the internal war against the Jews, and other acts of grotesque barbarity, and it was highly plausible to think that these could only have been accomplished by a totally dominant state whose combined ideology and terror had subverted and destroyed autonomous society. An influential version of this thesis was Hannah Arendt's famous study *The Origins of Totalitarianism* (first published in 1951), in which she argued that the totalitarian movement sprang from the break up of the class structure of civil society, the decay of its social ties and the 'atomization' of individuals torn out of their customary roles and allegiances by World War I and the economic catastrophes of the inter-war period. In power, Arendt argued, the movement made this atomization a fundamental principle of its rule by tolerating no ties except those which bound the masses to the leader and his élite.

The crucial flaw of this interpretation was that its view of the German 'masses' (a term with a heavy conceptual load which harked back to the theory of mass society) was no different from that enjoyed by Hitler from his podium. The Nazis' own claim to have eradicated class divisions and class consciousness, as well as other sectional ties, and to have created a mass community of sentiment between leader and led, was taken as an achieved fact. The traditional preoccupation of German historiography with the state and high politics, and the fact that the sources for the study of the regime are almost entirely official, have meant that, even for scholars sceptical of the totalitarian concept, the same view from the podium has been the dominant perspective on the Third Reich. Only relatively recently have historians begun to look at Nazi Germany 'from the bottom up' by reconstructing everyday experiences and popular mentalities. Research into these social aspects of the Third Reich has revealed the incompleteness of the regime's hold on the hearts and minds of the people and the existence of strong currents of popular dissent, amounting (in the opinion of some historians) to a massive challenge to the regime. Even if the challenge has been exaggerated, it is clear that German society was not simply the passive instrument of the Nazi state.

Admittedly research into popular mentalities has confirmed the extraordinary position of Hitler in the affections of his people; that the regime was able to function effectively was in no small part due to the fact that Hitler was loved rather than feared by the Germans. However, Hitler's role in domestic politics was symbolic rather than executive (with the crucial exception of anti-Semitism), and the myth built around him was all the more effective because he was perceived as being above the party and the bearer of traditional values that emanated from society. Wherever the Nazis confronted these values, especially religious senti-ments, then their ideology was relatively weak. It was where they worked with the grain of existing values that they were successful in carrying public opinion with them and pushing on with their political goals. (Bessel, 'Living with the Nazis', 1984).

Case I: Anti-Semitism

In 1933, approximately half a million German Jews formed less than 1 per cent of the total population. They were concentrated in commerce and the liberal and intellectual professions, most notably the law where 16.6 per cent of practitioners were Jewish (Noakes and Pridham, eds, 1984, p.522). This strong presence in the most conservative of professions was testimony to the secularization and assimilation of Germany's Jewish community. Although Jews were often identified with the subversive qualities of modernism, there were no political and cultural attitudes which could be said to be typically Jewish, and those held by Jews were as diverse as among any other cross-section of urban Germans (Gay, *Freud, Jews and other Germans*, 1978, ch.2). Why, then, was anti-Semitism such an obsessive and central part of Nazi ideology?

Nazi anti-Semitism did not spring from religious intolerance (and indeed flew in the face of Christian traditions because conversion was for the Nazis irrelevant in deciding Jewish identity), but rather from a chiliastic doctrine which made race and racial struggle the determining force of all history. Propagating anti-Semitism had, for the Nazis, the functions of raising a more general race consciousness and universalizing that sense of incessant struggle which was central to their 'world view'. The values attached to anti-Semitism – martial hardness, rejection of common humanity, indifference to human suffering – were the values needed for the primitive tribal warfare and domination which Hitler envisaged as the more or less permanent future of Eastern Europe (Nolte, *Three Faces of Fascism*, 1965, p.516). Sexual paranoia was an important factor in the psycho-pathology of anti-Semitism: the most vicious of the Nazis' racist papers, *Der Stürmer* (which had a semi-official status after 1933), frequently portrayed Jews as monstrous sexual perverts. Significantly, the element of anti-Jewish legislation which seems to have given the party rank and file greatest satisfaction was the outlawing of miscegenation. Anti-Semitism also accorded with the Nazis' more explicitly political notions, especially their hostility to parliamentary democracy and to the fissure between state and society in liberal polities. As we have seen, the inclusion of Jews within the nation-state exemplified a more general process of emancipation which the Nazis strove to reverse. Their anti-Semitic legislation set at nought the category of secular citizenship and was a crucial expression of the new political totality created by the Nazis.

The National Socialist programme demanded the disfranchisement of Jews and their exclusion from economic life, but the Nazis had few detailed proposals as to how these measures were to be effected. During the seizure of power after the March elections, anti-Semitism chiefly manifested itself as SA violence and local boycotts of Jewish businesses which, though condoned from above, were part of the 'revolution from below' (discussed on pp.157–8). Partly to reassert its authority over the rank and file and restrain random violence, the Nazi leadership called for a national boycott of Jewish businesses on 1 April. Despite the regime's claims, it was not a complete success; though the boycott was generally peaceful, the public responded in a number of places by demonstratively buying from blacklisted businesses. Some Nazis were sufficiently dismayed by the failure to mobilize anti-Semitism among the general population as to suggest that future actions against Jews should be kept secret (Bessel, *Political Violence and the Rise of Nazism*, 1984, pp.107–8). Hitler's concern at the hostile foreign reaction was such that the boycott was broken off prematurely, and the regime turned to legislation to provide more orderly and systematic means for excluding Jews from public life. On 7 April, a hurriedly prepared Law for the Restoration of the Professional Civil Service was promulgated; Article 3 required the retirement of civil servants of 'non-Aryan' descent. A similar law of the same date attempted to exclude Jews from the legal profession; as a result of local initiatives by Nazi bureaucrats, Jewish doctors were excluded from the state health insurance system. The effect of these measures was considerably mitigated by President Hindenburg's insistence that those who had been in office or their professions in 1914, or had fought in the war, or whose sons or fathers had been killed, should be exempted. Because of these exemptions, over 70 per cent of Jewish lawyers remained in their profession (Noakes and Pridham, eds, 1984, p.528). In January 1934, as part of the moves to restrain the radicalism of the SA, the Minister of the Interior instructed local authorities not to extend 'Aryanization' to the economy, and the year proved to be one of relative calm for German Jews.

It is pertinent to ask why the boycotting of Jewish businesses and anti-Semitic violence did not revive until May 1935, and why the regime waited until the party annual rally in September to promulgate the racist Nürnberg Laws, criminalizing marriage and sex between Jews and Gentiles and depriving Jews of their citizenship. (Shortly afterwards most of the Jewish civil servants exempted under the April 1933 Law were dismissed.) The renewal of SA violence is probably best explained as the stormtroopers' disgruntlement with Hitler's conciliation of the conservative élites and his failure to implement the social radicalism of the Nazi programme; anti-Semitism expressed SA race hatred but was also a tolerated way of venting other resentments. Several factors may explain the regime's delay in introducing the laws: apprehension about foreign reactions and the direct and indirect effects of anti-Semitic laws on the economy; the practical difficulties of defining 'Jewishness' and identifying a tiny, well-assimilated minority; conservative and religious objections; even sheer bureaucratic inertia. What is important to stress here is that, for the historian explaining the institution of anti-Semitism in Nazi Germany, reference to intentions and ideology is necessary but not sufficient for a full account.

The years 1936–1937 were comparatively peaceful for German Jews and many were persuaded that they could retain a tolerable niche within German society. Nazi propaganda had only a limited success in raising popular race consciousness; although anti-Semitism was a widespread prejudice, relations between individual Jews and their Gentile neighbours were often cordial. Attacks on Jewish property by Nazi stormtroopers were frequently condemned as sheer hooliganism, and police reports noted with regret that Jewish middlemen still enjoyed the confidence of their clients. The Munich Gestapo complained in August 1937 that 80–90 per cent of the cattle trade in one Bavarian locality remained in Jewish hands. 'The deeper reason for it', according to the report, 'lies in the attitude of the peasantry who show a complete lack of awareness of race . . . particularly in those districts where political Catholicism is still in control, the peasants are so infected by the teachings of an aggressive political Catholicism that they are deaf to any discussion of the racial problem' (Noakes and Pridham, eds, 1984, p.546). Protestant, as well as Catholic clerics opposed the Nazis' racist extremism, as did conservatives in the government (such as Schacht), the bureaucracy and the army; and they acted as a brake on anti-Semitic policies.

During these 'quiet years' the SS, that most ideologically rigid but also most methodical of Nazi power machines, became increasingly important in formulating official policy towards Jews. It pressed for the radical solution of mass emigration and, logically, persecuted assimilationist and encouraged Zionist organizations. Two difficulties hindered the implementation of this solution: firstly, the regime had introduced measures which stripped Jewish emigrants of virtually all their property when they left Germany, so there was a strong disincentive to leave. But, secondly, a wave of anti-Semitism in Poland, Romania and other parts of Eastern Europe had left a flood of stateless people trying to enter developed countries who now had strict controls over immigration. Furthermore, Britain, the mandate authority over the Jewish Home in Palestine, restricted settlement in order to appease Arab opinion.

A radicalization of anti-Semitic measures was initiated in the autumn of 1937, at the same time as important conservatives were removed from the bureaucracy, the diplomatic corps and the army, and the regime quickened the tempo of its rearmament programme and aggressive foreign policy. The scale of the changes was such as to be likened to a 'second seizure of power', and the quickening pace of anti-Semitism was no coincidence: it signalled the determination to grapple with the internal as well as the external enemy, to remake society as part of the drive to make war. At the September party rally, Hitler launched his first major attack on the Jews since 1935 and in the following months the 'Aryanization' of Jewish businesses accelerated as their owners came under increasing pressure to sell out at silly prices. The occupation of Austria led to the unrestrained seizure of Jewish companies by Nazi officials; to regulate this rapacity, and ensure that his Five-Year Plan organization benefited most from Aryanization, Goering ordered a general registration of Jewish property which was clearly a preliminary to its confiscation. Simultaneously the regime introduced further restrictions on Jewish professionals and excluded them from many commercial occupations. In July 1938 a decree compelled all Jews to adopt the names 'Israel' or 'Sarah' if they did not already bear identifiably Jewish names.

On the night of 9/10 November Goebbels seized the opportunity of the assassination of a German diplomat in Paris by a young Polish Jew to instigate a massive pogrom, the *Kristallnacht* (so-called because of the smashed glass littering the pavements after Nazi thugs ransacked Jewish shops). About a hundred Jews were murdered, thousands tormented and abused, their synagogues were burnt down and graves defiled in what has been called a 'quasi-medieval orgy of destruction' (Kershaw, *Popular Opinion and Political Dissent . . .* , 1983, p.261). Seven thousand businesses were destroyed and 20,000 Jewish men were arrested and placed in concentration camps. The pogrom gave a huge impetus to Jewish emigration: 40,000 Jews left Germany in 1938, and 78,000 in the first five months of 1939.

Exercise   The American Consul in Leipzig wrote, on the basis of personal observation and interviews, an account of events in the city. This is reproduced in document I.13 in *Documents 2*. What does it tell us about the reaction of the general population to the atrocities? ∎

Specimen answer   The Consul describes local crowds as benumbed over what had happened and aghast over the unprecedented fury of Nazi acts. Spectators viewing the wreckage and the gutted synagogues were bewildered. Witnesses to the sadistic humiliation of Jews recalled the spectacle with nausea. The account makes clear that only its perpetrators condoned the wanton violence, although it also indicates how ineffective were their opponents. □

The reaction described by the Consul appears to have been quite representative of German popular opinion. Although some reports spoke of casual bystanders looting shops and baiting Jews, most indicated a general abhorrence at the senseless destruction, and in Catholic areas the condemnation of barbarity was particularly vociferous. The alienation of opinion appears to have persuaded the Nazi leadership that such a tactic should never again be tried, and that anti-Jewish measures should take a more 'rational' course (Kershaw, *Popular Opinion and Political Dissent . . .* , 1983, pp.257–71). But Nazi propaganda had not entirely failed in its aim of instilling racism: despite evidence for much human sympathy and good neighbourliness, the dominant concern of popular opinion appears to have been with property, rather than human rights. There was widespread approval of the further legal discrimination which followed the pogrom and of the imposition by Goering of a 1 billion Reichsmark fine on the Jewish community as 'reparation' for the murder of the German diplomat. Most crucially the Germans were now generally persuaded by Nazi propaganda that there was a 'Jewish Question'. There is no evidence that genocide was seriously contemplated before the war, but the Nazi leadership may have concluded that, if the methods to solve the Question did not visibly offend Germans' sensibilities, they would be indifferent to its solution. Even before the outbreak of war, the Nazi state had instituted a type of social change for which we have to go back to the religious strife of the seventeenth century to find parallels: it had stripped a religious community of its property, deprived it of political and civil rights, instituted social and sexual apartheid, and driven more than half its members into exile.

Case II: Catholics and the Nazi state

You will recall that political Catholicism had withstood the rise of Nazism until the signing of the Enabling Law, and the previous section has indicated how Catholic communities could be points of moral resistance to Nazi anti-Semitism. What explains this? Chiefly the fact that during the conflict with the Wilhelmine Reich (known as the *Kulturkampf*) the Catholic Church had developed a defensive armour against the state. The Church gave the faithful a firm and coherent 'world view' and it had secured a popular loyalty through its newspapers, trade unions and a dense network of youth and welfare organizations. Catholicism was an ideological community which the Nazis envied and tried to emulate; its autonomy was an affront to their 'totalizing' ambition.

   A cynic might argue that the political views of the Catholic hierarchy, especially in Bavaria, were such that the Church should have been able to accommodate itself fairly comfortably to the new regime, provided that the near paganism of a minority of Nazi zealots was held in check and the rights of Catholic schools and congregations acknowledged. A regime that proclaimed itself the bastion of Western cultural values against atheistic Bolshevism was bound to strike a sympathetic chord among churchmen; the attack on the USSR in June 1941 was applauded by Catholic bishops as a 'holy crusade' (Kershaw, *Popular Opinion and Political Dissent . . .* , 1983, p.340). Many leading clerics were patriotic and authoritarian conservatives, detested socialism, had a pronounced antipathy for parliamentary democracy and hankered after a monarchical state. The head of the Church in Bavaria, Cardinal Faulhaber, was such a type; though he had roundly condemned anti-Semitism from the pulpit, and strongly protested during the violence suffered by Catholic youth and other organizations at the hands of the SA during the seizure of power, he wished to avoid conflict with the Nazi state with which he had much in common politically. Priestly and lay sub-ordinates were generally behind their superiors in seeking a *modus vivendi*; for example, Catholic teachers' associations at national and local levels voluntarily 'co-ordinated' with the Nazi teachers' organization during 1933.

The basic cause of the long-running 'Church struggle' in Nazi Germany was not political incompatibility, but the constant friction of the Nazi *Volksgemeinschaft* against the Catholic 'way of life' with its rich pattern of custom and ritual. In the Nazi ideal, the local party leader would have taken on most of the pastoral functions of the priest and the ceremonies, which gave common meaning to social life, would have been Nazi-inspired. Both priests and congregations were determined that this would not happen, and they reasserted the distinctiveness of Catholic culture in response to the 'totalizing' pretensions of the regime. For example, the first mass of a newly ordained priest in Bavaria (often celebrated in the priest's home parish) became a particularly marked demonstration of Catholic feeling and solidarity. These were occasions for the expression of a form of dissent which was anxiously monitored but proved difficult to repress (although in 1939 the Gestapo banned all festivities outside the church building itself) (Kershaw, *Popular Opinion and Political Dissent . . .* , 1983, pp.196–7).

To assert that the 'Church struggle' arose basically over social practices is not to deny doctrinal divisions between Catholicism and the state. One source of Church–state conflict was the anti-Catholic fantasies of Alfred Rosenberg, the Nazis' leading ideologist. He wanted to make a religious myth of the blood community of the *Volk*, a myth so exalted that it would tolerate no values in its vicinity higher than its own. Hatred for the Church – which contested this supremacy (and was anyway Jewish inspired) – ran through his writings. It is doubtful whether even Hitler took them seriously (they rivalled his own in tedium) but they had an impact when local party zealots seized state offices regulating the churches and schools, and expected teachers to treat them with respect. This occurred in Oldenburg, a state with a very pious Catholic minority, as the prelude to a protracted struggle over the attempt to ban crucifixes in schools (or other denominational symbols such as portraits of Luther) and to forbid their religious consecration (Noakes, 'The Oldenburg Crucifix Struggle . . .', 1978, pp.210–34). The ban, proclaimed in November 1936, was a piece of 'private enterprise' by a local Nazi on the make that appalled the regional authorities who correctly anticipated the public outcry it would provoke. That the ban was decreed at all was due to the chaos of Nazi administration. Protests took various forms: a virtual mass demonstration of ex-servicemen (where a priest declared their determination to 'fight and bleed, and if necessary die for Christ and . . . the crucifix'); a flood of protest letters; deputations to the Oldenburg government; the setting up of an illuminated cross that could be seen for miles; even the ostentatious wearing by women of jewellery crucifixes. A local mayor warned that 'Trust in the state has been as seriously shaken by this decree as one can possibly imagine'. As well as dividing the people from the regime, it split the party apparatus in the districts most affected; many resigned their membership and in one village the SA disbanded itself. In the face of this opposition, the offending decree was revoked. The public humiliation of the Nazi authorities was all the greater because at the packed meeting announcing the revocation, the *Gauleiter* was furiously barracked and the SA and police openly defied.

This dramatic victory of the Nazi state was, however, a short-lived triumph for religious symbolism, made possible by the solidity and piety of local Catholic communities and the simplicity of the issue. In 1938 the authorities were able to abolish denominational schools in Oldenburg (as they had already done in other regions after referenda held under conditions of intimidation), although they felt obliged to proceed circumspectly. When they did encounter parental opposition in the villages, the Gestapo arrested the protesters and sent them to concentration camps.

The 'Church struggle' subsided into an uneasy and partial truce during 1938–39, but then revived into bitter opposition between Christian denominations and the state over the 'euthanasia action' of 1939–41. For the sake of completeness I will touch on it here. Shortly after the beginning of the war, Hitler secretly ordered the murder of the mentally and physically handicapped, many of whom were patients in Catholic and Protestant asylums. The order was inspired by racist-eugenic ideas quite widely current in the medical profession, and resulted in the deaths of more than 70,000 helpless victims. The action violated Christian doctrines on the sanctity of human life and was undertaken clandestinely for fear of popular outrage had the public been informed. Murder on this scale is difficult to keep secret and, inevitably, knowledge of the action seeped out, provoking categorical condemnation by Catholic and Protestant leaders and great public unease. Admittedly many lay protesters did not dispute the principle of euthanasia so much as the utter lawlessness of instituting it by administrative fiat. The reception of the feature film, *I Accuse*, a piece of pro-euthanasia propaganda, suggested to the authorities that the termination of life on ethical-medical grounds was widely acceptable. Catholics were the most resolutely opposed to it; priests organized demonstrations against the action and its most famous condemnation came from the Catholic Bishop of Munster. The Nazi leadership was urged to hang him, but Goebbels advised that this would lose Munster – indeed the whole of Westphalia – to the war effort. Hitler ordered the action to cease. Ian Kershaw has described this as a victory without parallel during the Third Reich for the force of popular opinion in a matter which lay not far from the heart of the Nazi racial-eugenic creed of Social Darwinism. He attributes this to the willingness of Church leaders not merely to respond to public opinion, but to channel and direct it. Sadly it was the only occasion when they gave this leadership in an issue which concerned not merely their denomination, but the most basic human right to life itself.

Case III: The state and the working class

We turn now to the most controversial topic in the historical analysis of Nazi society: the relationship between the regime and industrial workers, particularly those who had supported the SPD and KPD before 1933. The controversy has a dual significance for our course: it makes us examine the nature and extent of conflict between the working class and the employers and state in Nazi Germany; and it leads us to ask whether this conflict was a determining factor in the decision to go to war in 1939. In various publications, T. W. Mason has been the chief protagonist of the views that class conflict was the 'fundamental reality' of the Nazi system; that it re-emerged in the form of a 'Workers' Opposition' to the regime with the restoration of full employment; and that working-class intransigence generated an 'inner' socio-economic crisis which affected not just the decision for war, but its strategy. If – as many would agree – the wars which the Third Reich actually fought bore very little relation to the wars which Hitler appears to have wanted to fight, then (argues Mason) 'this was so because of the domestic pressures and constraints which were economic in origin and also expressed themselves in acute social and political tensions' (Mason, 'Intention and explanation', 1981, p.39). The gist of his interpretation of the 'inner crisis' of 1938–39 is that economic instability, autarky and aggressive expansionism became locked into a self-reinforcing cycle. As the economic problems of the regime mounted, so the temptation to solve them by a war of conquest and plunder grew.

The relationship between military strategy and internal, social politics is something we return to in the final section. Here I want to explore the nature of workers' opposition to the regime, and question some of the significance which Mason attaches to it by drawing on research into industrial relations in the Ruhr coal mines.

In 1933, workers were neither politically nor industrially united and their disunity goes far to explain the speed and completeness with which the Nazis destroyed the working-class movement. Moreover, the Nazis' intentions were poorly gauged; even in April, some leaders of the free trade unions hoped that their organizations would retain their independence in exchange for dissolving the tie with the SPD. Corporatist ideas were influential among labour leaders and they publicly offered 'to cooperate in the corporative structure of the . . . economy as planned by the Government' (Noakes and Pridham, eds, 1984, p.329). In fact corporatist policies were never seriously entertained by the Nazis; they ordered the 'co-ordination' of the trade unions, under the provisional local leadership of their own factory cell organization (the NSBO). This was too radical a body to be permanently entrusted with workers' interests and in May new Reich Trustees of Labour (that is, state officials) were created with ultimate authority for the regulation of wages. At the same time the German Labour Front (DAF) was set up under the leadership of Robert Ley as a sop to the workers for the destruction of their unions, and to keep the NSBO in hand. DAF was to become the largest of Nazi social organizations, with about 25 million members, that incorporated employers as well as workers and, for Hitler, symbolized the new class harmony. An agreement with the Ministries of Labour and Economics narrowly defined its role as educating all Germans at work to support the state and indoctrinating them in the National Socialist mentality.

The basic legal instrument governing labour in the Reich was the Law for the Ordering of National Labour of January 1934. It brought a neo-feudal division of industry into 'leaders' (employers) and their 'retinues' (workers), set up advisory Councils of Trust to increase the mutual confidence within the plant community, and created Courts of Social Honour to try 'leaders' for maliciously exploiting labour and 'retinue' for endangering social peace. In practice, only small employers had anything to fear from the courts. The key adjudicating role on industry was taken by the Trustees of Labour, whose general support for 'leaders' was guaranteed. The fig-leaf of workers' representation was stripped from the system when, after anti-Nazi election results, the Councils of Trust ceased to be elected bodies. DAF had no part in drawing up this law, and initially none in an industrial relations system dominated by employers, but the growth of Ley's organization led him to extend its functions and it later pressed the interests of labour in small firms. DAF's educative and integrative roles were mostly pursued by two welfare organizations established under its aegis: 'Beauty of Labour', which tried to persuade employers to improve working conditions, and 'Strength through Joy', the workers' holiday and physical fitness outfit which has already been mentioned. Workers did take advantage of what was often their first opportunity for travel and tourism, but they appear to have seen this for what it was: the superficial glitter on a repressive industrial system (Kershaw, *Popular Opinion and Political Dissent . . .* , 1983, p.313).

Between 1933 and 1936 the restoration of employment and the threat of the Gestapo kept labour quiescent; many were grateful to the Nazis for providing jobs and shared the sense of national revival. But, after 1936, the discipline of the labour market was much less effective and, argues Mason, 'economic class conflict re-emerged in Germany on a broad front . . .' (Mason, 'The Workers' Opposition in Nazi Germany', 1981, p.120). It manifested itself through spontaneous strikes, defiance of work-place rules, absenteeism, going-slow, and such forms of collective pressure on employers as threatening to leave *en masse* unless wage demands were met. The last tactic was particularly successful in the building industry where smaller and medium-sized firms had to reckon with the solidarity of their whole labour force. Such was the truculence of workers in the Ruhr that DAF officials had to make wage demands on their behalf in order to maintain credibility. The rearmament boom brought acute labour shortages and the poaching of labour by one employer from another publicized the new balance of forces in the labour market and encouraged workers to assert themselves. By the end of 1938 there were one million vacancies in German industry; labour turnover was so rapid that on average workers were changing their jobs every twelve months. The state had to intervene by directing labour (see section 6) and workers responded by lowering productivity and poor discipline which 'was . . . the direct and conscious expression of resentment against the new measures of regimentation'. The outbreak of war brought no improvement; indeed, Mason discerns in workers' behaviour during its first months 'a broad denial of co-operation by the working class . . .' (pp.129–30).

Assessing the 'political' content of such sporadic and, in the absence of overall leadership, uncoordinated industrial action is obviously difficult. Virtually the only sources at historians' disposal are official (usually police reports) which tend to attribute unrest to unidentified communist subversives and deny large-scale political disaffection. Mason argues that 'Workers' Opposition' displayed the solidarity of a largely unbroken class consciousness, and drew upon notions of social justice nurtured in trade unionism and social democracy before 1933. Workers were manifesting a sense of collective independence fundamentally incompatible with the Nazi *Volksgemeinschaft*. Others have failed to discern in workers' industrial behaviour any general spirit of opposition to the political system as such; they explain it in terms of the increasing frictions in the German economy caused by labour shortages, official wage restraint, longer hours and a dearth of consumer goods on which to spend growing weekly incomes. Detlev Peukert's conclusions are particularly noteworthy: although he characterizes workers' attitudes as 'non-compliance', he argues that 'lack of enthusiasm for the character and policies of the regime, and lack of zeal in the workplace, went along with a wary retreat into privacy . . .'. The destruction of collective bargaining and workers' institutions gave rise, in his view, to 'a makeshift Schweikian individual-ism', and he suggests that the 'privatized' worker analysed by sociologists in the 1950s may have originated with the Nazi experience (Peukert, *Inside Nazi Germany*, 1987, pp.110–7).

The Ruhr coalfield is an interesting case in which to test Mason's thesis: labour–management strife had been frequent before 1933 and workers were often politically radical, although divided by confession and ethnicity. Because mining operations were inherently difficult to supervise, the management, through wage differentials and welfare policies, had tried to create a core group of skilled and loyal hewers, but after 1930 their wage levels declined relative to other industries, and mining lost the social status it had once enjoyed in working-class sub-culture. Germany was extraordinarily dependent on coal for energy supplies and syn-thetic products (much more so than any other great power), so the labour force was in a position to hold the rearmament programme and the war economy for ransom. These background conditions should have proved fertile soil for the growth of 'Workers' Opposition', but the brute fact is that they did not. Though there were problems with malingering, the regime succeeded in imposing max-imum production at minimum cost on the mining labour force. From 1937, record outputs were achieved because of the willingness of miners to work longer, even without adequate compensation. This growth in production continued during the war, in contrast to Britain where coal output slumped (both in aggregate and per manshift) and strikes and absenteeism rose. Of course, terror and the use of slave labour partly explain the German coal industry's far better wartime production record, but it seems inescapable that what Albert Speer called 'the soldierly bearing of our German workforce' was of fundamental importance (Gillingham, 'Ruhr coal miners and Hitler's war', 1982).

Exercise Consider the points I have drawn from Mason and Gillingham and say whether you regard 'Workers' Opposition' as a justifiable term to describe German industrial behaviour and whether we can characterize it as a form of political action. ■

Specimen answer The fact that there was more evidence for so-called 'Workers' Opposition' in British than in German coalfields in the early 1940s should have given pause for thought about what exactly the term means. For me the comparison underlines the fact that industrial militancy and labour-management conflict do not necess-arily entail opposition to the political form of the state. The term 'Workers' Opposition' strikes me, therefore, as an interesting but unproven thesis. □

8 ARMAMENTS AND ECONOMIC PREPARATIONS FOR WAR

In *Mein Kampf* Hitler had made clear that he was not interested in pursuing the *Weltpolitik* of pre-war Germany, nor did he make the recovery of the frontiers of 1914 one of his objectives. National Socialists, he wrote,

> . . . have purposely drawn a line through the line of conduct followed by pre-War Germany in foreign policy. We put an end to the perpetual

> Germanic march towards the South and West of Europe and turn our eyes towards the lands of the East. We finally put a stop to the colonial and trade policy of pre-War times and pass over to the territorial policy of the future.
>
> But when we speak of new territory in Europe today we must principally think of Russia and the border States subject to her.
> (document I.23 in *Documents 2*)

Hitler made far fewer public references to eastward expansion during the 1930s and his ostensible policy was the revision of Versailles. However, we have evidence that on his accession to power his ultimate goals were unaltered. At a meeting with the German generals on 4 February, Hitler asserted that Germany's economic prospects would improve only when it recovered its military and political power. He envisaged as the long-term solution to the problems of lost export markets and living space 'the conquest of land in the east and its ruthless Germanisation' (Carr, *Arms, Autarky and Aggression*, 1979, p.22). Although he often spoke for effect, and not all his listeners took his bellicose ramblings seriously, we have little reason to doubt his sincerity. True, the low level of Germany's military forces, and fear of a French attack during the early stages of the Nazi regime, dictated caution in foreign affairs, in whose conduct conservative professional diplomats initially had a major role. Moreover, Hitler's frequent public declarations of his desire for peace were in one sense quite genuine; his regime simply had negligible means of waging war. In 1933, Germany possessed only 80 aircraft and 450 flying personnel, and had none of the reserve strength on which states who had maintained conscription could call. The work of building modern armed forces would take years and Hitler, it would seem, did not contemplate war with the major powers before 1942. In February 1934, when the show-down with Röhm loomed and Hitler had to choose between the professional army and the SA, he reviewed foreign and military policy with local army commanders and party leaders and for the first time drew up a timetable for attaining his objectives. He anticipated a recurrence of acute economic difficulties in about eight years' time and stated that Germany would then be obliged to acquire living space to accommodate its surplus population and to avoid 'frightful destitution'. Opposition from the Western powers was certain; therefore, 'short decisive blows to the west and then to the east would be necessary'. Germany, he said, required a powerful mass army, based on the *Reichswehr*, ready for defensive action in five years and for offensive action in eight years (Carr, 1979, pp.36–7).

All historians accept that foreign policy was the sphere in which Hitler's personal power had freest rein; not surprisingly many have taken these and other pronouncements as evidence in support of 'intentionalist' explanations of the course of German policy after 1933. There is some dispute as to just how grandiose those intentions were. Certain scholars (most prominently Andreas Hillgruber) have argued that Hitler's ambition was a world dominion, to be achieved 'stage-by-stage': after the conquest of Europe and the establishment of an autarkic German-dominated *Grossraumwirtshaft* Hitler envisaged, it is argued, an apocalyptic inter-continental war between 'The Teutonic Empire of the German Nation and the American World Empire'. The ideological dynamic behind this global megalomania was an unshakeable belief in the racial superiority of the *Herrenvolk*. (The argument is summarized in Hauner, 'Did Hitler want a world dominion?', 1978.) Other 'intentionalist' historians have argued that Hitler's ambitions were continental, and that his expansionist plans did not go beyond territorial conquest in Russia and hegemony throughout Europe.

A minority of scholars has disputed the 'intentionalist' orthodoxy. The most famous heretic is A. J. P. Taylor, whose controversial study of the origins of World War II you will meet in another unit. More pertinent here are the views of Martin Broszat who asserts that *Lebensraum* should be understood as an essentially symbolic and metaphorical concept which represented untrammelled power politics in the international sphere rather than concrete territorial objectives. 'Living space', it could be said, had an ideological function comparable to that of 'The White Man's Burden' for late-Victorian imperialists. For Germans, *Lebensraum* connoted the mythology of the Teutonic knights, the ideal of a self-sufficient agrarian community and a master-race of yeoman farmers; it was these secondary significations which made it a crucial symbol in sustaining the dynamic momentum which Hitler had unleashed. In support of this interpretation, Broszat cites the absence before 1939 of any clear thinking on the position of Poland (despite the fact that its geographical position ought to have made it a central component of any concrete notions of an attack on Russia) as demonstrating the nebulous, unspecific and essentially 'utopian' nature of Hitler's foreign policy goals. (Broszat's views are summarized in Kershaw, *The Nazi Dictatorship*, 1985, p.110, which I have followed closely.) Whether you find Broszat's analysis of *Lebensraum* convincing or not, it is clear that with respect to his Eastern neighbour, Hitler initially behaved with a high degree of pragmatic flexibility. In January 1934 he concluded a non-aggression pact with Poland which was quite contrary to the nationalist and revisionist tendency of German *Ostpolitik* since 1919. Germans had resented the division of their state by the Polish Corridor, Polish suzerainty over Danzig (which local Nazis attempted to overthrow), and successive German governments had refused to recognize the Eastern frontier. Hitler brushed aside these powerful anti-Polish prejudices in the interests of detaching Poland from France and of pursuing an increasingly anti-Soviet policy.

While Hitler was displaying considerable diplomatic flexibility, he was also initiating the rearmament of Germany which was the prerequisite to its assuming a power-political role commensurate with its basic industrial and demographic strength. This led to the withdrawal in October 1933 from the Geneva disarmament conference and League of Nations – so bringing Germany's determination to rearm into the open – and could have resulted in international action, but Hitler correctly calculated that Anglo-French differences would neutralize this danger. (In March 1935 he similarly, and equally correctly, assumed that Britain and France would not unite to oppose effectively Germany's reintroduction of conscription in breach of the military clauses of Versailles.)

The domestic, financial obstacles to rearmament were more serious than the international, and Hitler was greatly assisted in surmounting them by the ingenuity of Hjalmar Schacht, a Nazi sympathizer appointed to the Presidency of the Reichsbank in 1933 who also served as Minister of Economics between 1934 and 1937. Hitler's intention of greatly increasing expenditure on armaments and defence-related projects appeared to be thwarted by the falling tax revenues of the German government and the constitution of the Reichsbank, which placed stringent limits on the amount it could lend to the state for deficit financing. To have breached the Bank's constitution by *force majeure* would have meant forfeiting the confidence of financiers both at home and abroad. Schacht escaped the dilemma by his system of Mefo bills. These were bills of exchange issued by a nominal company, Metall-Forschungsgesellschaft GmbH, accepted by government contractors and banks and discounted by the Reichsbank. The primary advantage of this arrangement was that it camouflaged the scale of the financing of rearmament during the first three years of the regime when the shake-up of Germany's forces was actually reducing their military effectiveness. Since Mefo bills earned 4 per cent and could be prolonged for five years, they became an attractive form of investment once the financial markets had recovered. During 1934–36 they accounted for 50 per cent of arms expenditure; thereafter, economic recovery and the decreasing need for secrecy enabled the government to resort to loans and taxation to finance rearmament. Mefo bills were discontinued in March 1938, when a total of 12 billion marks was outstanding.

Thanks to Schacht's measures, German military expenditure immediately rose rapidly both as a total sum and in proportion to the gross national product. By the eve of World War II, nearly a quarter of GNP was devoted to military purposes. Because many of the raw materials (metals, oil, rubber) for rearmament had to be purchased abroad and its export trade was stagnant, Germany was quickly faced by a severe balance of payments problem. This led in September 1934 to the imposition of exchange controls on German importers, the insistence that foreign creditors accept interest payments in Reichsmarks, barter transactions, and the search for autarkic solutions (such as investment in synthetic fuel production) to Germany's deficiences in *matériel*. In the interests of strategic self-sufficiency, German trade was reoriented away from North America and overseas regions dominated by Britain to Europe, particularly south-east Europe where states could be persuaded to take German manufactured goods in direct exchange for foodstuffs and raw materials, and agree to payment through blocked accounts which could only be spent in Germany.

These measures brought a temporary alleviation of the balance of payments crisis but did not permanently control the economically destabilizing consequences of rearmament. Towards the end of 1935, Germany's leaders were faced with a renewed crisis because the revival of employment had led to an increased demand for foodstuffs which German agriculture could not fulfil, and a consequent consumer pressure for more imports of food which would have used scarce foreign currency needed for imported industrial raw materials. The Nazi government was reluctant to impair its popularity by introducing rationing, but even more unwilling to slow down the rearmament programme. In this dilemma, the chemicals industry came to play a foremost part in Nazi economic and political

Table 18.2

	GNP (Rm Billions)	Military expenditure	%
1929	89	0.8	1
1932	58	1.8	3
1933	59	1.9	3
1934	67	4.1	6
1935	74	6.0	8
1936	83	10.8	13
1937	93	11.7	13
1938	105	17.2	17
1939	130	30.0	23

(Source: Noakes and Pridham, eds, 1984, pp.297–8)

calculations: since the 1920s, IG Farben had been developing synthetic methods for the production of petrol and rubber – methods which were intrinsically expensive but had the signal advantage that they used raw materials Germany possessed in abundance. In 1933, IG Farben had persuaded the Nazi government to underwrite a limited production of synthetic fuel and rubber; in 1935–36 it won important converts among the Nazi hierarchy for more extensive government support for the manufacture of synthetic materials and the company's directors began to play key roles in economic planning. The support of Hermann Goering, who needed aviation fuel for the new *Luftwaffe*, was crucial to the establishment of the chemicals industry as the economic pillar of the state. In April 1936 he was appointed Commissioner of Raw Materials with wide-ranging powers over the disbursement of foreign exchange by government departments.

Exercise   During the summer of 1936, the exchange crisis intensified; munitions factories were producing much below their capacity because of the shortage of raw materials. In this situation, Hitler intervened decisively and in a way wholly uncharacteristic of his method of rule. He composed, sometime in August, a lengthy memorandum which proved to be 'one of the basic documents of the Third Reich' (Noakes and Pridham, eds, 1984, p.280). This is reprinted as document I.14 in *Documents 2*. Read it and answer the following questions:

1   What fundamental premises did Hitler put forward in the first three sections ('The political situation', 'Germany', and 'Germany's defensive capacity') as the bases for political and economic policies?

2   How, throughout the memorandum, did Hitler view the economy and private capitalism in relation to his military-political objectives and his assessment of Germany's national needs?

3   In what way does Hitler's diagnosis of Germany's economic problems, and his proposed 'final solution', strike you as consistent with expansionist views formulated early in his political career? Does the document help settle the historiographical controversy I outlined on page 183?

4   What arguments did Hitler advance against the stockpiling of raw materials and the building up of foreign exchange reserves as economic preparations for war?

5   What were the key practical points of his 'programme' for the preparation of Germany's vital needs?

6   What example clearly affected his decision to implement a 'Several Years Plan'?

7   What seemingly irrelevant ideological obsession does Hitler betray in the document? ■

Specimen answers   1   Hitler depicted history as a Social Darwinian struggle for survival and argued that in the present epoch Germany was at the forefront of a life and death conflict with Bolshevik Russia. Though he did not predict when actual war would occur, he forecast its character in truly apocalyptic terms. National Socialism had to educate and strengthen the people for this struggle which demanded that 'the military development of our resources cannot be too large, nor its pace too swift'.

2   Hitler unequivocally argued that the economy had to be the handmaiden of military–political needs and his remarks were often contemptuous of, even threatening towards, private capitalist interests. For example, he states (p.34)

that if private industry could not perform the tasks the government set it, then the government itself would undertake them and 'in that case we have no further need of private industry'. (You probably noted other examples.)

3   Hitler argued that Germany was overpopulated and unable to feed itself from its own resources; the 'final solution' to this lay in 'extending our living space', an argument he had been advancing since the early 1920s. The reference to 'living space' is too brief to settle conclusively the controversy over what it meant for Hitler but, in my view, the general tone of the document with its quite specific analyses of the demographic and resource problems, indicates that 'living space' was a tangible reality, and not a symbolic or metaphorical concept.

4   Stockpiling of materials simply meant that the moment of their manufacture into munitions would be postponed until the outbreak of war; the building up of foreign exchange reserves would not guarantee that they could be spent to advantage during an actual conflict. You should have noted how Hitler deployed an historical argument against these measures, based on Germany's experience during World War I.

5   The key points were the saving of foreign exchange wherever possible, the stepping up of German synthetic fuel and rubber production, and the greater use of poor-quality domestic ores in Germany's iron and steel industry in preference to high-quality foreign ores. These measures were to be taken irrespective of the economic arguments against them.

6   Hitler makes a reference to the Soviet State 'setting up a gigantic plan' and it is a fair inference that this example influenced his own decision to inaugurate what became the Four-Year Plan.

7   In two places Hitler gave vent to his anti-Semitic paranoia: the Bolshevik menace was equated with the goal of eliminating the leading strata of mankind and replacing them with world-wide Jewry, and the Jewish 'community of criminals' was associated with economic sabotage (for which Hitler proposed draconic penalties). □

Hitler's memorandum was presented to the Cabinet by Goering on 4 September and he was made responsible for executing the tasks it set out. The Four-Year Plan decreed in October was not intended (unlike Stalin's) to create an industrial economy in an underdeveloped society, but rather to make an already powerful industrial economy 'fit for war within four years'. Much economic activity was untouched by the planning organization, the key department of which was an Office for German Raw Materials staffed by Luftwaffe personnel and representatives of private industry, notably Carl Krauch of IG Farben. Krauch was responsible for making Germany self-sufficient in about thirty major products and for allocating a huge slice of total annual industrial investment, much of it destined for IG Farben. This has inspired the charge that the private corporation was using the government agency to further its own interests, and it certainly lends colour to the characterization of the Reich as a 'monopolies' state. A major study of the company refutes this charge; although it is true the company prospered under the Plan, Krauch and his subordinates rapidly identified with their new tasks, not their old employers (Hayes, *Industry and Ideology*, 1987, p.178). In June 1938, when the tempo of Hitler's diplomatic offensive quickened, Krauch put forward 'an express plan' for the corresponding acceleration of the production of strategic raw materials.

8.1   Economic mobilization for *Blitzkrieg* or total war?

There can be no question that from 1936 Germany mobilized economically for war, nor that from late 1937 its strategic planning switched from a defensive to an offensive posture, as an amendment to a high command directive of December makes clear:

> When Germany has achieved complete preparedness for war in all fields the military conditions will have been created for carrying out an offensive war against Czechoslovakia so that the solution of the German problem of living space can be carried to a victorious end even if one or other of the Great Powers intervene against us. (Quoted in Carr, *Arms, Autarky and Aggression*, 1979, p.80)

It is important, nevertheless, to ask for what sort of war was Germany mobilizing its economy? The conventional answer is *Blitzkrieg*, or short victorious campaigns with limited objectives, for which Germany required rearmament 'in breadth, not in depth' and which demanded only a partial mobilization of the economy. The military–economic strategy of *Blitzkrieg* was, supposedly, determined by Hitler's unwillingness to impose on the Germans the hardships they suffered on the home front during World War I for fear that his regime would collapse internally. *Blitzkrieg*, supposedly, was the military solution to the 'internal crisis' discerned by Mason whose views I outlined above.

Exercise   In his article in the Course Reader, Richard Overy raises some important objections to *Blitzkrieg* as an economic concept. I want you to read that article, 'Hitler's war and the German economy', now and summarize his objections. What explanations does he offer for the fact that the German economy appeared to have been only partially mobilized for war until 1942? How does he assess the part played by economic and social considerations in Hitler's foreign policy calculations? ■

Specimen answer   Basically, the *Blitzkrieg* thesis does not fit the actual facts of German economic life between 1936 and 1942. Hitler planned for a long, continental war of conquest to be fought some time after 1939, when the requirements of the army would be a 'bottomless pit'. The lesson he drew from World War I was not the threat to his regime of 'internal crisis', but the need for a total and unrestricted use of all resources. If looked at from a pre-war perspective, military expenditure was very large up to 1940, and all the plans suggest that Hitler wanted further huge increases even if war had not broken out in 1939. These plans do not at all suggest that Hitler envisaged the easy shifting of resources from normal economic needs to those of 'lightning war'. His military–economic preparations (the naval and fortifications programme, synthetic products) would only come into effect in the long term and made no sense if the prospect was a '*Blitzkrieg* economy'. The fact that Germany's economy appeared to have been only partially mobilized for war up to 1942 was because foreign policy got out of step with economic planning. Economic and social considerations, according to Overy, played only the smallest part in Hitler's foreign policy calculations. □

Discussion   In a subsequent article, Overy has argued that most of the evidence for a 'domestic crisis' in 1938–39 originated with conservative opponents of the regime and British sources with an interest in the economic appeasement of Germany. If we discount such evidence there were few indications of a crisis, as economists understand the term, and 'the working class was demoralized, powerless and fearful'. The Nazi leaders did not generally perceive a crisis, and one cannot, therefore, be invoked in explaining the outbreak of war in September 1939 (Overy, 'Germany, "Domestic Crisis" and War in 1939', 1987). This has provoked a lively debate between Overy, David Kaiser and Mason, in which Overy was accused of ignoring the critical problems of German trade and industry (which had lost its capacity to meet its orders because of labour and material shortages) and of putting forward a long-outmoded image of Nazi Germany as a unified monolith. From the tone of the exchanges between Overy and Mason, one senses that this is a debate which will run and run.

9 CONCLUSIONS

So we end as we began on the clash of historical interpretations. The capacity of the Third Reich to generate scholarly controversy is quite unabated; indeed, while drafting this unit there were lengthy articles in the serious press over the hornets' nest stirred up by Nolte's hypothesis that Nazi racial extermination was, in some sense, a response to (maybe even determined by) Bolshevik class extermination. Some controversies arise because the evidence simply doesn't suffice to settle disputes, others because the evidence is itself disputable. Running through this unit we have encountered a rather different source of controversy over the nature of historical explanation as such: it's a debate between those who think the essence of explaining the past lies in identifying the intentions and meanings behind human actions, and those who prefer a more natural scientific model of explanation, the essence of which is the search for more general causes than individual mental states. Where you stand in relation to this debate will partly be a matter of philosophical cast of mind, and in one form or another the debate is recurrent in history and social sciences. I've not attempted to 'settle' this debate, but I hope that you have found it useful to approach the history of Nazi Germany in its terms.

References

Arendt, H. (1951) *The Origins of Totalitarianism*, André Deutsch.

Aycoberry, P. (1981) *The Nazi Question*, Routledge.

Bessel, R. (1984) 'Living with the Nazis: some recent writing on the social history of the Third Reich', *European History Quarterly*, 14.

Bessel, R. (1984) *Political Violence and the Rise of Nazism*, Yale.

Bracher, K. D. (1971) *The German Dictatorship*, Penguin.

Broszat, M. (1981) *The Hitler State*, Longman.

Broszat, M. (1987) *Hitler and the Collapse of Weimar Germany*, Berg.

Carr, W. (1976) 'National Socialism: foreign policy and Wehrmacht' in Laqueur, W. (ed.) (1979).

Carr, W. (1979) *Arms, Autarky and Aggression*, Arnold.

Craig, G. A. (1981) *Germany 1866–1945*, Oxford University Press.

Eyck, E. (1957) *A History of the Weimar Republic*, Wiley.

Fest, J. C. (1977) *Hitler*, Penguin.

Gay, P. (1978) *Freud, Jews and other Germans*, Oxford University Press.

Geary, D. (1983) 'The industrial élite and the Nazis in the Weimar Republic' in Stachura, P. D. (ed.) (1983).

Gillingham, J. (1982) 'Ruhr coal miners and Hitler's war', *Journal of Social History*.

Gillingham, J. (1985) *Industry and Politics in the Third Reich: Ruhr Coal, Hitler and Europe*, Methuen.

Hardach, K. (1980) *The Political Economy of Germany in the Twentieth Century*, University of California.

Hauner, M. (1978) 'Did Hitler want a world dominion?', *Journal of Contemporary History*, 13.

Hayes, P. (1987) *Industry and Ideology: IG Farben in the Nazi Era*, Cambridge University Press.

Hirschfeld, G. and Kettenacker, L. (eds) (1981) *Der Fuehrerstaat: Mythos und Realitat*, Klett-Cota.

Jaeckel, E. (1972) *Hitler's 'Weltanschauung'*, Wesleyan University Press.

Jaeckel, E. (1984) *Hitler in History*, University Press of New England.

Kershaw, I. (1983) *Popular Opinion and Political Dissent in the Third Reich*, Oxford University Press.

Kershaw, I. (1985) *The Nazi Dictatorship*, Arnold.

Kershaw, I. (1987) *The Hitler 'Myth'*, Oxford University Press.

Landes, D. (1969) *The Unbound Prometheus*, Cambridge University Press.

Laqueur, W. (ed.) (1979) *Fascism: a Reader's Guide*, Penguin.

Mason, T. W. (1968) 'The primacy of politics – politics and economics in National Socialist Germany' in Woolf, S. J. (ed.) (1968).

Mason, T. W. (1981) 'Intention and explanation: a current controversy about the interpretation of National Socialism' in Hirschfeld, G. and Kettenacker, L. (eds) (1981).

Mason, T. W. (1981) 'The Workers' Opposition in Nazi Germany', *History Workshop*, 11, Spring.

Milward, A. S. (1976) 'Fascism and the economy' in Laqueur, W. (ed.) (1979).

Mommsen, H. (1979) 'National Socialism: continuity and change' in Laqueur, W. (ed.) (1979).

Neumann, F. (1942) *Behemoth*, Gollancz.

Noakes, J. (1978) 'The Oldenburg Crucifix Struggle of November 1936: a case study of opposition in the Third Reich' in Stachura, P. D. (ed.) (1978).

Noakes, J. (1980) 'The Nazi Party and the Third Reich: the myth and reality of the One-Party State' in Noakes, J. (ed.) (1980).

Noakes, J. (ed.) (1980) *Government, Party and People in Nazi Germany*, University of Exeter.

Noakes, J. and Pridham, G. (eds) (1984) *Nazism, 1919–1945, Vol. 2: State, Economy and Society 1933–1939, A Documentary Reader*, University of Exeter.

Nolte, E. (1965) *Three Faces of Fascism*, Weidenfeld and Nicolson.

Overy, R. J. (1982) 'Hitler's war and the German economy', *Economic History Review*, second series, 35.

Overy, R. J. (1982) *The Nazi Economic Recovery, 1932–1938*, Macmillan.

Overy, R. J. (1987) 'Germany, "domestic crisis" and war in 1939', *Past and Present*, 116, August.

Overy, R. J., Kaiser, D. and Mason, T. W. (1988) 'Debate: Germany, "domestic crisis" and war in 1939', *Past and Present*, 112.

Peukert, D. (1987) *Inside Nazi Germany*, Batsford.

Poulantzas, N. (1974) *Fascism and Dictatorship*, Verso.

Schoenbaum, D. (1966) *Hitler's Social Revolution: Class and Status in Nazi Germany 1933–1939*, Weidenfeld.

Stachura, P. D. (ed.) (1978) *The Shaping of the Nazi State*, Croom Helm.

Stachura, P. D. (ed.) (1983) *The Nazi Machtergreifung*, Allen and Unwin.

Turner Jnr, H. A. (1985) *German Big Business and the Rise of Hitler*, Oxford University Press.

Woolf, S. J. (ed.) (1968) *The Nature of Fascism*, Weidenfeld.

UNIT 19 MASS SOCIETY 1918–1939

Tony Aldgate

Open University students of this unit will need to refer to:

Set book: J. M. Roberts, *Europe 1880–1945*, Longman, 1989

Documents 2: 1925–1959, eds Arthur Marwick and Wendy Simpson, Open University Press, 1990

Offprints Booklet

Video-cassette 1

Audio-cassette 3

INTRODUCTION

The aims of this unit are:

• to discuss the meaning and validity of the term 'mass society';

• to assess the reaction of European political and cultural élites to the emergence of mass society;

• to discuss the part played by World War I, and subsequent political and social developments, in heightening élitist 'fears' of the masses;

• to explore political attempts to mobilize and control mass opinion in the inter-war period;

• to examine the role of the mass media in propagating post-war responses to the experience of World War I and the prospect, and nature, of a future war.

'Mass socialization', according to the historian Michael Biddiss, must be recognized as 'the most fundamental fact confronting those in dialogue with the historical situation of the last hundred years'. 'In the context of European history', he states at the outset of *The Age of the Masses. Ideas and Society in Europe since 1870* (1977, p.14), 'it is the emergence of mass society, and the associated developments of mass politics and culture, which most essentially and dramatically distinguishes this period from what has gone before.' What, though, distinguishes mass society?

At its simplest, Biddiss continues, 'mass society is differentiated from what precedes it by an enlargement in the scale of activities, institutions and loyalties'. Thus it has been characterized by the presence of such features as widening electorates, mass markets, increasing educational provision and enhanced literacy, the spread of mass communications, material improvements, greater leisure, and rising expectations. At its most complex, Biddiss elaborates, mass socialization has given rise to a host of conflicting ideas and theories. Some of these stressed the beneficial results accruing from the process – enlarged areas of public participation in politics, for example, and increased consensus about social needs. Others sought to highlight the debilitating and detrimental effects for society – the tendency to conformity, mediocrity and alienation, with the masses responsive to the direct manipulation of governing élites. The ensuing debate over the consequences of mass society, furthermore, has embraced writers and thinkers as diverse in background and approach as Matthew Arnold, T. S. Eliot, Friedrich Nietzsche, José Ortega y Gasset, John Stuart Mill, Alexis de Tocqueville, Gustave Le Bon, Hannah Arendt, Vilfredo Pareto and Karl Mannheim, to name but a few.

You will encounter some of their ideas, albeit briefly. There is neither the time nor the space, however, to go into all aspects of the matter and it is necessary to be selective. 'Mass society' is a wide-ranging topic and the questions and arguments arising from it are still very much with us today. The term 'mass society' itself begs many questions. It is a convenient generalization used to describe societies which evolved as a result of industrialization and urbanization. But are all twentieth-century European societies necessarily examples of 'mass society', whether they be democracies or dictatorships? What kind of society is 'mass society' being contrasted with? Mayer has spoken of the persistence of 'the old regime'. Presumably mass society is different from this? And presumably, also, a distinction should be made between the genuine existence of something which can appropriately be described as 'mass society' (bearing all the hallmarks of social change, for example, as outlined by John Golby in Unit 15), and the perceptions (sometimes distorted, as you will see) of certain intellectuals and political leaders.

Throughout this unit I shall refer to Roberts, chapter 14 'Social and cultural change, 1918–1939', which you were instructed to read in Unit 15. I shall not be setting an exercise on this chapter here, but I should like you to remind yourself of its contents by re-reading it now. Please note what Roberts has to say on the following areas: élites and the masses/the movement from status to market society (pp.478–9, 481–2, 499–501); mass communications/the social and political role of broadcasting and cinema (pp.480–1, 494); post-war 'disillusionment' (pp.491–4); and mass bombing (p.503).

There are some written documents that accompany this unit, though overall you will find there is probably less reading to be done in association with this unit than with previous units on the course. This is because I expect you to spend a larger proportion of your time – I estimate about a quarter of your normal weekly workload – examining a selection of audio and visual documents. After all, as Roberts points out (p.480), the inter-war years were a period in which the mass media of cinema and radio were increasingly perceived as powerful agents in helping to shape public attitudes. They inevitably attracted the attention of social and political élites in all European countries. Thus I have given you a variety of film and radio extracts which are intended to further your skills in the critical analysis of such sources and to illuminate aspects that are directly related to our study of mass society.

Let me illustrate the point immediately with a clip (item 20 on video-cassette 1) from the Gaumont British newsreel of 14 November 1938. The story is entitled 'Armistice 1918–1938'. The newsreels were issued twice weekly and they formed part of an evening's viewing for between 18 and 20 million cinemagoers in Britain. Five companies produced them and the Gaumont reel had one of the largest circulations of the lot.

Exercise   Look at item 20 on video-cassette 1. What are the the major points of emphasis in this report and what strikes you as surprising about it? What do you think prompted the report, what questions does it raise, and what, finally, does it demonstrate? ■

Specimen answer   It is a report on the Armistice Day ceremony at the Cenotaph in Whitehall and
and discussion   pays homage and respect to those who died fighting for Britain in the Great War. There is much stress, as the captions emphasize, on the fact that 'the glorious dead' sacrificed their lives 'to give us peace', and 'they have given us peace for twenty years', and that 'it is the duty of all nations to preserve peace for ever'. After that, however, another message is evident.

Given this emphasis upon peace, I am struck by the fact that the story takes on a distinctly martial aspect. We hate war, it states, but the best way to prevent war is to be prepared for it. The people must be fit, Britain must be strong, and our military forces ready for any eventuality. The wish is that all men may live together in peace. Yet, as you see, we are treated to a visual display of massed warplanes in the sky and a mighty navy at sea, to the heartening accompaniment of 'Rule Britannia' on the soundtrack.

It is surprising, and somewhat ironic, that twenty years after the conclusion of 'the war to end wars', a newsreel report like this should be so preoccupied with Britain's ability to wage another war. You might be forgiven, there again, for thinking you are witness to a nation actively engaged in preparations for war rather than one just entertaining hopes for peace (which makes this report doubly surprising if you remember also that it came out barely six weeks after Neville Chamberlain's return from Munich with the promise of 'peace in our time'). But then, of course, this newsreel is clearly trying to mobilize public opinion in favour of continued rearmament, and it is seeking to secure popular consent for its message of 'peace through strength'. It is an obvious attempt at mass persuasion with propaganda designed to fulfil political objectives. In this regard, the questions which spring to mind are: 'Who, precisely, was trying to persuade the public in this way?'; 'Were they acting on their own or in unison with the government of the day?'; 'How widespread was the practice of mass persuasion in Britain at the time, and what were the results?' We shall be returning to these questions later. What the use of such propaganda demonstrates, though, is that its purveyors plainly believed it could prove effective. And there, one is prompted to ask: 'On what basis did they reach such a judgement?'; 'What reasons did they have for thinking the masses would react positively to propaganda?' It is these questions that will concern us now. □

1 THE ÉLITES' PERCEPTION OF THE MASSES

Roberts broaches this topic briefly at the outset of his chapter with an anecdote about the Polish aristocrat, Count Potocki, at the Paris Peace Conference in 1919. The war had compelled the count to rethink the values and assumptions of the hierarchically structured and well-ordered society which had obtained in 1914. He was now surprised to find himself conversing with a man from one of his villages (albeit the president of the new Polish republic) as though with 'an equal'. I shall broach the topic with a visual anecdote from a film made in 1936, Jean Renoir's *La Grande Illusion*, which Roberts mentions fleetingly (footnote on p.226). Look at his comment.

La Grande Illusion was the most popular film of 1937 in France, the top box-office attraction in Paris and the provinces, winning the major French film prizes for that year. It was also a considerable international success. Its title was inspired by Sir Norman Angell's bestselling anti-war book, *The Great Illusion* (1909). Renoir's own experience as a cavalry officer and aviator in World War I apparently prompted his desire 'to express all my deep feelings for the cause of peace'. You may already be familiar with the film and, if so, will know that a broadly pacifist message is evident, in keeping with other notable films of the period, such as *All Quiet on the Western Front* (1930), *Westfront 1918* (1930) and *Kameradschaft* (1931). Its plea for greater French–German unity in particular, and its sympathetic portrayal of a Jewish character, did not exactly recommend the film to Joseph Goebbels, who thought it pernicious and promptly banned it in Germany. (Earlier in the decade, even before assuming power, the Nazis had managed to exert enough pressure on the censorship authorities to ensure that *All Quiet on the Western Front* would be banned – ostensibly because it was slanderous to the image of Germany.) Given

Renoir's undoubted artistry in evoking his themes, however, it is little wonder that *La Grande Illusion* has gained a reputation as 'a timeless masterpiece of humanist cinema'.

In the midst of all the praise heaped upon the film, what is all too easily neglected is that Renoir set it firmly in the context of World War I. And he did so because he had something precise to convey about the effects of that war in particular. The plot concerns three very different French officers – Captain de Boeldieu, Lieutenants Maréchal and Rosenthal – who are incarcerated in a German prisoner-of-war camp, under the command of Major von Rauffenstein, until Boeldieu loses his life in helping his two comrades to escape to Switzerland.

Exercise   Watch the two sequences from *La Grande Illusion*, items 21 and 22 on video-cassette 1. What sort of relationship is depicted between the three principal French officers and Rauffenstein? What do you see as the cause of their differences? ∎

Specimen answer   It is not harmonious, that is for sure, and for reasons beyond the fact that the French officers and Rauffenstein are wartime enemies, and they are his captives. There is an obvious divide between the two aristocratic career officers, Boeldieu and Rauffenstein, who have much in common, and 'the rest'. Not that the rest, mind you, easily equate with the masses. The French are all officers and there is not a private soldier in sight. They include a Greek scholar and an artist among their ranks, as well as the *nouveau riche* Jewish businessman, Rosenthal, and Maréchal who is, incidentally, an engineer. Still, Rauffenstein plainly sees them, with the exception of Boeldieu, as the lower classes, and to him they are the masses. He is contemptuous of them and racist as well – notice his scrutiny of the scholar's features and his scorn of Rosenthal.

As Roberts comments, the film admirably dramatizes the shared aristocratic assumptions of Rauffenstein and Boeldieu. They are both well educated, enjoy horses, converse as naturally in English as in their native languages, and in peacetime travelled abroad and frequented the same prestigious social occasions, such as a royal horse-race meeting in England in 1909. Boeldieu, for his part, gets on well with his fellow French officers. He can easily share a joke with them, at his own expense, but he is definitely not one of them. As Maréchal and Rosenthal recognize when they chat together, he is 'a good bloke', 'a fine chap', but 'you never feel completely at ease with him'. There is 'a barrier'. He had 'a different sort of education' and if they all fell on hard times, the contrasts would be obvious. They would be beggars, he would always be addressed more formally.

But Boeldieu has more of an egalitarian instinct than Rauffenstein. He is aware of 'the march of time', wonders whether aristocrats are superfluous, notes their former privileges are fast disappearing, and that there is a continuing process of democratization at work in society. Rauffenstein mocks 'the legacy of the French Revolution' and laments modern warfare which brings an influx of conscript officers. (In a line cut from the final release version of the film he describes modern warfare as 'the nation in arms'.) To him the war spells 'the end of the Rauffensteins and the Boeldieux'. It does, certainly, for Boeldieu who dies (albeit with the saving grace that his sacrifice allows his comrades to escape to freedom). And Rauffenstein, who symbolically cuts the flower off his plant (the only concession to beauty in his stark environment), is consigned, as he puts it, to 'dragging out a useless existence'.

Discussion Renoir's film was, of course, a fictional account, dramatically rendered and with a considerable amount of artistic licence. But his representation of Rauffenstein, especially, evoked a real note of pessimism that distinguished the élites' perception of the masses. Earlier more scientific studies had already contributed to the same gloomy outlook. There was, quite simply, a lot of them. The notion that 'mobs', 'multitudes' and the 'lower classes' constituted a threatening presence in society was nothing new. At the turn of the twentieth century, however, social scientists in France and Britain developed the idea further and produced disturbing findings about the suggestibility of the masses. □

'The age we are about to enter', wrote the social psychologist, Gustave Le Bon, in 1896, 'will be in truth the era of crowds'. He examined the changes that overcame individuals when herded together with their fellows and concluded that the crowd was too easily persuaded by the affirmation and repetition of certain basic ideas, resulting in 'mental contagion'. By the application of the techniques of mass persuasion which he outlined, skilled leaders could therefore manipulate collective behaviour that much more easily.

Though in many respects he simply plagiarized the work of his fellow Frenchman, Gabriel Tarde, and the Italian, Scipio Sighele, it was Le Bon who proved to be the best popularizer and publicist of all the crowd theorists. His book, *The Crowd: A Study of the Popular Mind*, went through twenty-six printings in French between its publication in 1896 and 1920, the English edition was reprinted twelve times in the same period, and, in all, it was translated into thirteen different languages. 'Le Bon's *The Crowd* was a great publishing success', John McClelland has argued, 'because it was able to summarize what had been worrying the *savants* within the academic world of social sciences at a time when the literate public were themselves worrying about much the same thing'. 'The secret of Le Bon's success', he continues, 'was to use science to frighten the public, and then to claim that what science could understand it could also control' (*The Crowd and the Mob*, 1989, p.196). Le Bon's ideas on crowd leadership, furthermore, had a considerable influence on the French army, where they were adopted for training purposes. And in case the politicians should fail to grasp the wider implications of his arguments, he published *Political Psychology and Social Defence* in 1910. (His arguments were not lost, finally, on Goebbels and other Nazi leaders who were especially fond of quoting him. Whether Hitler read Le Bon is uncertain, but his ideas on the crowd in *Mein Kampf* are very similar and McClelland claims that some of the phrases used there look as though they have been borrowed from a German translation of Le Bon's *The Crowd*.)

The contemporary British social psychologists William McDougall and Wilfred Trotter were somewhat more guarded and optimistic in their assessment of the masses, as Roberts notes, though Trotter's *Instincts of the Herd in Peace and War* (first published in 1916) still insisted that 'the cardinal quality of the herd is homogeneity'. Moreover, in that same year Le Bon wrote a treatise on *The Psychology of the Great War*, which purported to show how the German population had been mobilized for war through the control exercised by the military authorities over the country's propaganda machine.

For many of the crowd psychologists, indeed, World War I proved their worst fears about mass gullibility to be correct, not least because of the extensive use made of propaganda by the belligerent nations. 'To the social psychologists who had been warning the world of the terrors of propaganda for twenty years and more', Anthony Smith concludes, 'the wave of mass propaganda which accompanied the war operated exactly according to the old textbooks' (*The Shadow in the Cave*, 1976, p.26). By 1918 all the belligerents had recognized its value and had employed it to greater or lesser effect in waging total war. (You have seen an example of the British effort, of course, with the clip from the highly popular 1916 film, *Battle of the Somme*, cited in Book II, Unit 7.) Most, like the British, proceeded to dismantle their propaganda organizations immediately at the end of the war. But the lessons to be learned from wartime propaganda were not lost, as we shall see. And various post-war scholarly and popular European publications appeared merely to confirm its worth and importance. These included H. Wickham Steed's *Through Thirty Years* (1924) and Arthur Ponsonby's *Falsehood* (1925), not to mention *Mein Kampf* (1925), which we shall return to later. From America, there were H. Lasswell's *Propaganda Technique in World War I* in 1927, and G. C. Bruntz's *Allied Propaganda and the Collapse of the German Empire* (1938) among others.

In post-war Europe, furthermore, a wave of cultural critics emerged who identified what they saw as the threat to society emanating from below, from 'mass man'. For Roberts, as for many commentators, their work is evidence of 'the alienation of the writer from society' (pp.497–9). Below you will find two short extracts from the poetry of T. S. Eliot and D. H. Lawrence. The first, (a), is from *The Waste Land* (1922, Part 1 'The Burial of the Dead', lines 60–8), and the second, (b), 'The Cry of the Masses', is from a collection entitled *Nettles* (1930), which was published by Eliot's magazine, *Criterion*. Extracts (c) and (d) are two commentaries which will help to put them into context.

> *Extract (a)*
> Unreal City,
> Under the brown fog of a winter dawn,
> A crowd flowed over London Bridge, so many,
> I had not thought death had undone so many.
> Sighs, short and infrequent, were exhaled,
> And each man fixed his eyes before his feet.
> Flowed up the hill and down King William Street,
> To where Saint Mary Woolnoth kept the hours
> With a dead sound on the final stroke of nine.

> *Extract (b)*
> Trot, trot, trot, corpse-body, to work.
> Chew, chew, chew, corpse-body, at the meal.
> Sit, sit, sit, corpse-body, in the car.
> Stare, stare, stare, corpse-body, at the film.
> Listen, listen, listen, corpse-body, to the wireless.
> Talk, talk, talk, corpse-body, newspaper talk.
> Sleep, sleep, sleep, corpse-body, factory-hand sleep.
> Die, die, die, corpse-body, doesn't matter.

> *Extract (c)*
> T. S. Eliot was happy to publish that kind of thing [D. H. Lawrence's 'The Cry of the Masses'] because he'd held for some time that the urban masses were dead: in fact in *The Waste Land*'s 'Unreal City' section the crowd ('so many') flowing to work over London Bridge of a morning isn't only dead, it's in a Dantesque Hell. 'I had not thought death had undone so many' the poem's narrator is made to think, in words out of the *Inferno*. Nobody

abhorred a collective more strenuously than Eliot. His articles in the *Criterion*, his book *The Ideal of a Christian Society* (1939), his talks on the wireless, his other essays and lectures, sustain a horrified rhetoric against mass-education, mass-production, mass-meetings, mass-identity, mass-civilisation. How the contemptuous Arnoldian phrases ring repeatedly out: 'masses of the people', 'great mass of humanity', 'mass of the population', 'mass society organised for profit', 'the mass', 'bodies of men and women – of all classes – detached from tradition, alienated from religion, and susceptible to mass suggestion: in other words a mob', 'illiterate and uncritical mob', 'a state secularised, a community turned into a mob, and a clerisy disintegrated', 'herd-feeling'. Even in his dramatic piece *The Rock* (1934) with its flaunted cockneyfied proles and its apparent interest in the souls of the people at large, Eliot is bluntly hostile to 'mass-made thought': for mass man is probably the dupe of bolshevik agitators, and certainly sinful ('masses of my fellow creatures living without God in the world'; 'the ordinary deadly sins of ordinary men like the mass of men living today') . . . (From Valentine Cunningham, *British Writers of the Thirties*, 1988, p.277)

Extract (d)
The prevailing mood was largely pessimistic. Mass civilization, it was commonly asserted, was incompatible with culture. Culture was the work of minorities, and the domination of the masses, in conjunction with 'levelling', standardization and commercialization, implied the decline of civilization to the level of dull, mechanical uniformity. 'Civilization and culture', F. R. Leavis wrote in 1930, 'are coming to be antithetical terms', and Yeats foresaw 'the ever increasing separation from the community as a whole of the cultivated classes'. Writers and artists recoiled from the empty facade of urban life and the routine of mechanical civilization. Science, I. A. Richards declared, had deprived man of his spiritual heritage; a God who was subject to the theory of relativity could not be expected to provide inspiration for the poet. But the main burden of complaint, explained with particular force by T. S. Eliot, was that 'mass culture' would always be a 'substitute-culture', and that in every mass society there was a 'steady influence which operates silently . . . for the depression of standards'. (From Geoffrey Barraclough, 'Art and literature in the contemporary world', 1967, pp.250–1)

In 1927, the Frenchman Julien Benda, somewhat exceptionally, diagnosed the source of society's problems as 'the treason of the intellectuals' who had abandoned the realms of cultural leadership (*La Trahison des Clercs*, translated in 1929 as *The Great Betrayal* – see Roberts, p.493). But the Spanish philosopher, José Ortega y Gasset, in yet another evocatively titled book, published in 1930 with an English edition in 1932, held to the élitist view that the fault lay with 'the revolt of the masses' (*La Rebelión de las Masas* – Roberts, p.482).

'The political innovations of recent times signify nothing less than the political domination of the masses', Ortega y Gasset asserted in reference to the increasing enfranchisement which was evident throughout Europe. He coined the term 'hyperdemocracy' to describe the results and doubted 'whether there have been other periods in history in which the multitude has come to govern more directly than our own'. Nor, indeed, were his fears confined to political domination alone. 'There is one fact which, whether for good or ill, is of utmost importance in the public life of Europe at the present moment', he continued, and 'This fact is the

Visual illustrations of the masses

(a) *Print by Hans Schmitz* Die Masse, *1923. (From* Prints and Drawings of the Weimar Republic, *1988, p.216, Institut für Auslands-beziehungen, Stuttgart)*

(b) *Film still from Fritz Lang's* Metropolis, *1926. (British Film Institute. Copyright: Transit Film, Munich)*

(c) *Film still from René Clair's* A Nous La Liberté, *1931. (British Film Institute)*

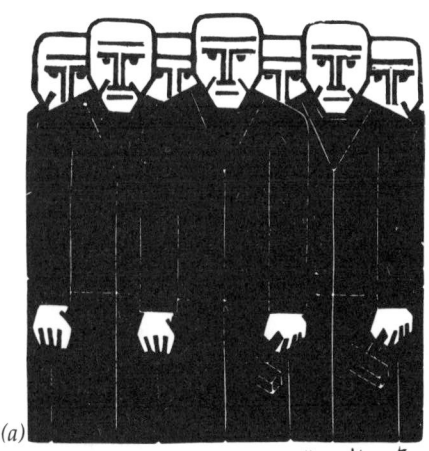

(a)

(b)

(c)

accession of the masses to complete social power'. The outcome, he concluded, was plain to see: 'The characteristic of the hour is that the commonplace mind, knowing itself to be commonplace, has the assurance to proclaim the rights of the commonplace and to impose them wherever it will' (*The Revolt of the Masses*, 1932, p.9).

For many such intellectuals, then, mass society was perceived as a grim reality. No matter that with hindsight one might query the validity of their perceptions – how, for instance, could Ortega y Gasset write in 1930 of 'hyperdemocracy' or fear 'the political domination of the masses' when women still did not have the vote in his native Spain (and only voted for the first time in the 1933 elections)? The point is that their perceptions held good as far as they were concerned and their perception of the masses was of a threatening entity. Just as valid for many among the political élites was the perception that the masses could be manipulated and that the media provided the means of manipulation. And it was the political leaders, of course, who had to contend with the effects of mass society.

2 MASS PERSUASION

2.1 Soviet Union

In Russia, after the revolutions of 1917, the Bolsheviks were faced with both external and internal threats. The external threat was posed by Britain, France and America who sent in armed forces in an attempt to crush the revolutionaries. The internal threat was posed by the White forces and those among the population who continued to oppose the new regime. The immediate problems were therefore of a military nature. But in order to mobilize the masses across such a vast country and to secure the revolution generally it was necessary to disseminate the principles of Bolshevik ideology to the many peoples of Russia.

A massive propaganda programme was devised which envisaged utilizing posters and leaflets, theatre, the press and a fleet of 'agit-prop' trains, ships and lorries. The main emphasis was put on the visual media of communication to obviate the problems of differing languages and cultures and here, as Roberts states (p.480), the cinema was especially valuable in a country with a mainly illiterate population. All the Bolshevik leaders testified to its significance. Lenin commented that 'of all the arts for us the cinema is the most important'; Stalin called it 'the greatest means of mass agitation'; and Trotsky considered it 'the best instrument for propaganda'. Anatoli Lunacharsky, the People's Commissar for Enlightenment, set out 'The tasks of the state cinema in the RSFSR' in 1919, which you will find as document I.15 in *Documents 2*. Its major purpose, he stated, was to reach 'the mind and the heart' of the people with 'revolutionary propaganda'. Read this document now.

The cinema was nationalized in August 1919 and a state film school was established in the same year. Such moves, however, belied the reality of the situation and the fact that the Communist Party did not easily gain control of the cinema. For one thing, the Soviet cinema depended upon the import of foreign films (not least from America) to sustain its exhibition sector. For another, the domestic film industry, like many other realms, suffered from acute shortages as a result of wartime devastation and deprivation. Cameras, projectors, film stock,

technicians, artists and money were all in short supply and desperately needed before the Soviet film-makers could begin to provide their political masters with the quantity and quality of propaganda they required.

Some areas, such as newsreels, were afforded priority and granted scarce resources to depict the struggle being waged in the civil war. Although the first newsreels were pretty perfunctory, later series, especially *Kino Pravda* ('cinema truth') which appeared in 1922, presented events in a dramatic and original fashion under the direction of talented film-makers like Dziga Vertov. But, in fact, it was not until 1924, when the economy began to revive with NEP, that Soviet film production really got under way. And it was only in 1928 that box-office receipts from domestic production exceeded those of imported films for the first time. In 1923, twenty-six feature films were made, but by 1928 that number had risen to 123. In 1923, the receipts from imported films exceeded those from Soviet films by 2,991,064 roubles. By 1928, when 300 million cinema tickets were sold, the income from Soviet films exceeded foreign films by 627,829 roubles.

It was during this period, furthermore, that Eisenstein, Dovzhenko, and Pudovkin, among others, produced many of the 'revolutionary epics' for which the Soviet cinema has become renowned. (You are probably familiar with some of them and most are now available on an excellent series of videos entitled 'Russian Classics' – see p.228.) They served, essentially, to legitimize the revolution and the Bolshevik regime by highlighting the plight of the masses in the tsarist era.

Eisenstein's *Strike* (1925), for instance, dealt with the subject of industrial conflict in tsarist society. In this film, the workers at a factory go on strike and thereafter suffer hardship, intimidation and finally death at the hands of the police and army authorities. Throughout the factory owners are presented as fat, cigar-smoking capitalists, intent only on their own gratification and profits, who care nothing for the grievances and misery of the downtrodden workers and their children. Its emotional message was enhanced by skilful and innovative editing – 'intellectual montage' – which juxtaposed disparate images so as to bring out the point being made. Thus, at a moment when police spies are introduced to the viewer, each spy is given the characteristics of an animal, such as an owl or a fox, and visually contrasted with the same, in order to emphasize the base and furtive nature of their roles. Similarly, at the climax of the film, the scenes of massacre of the workers are compared with gruesome images of bulls being slaughtered.

Eisenstein's concept of montage was put to even greater effect with his next film, *Battleship Potemkin* (1926). It was produced as part of the celebrations to commemorate the twentieth anniversary of the unsuccessful 1905 revolution and, in particular, an incident during which sailors in the tsarist fleet rebelled against their officers and sailed into the Black Sea port of Odessa. Again, great use is made of caricatures of the enemies of the working class. And once more there is a massacre of the people, this time in the course of the much praised Odessa steps sequence. Eisenstein's trilogy of films (*October*, celebrating the 1917 revolution, followed in 1927), together with Pudovkin's *Mother* (1926) and *The End of St Petersburg* (1927), and Dovzhenko's *Arsenal* (1929), amply chronicled the development of revolutionary consciousness – albeit by resorting, as often as not, to the creation of grandly heroic, large-scale if somewhat fictitious episodes in evoking their themes (the Odessa steps sequence, for example, was a wholly fictional and fabricated incident).

The ideological import of these Soviet epics was well recognized by censorship authorities in Britain and France who proceeded to ban them from public exhibition, though that did not always stop their exhibition in private cinema clubs, film societies and other non-theatrical outlets, where they acquired a considerable reputation. In Germany, despite attempted bans, *Potemkin* was released in 150 cinemas and proved a popular success. For all its achievements abroad during the mid to late 1920s, however, questions were increasingly asked about the domestic relevance of the Soviet cinema and the way it was evolving.

Exercise   Read document I.16 in *Documents 2*, 'We have no Soviet cinema', written and published in 1929 by Pavel Petrov-Bytov. In what respects did he feel the Soviet cinema was failing to achieve its objectives, and why? ■

Specimen answer   It was failing because the films produced were often not watched by the people for whom they were primarily intended. They were, Petrov-Bytov considered, largely irrelevant to the current needs of the people and that is why they did not go to see them. He complained that the leading film-makers were out of touch with the mass of the population and that their films were unintelligible. While he acknowledged their films had formal qualities, he plainly believed that directors like Eisenstein were patronizing aesthetes and élitists, who displayed scant knowledge of the workers' and peasants' way of life, and therefore could not possibly hope to engage 'the thoughts and feelings' of the masses.

Discussion   It was a scathing attack and typical of those radicals demanding 'proletarian hegemony' (see Bernard Waites's comments on the same in Unit 16). But unfortunately for Eisenstein and the rest, they were vulnerable to such criticism. Many of their films had not proved especially popular with Soviet audiences. *Potemkin*, for example, had been taken off less than a month after its release in Moscow on 19 January 1926. Though it was re-released on 15 June, following its immense success in Germany, it only lasted for a further two weeks before it was replaced by an American film. Moreover, several of their films, including Eisenstein's *October* and *The General Line* (1929), were considered to be ideologically suspect and re-edited to make them acceptable. Finally, Petrov-Bytov's call for mass intelligibility was a call that was echoed in many important quarters of the Communist Party. □

It had emerged at the First All-Union Party Conference on the Cinema, in March 1928, when A. I. Krinitsky, head of the Agitprop Department of the Central Committee, urged that more films be produced which would prove 'comprehensible to the millions'. And it had been evident when the Party's Central Committee took the first steps, on 11 January 1929, to implement that Conference's decisions. The result was that the Party determined 'to use all measures to strengthen its leadership of the work of the cinema organizations' and to aim for greater 'ideological consistency of the films produced'. Subsequently, the importing of foreign films was stopped and the Party exerted increasing control to ensure the cinema would play its full part in mobilizing society to meet the needs of the First Five-Year Plan and the drive towards industrialization and collectivization. 'Social realism' was now the order of the day and a film like *Chapayev* (1934, S. and G. Vasiliev) was held up as a model to follow. It was, indeed, a box-office success, but most of all its plot demonstrated the superiority of Party organization over individual spontaneity. To be 'comprehensible to the millions' came, in effect, to mean 'in accordance with the Party line'. As one leading historian of the Soviet cinema has put it: 'in the 1920s Soviet film-makers had been able to portray reality as they saw it; in the 1930s they had to portray reality as the Party saw it' (Richard Taylor, *The Politics of the Soviet Cinema 1917–1929*, 1979, p.157).

2.2   Nazi Germany

Like the Communist Party in Russia, the National Socialist Party in Germany was determined not just to achieve power but also to maintain it. Thus it too was compelled to adopt a dynamic yet pragmatic approach to propaganda to meet changing needs and circumstances. One of the major charges it had to confront, at least initially, was the oft-repeated claim that Hitler only acceded to office as Chancellor by means of 'backstairs intrigue' in the wake of the collapse of first Papen's then Schleicher's governments. Given Hitler's intention at this stage to follow 'the tactic of legality' (outlined by Bernard Waites in Unit 18), it was important to dispel the charge in order to project Hitler as the only leader capable of uniting the country and to establish the popular legitimacy of his regime.

> The way Hitler came to power by the invitation of those bourgeois and reactionaries whom Nazism was intended to supplant, was something which had to be lived down. The Nazi Dr Goebbels, minister of propaganda, understood that very well. After the Nazi accession to power, propaganda by film, wireless and newspaper treated Hitler *as if* he was the leader who had been swept to power by the crowd from outside. Goebbels used the state control of the media of mass persuasion to complete the portrait of Hitler as the kind of leader that crowd theory had always predicted. Of course, this was to a degree fraudulent, the cart having come before the horse. Crowd theory was being used not only as a means, but also as an *ex post facto* justification. This was the true sense in which the Nazis drew a technique of political persuasion out of crowd theory, but they did not thereby relinquish the rest of it, least of all the theory of crowd leadership. What Goebbels did after 1933 was to use one part of crowd theory, its techniques of persuasion, to persuade Germans that another part of crowd theory, its expectation of charismatic leadership, was realised in the person of Adolf Hitler. *Then* the Führer principle could itself be used as a technique to bind the people to its leader. (McClelland, *The Crowd and the Mob*, 1989, p.291)

Hitler's opinions on the masses and propaganda, of course, were well outlined in *Mein Kampf* (1925), several years before he became Chancellor of Germany. Although the book has been dismissed by some historians, the chapter on war propaganda has invariably been singled out for praise. Alan Bullock, for instance, a proponent of the view that Hitler's political ideas were 'entirely unoriginal', still manages to describe that chapter as a 'masterly exercise' (*Hitler*, 1962, pp.55 and 69). James Joll, who, by contrast, feels the book should not be underestimated (a view shared by Antony Lentin in Unit 20, as you will see), also agrees that the chapter demonstrates that Hitler had 'some shrewd things to say about the value and use of propaganda' (*Europe since 1870*, 1976, p.332).

As an effective example of his propaganda once the National Socialists had assumed power in 1933, furthermore, one need only look at the film of the 1934 Party rally in Nuremberg, which was made 'by order of the Führer' and released with the title he coined for it, *Triumph of the Will* (*Triumph des Willens*). Certainly there were enough people engaged in bringing it to fruition. Leni Riefenstahl was credited with overall responsibility for the production (though recent research would suggest she shared the editing with Walter Ruttmann, who remained unacknowledged). No fewer than 172 people were employed in the production crew, including sixteen cameramen, each with an assistant, utilizing thirty cameras with four sound trucks and backed up by twenty-nine newsreel cameramen, with everybody dressed in uniform so as to blend into the proceedings. Far from being a literal record of the assembly, however, many scenes were rehearsed beforehand and the sequence of events in the film did not accord with their order of presentation in the course of the rally. In all, some 280,000 Reichsmarks were spent and the result was sixty-one hours of film which, after five months' editing, ended up as a final version with a running time of two hours. The completed film was given its premiere on 28 March 1935 at the Ufa-Palast in Berlin, the city's largest cinema, before an invited audience consisting of foreign diplomats, the highest military staff, top Party officials, and Hitler himself. Few documentaries received the publicity and measure of official support that was afforded *Triumph of the Will*. But then, of course, it was a special case.

Exercise Read the chapter entitled 'War propaganda' from *Mein Kampf*, reprinted in the *Offprints Booklet*. Then watch the sequence from *Triumph of the Will*, item 23 on video-cassette 1. The translation of the speech by Hitler in this sequence can be found as document I.17 in *Document 2*.

1   How did Hitler view the masses?

2   What did he see as the purpose of propaganda?

3   In what ways did the film fulfil that purpose? (Analyse both the form and content.) ∎

Specimen answers 1   The simple and obvious answer is with a great deal of contempt. Their receptive powers are restricted, he asserts, and their understanding feeble and slow. They quickly forget and vacillate like children. They are ruled by sentiment rather than reason and their overall intellectual level is pretty low.

2   The purpose of propaganda is to win over the masses to serve a leader's ends. To do this it must be presented in a popular form, confined to a few bare essentials and simple themes, expressed in stereotyped formulas; it must reiterate certain basic slogans and generally be emotionally engaging. (I hope you noticed, incidentally, how successful Hitler thought British propaganda had been during World War I in achieving its objectives.)

3   Well, for a start it 'confined itself to a few themes', to borrow Hitler's words, and 'it repeated these themes with untiring perseverance'. The themes covered in this sequence, as elsewhere in the film, are: loyalty, unity, strength, German superiority and, above all, leadership. They are most evident in the course of Hitler's speech but the principal theme is reinforced throughout. The means whereby it is conveyed here, especially, have been well summarized by one scholar as follows (and I hope you spotted some of the points he mentions):

> The stage and the podium are constructed to place Hitler apart from his immediate entourage and, more important, high above the crowd. Here the people are reduced to architectural patterns, deprived of their individuality in favor of some larger communal ideal. This is accomplished through the use of flags, as if they were costumes, to cover the participants and through the distorted visual effects created by a telephoto lens. This reduction of people into masses is juxtaposed to an equally distorted

elevation of the *Führer* . . . From this point on, Riefenstahl continues to develop the godlike presence that began with motif and music in the early moments of the film. Now the controlling images are the recurrent shots of the huge architectural eagle and swastika and, of course, the forest of flags. Now while the canvas is crowded to the borders with men, we are given a clear picture of only one of them; the rest are supporting characters, faceless and unidentified.

Standing behind and away from the microphones on a high platform, with hands folded in front of him, Hitler addresses the assembled crowd. . . .

Moving from its position on tracks below and to the side of the high podium, the camera records Hitler's speech in a series of shots looking up at him, shots from behind, and close-ups, medium and long shots. These shots are intercut with shots of the faces of the listening audience of flag bearers; indeed, it is in these brief shots that we realize that there are actual men alive in the forest of flags. The architectural setting is severe, and the crowd seems lost in its vastness and in the murky haze which comes from the smoking torches. Although there are some 200,000 men marching in the stadium, we are aware of them only as a mass, not as individuals. At times the screen seems dark except for the spotlight on the eagle, the swastika, and Hitler, but it is only the mass of people that makes it seem dark.

Overall, it is a memorable scene. Maintaining the consistent growth of her principal theme, Riefenstahl has now advanced Hitler to yet a higher level. In his speech, he makes reference to the 'lord who has created our nation'; through the theater and film of this spectacle, he has become that lord of creation. Now the early sequences of the film assume an added significance; here, Riefenstahl suggests that the *Führer* is the lord, that he has descended to walk among his people, to bring them food, and to receive their vows . . .

In actuality, Hitler did not have many duties at the rally. He arrived by plane, observed the events, and spoke to his supporters. With music, motif, and movement, Riefenstahl creates the impression that he descended from an ethereal height, delivered sacred words, and infused the people with his spirit. The title of the film was the theme of the rally; Hitler chose it to underscore the triumph of his will over diverse party factions. (From Richard Meran Barsam, *Filmguide to Triumph of the Will*, 1975, pp.49–52) □

Triumph of the Will, then, neatly encapsulated what Hitler expected of successful propaganda. Not surprisingly, it was shown all over Germany, particularly by means of mandatory screenings in schools, local halls and the like, and it continued to be exhibited throughout the period of the Third Reich. Although it has often been held up as a typical example of Nazi film propaganda, however, in fact it proved somewhat exceptional. For one thing, as we have said, it was made at the personal instigation of Hitler himself and enjoyed unusually lavish resources. For another, it was made outside the auspices of Goebbels's Propaganda Ministry. Indeed, Goebbels expressed misgivings about the project at its outset, though on completion he recognized its achievements and recommended it be awarded the National Film Prize for 1935 (it also won the Gold Medal at the 1935 Venice Film Festival and the Grand Prix at the 1937 Paris Film Festival). Goebbels preferred to concentrate such direct propaganda in the newsreels and, besides, he had evolved his own ideas about what constituted the best means of reaching the population through feature-length film propaganda.

Although Goebbels shared both Hitler's contempt for the masses and the conviction that 'films constitute one of the most modern and scientific means of influencing the masses', he soon came to realize that sometimes more was required than simply party propaganda. The first Nazi efforts, on assuming power, at utilizing feature film as a vehicle for this purpose – *Hans Westmar, Hitler junge Quex* and *SA-Mann Brand*, made in 1933 – were devoted to the depiction of 'heroism in the Party and the movement', and all were commercial failures. Thereafter, Goebbels was increasingly of the opinion that feature films could be of greater service if they provided 'entertainment for the masses'. Of course, this did not mean that they were wholly escapist, ideology-free or apolitical. But Goebbels was sensible enough to appreciate that cinemagoers would not be sustained on a diet of unadulterated propaganda. The German cinema in the Nazi era had more than its fair share of love stories or comedies, crime thrillers and musicals, as the following table suggests:

Table 19.1

Year	Comedies (%)	Dramas (%)	Political (%)
1934	55	21	24
1935	50	27	23
1936	46	31	23
1937	38	34	28
1938	49	41	10
1939	42	40	18

(Extracted from David Welch, *Propaganda and the German Cinema 1933–1945*, 1983, p.43)

Goebbels was also less inclined than Hitler, incidentally, to do away altogether with American films, which continued to be important to German exhibitors. However, new found censorship laws reduced the number of American films shown in Germany, and some were withheld for fear of causing disturbances in cinemas. Their numbers were almost halved within a matter of a few years.

But despite calls from more extreme Party ideologues for their total withdrawal and his own concern about the dangers that Hollywood *Unkultur* posed to the true Aryan culture, Goebbels continually refused to ban them on economic grounds, claiming that the cost of removing them was prohibitive. In fact, he did not completely ban them until the spring of 1941 and they finally disappeared from German screens around February 1942.

Table 19.2

Year	German films	Foreign films (total)	American films
1933	114	92	64
1934	129	81	41
1935	92	96	41
1936	112	64	28
1937	94	78	39
1938	100	62	36

(From Phillips, 'The Nazi control of the German film industry', 1971, p.48)

By the same token, Goebbels did not feel that state control of the cinema was economically desirable in 1933 and it was not until 1937, when the film industry was suffering from falling export revenue and increased production costs, that a state-directed reorganization took place. Alfred Hugenberg was persuaded to sell his holdings in UFA, and Tobis, the other large film company, was bought out. Along with four smaller companies, they were now told to work in co-operation rather than as business rivals. But full nationalization of the film industry did not take place until the spring of 1942, when all the film companies were placed under the control of one central administration. It has also been estimated that of the 1,097 films produced during the Third Reich, only ninety-six were commissioned directly by the Ministry of Propaganda. Few of the other films, however, escaped the eyes of the *Reichsfilmdramaturg*, a state official whose function was to vet all scripts in advance of production. He was available to advise producers whether the ideas contained in their scripts were acceptable to the regime. And at the post-production stage, films could also easily be censored or even banned from exhibition. Nothing, in short, would have been shown that the National Socialists did not want to be seen. They controlled the German cinema as comprehensively as the communists did the Soviet screen.

2.3   Britain

'The new electorate contains an immense mass of very ignorant voters of both sexes whose intelligence is low . . .' (Neville Chamberlain, 1923)

'The modern, democratic world contains so many newly enfranchised and very slightly educated minds that it is more important than ever before to prevent their being led astray by ill-chosen ideas . . .' ('False Values', *The Times*, 1927)

'Democracy has arrived at a gallop in England and I feel all the time that it is a race for life; can we educate them before the crash comes?' (Stanley Baldwin, 1928)

Radio

Radio, as Roberts notes (p.481), provided governments with an ideal instrument of propaganda and the political use of broadcasting was very much in evidence during the inter-war period, not least in Russia and Germany. By 1938, of the thirty European national broadcasting systems in existence, thirteen were state owned and run, nine were government monopolies, four were directly operated by governments, and only three were privately owned.

Control of wireless technologies in Britain lay with the state. The 1904 Wireless Telegraphy Act laid down that no person could establish a wireless telegraph station without a licence from the Post Office. Receivers as well as transmitters fell within the control of the Postmaster-General when they were compelled to buy a licence from the GPO. The transition to broadcasting came in 1922, when nearly 100 applications were made seeking permission to set up transmitting stations and the Postmaster-General granted a broadcasting licence to a single cartel, a combination of the six main companies. This cartel, the British Broadcasting Company, received its licence to broadcast on 18 January 1923, though transmissions had actually started in November 1922. At the end of 1922, the number of licences issued to receivers amounted to 36,000. But by 1926 the figure had increased considerably to 2,178,000.

In 1926 the British Broadcasting Company's two-yearly broadcasting licence came up for renewal. The government, adopting in the main the Crawford Committee's conclusions, decided that henceforth broadcasting should be conducted by a public corporation, acting in the national interest and with a Board of Governors whose responsibility was to maintain broadcasting as a public service. The Company was considered the right body to perform the task and it became the British Broadcasting Corporation on 1 January 1927. John Reith, the Company's managing director, became the BBC's first Director-General and was knighted in the same month.

From the outset, public broadcasting in Britain was infused with a sense of purpose. It came, in part, as a reaction of some of the men who laid the foundations of broadcasting to their experiences of propaganda in World War I. Arthur Burrows, for example, the first Director of Programmes at the BBC, had worked for the British government in the war collecting and editing the wireless propaganda of the enemy. He was a great believer in the social potential inherent in broadcasting. So, too, was John Reith, to judge from his book *Broadcast over Britain*, which was written in 1924 and published in 1925. You will find an extract from this book in document I.18 in *Documents 2*. Read it now. Note in particular, Reith's emphasis on the 'educative influences' of broadcasting.

There was also a strong sense of hostility towards the popular press of the day and the generally debilitating effects it was believed to have upon the population. Against the idea of 'giving the public what it wants' was the idea that it was better that they should be given 'the best of everything'. There was a reaction, also, against anything remotely approaching the sort of commercial broadcasting that had taken hold in the United States. 'It would not have been difficult to make the service a clearing house for sensationalism', Reith commented, but he had a larger, more uplifting purpose in mind: 'Our responsibility is to carry into the greatest possible number of homes everything that is best in every human department of knowledge, endeavour and achievement, and to avoid the things which are, or may be, hurtful'. Along with such well-meaning ambitions there went a strong feeling of moral certitude, a good deal of paternalism and, last but not least, 'the brute force of monopoly'.

The General Strike of 3 May to 12 May 1926 occurred at a vitally important moment for the BBC: in the period between the publication of the Crawford Committee Report and the Postmaster-General's decision to act upon the committee's recommendations. As a result of the strike, furthermore, radio became virtually the sole means of communicating the course of events to the nation at large. Several provincial newspapers continued publication of a sort after the TUC brought out the printers, as did *The Times*. And they were joined after 5 May by the *British Gazette*, the government paper that was edited by Winston Churchill, and the TUC's official organ, the *British Worker*. But the mass newspapers in effect disappeared.

Because the radio was able to continue with a regular supply of news, it greatly assisted the government of the day. Asa Briggs suggests it did so in two ways (see his chapter on the General Strike in volume 1 of *The History of Broadcasting in the United Kingdom*, 1961). For a start it helped to dispel rumours, doubt and uncertainty, and then, on a more positive note, it spread good cheer and boosted morale. With news bulletins at 10.00am, 1.00pm, 4.00pm, 7.00pm, and 9.30pm each day, and a stream of programmes designed to dispel 'strike depression' while reminding listeners of 'the cheerfulness and confidence maintained by Londoners', it is little wonder the BBC was credited by many with having a steadying influence on public opinion.

But there were others at the time who felt that the BBC ought more appropriately to be called the BFC, or 'British Falsehood Company'. The TUC had from the first warned its members not to believe anything broadcast during the strike because it was likely to be 'just another tool in the hands of the Government'. (One section of the Cabinet, led by Churchill, had in fact wanted to take over the BBC completely, and use it simply as another source of government propaganda. Baldwin did not agree to the proposal and thought it wiser to leave the BBC with a 'measure of autonomy and independence'.) The sin of omission, furthermore, sometimes rankled more than the sin of commission. It was not always what the BBC actually broadcast that caused concern but what it did not broadcast. Labour Party members agreed, for instance, that while little was said against the miners, there was certainly nothing said in their favour. Nor was anything heard of the other strikers' points of view. Briggs has examined all the news bulletins from the period of the strike and he concludes that 'there was no fabrication, no attempt to twist or to distort'. But he too makes a point of stressing that 'much news was excluded'. So, indeed, it was. And more went on besides.

Exercise   Read document I.19 in *Documents 2*, which is a confidential memorandum that Reith sent out to his senior staff on 15 May 1926, and listen to item 1 on audio-cassette 3, a period reconstruction of a news bulletin of 9 May 1926.

1   What would you say was the major factor governing Reith's thinking on the role of the BBC during the General Strike?

2   What does this news bulletin reveal? ■

Specimen answers   1   Reith's thinking on the matter was governed by one over-riding argument: since the government was acting for the people in the crisis, and the BBC was a national institution, then the BBC was for the government. There was no feasible alternative in his eyes. As a result, Reith followed the government line and no Labour speakers, for example, were heard on the air. (He did, in fact, consider giving broadcast time to Ramsay MacDonald but a government veto settled that issue. The speeches of Labour leaders and the TUC were reported in the news but they were not allowed to broadcast for themselves.) Reith set great store, furthermore, on his reading of a High Court judgement which laid down that the strike was illegal (a point also expressed in Parliament by Sir John Simon, though the view was later challenged). Of course, as Reith well recognized, the fact was that at any time during the strike the government had the legal right to commandeer the BBC and to order it to broadcast whatever messages it chose, had it wished to do so. Thus, the 'measure of independence' which he won for the BBC was a compromise solution that suited the interests of the BBC and the government alike. Plainly, though, the paramount role, in Reith's words, had been to support 'the preservation of law and order'.

2   A bulletin like this one could do no other than aid and abet the government's cause and it was clearly chosen for broadcast because of that. Cardinal Bourne's speech lent moral force to the argument that the General Strike was 'against lawful authority'. As far as he was concerned, 'moral principles' were involved,

the strike was 'a sin against obedience which we owe to God', and it therefore transgressed the laws of both God and man.

Discussion   Bias, then, could be reflected in many ways, as this incident well shows. In this instance, the speech by the Roman Catholic Archbishop of Westminster on 9 May was reported on the same day. By contrast, a 'peace appeal' for the resumption of negotiations to seek a compromise between the strikers and the government, which was made by the Archbishop of Canterbury and other churchmen on 5 May, was not reported until 11 May, one day before the end of the strike. The delay was caused by the fact that on reading a draft of the appeal, Reith decided to consult J. C. C. Davidson, the Deputy Chief Civil Commissioner and his 'contact man' with the government. He advised against broadcasting it 'on the ground that it would provide Churchill and his group with just the opportunity they had been wanting to take over the BBC' (Briggs, 1961, p.379). Only after consultation between Reith and the Archbishop, and when questions were asked on the matter in the Commons, was it possible to broadcast the appeal. □

With the exception of item 2 (which John Golby has already dealt with in Unit 15) and item 8 (which Antony Lentin will cover in Unit 20), the remaining items on audio-cassette 3 have been assembled primarily to allow you to follow through the sort of issues raised here on the BBC coverage of the General Strike. Obviously the BBC continued to evolve in the period leading up to World War II. New programmes were fashioned, policies were refined, and the corporation expanded considerably. So, too, did the audience for its product. By 1939, some 8,900,000 radio licences were sold in Britain. This collection of broadcasts will enable you to pinpoint many of the changes which ensued with regard to programme format and content. One can hardly call it a representative sample, however, given the mass of material in the BBC Sound Archives. There are notable omissions, it must be said, such as variety and entertainment (which I shall broach on audio-cassette 4 when we come to World War II), music, and regional programmes. For the most part, my selection draws upon current affairs sources such as talks, news and the like. It was made on the basis of highlighting topics, issues and presentation. The items chosen are relevant to several units in this part of the course but, as will be evident, all are related to this unit and to this section in particular. Bear in mind the general questions raised so far – not least the matter of the relationship between the BBC and government – and address them to the material you hear. I have posed one or two more specific questions and, to help contextualize the individual broadcasts, I have appended some commentaries which bear directly upon them.

Exercise   Listen to the remaining items on audio-cassette 3, from item 3 onwards. Refer to the notes which follow before you listen to the appropriate item.

Items 3 and 4: 'General Election Speech' by David Lloyd George (15 October 1931), and 'General Election Broadcast' by Ramsay MacDonald (24 October 1931).

> . . . the General Strike was not the only cause of bitterness between the wars. Anger at obvious bias was powerfully reinforced during the 1931 election, which ended in Labour's catastrophic defeat. If the exploitation of the fraudulent Zinoviev letter by the press was often blamed for Labour's loss of office in 1924, a broadcast allegation by the turncoat Chancellor,

Philip Snowden, that Labour's programme was 'bolshevism run mad', was widely taken as a cause of the 1931 calamity. Clement Attlee, one of the few survivors, later described the 1931 election as 'the most unscrupulous in my recollection'. The complaint against the BBC was that Labour had been denied a right of reply. It seemed that in this most one-sided of contests, the Corporation abandoned all pretence at neutrality, arbitrarily weighting the scales to the benefit of the 'National' coalition.

One issue concerned an interpretation of the rules: the BBC decision to treat each of the three elements in the government – Conservative, 'National' Liberal and 'National' Labour – as if they were separate and independent bodies, when, in reality, all were dependant on the National ticket and did not compete electorally among themselves. On this basis, eight out of eleven pre-election broadcasts went to government speakers, and only three to the official Labour Party. A second grievance, after the campaign, concerned the broadcast of speeches by the Prime Minister and the Chancellor during the gold crisis which preceded the election. 'Under the guise of national appeals and statements on the financial emergency', protested the Labour Executive, 'Ministers and their supporters had a complete monopoly of broadcasts'. A third accusation was that the BBC presented National Government slogans as though they were the Corporation's own moralisms. 'On your action or failure to act', the BBC had admonished listeners just before polling began, 'may depend your own and your children's future and the security and prosperity of the country'. These were almost precisely the terms in which the 'National' parties had pushed their 'national unity' platform. (Jean Seaton and Ben Pimlott, 'The struggle for "balance"', 1987, p.135)

Why do you think the BBC permitted these two speeches to be broadcast? Notice the basis of Lloyd George's appeal to the voters and the arguments (and tone) used by MacDonald to condemn the last Labour government.

Items 5, 6 and 13: 'Whither Britain? No.1 "Taking stock"' by H. G. Wells (9 January 1934), and 'No.7' by Quintin Hogg (20 February 1934); 'Rearmament and un-employment' by John Maynard Keynes (23 May 1939).

That the BBC sought to establish itself as a national institution we have already seen. The ease and speed with which it was recognized and accepted as such was due to a number of factors. In the first place it had no competition. Moreover it was in the nature of the programme service itself to fuse together social needs and interests which had previously been separated and unconnected. Sport, music, drama, news – social needs and pleasures which became so rapidly taken for granted as programme categories – entered into new relationships and were transformed by radio. This was especially true of such things as the Cup Final, the Boat Race and the Grand National. These, through the running commentaries broadcast as they happened, became for the first time truly national events to which the whole country could listen. The Monarchy, too, through the microphone, became accessible to the people in a wholly new way.

There is no doubt that such programmes along with the Christmas and New York specials were widely regarded as the outstanding achievements of broadcasting before the war. More than anything else they established the popularity of the medium with a public which grew each year. They were ritual expressions of a corporate national life. But the legitimation of the BBC's enterprise, of its service to the nation, came not from the majority audience but from the great and the good who trooped into the studios to educate and inform on every subject, from unemployment to the origin of species: Shaw, Wells, the Webbs, Beveridge, Keynes, Huxley – the roll call is endless. These accredited spokesmen, not merely in the areas of their particular expertise, were endorsed in their public personas by the microphone, and *quid pro quo* endorsed the BBC as an agent and institution of the educational and cultural life of the nation. (Open University, DE353 *Mass Communication and Society*, Offprint, 1977, p.10)

In broad cultural terms, the BBC was far from conservative. Even in the field of economic or social ideas (when detached from immediate events) the accusation of rightward bias could scarcely be maintained. Maynard Keynes, still officially out of favour, was a frequent speaker, so was William Beveridge. Indeed, the list of pre-war broadcasters, which included many of the most fertile and imaginative speakers of the day, has led some historians to suggest that the spirit of reform of the 1940s had been nurtured by radio during the previous decade. Party or organisational politics, on the other hand, were another matter. The BBC would only countenance reform in the terms of which it approved: 'non-partisan', advocated by speakers talking in an individual capacity, who had been invited on the basis of their particular achievement or of personal friendship with somebody at the BBC. 'Contacts' was a key word in Corporation circles. Trade unionists did not count as 'contacts'. (Seaton and Pimlott, eds, 1987, p.135)

Wells's talk is especially rich in ideas and illuminates many of the aspects I have been talking about with regard to mass society. Notice the distinctly pessimistic note, the patronizing tone, the feeling that World War I was a great watershed, and the fear that Europe is drifting towards another war. Interestingly, later in the same year, Wells set about adapting his book, *The Shape of Things to Come* (1933), as a film treatment for producer Alexander Korda. He initially called it *Whither Mankind?* and we shall see an extract from the completed film, *Things to Come* (1936), towards the end of this unit. Keynes, you will note, ties war in with the tantalizing prospect of increased employment – a link also forcefully made by the cinema newsreels which, once again, you will encounter later. (Keep these two items in mind for future use.) Hogg, now Lord Hailsham, hardly qualified at the time he was delivering this talk as the sort of 'expert' cited in the passages above, though he was certainly 'up-and-coming': twenty-six years old, Eton and Christ Church, former President of the Oxford Union, Fellow of All Souls, son of a peer and cabinet minister, he stood as a candidate in the 1938 Oxford by-election and retained it for the Conservatives.

Items 7 and 12: '2nd General News: German Conscription' (16 March 1935), and 'Sudeten Dispute' (7 September 1938), both by F. A. Voigt.

As for news, it is true that the BBC was in the beginning forbidden to broadcast news, and won the right from the national press to transmit news bulletins only after protracted negotiations. By 1932 it had won the right to run commentaries on events by its own reporters, and to recruit journalists onto its new production staff; yet it did very little with these new freedoms. As Francis Williams observes, 'It is remarkable how little radio reporting contributed to the serious reporting of current affairs . . . Right up to the Second World War the BBC was astonishingly unconcerned with radio as journalism'. Undoubtedly the major inhibiting factor in the development of live actuality in news and documentary programmes was the BBC's self-imposed censorship system, whereby *all* material broadcast over the air had to be written down and checked before it could be transmitted. Only in rare and exceptional cases were people allowed to speak spontaneously into the microphone in the pre-war period; in, for instance, occasional live studio debates on carefully selected topics, with carefully selected speakers. The live news interview appears to have been unknown or unthought of in the thirties. (Open University, DE353 *Mass Communication and Society*, Offprint, 1977, p.11)

Although his [Voigt's] relations with the Foreign Office were good and his attitude from their point of view sound, the medium of radio itself posed a problem. There was a considerable difference between the reactions to a responsible newspaper and to a popular broadcast. A report on German rearmament in March 1935 [the first of the two broadcasts you hear now] caused considerable press comment and prompted the editor of the *Manchester Guardian*, W. Crozier, to question Voigt's use of material not previously submitted to the paper. (A condition of employment by the BBC had been that Voigt should not broadcast anything not previously contained in his press reports.) He replied that all the information in the talk had in fact been published and he was surprised 'that the particular passage (on the scale of rearmament) should be lifted out'. What to the reader of the serious press should have been familiar knowledge was, apparently, sensational revelation to radio listeners. The very impact of the wireless, as Sir John Simon had earlier pointed out to the cabinet, was the important factor, rather than the content of the disclosure. . . .
Undoubtedly, for the BBC, such incidents reinforced the wisdom of using known and 'safe' people. Journalists had divided loyalties and were subject both to unpredictable pressures and independent thought. (Bryan Haworth, 'The BBC, Nazi Germany and the Foreign Office, 1933–1939', 1981, pp.53–4)

The extracts above describe succinctly the constraints on BBC news reporting. But, clearly, Voigt at least continued to broadcast despite the difficult circumstances. Some officials welcomed his engagement by the BBC as a step towards informing the public of 'how serious the European situation is'.

Items 9 and 10: 'Radio Gazette No. 1 – review of events at home and abroad' (10 October 1936), and 'Children's Hour Talk' by Stephen King-Hall (9 July 1937).

The first broadcast here is a fascinating example of the kind of compendium news review the BBC experimented with at various points during the late 1930s. As you will hear, it contains dramatized re-enactments of topical events, a lot of sound effects to lend substance to the proceedings, some more lighthearted items, and the announcer adopts an altogether different and jokey tone to that normally employed – this was the era, remember, when announcers invariably donned formal evening wear to read the news. Notice, in particular, the use of an American (supposedly more disinterested?) to report upon 'The Battle of Cable Street', though it is not described in such emotive terms. Notice, also, the commentator's emphasis upon 'the crowd' and 'the mob' which gets out of hand only to be put firmly in its place by the valiant 'cops'. The report, in short, ends up as a fulsome tribute to the British police and the events are presented solely as a matter relating to the question of 'law and order' – an interpretation which was reinforced constantly in many a newsreel story of the day, regardless of the event being covered. The political ramifications of Mosley's march through the East End are completely ignored. Then, the BBC announcer proceeds to mock the American's accent as he leads into the lightweight report on a dog show. This, in itself, proves very revealing. Note the patronizing and pompous air he adopts as he proceeds to spell out the names of the more exotic dogs (quiz shows called 'spelling bees' were quite common on the radio at the time and they generally manifested the same condescending tone). This is a rich and rewarding item which deserves repeated scrutiny for the insight it gives on British broadcasting of the period – the values it represented and the view it took of the audience. Though by no means as rich, the King-Hall talk is interesting because of the way it inserts reference to pressing current affairs into the midst of a 'Children's Hour' broadcast; only to end, as you might expect, with some fatherly advice and a reading from the Bible.

Item 11: 'The cinema and censorship' by Lord Tyrrell (21 March 1938).

I have included this for two reasons. First, Lord Tyrrell, the President of the British Board of Film Censors, was yet another 'expert' of the sort so often used by the BBC. Second, his talk serves usefully to summarize the bounds which the BBFC set for the mainstream British cinema. Although established by the film industry in 1912 as a self-regulating body, the BBFC's president was in practice appointed by the Home Secretary. And it worked according to a fairly comprehensive list of censorship rules covering religious, moral, social and political matters, among many others. These rules were rigorously applied to feature films throughout the period at both the pre-production stage (with the submission of scripts and scenarios for scrutiny in advance of going into production), and post-production stage (when a film was completed and awaiting the award of a BBFC certificate, without which it could not be shown in a cinema). The rules did not apply, however, to the cinema newsreels, but other means were employed there to achieve the desired effect, as you will learn.

Thus, for example, in one of the better known and well-documented cases, the BBFC suggested to the Gaumont British company on 15 March 1936 that it would not be a good idea if they proceeded with the filming of Walter Greenwood's best-selling Depression novel, *Love on the Dole* (1933). One BBFC criticism was that it contained 'too much of the tragic and sordid side of poverty' and so it 'would be very undesirable as a film'. In contrast they were happy to allow director John Baxter to proceed with his proposed film of *A Real Bloke* (1935). Although it also told the story of an unemployed labourer and 'the pathetic side of life is well shown', the BBFC were heartened by the fact it depicted a character who 'doesn't whine and whimper but tries to keep his chin up bravely'. Spirit and fortitude in the face of adversity were what the BBFC wanted to see on the screen.

The talk here by Lord Tyrrell explains broadly why the BBFC took the line it did. Note, in particular, his concluding remarks that 'The cinema caters for millions whereas other forms of art cater only for thousands' and that 'To a degree which has not been reached by any other form of entertainment, the cinema is the resort of the family'. He appears to have forgotten the existence of radio, it is true. But given that there were between 18 and 20 million people frequenting the cinema each and every week in Britain at the time, he was right to single out the cinema as the mass medium *par excellence*.

Newsreels

For this section, I would like you to begin immediately with an analysis of the film evidence I have assembled, without any preamble from myself. We shall then discuss the background to these documents. Once again, my selection of source material cannot claim to be either representative or comprehensive. The newsreel libraries for the period contain many millions of feet of film. My choice was made this time in order to highlight certain themes, some of which I have already broached, some of which are new. You will recognize a portion of the material, however, since John Golby has used it for Unit 15. But I expect you to view it again looking for rather different aspects from those raised in Unit 15. Please watch the items in the order I specify. There are only a couple of occasions, in fact, when my preferred viewing order differs from the running order you will find on video-cassette 1.

Exercise   Watch the following items on video-cassette 1:

Item 14: 'Hunger trek ends', British Paramount News Issue No.175, 31 October 1932.

Item 11: 'Jarrow unemployed march to London', British Movietone News Issue Vol.8 No.383A, 8 October 1936.

Item 12: 'Jarrow marchers reach London', British Movietone News Issue Vol.8 No.387, 2 November 1936.

Item 13: 'Demonstration – police kept busy by street clashes in a tale of two cities', British Movietone News Issue Vol.8 No.383A, 8 October 1936.

1   What obvious points of contrast do you detect in the newsreel presentation of the NUWM Hunger March story and the two stories on the Jarrow March?

2   What contrasts, once again, are being drawn in the depiction of the East End street clashes (remember, here, the BBC sound coverage of the same event, 'The Battle of Cable Street') and the Paris demonstrations?

3   What would you say was the overall purpose behind the newsreel characterization of the NUWM story and the East End story? ■

Specimen answers   1   Well, I trust you noticed straight away that the Jarrow march received sympathetic and favourable treatment in a way that the earlier NUWM march did not. The coverage of the first march, in 1932, makes reference to 'extremist speeches', it stresses that the Hyde Park meeting was 'completely disorganized', and got out of hand when 'the hooligan element' took over. Although it concedes that 'ruffians unconnected with the marchers' caused the bother, nevertheless 'mob' violence ensues and rioting is brought to an end only by the timely intervention of the police.

By contrast, as you see, the 1936 Jarrow 'crusade' was greeted by the newsreels, as indeed it was by much of the news media, in terms of positive approval. It was 'an orderly demonstration' with 'a deserving object', later in the second report, reiterated as 'most orderly' and 'their object . . . a worthy one'. Mind you, the newsreels are still selective in their treatment. They minimize many of the larger issues at stake by concentrating upon the plight of one town – a notorious 'black spot' – and they personalize the story by highlighting some of the individuals involved, notably the MP, Ellen Wilkinson. Notice we are not told that she was an

MP for the Labour Party. (But then this was an unsurprising omission, really, given the supposedly non-partisan nature of the march and the fact that it was not overtly anti-government. The local Conservative agent also accompanied it for part of the way.) In short, this was considered to be a respectable march conducted by responsible people. Thus, the newsreels' sympathies were clear, their approbation obvious, the march was sanctioned, space was found to mention such comforting features as the presence of a dog 'that joined the crusade', and, in all, the event merited, as you hear, a constant stream of good wishes for 'a happy march' and 'the very best of luck'.

2   The immediate point being made, which John Golby has already covered, is that the riots in France 'appear' more violent than they do in Britain. And this was a common enough feature in British newsreels of the day – the current situation was always presented as being worse abroad than in Britain. They were nothing if not patriotic and nationalistic, as you would expect, and we shall see more examples of this trait shortly. That said, however, I hope you spotted just how comforting and reassuring this story was, in the final analysis, whether dealing with France or Britain. Indeed, the commentary goes out of its way to stress that these pictures should not lead one to infer there is profound 'political upheaval' in either country. The implication is that these are only rare and unusual outbursts, and are easily contained. How could things be otherwise when there is always a French gendarme or British bobby on hand, to restore law and order? 'It's not a riot. It's a policeman's holiday.' Which reminds me of the interpretation forth-coming in the BBC coverage of Mosley's British Union of Fascists march through the East End, and leads on to the final point.

3   Once again, as with the BBC, the newsreels were especially prone to present issues like the NUWM march and the BUF demonstration without adequate contextualization or analysis. They were incorporated within the framework largely of one specific debate, that of 'law and order' news, and served, quite simply, as an excuse for a panegyric on the British police.

Discussion   Where, though, did the newsreel companies find the inspiration for the line they took? Well, the agenda for the media coverage of the NUWM marches, for instance, was very much set by the government response to them. It viewed them with hostility and, as Stevenson and Cook have argued, sought 'to give a lead to public opinion by suggesting that the [NUWM] hunger marches were a major threat to public order' (*The Slump*, 1977, p.222). Sir John Gilmour, the Home Secretary of the day, vehemently condemned the first of the NUWM marches in the House of Commons on 19 October 1932, even before it arrived in London. He pointed out that the NUWM had close connections with the Communist Party of Great Britain and cited an article in the *Daily Worker* which called for 'mass struggle in the streets'. Subsequently, the bulk of the British news media took up the same line, adopted an antagonistic stance, and denounced them accordingly. The newsreels were little different, as we have seen, except that they tended to ignore most of the political connotations and their reportage, such as it was, rested solely on emphasizing the general threat to public order.

The Jarrow march escaped this sort of vilification, basically because it was considered to be of a 'non-political' nature and because its organizers consciously disavowed any sort of connection with the NUWM or the Communist Party. They rejected the former's offer of co-operation and carefully followed the stringent conditions laid down by the police for their march.

Still, the government view on law and order provided a ready-made mould into which any such story could be cast. And the newsreel depiction of the marches by the BUF showed, once again, much the same sort of emphasis and reassurance. Indeed, if anything, it revealed even less inclination to delve into the issues at stake. To add to the BBC and newsreel stories I have given you, take a look finally at the script for the Universal Talking News report on 'The Battle of Cable Street'. Unfortunately, in this case I do not have the film which accompanied the report but the script for the commentary alone is revealing enough and bears out the points I have been making. In view of what you have already seen and heard, I think you will agree. Anyway, the story in Universal Issue No.652 for 8 October 1936 read as follows:

> All this shemozzle arose because one man in whom a lot of people placed faith said 'We'll take a walk through the East End of London'. Then several other men, in whom a lot of people placed faith, said 'Not on your —— life, you don't.' Then the police said 'Now, now, you children, you can't do that there 'ere', and started sorting them out. It wasn't easy but they did it because if you want to place faith anywhere safe, put your money on the police.
>
> Batons and truncheons were drawn, exhibited quite a lot, but used comparatively little. A look was usually sufficient. A hundred arrests were made and, while watching, I realised how right film stars don't know they are when they say, 'I think your police are wonderful.'
>
> The way they kept their heads in the middle of a mob which had lost theirs, was an object lesson. Watch how this baton doesn't hit! You've read all about the whys and wherefores of the riot, so I needn't go into that . . . it's been written about enough, or too much, already. But whatever colour of political roulette you back, pink, red or black, every perfervid party punter will, I think, agree that blue is a wonderful saver.

The fact that the clashes on Sunday 4 October proved the final straw before the government set about legislating for its Public Order Act was subsequently acknowledged by Universal, albeit briefly and in the same lighthearted, punning vein. Its Issue No.675 for 28 December 1936 contained a short item looking back on the events in October, which stated:

> Disorderly scenes in London's East End, caused by the clashing of political factions, took place and gave rise to a few new laws regulating or banning the use of uniforms for political bodies . . . Arthur and Ernest didn't want them – it was Oswald Mos-ley.

Beyond that Universal was not prepared to comment. But then that was virtually as far as any newsreel was prepared to go in reporting upon these matters. □

Exercise   Now watch the following items on video-cassette 1:

Item 15: 'General Election Section', Gaumont British News Issue No.192, 31 October 1935.

Item 16: 'National Government Returned', Gaumont British News Issue No.197, 18 November 1935.

Item 10: 'The Prime Minister speaks out', Gaumont British News Issue No.303, 23 November 1936.

Item 24: 'The World Today', Gaumont British News Issue No.278, 27 August 1936.

1   Compare the treatment of Attlee's speech with that afforded to Baldwin in the first item. Which one, would you say, did the newsreel favour and in what ways does the report on the election results further substantiate the newsreel producer's attitude?

2   To judge from the last two stories, in particular, what picture did the newsreels present of the state and condition of Britain, and how did they seek to convey it?

Specimen answers   1   The opening title to this story, of course, insists that Gaumont British is 'non-party' in regard to the forthcoming general election. Yet despite that fact, and the obvious attempt to achieve a balance of sorts by including speeches from the Labour leader and the Prime Minister, it is pretty obvious the newsreel favours Baldwin. Attlee looks distinctly uncomfortable, being precariously perched on the edge of an armchair with his notes balanced on his knees. He is hardly very convincing when delivering his speech and altogether looks ill at ease. By contrast, Baldwin is set in what appears to be typical prime ministerial splendour and talks with authority, as befitting a man who has already accumulated considerable experience in office. The partisan attitude of the newsreel company is reinforced, furthermore, with its coverage of the election results where it clearly contrives to emphasize that the country took the right and proper course in electing Baldwin's National Government – did you notice the way in which Baldwin's speech was selectively re-edited and re-used, with captions added to spotlight the measure of agreement between Baldwin and the electorate, between the leader and the led?

2   Both stories obviously stress that Britain is best not least when compared with conditions abroad. In both instances there is a cursory review of the turbulent state of affairs existing in other countries accompanied by a heartening and reassuring report upon the situation obtaining in Britain. In the first example, of course, the message is self-evident and the country's case is plainly outlined in glowing terms by the Prime Minister. It is a pretty straightforward state of the nation speech and all very predictable, you might say, with the newsreels simply presenting the prime minister's assessment for endorsement. (All five of the newsreel companies, incidentally, carried exactly the same story on the same release date though Paramount entitled it, 'Premier takes stock, finds Britain best'.)

But the last story goes further and illustrates the way in which the newsreels utilized the full array of cinematographic effects to achieve their purpose. It is especially well constructed with its literary turn of phrase ('fortunate Britain . . . the rock of steadying influence amid the eddying stream of world affairs'; 'Britain's industries . . . have arisen from the slough of despond which clogged the wheels of progress in the depression of the last decade'), some neat visual touches (notice the wipe from foreign to home affairs), and the calculated use of comforting imagery and symbols (everything from rural idyllic country cottages to the Queen Mary – 'unquestionably supreme upon the mercantile lanes of the sea', from 'the vital factor of British justice' to the power and might of the armed forces, then, at the end, the royal family is dutifully and patriotically trooped out to bring the proceedings to a suitable climax and to reinforce the overall message that Britain is definitely best).

Discussion   The newsreels, then, as you have seen, were nothing if not highly partisan in their approach to political issues, politicians and current affairs. For all that they consciously invoked, as they did, the neutral ideology of the contemporary news media and supposedly sought to manifest the professional goals of balance, fairness and impartiality, in fact they invariably selected and interpreted the news within a framework which supported the government of the day. Indeed, they went even further than these film reports might suggest in ensuring that the 'correct' views and opinions came across in the manner that was intended.

The historian, John Ramsden, tells us that in the case of the Baldwin pre-general election story, a special set was constructed so that he would appear convincingly as in a prime minister's study, with the solid looking desk, imposing columns, and all the other trappings of authority you see. By contrast, as Ramsden points out, Attlee looks as if he has been placed in a traditional suburban sitting room. There again, Baldwin was provided with a roller mechanism carrying his speech, which was attached to the camera and allowed him to talk comfortably. Attlee, of course, looks down constantly to read from his notes. Last, but not least, Baldwin had a distinct advantage over Attlee in that he had been shown a copy of the latter's speech in advance of it being recorded and so could amend his own speech to anticipate his opponent's arguments – though this bit of sharp practice owed more to Conservative Central Office than the newsreel companies (see John Ramsden, 'Baldwin and film', 1982, pp.126–43.)

The Baldwin speech on the state of the nation is perhaps less impressively rendered. But then that was actually filmed in Downing Street, under less favourable and controlled conditions, and in something of a rush. Notice the date of the release, 23 November 1936 – barely a week or so before the Abdication Crisis became public knowledge. John Golby has already explored the newsreel coverage of this affair in some detail (video-cassette 1, items 17–19) and pointed out the many compromises that were made. So, I shall only add a few words. The newsreel reaction to the constitutional crisis, like much of the rest of the British media, was to follow the line dictated by Baldwin, which was to say nothing at all until they had something positive to report, namely the advent of a new king in George VI. Then, as with so many other matters, the newsreels largely ignored the controversial and potentially divisive aspects surrounding the issue. After all, they had spent so much time glorying in the image of the monarchy in earlier stories – such as 'The World Today' which was, by the way, originally meant to be titled 'Wonderful Britain' – that to do otherwise would have undermined their point about the essentially stable nature of the country, and the idea they had conjured of the nation as one great family with the monarchy at its head. Hence they settled for the course of action they followed when the story of Edward VIII's intention to abdicate became public knowledge. But the timing of release to the cinemas of this particular speech by Baldwin, a week before the crisis story broke, shows it was clearly intended to prepare the way and to reassure the country at large about the state of the nation in anticipation of the dramatic events that were to follow. □

There were, however, some matters the newsreels did not wish to play down or defuse in the manner they employed over the abdication crisis. Rearmament was one such issue. It was given increasing prominence as the European situation gradually worsened throughout the latter half of the 1930s and here, it is evident, the newsreels felt they had an important job to do in 'educating the public'. Once again, though, it is interesting to note how closely this process of 'psychological rearmament', as it has been described, linked with the official government view of the matter. The final selection of newsreel items in this section has been chosen to highlight the process at work.

Watch the following items on video-cassette 1, referring to the notes below in advance of the appropriate report:

Item 25: 'Is there to be an armaments race?', British Movietone News Issue Vol.6 No.300A, 7 March 1935.

Item 26: 'Where stands peace?', British Paramount News Issue No.597, 16 November 1936.

Item 27: 'Britain's re-armament plan', Gaumont British News Issue No.328, 18 February 1937.

Item 28: 'Austria abolished', Gaumont British News Issue No.440, 17 March 1938.

Item 29: 'Britain's reply – Re-arm on a war basis', Gaumont British News Issue No.440, 17 March 1938.

Item 25, from Movietone, was released three days after the Government's 'Statement Relating to Defence' had been issued as a White Paper. Though the latter was somewhat watered down by the time of publication, for fear of offending Hitler, A. J. P. Taylor considers it 'a remarkable innovation' since 'it announced that the British government had ceased to rely on collective security and were now going to rely on the older security of armed force' (*English History 1914–1945*, 1965, p.464). As you see, Movietone's report was unequivocal in vindicating the government's standpoint with regard to rearmament. The opening lines to the commentary suggest that Britain was being compelled to prepare itself militarily because other nations were now rearming (though subsequent stories made it clear that Germany was the major source of concern – see, for instance, Movietone's report of exactly two weeks later, 'Germany Asserts Right to Re-arm', video-cassette 1, item 35, which Antony Lentin mentions in the next unit).

The use of the terms 'imperial defence' and 'defensive ratio' emphasizes, however, that Britain should not be seen as a potential aggressor. And the review which scans the rearmament by the world powers leads quite logically, albeit somewhat apologetically, into a final rejoinder stating Britain's case. The spirit of peace exists by implication, although throughout the visual accompaniment is of a decidedly aggressive nature, not resting simply within the realms of military preparedness but pointing most of all to armaments in action. The same mixture of peaceful intent and military power is to be found in the Paramount story, 'Where stands peace?'. It culminated, of course, in the Gaumont report on the 1938 Armistice Day ceremony which you saw at the beginning of this unit.

The item on 'Britain's re-armament plan' has been described by the historian, Nicholas Pronay, as 'one of the most brutally effective pieces of screen propaganda of the inter-war years' (in 'Re-armament and the British public: policy and propaganda', 1987, p.83–4). He elaborates as follows:

> The running refrain of 'every aeroplane' (or tank or ship, or training establishment or storage depot) 'means more work; more wages; for more men' on the soundtrack was rammed in by the use of some really dubious

cinematic devices, some of which in later times came to be banned in screen advertising as psychologically damaging. One such was cutting in at the refrain point a close up shot of a steam hammer striking towards the audience, over which for just a couple of seconds was superimposed in huge white letters *Men Wanted*. The combined impact of the steam hammer rushing at the viewer as if he were right under it and the sudden blinding of his eyes by large white areas on the screen is really overwhelming. This was classic, brainwashing, 'forced association' technique; for a generation for whom the sign 'Men Wanted' became the symbol of hope, cruelly effective too.

Notice, also, that the forced association of rearmament with the prospect of new-found employment recurred in the BBC talk by Keynes which you have already heard. It was by no means confined to one medium alone. As you see here, however, the technique was put to best effect in the cinema newsreels.

The final two stories were released in the same newsreel issue (indeed, the last one followed immediately upon the former and consciously sought to capitalize on it, as the captions indicate). By now the message is all too evident, though, with little need to resort to extraneous cinematic devices to reinforce it. The point being made, quite simply, is that rearmament is necessary to guarantee 'security' and 'the safety of our homes and our own people' – '*Your* safety'.

In the vast majority of cases, then, the newsreel companies adhered to the government view on whatever issues were considered to be significant throughout the period of the 1930s. And it showed in their coverage of events. You have seen enough film evidence to bear out this point. On one notable occasion, however, the British Paramount News chose to depart from the agreed consensus in their coverage of a story related to the Czechoslovak crisis in September 1938. So, to conclude this section, let us look now at what happened to bring the offending company back into line in that instance, bearing in mind, as I have already indicated, that the newsreels were not subject to the censorship generally exercised over the cinema by the British Board of Film Censors. The incident did not go unnoticed, as you would expect, and it was cited in some quarters, not least in the House of Commons, as an obvious case of government interference with a supposedly free medium of communication. It certainly raised many pertinent questions about the relationship between the government and the media, and the notion of free speech in a liberal democracy. The means whereby the government achieved the effect it desired, however, demonstrates all too clearly how pressure was brought to bear on the news media without recourse to any sort of overt control.

Exercise   Read document I.20 in *Documents 2*. It is extracted from the Commons proceedings of 7 December 1938, and relates to the debate on the motion which was put by Geoffrey Mander, Liberal MP for East Wolverhampton, that:

> This House, attaching the utmost importance to the maintenance undiminished of British democratic traditions of the liberty of expression of opinion, both in the Press and in public meetings and also in other media such as cinema films, would greatly deplore any action by the Government of the day which tended to set up any form of political censorship or which exercised pressure direct or indirect.

1 Why does Mander believe the government wanted to cut Paramount's story on the Czechoslovak crisis?

2 How did the government effect the cut? ■

Specimen answers 1 For the obvious reason that it gave vent to feelings which were highly critical of Chamberlain's policy in his dealings with Hitler over the Czech crisis. Although the newsreel was ostensibly expressing the personal opinions of Wickham Steed, A. J. Cummings and Herbert Hodge, they were plainly being put in the position of political commentators. Steed and Cummings were intended to represent informed and independent 'expert' opinion, while Hodge was meant to convey the ordinary man-in-the-street's viewpoint.

2 By the simple expedient of letting the American Ambassador know of the British government's misgivings and concern. The argument being used here was perfectly precise if, Mander felt, somewhat difficult to credit: the newsreel report might prejudice the negotiations taking place in Godesberg between Chamberlain and Hitler. The American Ambassador, Joseph P. Kennedy, then proceeded to contact the Hays organization (the American equivalent of the BBFC). They got through in turn to the head of Paramount News. Clearly, as a result of the right word being dropped in the right place, the story was excised. And I hope you noticed how speedily this process of contacts worked: the newsreel was withdrawn within twenty-four hours of its release.

Discussion Mander was well informed and his deductions were essentially correct. Moreover, his allegation that 'the Conservative Central Office is not wholly disinterested in or without knowledge of what is going on' was right on the mark. As recent research has confirmed, it was Sir Patrick Gower of Conservative Central Office who started the ball rolling by writing to the Foreign Office demanding the newsreel's withdrawal. Thereafter, Halifax requested Kennedy to intervene with the American parent company of British Paramount News. Kennedy, it transpires, wisely advised caution on the grounds that censorship would raise an inevitable storm of protest and, after all, Steed and Cummings were well-known and much respected journalists. But Samuel Hoare was consulted and provided the winning argument. He considered 'it was definitely undesirable that such speeches should be heard in the cinemas while the talks at Godesberg were actually in progress. Whilst he did not wish to apply any pressure and there was no question of censorship, he would prefer that the speeches should be taken out on these grounds'. 'This clinched the matter', as Anthony Adamthwaite puts it, 'and Kennedy secured the withdrawal of the offending reel' ('The British government and the media, 1937–1938', 1983, pp.288–89). □

In the event Mander lost the debate when, as you see, a Conservative MP amended his motion to read that the House 'is fully satisfied that His Majesty's Government have maintained these traditions unimpaired', and the newly formulated motion won the vote. Furthermore, British Paramount quickly atoned for its sin and rejoined the ranks of those for whom, to borrow Mander's words, 'nothing anti-Government, nothing anti-Fascist is permitted, but anything that is favourable to the policy that the Government are pursuing is allowed to go forward'. The three speakers were replaced by a new story entitled 'Premier flies for peace' in which Neville Chamberlain appeared and talked of 'A peaceful solution to the Czechoslovak problem', of seeking 'a better understanding between the British and the German peoples', and in which he promised: 'European peace is what I am aiming at'. Appeasement was definitely the order of the day as far as a contrite Paramount News was concerned and subsequently, with Chamberlain's return from Munich, it proved only too happy to go along with the other newsreels in stating that he had secured 'peace in our time'.

Obviously, for all that the newsreels fell outside the remit of the BBFC, it was a relatively simple job to ensure they did not step out of line. But then, of course, they rarely wished to do so. The Paramount case was exceptional and, in my opinion, born of a maverick news editor's attempt to try his hand at something new, to scoop the rest. Tom Cummins was an independent-minded newshound who clearly fancied experimenting with the novel idea of political commentators. But he was not a political radical. Moreover, it was hardly as though the newsreel companies in general were seething with radical intent and only contained or kept in their place by extreme and repressive measures. Far from it, as we have witnessed from the film evidence. To judge from remarks made in 1938, furthermore, emanating from the highest echelons of both the Newsreel Association of Great Britain and the Conservative Central Office, it is abundantly clear that the newsreel companies were motivated, for the most part, by feelings of loyalty towards the National Government.

In June of 1938, for instance, the executives of the Newsreel Association invited Sir Albert Clavering of the Conservative and Unionist Films Association along to one of their council meetings. It was not the first such meeting, nor indeed the last, at which they 'emphasised the readiness of all the newsreel companies to assist the government and public departments on all suitable occasions in reproducing items deemed to be of public interest, although not necessarily of great news value'. In that same month, Sir Joseph Ball, director of the Conservative Research Department, confided to Neville Chamberlain that he had cultivated close personal contacts with the leaders of the British film industry, including the chairmen of the five newsreel companies and certain key producers like Alexander Korda. And he felt satisfied that he could 'count upon most of them for their full support to any reasonable degree'. It is little wonder the government did not need to resort to overt control when the newsreels, plainly, were such natural allies in helping to 'educate' the masses.

Mass bombing

> I think it well . . . for the man in the street to realise that there is no power on earth that can protect him from being bombed. Whatever people may tell him, the bomber will always get through. (Stanley Baldwin to the House of Commons, 19 November 1932)

Exercise   Read what Roberts has to say about the bombing of Guernica (p.522), and then watch the following items on video-cassette 1.

Item 30: Extract from *Things to Come* (1936).

Item 31: 'Guernica wiped out by air-raid', Gaumont British News Issue No.350, 6 May 1937.

Item 32: 'Die Ruinen von Guernica', UFA Ton-Woche Issue No.349, May 1937.

Item 33: 'Espagne dans les Villes en Ruines de Guernica et Durango', France Actualités Gaumont Issue No.19, 7 May 1937.

Item 34: 'Soviet display of air strength', Gaumont British News Issue No.419, 3 January 1938.

1   What according to the British, German and French newsreels caused the destruction of Guernica and who was responsible for it?

2   To judge from this extract, what would you say was the major purpose of *Things to Come?* ■

Specimen answers   1   The British newsreel plainly states that Guernica was destroyed by aerial bombardment, though it does not say who did the bombing; the German newsreel states it was destroyed by retreating Bolshevist incendiarists and categorically denies the claim that it was bombed by German planes; while the French newsreel states simply that Guernica was destroyed but it does not say how or by whom.

2   *Things to Come* was clearly intended to warn against the horrors of aerial bombardment and vividly highlights, in particular, the consequences of mass bombing for the civilian population and the havoc and devastation it would cause. One might almost see this extract as a graphic illustration of Baldwin's maxim 'The bomber will always get through'.

Discussion   I hope you also noticed, in regard to the three Guernica newsreels, that the newsreel companies were using the same source of film. It was shot by a French cameraman, Raymond Méjat, who was working for the Hearst Metrotone News and who arrived in Guernica on Thursday 29 April, three days after it had been destroyed. His film was syndicated, picked up by Gaumont British, UFA Ton-Woche and Gaumont Actualités, and put to use in the manner you see.

As is clear, however, it was used for varying ideological purposes, all of which reveal the immense potential for manipulation of the image. The manipulation by the German newsreel is the most blatant since it used the original film to fabricate a story which best suited the German (and Franco's) propaganda machine. In view of the immediate and widespread public condemnation of Guernica's destruction, the Germans and Spanish Nationalists acted quickly to try to scotch the argument that German planes had been responsible for it and, it should be noted, their story about Bolshevist incendiarists attracted a measure of support, in some quarters, for a considerable time.

The French report is the least informative. It apportions no blame for the incident, there is no mention of what caused the destruction, and it settles instead upon emphasizing the tragedy, in human terms, comparing it with the devastation which befell French villages in World War I (though the fact that the latter had been caused by German forces may just have been intended to infer who was responsible for Guernica). The British newsreel, of course, carefully treads a path which highlights all the features they wanted, while at the same time making the appropriate compromises. Thus there is no mention of the controversial aspects surrounding Guernica's destruction – no less a paper than *The Times* admitted initially that Guernica had been bombed by German planes, though it later claimed it may have been over-hasty in reaching that conclusion and afforded space and credence to the Basque incendiarists argument. To that extent, Gaumont British was of the same mind as those who wished to appease Hitler's Germany. It joined the ranks of those for whom responsibility for the bombing was never definitely apportioned. In fact, like the rest of the British newsreels, it did not even acknowledge that any Germans were fighting in Spain.

Yet at least Gaumont British acknowledged that Guernica had been bombed. The reasons why it did so, there again, are not difficult to fathom and are revealed, most of all, in the final sentence of the newsreel commentary: 'This was a city and these were homes, like yours.' The fact of the matter is that, as we have seen, the newsreels at this point were conducting a campaign to bolster the government line on rearmament. This report fitted neatly into that campaign. At the same time it emphasized the importance which the government now attached to the power of aerial bombardment. □

After Guernica, not surprisingly, stories on air power proliferated. Gaumont's Issue No.363 of 21 June 1937, for example, showed that 'Flying over Henlow, our cameraman with the Royal Air Force secured pictures of parachute training' and went on to reveal: 'The most spectacular of all exercises, a mass formation of flight. Two hundred and fifty planes darkened the sky and the roar of engines set the earth athrob. It was the biggest mass flight ever attempted'. Gaumont's Issue No.378, for 12 August, also centred on Britain and showed how '398 planes test London's air defence plan' in a story noting that the mock raiders were foiled and that the plan 'claims 80 per cent success'.

Shortly after that occasion, Gaumont spotlighted Air Ministry and War Office representatives at a mock air-raid during the rush hour in Berlin. 'At the first warning', the story ran, 'houses, offices, shops, buses, cars and trams were all deserted for bomb and gas-proof shelters'. It concluded by stating: 'Overhead, squadron after squadron of bombers darkened the sky, playing a duet of death with defending anti-aircraft guns. This is peacetime make-believe, in war it would be worse than this.' The same issue, No.390 for 23 September, complemented Germany's show of strength by observing Hore-Belisha, the British War Minister, as a representative at French army manoeuvres. The filming of aerial power continued into the following year with such stories as the one you have seen as item 34 on video-cassette 1, the mass parachute descent near Moscow. (Did you notice, incidentally, how similar the concluding images on this report were to some of the shots in *Things to Come?*)

Nor indeed on the general question of aerial power and warfare were other newsreels lacking in stories. Indeed, it was British Movietone News which, in effect, had started these reports, drawing parallels with Spain, in its Issue No.394 on 12 December 1936. There Sir Malcolm Campbell had made one of his occasional appearances before the Movietone cameras with an item entitled 'Preparedness: the grim face of Madrid brings home the moral of air-raid danger'. He proceeded to recount how he had made an air-raid shelter in his back garden, to see what it would take to construct. He concluded by commenting: 'I hope these pictures will not mar your Christmas festivities, but we shall have to take real steps to grapple with this menace from the skies in the immediate future.' Campbell reappeared again on 14 January 1937 in a Movietone report entitled 'Gas respirators for all is a timely answer to the danger of air-raids'.

Clearly, as far as the newsreels were concerned, aerial warfare had become an awesome reality and mass bombing was the likely prospect of any future war. But then, as we have seen, Alexander Korda had already speculated upon the effects of this force. What his film had demonstrated most of all was an élitist fear about the collapse of morale and the likelihood of social unrest as a consequence of the mass bombing of the civilian population. His film predicted panic, anarchy and the breakdown of civilization. This did not materialize, even under the testing conditions of the total war that followed. In Book IV we shall explore the extent to which war rendered mass society acceptable and exposed as illusions many of the élite's fears about the masses.

Bibliography

Adamthwaite, A. (1983) 'The British government and the media, 1937–1938', *Journal of Contemporary History*, vol.18, no.2, April.

Aldgate, A. (1979) *Cinema and History. British Newsreels and the Spanish Civil War*, Scolar.

Armes, R. (1985) *French Cinema*, Secker and Warburg.

Barraclough, G. (1967) 'Art and literature in the contemporary world', *An Introduction to Contemporary History*, Penguin.

Barsam, R. M. (1975) *Filmguide to 'Triumph of the Will'*, Indiana University Press.

Biddiss, M. (1977) *The Age of the Masses. Ideas and Society in Europe since 1870*, Penguin.

Briggs, A. (1961) *The History of Broadcasting in the United Kingdom. Volume 1. The Birth of Broadcasting*, Oxford University Press.

Brown, G. with Aldgate, A. (1989) *The Common Touch. The Films of John Baxter*, British Film Institute.

Bullock, A. (1962) *Hitler: a Study in Tyranny*, Penguin.

Cunningham, V. (1988) *British Writers of the Thirties*, Oxford University Press.

Curran, J. and Porter, V. (eds) (1983) *British Cinema History*, Weidenfeld and Nicholson.

Curran, J., Smith, A. and Wingate, P. (eds) (1987) *Impacts and Influences. Essays on Media Power in the Twentieth Century*, Methuen.

Haworth, B. (1981) 'The BBC, Nazi Germany and the Foreign Office, 1933–1939', *Historical Journal of Film, Radio and Television*, vol.1, no.1, March.

Joll, J. (1976) *Europe since 1870*, Penguin.

Kenez, P. (1985) *The Birth of the Propaganda State. Soviet Methods of Mass Mobilization 1917–1929*, Cambridge University Press.

LeMahieu, D. L. (1988) *A Culture for Democracy. Mass Communication and the Cultivated Mind in Britain Between the Wars*, Clarendon Press.

McClelland, J. S. (1989) *The Crowd and the Mob*, Unwin Hyman.

Open University (1977) DE353 *Mass Communication and Society*, Offprint (Scannell, P. and Cardiff, D. 'The social foundations of British broadcasting'), The Open University.

Ortega y Gasset, J. (1932) *The Revolt of the Masses*, Norton.

Phillips, M. S. (1971) 'The Nazi control of the German film industry', *Journal of European Studies*, vol.1, March.

Pronay, N. (1987) 'Re-armament and the British public: policy and propaganda' in Curran, J., Smith, A. and Wingate, P. (eds) (1987).

Ramsden, J. (1982) 'Baldwin and film' in Pronay, N. and Spring, D. W. (eds) *Propaganda, Politics and Film 1918–45*, Macmillan.

Reader, K. (1981) *Cultures on Celluloid*, Quartet.

Richards, J. (1984) *The Age of the Dream Palace*, Routledge and Kegan Paul.

Richards, J. and Aldgate, A. (1983) *Best of British. Cinema and Society 1930–1970*, Basil Blackwell.

Seaton, J. and Pimlott, B. (eds) (1987) *The Media in British Politics*, Gower.

Short, K. R. M. (ed.) (1981) *Feature Films as History*, Croom Helm.

Smith, A. (1976) *The Shadow in the Cave. The Broadcaster, the Audience and the State*, Quartet.

Stevenson, J. and Cook, C. (1977) *The Slump*, Cape. (Chapter XIV is reproduced in the *Offprints Booklet*.)

Taylor, A. J. P. (1965) *English History 1914–1945*, Clarendon Press.

Taylor, R. (1979) *Film Propaganda*, Croom Helm.

Taylor, R. (1979) *The Politics of the Soviet Cinema 1917–1929*, Cambridge University Press.

Taylor, R. and Christie, I. (eds) (1988) *The Film Factory. Russian and Soviet Cinema in Documents 1896–1939*, Routledge and Kegan Paul.

Vincendeau, G. and Reader, K. (eds) (1986) *La Vie est à Nous. French Cinema of the Popular Front 1935–1938*, British Film Institute.

Ward, K. (1989) *Mass Communications and the Modern World*, Macmillan.

Welch, D. (1983) *Propaganda and the German Cinema 1933–1945*, Clarendon Press.

Selected filmography

1   Feature film

'The Alexander Korda Classic Film Library' (Central Video)
    Things to Come (1936, William Cameron Menzies)

'Russian Classics' (Hendring Video)
    Battleship Potemkin (1926, Sergei Eisenstein)
    End of St Petersburg (1927, Vsevolod Pudovkin)
    Mother (1926, Vsevolod Pudovkin)
    October (1927, Sergei Eisenstein and Grigori Alexandrov)
    Storm over Asia (1928, Vsevolod Pudovkin)
    Strike (1925, Sergei Eisenstein)

2   Newsreel

'Music, Memories and Milestones' (Visnews Video)
    Volume 1. The 1930s

'The Silver Heritage Collection' (British Movietonews Video)
    Volume 2. Great Events

UNIT 20 ORIGINS OF WORLD WAR II

Antony Lentin

With grateful acknowledgement to Richard Bessel, Arthur Marwick, Peter Neville and Bill Purdue

Open University students of this unit will need to refer to:

Set book: J. M. Roberts, *Europe 1880–1945*, Longman, 1989

Documents 2: 1925–1959, eds Arthur Marwick and Wendy Simpson, Open University Press, 1990

Course Reader: *War, Peace and Social Change in Twentieth-Century Europe*, eds Clive Emsley, Arthur Marwick and Wendy Simpson, Open University Press, 1990

Maps Booklet

Video-cassette 1

Audio-cassette 3

INTRODUCTION

The aims of this unit are to enable you:

● to identify the main developments and characteristics of international relations in Europe 1919–1939, geopolitical, diplomatic and ideological;

● to examine and evaluate a variety of documentary and other primary sources as evidence of the origins of World War II;

● to engage in part of the historiographical debate on the origins of World War II and to reach your own informed conclusions.

Specifically, you are asked to consider the following four questions, discussed in the corresponding sections of the unit:

1   How far did the Versailles settlement and the Locarno agreements solve the 'German problem' in the 1920s?

2   Did Nazi foreign policy differ materially from its predecessors?

3   In what ways was the Rhineland crisis of 1936 a crucial turning-point to war?

4   Was the 'Appeasement' policy of Neville Chamberlain a contributory cause of war?

In 1919 the Allied Commander-in-Chief, Marshal Foch, described the Treaty of Versailles as 'the twenty-year armistice', implying that it would not be adequate to control Germany for more than twenty years and that a second German bid to dominate Europe by war would be the consequence. His remark presupposes the existence of a 'German problem', 'the problem of fitting Germany into the European political system without endangering the independence of other states and the self-determination of other peoples' (Bull, *The Challenge of the Third Reich*, 1986, p.10).

It is common ground among most historians that the 'German problem' which had been in existence at least since 1900, perhaps since 1870, *was* the over-riding international problem in Europe between the wars. The failure to solve it whether by the use of military force (by the Allied victory of 1918 or by the invasion of the Ruhr in 1923) or by diplomacy (by the Treaty of Versailles in 1919, the Treaty of Locarno in 1925 or the Munich Agreement in 1938) – was an operative cause of World War II. Other threats to peace in Europe – Italian aggression under Mussolini, Hungarian revisionism, rivalries among the succession-states, discontented national minorities – were secondary to the 'German problem' and became serious disturbances to international stability only when linked with it. Hence this unit focuses on the 'German problem' in Europe between the wars.

Was World War II essentially a replay of World War I, the second round of a struggle for German predominance in Europe? Some historians (notably Fritz Fischer) point to strong similarities between German policies in both wars, and argue for an underlying continuity in German history. Such historians stress the similarity of war-aims evolved in both wars. World War I produced an 'almost megalomaniacal annexationism of the German leadership, civilian as well as military' (S. A. Schukman in Martel, *The Origins of the Second World War Reconsidered*, 1986, p. 57). Was this linked with similar annexationism in World War II? And if so, how does Weimar foreign policy fit into the pattern? As an interval? Or as a connecting link?

Other historians see the two wars as basically unconnected. The second did not flow inevitably out of the first. The peace after 1919 was not 'doomed' to be a mere truce. While Mayer (Course Reader, p.45) sees both wars flowing directly from an underlying chronic European crisis, the *causa causans* of both wars, others see World War II as the result of a *novus actus interveniens*, a new supervening element which was itself the substantial cause of World War II. This was the advent of Hitler and Nazism in Germany, which, while building on existing trends towards expansionism, added a wholly new impetus and ideology, going far beyond those of Weimar or Imperial Germany.

1 THE VERSAILLES SETTLEMENT AND THE 'GERMAN PROBLEM' 1919–33

This unit is concerned with the origins of World War II as manifested in the decline, fall and overthrow of the Versailles settlement across the twenty years 1919 to 1939. Therefore the first task is to consider the nature of that settlement.

Exercise   Please re-read Bill Purdue's analysis in Book II, Units 8–10, section 1.2, and/or Roberts, pp.323–31, and consult map 7 in the *Maps Booklet*. Then make brief notes on the impact on Germany of the Treaty of Versailles.

Now please consider the following, and use them to flesh out your notes on the impact of Versailles on Germany:

● Document I.21 in *Documents 2* (from the reply of the Allied and Associated Powers to the Observations of the German Delegation on the Conditions of Peace, 16 June 1919).
● A cartoon from the German satirical magazine *Simplicissimus*, 1919, reproduced opposite. ■

Versailles: a *Diktat*?

Individually and cumulatively, the 440 terms of Versailles do seem to represent a harsh and crushing imposition, a 'Carthaginian peace' as Keynes called it, a *Diktat*, to use Hitler's word. Almost every aspect of it offended some section of German opinion: the territorial amputations (especially the territories and nationals lost to Poland), the loss of raw materials in Alsace-Lorraine and Upper Silesia; the loss (albeit temporary) of the Saar, with its mines; occupation of the Rhineland by allied troops (albeit for a maximum of fifteen years); confiscation of all the German colonies; exclusion (albeit temporary) from the League of Nations; disarmament and massive cuts in Germany's armed forces.

The treaty was certainly a *Diktat* in the sense that its terms were first settled between the Allies and then imposed unilaterally on the Germans without face-to-face negotiations and with few changes.

In addition to all this was the opprobrium of Article 231, the notorious 'war-guilt' clause, which imposed historical, moral and financial responsibility on Germany for causing the war and for the losses brought about by its 'aggression'.

Document I.21 shows the thinking of the 'Big Three' and reveals why reparation, war-guilt and the trial of the Kaiser were felt to be integral parts of the treaty as a 'settlement of the accounts of this terrible war'. It was written for the 'Big Three' by Philip Kerr, secretary to Lloyd George, as the victors' final word to the

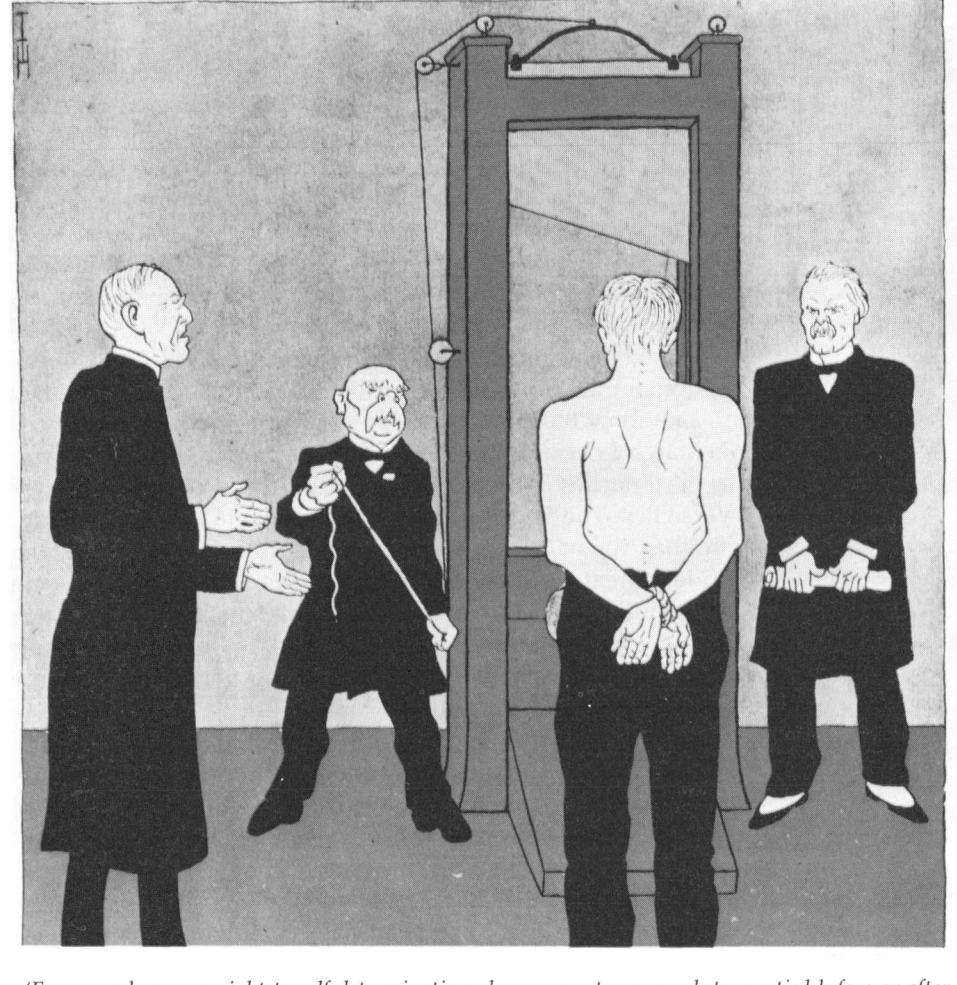

'Even you have one right to self-determination: do you want your pockets emptied before or after execution?' (A cartoon in Simplicissimus, *3 June 1919. Bildarchiv Preussicher Kulturbesitz, Berlin)*

German delegation in reply to the latter's objections, and as an explanation and justification of the treaty overall as inspired by and founded on 'justice' and 'reparation'. The document formed an introductory covering-note to the treaty; and its purpose, and that of the treaty, was emphasized by Lord Curzon when presenting the treaty to the House of Lords: 'The bringing home to Germany and its rulers of their responsibility for having inflicted on the world the sufferings and calamities of the last five years fundamentally distinguishes the Treaty of Versailles from any previous peace treaty' (quoted in Lentin, *Guilt at Versailles*, 1985, p.xi). Language like that of Article 231 and document I.21 was without precedent in a treaty of peace. Was it likely to conciliate German opinion?

At the time of the armistice, Wilson and the Allies had promised 'a peace of justice' on the basis of the Fourteen Points, especially if Germany got rid of the Kaiser and adopted a democratic form of government. Germany had duly declared itself a Republic, and the Kaiser had fled to Holland. But under the treaty not only was the new Germany saddled with moral and financial responsibility for the war as 'a crime against humanity and right', but there were numerous and obvious violations of the Fourteen Points (for example, the principle of open diplomacy and the refusal to negotiate; the principle of self-determination and the prohibition on Austro-German union; the principle of fair arbitration of colonial questions and the wholesale confiscation of Germany's overseas possessions).

In Germany, the suspicion gained currency that Wilson's offers had been no more than a *ruse de guerre* to trick Germany into armistice; and even that the German army had not been defeated in the war, but betrayed by left-wing politicians and revolutionaries at home – the notorious *Dolchstosslegende*, the legend of the 'stab in the back' by the 'November criminals' who signed the armistice. There were few symbols of military defeat; no war damage in Germany; no Allied invasion of its territory or march to Berlin; only the post-armistice occupation of the Rhineland. The psychological shock of Versailles was all the greater to a nation which had felt assured of victory, which had dictated terms to Russia in March 1918, and which now felt bewildered, deceived, betrayed and cheated.

No one in Germany had, or could be expected to have, a good word for Versailles. The first Weimar government refused to sign it and resigned, protesting that 'the hand that signed would wither'. A German signature was extorted under threat of a renewal of hostilities, the Social Democrat President Ebert complaining of the Treaty's 'unheard-of injustice'. No German statesman or party in the Weimar period was reconciled to the 1919 settlement, and German perceptions of Versailles were at least as important as Allied ones when it came to willingness to comply with it.

The cartoon from the left-wing satirical magazine, *Simplicissimus*, shows Versailles from a German point of view: the new, young Germany of Weimar is depicted stripped and bound, ready for execution. Lloyd George wields the death sentence; Clemenceau is the executioner and Wilson, the chaplain, vindictive and pharisaical. Germany is the innocent victim of 'unheard-of injustice'.

Throughout the 1920s Versailles was denounced, especially from the Right, as a *Schandvertrag* (treaty of shame). For Hitler's view of Versailles and the use which he sought to make of it, see document I.23(a) in *Documents 2*.

Wilson, Clemenceau, Lloyd George and the 'German problem'

Exercise What were the policies of the 'Big Three' (Wilson, Lloyd George, Clemenceau) who drew up the treaty? ■

Discussion You may feel – the Germans, Smuts and Keynes certainly did – that the conditions imposed on Germany suggest quite extraordinary vindictiveness or irresponsibility on the part of the victors. An alternative view is that the treaty stemmed from serious but conflicting and often contradictory attempts to deal with the 'German problem'. All three agreed that Imperial Germany had come close to pulling off a bid for domination of the European continent: at the height of its military success in March 1918, German troops were entrenched from the Belgian coast to the Black Sea. Only American intervention had turned the scales. How to prevent the tragedy of the world war from repeating itself was foremost in the victors' thoughts. Whatever their views on a solution, however, their freedom of action was crucially predetermined by their acceptance that a German state of some sort would continue to exist. There was no real expectation – despite appeals from Marshal Foch to detach the Rhineland from the Reich – of partitioning Germany in order to remove the German threat. It therefore followed, as Smuts pointed out to

Lloyd George, that 'the Germans are, have been, and will continue to be the *dominant* factor on the Continent of Europe, and no permanent peace is possible which is not based on that fact' (document I.22 in *Documents 2*). Each of the 'Big Three' agreed with Smuts's proposition. □

Wilson and self-determination

Wilson sought to accommodate legitimate French desires for security within a more liberal and lasting system of international relations based on national self-determination, the denial of which he believed to have been an underlying cause of the war. Hence his insistence on the return of Alsace-Lorraine to France. Hence the creation of the new nation states, based on the principle that 'No people must be forced under sovereignty under which it does not wish to live' (quoted in Lentin, *Guilt at Versailles*, 1985, p.5).

The problem here, as Wilson soon discovered, was that the rights of different nationalities (including Germans) could not always be reconciled, especially in areas of mixed population (such as Upper Silesia and the Polish Corridor). Any settlement which discriminated against Germans was bound to stir German national resentment, notably in the areas ceded to Poland, but also among German nationals in the former Austro-Hungarian Empire who sought unification with the Reich, such as the Austrians, forbidden by the 'Big Three' to join Germany. Wilson looked to his 'brain-child' the League of Nations to appease and conciliate, once the atmosphere of war hatred had died away, and even, where necessary, to consider revision of the peace treaties. However, America repudiated both the treaty and the League, leaving Europe to sort out its own problems. This left Britain and France with effective responsibility for Versailles.

France and security

France's basic concern was not so much punitive as compensatory. Clemenceau knew that, in the long run, time was on Germany's side. Its territory, population and resources, even after Versailles, were superior to France's. Its birthrate was higher. (See the demographic and economic analysis in Book II, Units 8–10.) The war seemed to have left France with old men, widows and cripples.

France sought first to weaken German power and hold it down, and second to require Germany to contribute towards making good in payments and in kind the devastation of its war-ravaged north-east. Scores of French towns and villages had been destroyed, and mines and industries wrecked and pillaged, while (outside East Prussia) Germany suffered no physical war damage. Obviously Germany would one day recover something of its strength in Europe; France's purpose was to restrain it by means of a fresh alliance system with the new succession states to the east and south of Germany (Poland and Czechoslovakia in particular), viewed by France as an 'eastern barrier' against Germany and at the same time as a *cordon sanitaire* against Russian bolshevism. Thus France, said Clemenceau's Foreign Minister, Pichon, wanted a Poland *'grande et forte – très forte'*.

For France, the key to enforcement of the treaty was the permanent demilitarization by Germany of the Rhineland and its occupation by allied forces for a fifteen-year period (theoretically extendible). Clemenceau saw occupation of the Rhineland (a) as a general deterrent against German aggression and (b) as a sanction and means of retaliation and enforcement in case of any lesser breach of the treaty (for example, default in payment of reparations).

Additionally, Clemenceau secured from Wilson and Lloyd George a pledge to come to France's aid in the event of a future attack by Germany. America, however, refused to ratify Versailles, whereupon Britain withdrew its military commitment to France. This threw the onus of responsibility for enforcing Versailles onto France alone.

Britain

Britain secured most of what it wanted at the armistice. British policy was essentially satisfied with the disappearance of the German navy and the confiscation of the German colonies, that is, with the removal of Germany as a naval and colonial rival. Additionally Britain was committed to exacting reparations, which Lloyd George had made a main plank of his election platform in December 1918. Once popular tempers had cooled, however, Lloyd George was ready to join in efforts to scale down reparations. While hoping that Wilson's policy of national self-determination would bring lasting peace, Britain worried about new trouble-spots, especially in Eastern Europe. Unlike France, therefore, once the treaty was signed, Britain was not whole-heartedly committed either to the full exaction of reparations or to the immutability of the settlement in Eastern Europe. There were misgivings among the British delegates at Versailles about French 'harshness'. Such qualms were crystallized in Keynes's polemic, *The Economic Consequences of the Peace* (1919), with its critique of the economic dislocation caused to the European system by the peacemakers' emphasis on the principle of nationality. After 1919 Britain backed away from commitment to the treaty. It was unwilling and unable to enforce militarily the 1919 settlement by continuing to act as the 'policeman of the world'; having made peace, Britain expected the treaties to enforce themselves.

Versailles: 'an impossible peace' (Smuts)?

Recapitulation exercise

Read document I.22 in *Documents 2* (Smuts's letter to Lloyd George, 26 March 1919). Can you identify the principal authors of particular proposals criticized by Smuts? Outline the relevant provisions of the treaty. ∎

Discussion

1   *Danzig*. America and France wanted to cede the German city of Danzig to Poland outright, Wilson having, in the Fourteen Points, promised Poland 'free and secure access to the sea' and Clemenceau wishing to strengthen Poland. A compromise was imposed at Lloyd George's suggestion, whereby Danzig was made an autonomous 'Free City' under League of Nations' sovereignty and Poland was granted the right to use the port.

2   *The Polish Corridor*. America and France wanted to make Poland viable by granting a geographical corridor between Danzig and the Polish hinterland. The Corridor and Poznania included half a million Germans, and remained a running sore between Germany and Poland between the wars. Again at the promptings of Lloyd George, plebiscites were held in the contested areas of Marienwerder and Allenstein, in East Prussia, and in Upper Silesia. Eastern Silesia, Marienwerder and Allenstein voted to remain with Germany (1921), but neither Germany nor Poland was satisfied.

3   *The Saar Valley*. Clemenceau wished to annex the Saarland (which had last belonged to France in 1814) in part to compensate France for wartime destruction of its coal mines. Wilson and Lloyd George opposed this as a clear violation of

self-determination. Lloyd George again came up with a solution: that France should occupy and use the mines, but that sovereignty of the Saar should go to the League of Nations for fifteen years, after which its future would be decided by plebiscite.

4   *Separation of the Rhineland*. Clemenceau broached the possibility of detaching the Left Bank of the Rhine from Germany as a buffer-state under French tutelage; but was vetoed by Wilson and Lloyd George, who warned against creating 'Alsace-Lorraines' in reverse. In the early 1920s there were several French attempts to foment separatism in the Rhineland.

5   *Trial of the Kaiser* and others thought responsible for 'crimes against humanity'; and payment of reparations by Germany. Lloyd George was closely tied to these policies. Clemenceau was equally anxious to exact reparations and to claim the lion's share for France as the country most severely damaged by the war. The trial of the Kaiser was abandoned in 1920 when the Dutch refused to surrender him. Wilson strove to moderate the sums being demanded and (like Smuts) to persuade Lloyd George and Clemenceau to agree to a fixed figure, but a final sum was not laid down until 1921. Both the amounts demanded and the obligation to pay at all were fiercely resented in Germany, linked as they were with the *Schmachparagraph*, the offensive 'war-guilt' clause. Throughout the 1920s reparations remained a constant source of difficulties and friction between Germany and the Allies.

6   *The League of Nations and Germany*. Wilson and Lloyd George wanted Germany to be a member of the League from the start. Clemenceau opposed German membership so soon after the horrors of the war. The 'Big Three' agreed to Germany's joining the League after a few years' probation. □

Versailles: a compromise peace?

Few of the 'solutions' imposed at Versailles were clear-cut. They were the fruits of political compromise between the 'Big Three'. Without such compromise, the Peace Conference would probably have broken up. 'We were no more at liberty to make peace on our own terms than we were to make war', said Clemenceau. 'There has, unfortunately, to be a great deal of give and take', Wilson admitted (quoted in Lentin, *Guilt at Versailles*, 1985, p.72). Versailles was thus largely a compromise between French and American policies.

'What has become of Wilson's Fourteen Points?' Smuts (and the Germans) quite reasonably complained.

A literal application of Wilsonian self-determination, enclosing most German nationals within the Reich, would have made Germany even bigger and more preponderant in Europe than in 1914. (As Roberts points out on page 330, the demand for such a *Grossdeutschland* – 'Greater Germany' – was a feature of the emergent Nazi Party in 1920.) Hence, in deference to Clemenceau's veto, the treaty forbade union between Germany and the new Austrian state. A strict application of self-determination would likewise have assigned the Sudeten Germans to Germany. Again, this would have made Germany larger than in 1914 and, as Clemenceau objected, have deprived the new Czechoslovakia of vital industries and a defensible frontier.

Such compromises were not consciously cynical violations of the Fourteen Points, though they often seemed so to German opinion; but they served to make the treaty seem inconsistent and unjust at Germany's expense.

At the last moment, the revisionist arguments of Smuts began to find favour in the British delegation; and Lloyd George argued – too late and largely in vain – with Clemenceau and Wilson for greater leniency towards Germany. The most he could secure was their agreement to plebiscites in East Prussia and Upper Silesia. Clemenceau refused any further concessions; and he was supported by Wilson, anxious not to unravel the series of hard-won inter-allied compromises, and looking idealistically to the League of Nations to settle outstanding grievances.

As an attempt to come to grips with the 'German problem', however, the treaty, a collection of improvizations designed to suit the victors, was a failure. It wrested a German signature; it did not win German acceptance. Versailles neither destroyed Germany, nor did it pacify it. It left Germany with plenty of causes for resentment, without rendering it permanently harmless. It was, commented Jacques Bainville in 1919, 'too mild for its severity' (quoted in Lentin, *Guilt at Versailles*, 1985, p.132).

The enforcement of Versailles

The 1919 settlement was not self-enforcing. Germany would comply only reluctantly and under protest, not feeling morally bound by it. America refused to ratify the treaty, and repudiated most of its responsibilities under it. This left Britain and France the guarantors of the settlement. Italy, discontented with its spoils, was half-hearted in its attitude towards the settlements, and periodically sided with other revisionist states, such as Hungary.

The treaty once signed, Britain, soon beset by economic stagnation, looked to a revival of international trade, in which Germany would resume its pre-war role as a leading purchaser of British goods. British opinion thus favoured a peaceful German recovery, and was not averse to a peaceful readjustment of the 1919 frontiers in the east. Keynes's *The Economic Consequences of the Peace*, a root-and-branch denunciation of Versailles in the spirit of Smuts's letter to Lloyd George, had enormous influence on public opinion; and successive British governments spoke of peaceful revision, or the 'appeasement' of Europe – the word did not take on pejorative connotations until 1939. Apart from the occupation forces in the Rhineland, Britain and America withdrew their armies from the continent. France alone, fearful of German recovery, sought to enforce Versailles to the letter, particularly after the repudiation of the Anglo-American guarantee.

Post-war Germany: stronger in Europe after Versailles?

To suggest that Germany's position in Europe after Versailles was, both actually and potentially, more preponderant than in 1914, may seem paradoxical. Yet so it was (please look at Roberts, Map 6, p.603). France, Britain, Russia and Italy together had been unable to break Germany in the war; and as well as holding off the three Western Powers, Germany had over-run the Balkans and defeated Russia. It required American intervention to turn the scales against Germany in 1918.

After Versailles, America withdrew into two decades of political isolationism. Bolshevik Russia was increasingly shunned by Britain and France, who attempted to isolate communism from Europe. Conversely, Germany to some extent offset Versailles by coming to terms with Russia: by the Treaty of Rapallo (1922) it undercut the Allies by recognizing Soviet Russia and entering into close economic ties. The year before it had secretly secured facilities for military manoeuvres on Russian soil.

The succession states of Central and Eastern Europe were either small, relative to Germany (Austria, Hungary, the Baltic states); or, if large, contained dissident minorities (Poland, Romania, Yugoslavia; Czechoslovakia was both relatively small and contained minorities). They were often economically and politically unstable, and commonly at each other's throats. This fragmentation (or 'balkan-ization') and mutual hostility in Central and Eastern Europe underscores overall German predominance, as does the fact that the succession states failed to make common cause to uphold the 1919 settlement, but on the contrary often pursued irredentist aims of their own (for example, Poland's war against Russia (1920) and its claim to Teschen, which prevented co-operation with Czechoslovakia between the wars; and Hungary's ambitions against 'the Little Entente' – Czechoslovakia, Yugoslavia and Romania).

Even counting its losses at Versailles, then, Germany remained, as Smuts pointed out, by virtue of its size, population, resources and geopolitical situation, 'the *dominant factor* on the Continent of Europe'. It was acknowledged that by the early 1930s Germany would have recovered internally from the war; yet the early 1930s was precisely the time fixed by the treaty for the withdrawal of the allied armies of occupation. That was why, as Roberts says (p.324), France sought 'to wound Germany as deeply and as permanently as possible' by supporting Poland and Czechoslovakia and by insisting on its full right to reparation and to punctilious payment by Germany of the instalments as they fell due. France hoped that rigorous enforcement of the treaty and the maintenance of its Eastern alliance system would keep Germany under control. Hence alliance with Belgium (1920), Poland (1921), Czechoslovakia (1924), Romania (1926) and Yugoslavia (1927). Hence French support for Poland against Russia (1920–21) and for the Little Entente against Hungary. Hence direct French military intervention several times when Germany defaulted on reparations, culminating in the invasion of the Ruhr in 1923. Roberts refers to the years 1919–23 as France's 'brief Indian summer as a great power' (p.350). In reality the 'Indian summer' was mainly the reflection of temporary German weakness, and France's 'belligerence' – the reflection of its realization of the fragility of Versailles as a protection against German resurgence. The British elder statesman, Balfour, commented of the French: 'They are so dreadfully afraid of being swallowed up by the tiger that they spend all their time poking it' (quoted in Kitchen, *Europe Between the Wars*, 1988, p.59).

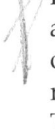

Britain accepted that Germany remained 'the dominant factor' in Europe, but felt that now that it was no longer a colonial or naval power, but disarmed and a democracy, there was no longer a 'German problem'.

The fact remains that the war completely destroyed the 1914 balance of power in Europe. Versailles did not supply anything to redress or replace it, but provided Germany with a set of ready-made grievances and at the same time left it with the potential for resurgence as a great power in a relatively weakened Europe. Versailles did not solve the 'German problem': it had 'scotch'd the snake, not killed it'.

'Enforcing' Versailles: the Ruhr 1923

Of the Allies only France was willing to attempt to enforce German compliance with Versailles. Rapallo, with its implicit challenge to Versailles, seemed brazenly provocative to Paris. In 1923, when Germany defaulted on reparations and requested a moratorium of several years, Prime Minister Poincaré insisted on action and French and Belgian troops were sent to occupy the Ruhr and ensure the delivery of reparations in kind.

Exercise   Please read Roberts, pages 351–3, on the invasion of the Ruhr, and also note its effects on the French and especially the German currency. How successful was the invasion of the Ruhr in enforcing Versailles? ■

Discussion   The use of force eventually compelled the German government to abandon passive resistance and to acknowledge its obligation to pay reparations, but these were soon rescheduled and scaled down in the Dawes Plan of 1924, under pressure from American bankers who now financed loans both to France and Germany. The United States, while continuing to eschew political involvement in Europe, and insisting on the repayment of allied war loans, favoured granting further loans in Europe generally as a profitable mode of economic investment and in the hope of encouraging political stability through economic recovery. As the world's greatest creditor-state, America imposed its terms on the borrowers and made its own assessment of their capacity to pay. As the central economic pivot in Europe, a liberal democratic Germany seemed the best prospect for American investors. Loans to France were conditional on French 'good behaviour' towards Germany over reparations. Thus France had to agree to forego its full entitlement from Germany under the figures agreed in 1921. Meanwhile, the Ruhr invasion profoundly alienated British opinion, and while the British government did not actively assist Germany, it questioned the legality of the invasion and in particular it condemned renewed French encouragement of Rhineland separatism, by which Poincaré had hoped to compensate for the dishonoured Anglo-American guarantee of 1919.

According to Roberts (pp.352–3), 'France had to show she meant to exact what Versailles gave her, or accept that she could not oppose the treaty's gradual withering-away under British and German pressure.' In the event, France was forced (as much by American financial pressure as by British political pressure) to accept a promissory note from Germany for considerably less than its entitlement under Versailles. More important still, France accepted that it could not single-handedly prevent the withering-away of the treaty. Unilateral armed force had won a pyrrhic victory. It was the last attempt of its kind to enforce Versailles and it left a deep impression on French policy-making. If military force under 'Poincaré-la-guerre' could not make Versailles work, how should France approach the 'German problem' in future? Coercion without British support had manifestly failed. □

'The spirit of Locarno' 1925

A new policy of conciliation was entered into with a will very largely as a result of the efforts of the foreign ministers of France, Germany and Britain, whose strategies (though not their objectives) happened to coincide. Briand abandoned the policy of attempting to *force* German compliance with Versailles, and sought to bind Germany to a modified version of the settlement through voluntary agreement. Stresemann, accepting the futility of resistance, whether military or passive, to overwhelming armed force applied against a disarmed Germany, sought, ostensibly in the name of a policy of fulfilment of Versailles (*Erfüllungspolitik*) and of understanding with France (*Verständigungspolitik*), to achieve radical revision of its terms. Austen Chamberlain sought to mediate between Briand and Stresemann and to assist in a general European 'appeasement'. All three were thought to embody 'the spirit of Locarno', where far-reaching agreement was reached in 1925. Both at Locarno and at the League of Nations at Geneva, which Germany, sponsored by France, joined in 1926 as a permanent member of the Council, the three statesmen were given to euphoric expressions of international amity and of hopes of the League as an instrument of pacification. 'Away with rifles, machine-guns, cannons,' exclaimed Briand, welcoming Germany to the League. 'Make way for conciliation, arbitration, peace' (V. Margueritte, *Briand*, 1932, p.283).

The three statesmen were jointly honoured as the architects of Locarno by the award of the Nobel Peace Prize. 'The spirit of Locarno' was heralded as a symbol of new-found stability and even cordiality in relations between France, Germany and Britain, and as a harbinger of still better things to come. Marked by American investment, general economic recovery and the surpassing of pre-war levels of production in France, Germany and Britain, the years 1925–29, as Roberts says, were years of 'optimism and confidence' (p.356), symbolized in 1928 by the adherence of the three states to the Briand–Kellogg Pact, renouncing war as an instrument of national policy.

Exercise   Please read Roberts, pp.353–6. Outline the main features of the Treaty of Locarno and assess how far it advanced a solution of the 'German problem'. ■

Discussion   Locarno provided mutual guarantees, underwritten by Britain and Italy, of the 1919 frontiers between Germany and France, and Germany and Belgium. It confirmed the continued permanent demilitarization of the Rhineland. Coupled with Locarno were sets of arbitration treaties between Germany and France, Germany and Belgium, and Germany, Poland and Czechoslovakia. Thus Locarno seemed to bring about the objective which had eluded the Allies since Versailles: a voluntary acceptance by Germany of the Versailles framework and the permanent integration of Germany within the post-war European system. Unlike Versailles, Locarno was freely negotiated and freely accepted by Germany as an equal. □

'Locarny-blarney' and the dismantling of Versailles 1925–30

Beneath what the humorist A. P. Herbert called the 'Locarny-blarney', however, Locarno should be seen clearly as the expression of a new balance of power: a French retreat, a German advance. It was a radically modified version of Versailles that Germany assented to. Under the Dawes Plan reparations were sharply scaled down to France's detriment.

Moreover, Locarno guaranteed only the *western* frontiers laid down at Versailles. Stresemann rejected French proposals for an 'eastern Locarno'. In the east, while Germany signed arbitration treaties with Poland and Czechoslovakia, it declined to recognize its 1919 frontiers with them as final, and these frontiers were not guaranteed by Britain and Italy. Austen Chamberlain pointedly dissociated Britain from any underwriting of the Polish Corridor. Britain would fight for France or Belgium against German aggression, but declared an unwillingness to do anything for Poland or Czechoslovakia. As Roberts says, 'certain sections of the Versailles settlement were given a privileged status: that very fact weakened the rest of it' (pp.355–6).

Locarno thus implicitly relegated Poland and Czechoslovakia to the status of second-class powers, whose very territorial integrity was put in question. From French client states, to be rallied against Germany at France's behest, Poland and Czechoslovakia now seemed more likely to drag France into conflict with Germany on their own account over some such trouble-spot as the Polish Corridor. And if France went to war for Poland, it would fight without Britain, whose commitment to assist France operated only in the event of an unprovoked German invasion of France, but not if Poland were the *casus belli*. But for France to fight Germany without Britain was unthinkable. Here was a circle that could not be squared. Stresemann boasted justifiably that Locarno broke the back of the Franco-Polish alliance. It did more: the British guarantee of the Franco-German frontier benefited Germany more than France; it meant that France had finally renounced its dream of detaching the Rhineland and had given up the notion of any future invasion of the Ruhr. Locarno left France without means of enforcing what was left of Versailles, and reliant on German goodwill, the price of which was continually rising. France was the loser at Locarno: the treaty was the price it had to pay for British commitment. Henceforth France retreated into the defensive 'Maginot' mentality: it would fight only in its own defence, if attacked by Germany; its troops would fight defensive actions from the protection of the Maginot Line (begun in 1930); and Britain would assist it in accordance with Locarno.

For Britain, Locarno offered the prospect of continuing 'appeasement', which, to the British meant 'appeasement' of Germany, a continuing search for settlements of the 'German problem' whereby alleviation of further parts of Versailles was granted in return for German undertakings to fulfil successively less. Since the Ruhr, Britain had moved from at least ostensible solidarity with its ex-ally to a position of 'honest broker' between France and Germany. Objectively this represented a crucial weakening and isolation of France and a corresponding strengthening of Germany's weight in the balance of power.

For Stresemann, Locarno was a starting-post for revisionism and for Germany's rapid recovery as a great power. An admirer of Ludendorff and an extreme annexationist in World War I, Stresemann as Foreign Minister adopted Bismarck and Metternich as his models. His policy of energetic diplomacy was only nominally 'fulfilment' of Versailles; privately he described it as one of 'finessing' (*finassieren*). Germany gained enormously by continually stepping up the price of agreement. For Stresemann 'the spirit of Locarno' was a process of continually pressing further demands: for further downgrading of reparations, for reductions in the occupation forces, for the accelerated evacuation of the Rhineland, for the withdrawal of the Inter-Allied Military Control Commission and for recognition of Germany's right to military equality. For good measure, he regularly threw in demands for the revocation of the war-guilt clause, the return of the Saar, and of Eupen-Malmédy from Belgium, the restoration of the German colonies and even *Anschluss* with Austria. In the League he championed the German minority in Poland, and to his own German People's Party he made no secret of his desire to revise the Polish frontiers and even to recover Alsace-Lorraine, despite Locarno.

Recapitulation exercise   How successful was Weimar revisionist policy after Locarno in undermining the Versailles settlement? ∎

Discussion   Extremely successful:

- Reparations were reduced and regulated by the Dawes Plan (1924) and again under the Young Plan (1929), whereby Germany's total capital debt was reduced to less than one-third of the amount fixed in 1921. The annual instalments were sharply revised, and a final date for payment (1988) was fixed. In 1931, in the face of the world economic crisis, payment of reparations was suspended by international agreement (the Hoover moratorium). It was never resumed.

- The Inter-Allied Military Control Commission was withdrawn in 1927.

- The Allied Armies of occupation completed a phased withdrawal from the Rhineland by 1930, five years ahead of time.

- From pariah nation of 1919 and the invasion of 1923, Germany had won international recognition and respect as an equal and one of the great powers. At the Geneva Disarmament Conference of 1932, Germany won approval in principle to military equality with France.

- Furthermore, while Weimar Germany was never in a position to engage successfully in a war with France, the prohibitions on rearmament laid down at Versailles were notoriously defied, both by agreement with Russia, permitting German rearmament and training on Russian soil, and by continual flouting of Versailles inside Germany, evidenced in damning reports by the Inter-Allied Military Control Commission, from which it was clear that 'Germany never was disarmed, never intended to disarm, and for seven years did everything in her power to obstruct, deceive and "counter-control" the Commission' (General J. H. Morgan, quoted in Eyck, *A History of the Weimar Republic*, vol.II, 1967, p.47).

Versailles limited the German army to 100,000 men. Plans were laid in the 1920s to treble this, and were put in motion in 1932. In 1931, during the Slump, the German army budget was nearly three times that of Britain (Marks, *The Illusion of Peace*, 1976, p.117) and the pocket battleship *Deutschland* was launched, with plans for more to follow.

The controls of Versailles having been shaken off by 1930, Germany was poised to resume its position as the leading military power in Europe, if it chose. □

Exercise   Was the resurgence of Germany's international standing by 1930 a threat to peace? ■

Discussion   Perceptions at the time differed according to national viewpoints. Austen Chamberlain, exhilarated by the 'spirit of Locarno', did not object to the shifting balance of power, and regarded Germany's recovery of its 'rightful' place as natural and beneficial to peace, so long as it evolved consensually in co-operation with Britain and France. Briand, powerless to prevent that recovery, sought at Locarno and after to keep Germany peaceful by treaty engagements and by offers of economic and even political ties, including, in 1929, a desperate but abortive bid for European federal integration, in the hope of taming German power. German nationalist opinion, by contrast, represented by the parties of the Right, denounced Locarno and each subsequent allied concession as inadequate, and seriously underestimated the magnitude of Stresemann's achievement.

Even Roberts does not, in my opinion, take sufficient measure of the foreign policy achievements of Weimar: continuing German resurgence, continuing French decline.

The basic answer depends on how far Germany intended revisionism to go and how far it was prepared to go in pursuit of it. The evidence does not suggest that the traditional power élites in Weimar Germany were satisfied with the radical revisions of Versailles achieved with the consent of Britain and France. The early evacuation of the Rhineland by the armies of occupation, far from being appreciated as a remarkable gesture of 'appeasement' in the 'spirit of Locarno', ignited an explosion of pent-up German nationalism and demands for more. Foreign policy dominated the election of 1930, in which Nazi representation in the *Reichstag* rose from 12 seats to 107, making the party the second largest in the *Reichstag*. The last governments of the Republic tried to outbid the Nazis in foreign policy demands, clamouring for the scrapping of reparations, for the right to rearm to a level with Britain and France and for an economic customs-union with Austria, no doubt as a prelude to *Anschluss*. □

How far, then, did German aims extend? And did Weimar Germany seriously contemplate a war with Britain and France to achieve them?

Germany could probably have gone to war with Poland to modify its eastern frontiers without involving Britain and France, since Britain had expressly and France by implication written off Poland at Locarno, and Russia's benevolent neutrality (to say the least) was secured by Stresemann at the Treaty of Berlin (1926) which reaffirmed Rapallo, isolated Poland, and reminded Britain and France that Germany could invoke Russian support for revisionism as an alternative to the 'spirit of Locarno'. 'Naturally,' Stresemann informed his Russian opposite number, 'we refuse to see any justification for the continued existence of the present Polish state' (quoted in Eyck, *A History of the Weimar Republic*, vol.II, 1967, p.25). Even at Locarno he explicitly refused to renounce the use of force against Poland, and the *Reichswehr* drew up plans for a limited war with Poland. In 1925 Stresemann secretly informed the Cabinet that his policy was to create a 'Greater Germany' in Central Europe, such a state to include non-Germans 'under German suzerainty' (Fischer, *From Kaiserreich to Third Reich*, 1986, p.84). Would he, as he boasted after Locarno, have sought to recover Alsace-Lorraine once Germany was rearmed? Recent research suggests that 'Stresemann's ultimate goal . . . went considerably beyond simple revision of the Versailles system: he intended on the ruins of Versailles to reconstruct and even to expand the pre-war Great Power position of the German Reich' (Lee and Michalka, *German Foreign Policy 1917–1933*, 1987, p.98). Would this, if true, necessarily have led to war? Or could the re-establishment of German hegemony in Europe have continued to evolve peacefully? We can only speculate about this, since Stresemann died prematurely in 1929, and the Republic came to an end soon after. The important point is that whatever Germany's political complexion after 1930, Stresemann's achievements would soon enable it to make wide-ranging foreign policy choices in defiance of what remained of Versailles.

2 THE CHALLENGE OF NAZI FOREIGN POLICY

Recapitulation exercise: the disintegration of Versailles to 1933

We have seen that by the end of the Weimar Republic, the Versailles settlement lay in tatters so far as its constraints on Germany were concerned. What was left of the treaty in this respect at the time Hitler became Chancellor in 1933? (See Map 7 in the *Maps Booklet* and Roberts, Map 7, p.604.) ■

Specimen answer 1   German inequality of armaments, despite continuous breaches of the disarmament provisions of Versailles. In 1933 Germany's armed forces were in no condition to fight a major war.

2   Control of the Saar by the League of Nations, the future of the territory to be decided by plebiscite in 1935.

3   Demilitarization of the Rhineland (freely accepted by Germany at Locarno).

4   Prohibition on *Anschluss* with Austria (an attempt to establish an Austro-German customs union in 1931, vigorously opposed by the French, was narrowly vetoed by the International Court as contrary to Versailles).

5   Inclusion of 3 million Germans in the Czech Sudetenland, though neither this territory nor its German minority had ever formed part of the Reich.

6   Inclusion of former German territory and half-a-million German nationals in the Polish Corridor and Poznania and control of Danzig by the League.

7   Grievances such as the loss of Memel to Lithuania, the loss of the former German colonies and the long-standing stigma of the war-guilt clause. □

Exercise: the reversal of Versailles after 1933   Taking the same items, what was left of Versailles by 1939? ■

Specimen answer 1   Germany withdrew from the Disarmament Conference in 1933 and began rearming in earnest.

2   The Saar returned to Germany after plebiscite (1935).

3   German troops reoccupied the Rhineland (1936).

4   Austria was united with Germany (March 1938).

5   Germany annexed the Sudetenland (September 1938), and then took over Bohemia–Moravia as a 'protectorate', Slovakia becoming a satellite state (March 1939).

6   Germany invaded Poland and re-took the lost territories (September 1939).

7   Germany re-took Memel (March 1939); Hitler repudiated the war-guilt clause (1937).

By March 1939, nothing was left of Germany's principal grievances at Versailles apart from the colonies, which barely interested Hitler, and the territories lost to Poland (which he re-took by force in the autumn).

By March 1939 Hitler had, without war, already more than reversed the balance of power in Europe in Germany's favour by annexing two independent states to the Reich. □

Historiography of the origins of World War II: Hitler's foreign policy 1933–37

In contrast to the complexities of explaining the origins of the 1914 war, the origins of World War II seemed obvious to contemporaries and could all be put down to one man. For twenty years after 1939, few doubted the explanation that World War II was intended, planned and ignited by Hitler, in absolute control of a Germany that was already the 'dominant factor' in Europe. To this was added the corollary of contributory negligence by Britain and France: their failure to check the undisguised and growing challenge for mastery in Europe after 1933. Failure to act in 1935, when Germany began *openly* rearming, or in 1936, when German troops reoccupied the Rhineland, meant inevitable European war and an uncertain outcome if resistance was finally offered.

The Taylor Thesis: World War II – 'the result of diplomatic blunders'

In 1961 this thesis was challenged by A. J. P. Taylor in *The Origins of the Second World War*. Taylor's views were radical, cogently put and argued with point and wit. Often they are full of illuminating insight. But his fundamental thesis flouted conventional wisdom, aroused passionate controversy at the time and continues to stimulate debate. (See E. M. Robertson (ed.) *The Origins of the Second World War. Historical Interpretations*, 1971; G. Martel (ed.) *The Origins of the Second World War Reconsidered. The A. J. P. Taylor Debate after Twenty-five Years*, 1986; and R. Boyce and E. M. Robertson (eds) *Paths to War. New Essays on the Origins of the Second World War*, 1989.) Taylor rejected the explanation accepted by the Allies at the post-war Nuremberg trials, just as historians after 1919 rejected the thesis of German 'war-guilt' laid down at Versailles. He denied that Hitler sought a war of territorial conquest for German 'living-space' (*Lebensraum*) at the expense of Poland and Russia, or that he contemplated a second European war should Britain and France intervene to prevent him.

According to Taylor, an expert in nineteenth-century diplomatic history, Hitler, like most modern statesmen, was a tactician and an opportunist, not a warmonger. Like most Germans, and like Stresemann before him, he wished to undo what was left of Versailles and as far as possible to reverse the verdict of 1918 by continuing to increase German predominance, particularly in Central and Eastern Europe. Again like Stresemann, he sought to do so by 'finesse', by a game of diplomatic poker, backed by bluff, by out-manoeuvring Western statesmen in a war of nerves. Since he was far better at this game than they were, he was continually more successful, and played for ever higher stakes: reintroduction of conscription 1935, remilitarization of the Rhineland 1936, annexation of Austria and the Sudetenland 1938, occupation of Bohemia–Moravia 1939. At most, he contemplated making limited gains by means of short, localized campaigns of the *Blitzkrieg* variety, and it was such a localized war that he intended in September 1939, not the European war which actually broke out when Britain and France declared war on Germany. 'Far from wanting war', says Taylor, 'a general war was the last thing he wanted' (p.16). 'The war of 1939, far from being premeditated, was a mistake, the result on both sides of diplomatic blunders' (p.269).

Taylor denies that Hitler had any serious long-term plans for conquest in Russia, still less for world domination. His utterances about *Lebensraum* were coffee-house babble or table-talk, without any effect on his actual pre-war foreign policy. We should not, Taylor urges, judge that foreign policy as the judges at Nuremberg allegedly did, with benefit of post-war hindsight. We should not conclude that Hitler always intended to dominate Europe by force and bring Western Russia under German sway simply because that was what he temporarily achieved, or that his rearmament policy meant that he was set on war, any more than rearmament in Britain meant that Chamberlain wanted war.

Taylor draws a clear distinction between domestic and foreign policy. At home, Taylor agrees, Hitler destroyed democracy and instituted a ruthless dictatorship by the Nazi party. However, his foreign policy, according to Taylor, was entirely conventional. 'His foreign policy,' Taylor writes, 'was that of his predecessors, of the professional diplomats at the foreign ministry, and indeed of virtually all

Germans' (quoted in Course Reader, p.191). Taylor makes the paradox that in some respects Hitler was less hidebound and more moderate in his foreign policy than his predecessors. Unlike Stresemann, he was willing to conclude a non-aggression pact with Poland in 1934, despite Danzig and the Corridor; and he renounced any claim to Alsace-Lorraine. Unlike the Pan-Germanists, he wrote off the South Tyrol in order to keep on terms with Mussolini. He never showed any interest in recovering the German colonies, except to embarrass the British. Unlike the Wilhelminian Imperialists, he was not interested in the Middle East, nor did he aspire to naval rivalry with Britain. 'Hitler,' Taylor argues sardonically, 'was treading, rather cautiously, in Bethmann's footsteps. There was nothing new or unusual in his aims or outlook' (quoted in Course Reader, p.197).

In both aims and methods, therefore, Hitler's foreign policy, according to Taylor, was conventional. Whoever had been in charge of German foreign policy in the 1930s would have continued in the tradition of Stresemann to exploit the international situation to Germany's advantage as its natural preponderance in the European balance continued to reassert itself. The Nuremberg explanation of Hitler as the author of long-premeditated plans for war, by placing responsibility for World War II on Hitler and his henchmen, absolves the German people. It also relieves historians of the task of explaining World War II in the context of German history, of which, in Taylor's view, it was the logical outcome. For all his insistence on the accidental and the contingent as causes of the war of 1939, at a deeper level Taylor sees the war as the inevitable outcome of the 'German problem', which the Allies had failed to solve in 1919. The 'German problem' was not Hitler, but the existence of Germany as the 'dominant factor' in Europe. Since 1870 a united Germany had proved incapable of peaceful integration within Europe, and the 'German problem' remained unsolved until the intervention of Russia and America and the partition of Germany in 1945. Hitler was not an aberration, but the culmination of German history.

Such is Taylor's thesis, argued both in *The Origins of the Second World War* and in his earlier book, *Course of German History* (1945).

Taylor continues to make us rethink several basic aspects of Hitler's foreign policy and their relation to the causes of World War II. First, what *were* Hitler's foreign policy objectives? Was there anything to distinguish them from those of Stresemann? The argument is not merely academic. If, as Taylor argues, Hitler's ambitions were limited to a *Grossdeutsch* programme in accordance with German self-determination, then 'appeasement' of Germany might have succeeded in satisfying him. If Germany could have been satisfied with the incorporation of Austria, the Sudetenland, Danzig and the Corridor, then 'appeasement' made sense and might have worked, and the British and French intervention in 1939 was a fatal error, leading straight to war on an issue in which Germany was in the right.

But what if Taylor's thesis is false? What if the *Grossdeutsch* policy was not the limit, but the start of Hitler's ambitions? Suppose that what he really wanted was not just Germany's 1914 frontiers or the *Grossdeutsch* frontiers achieved by him at Munich in 1938, but something far more ambitious – recovery of Imperial Germany's satellite conquests of March 1918 in the east, and their conversion into *Lebensraum*? In that case, eventual war was inevitable, unless Britain and France were willing to allow Hitler a 'free hand' in the east; and 'appeasement' of Hitler (which Taylor regards as morally and politically right) would place Germany in an ever better position to win, should Britain and France eventually decide to resist.

Exercise You are now invited to consider a critique of Taylor's thesis by Norman Rich, formerly Professor of History at Brown University. Please read his article entitled 'Hitler's foreign policy' in the Course Reader, pp.190–207. What is Rich's main objection to Taylor's interpretation of Hitler's foreign policy? ■

Discussion Any historical thesis must be based on *fact*, and its validity depends not on its 'brilliance' (which Rich concedes), but on its relationship to the evidence; that is, it must be judged on the author's treatment of the primary sources and on the inferences to be drawn from them.

   As a professional historian, Rich complains that Taylor's basic thesis is fundamentally flawed by unsound treatment of primary sources, which Taylor either ignores or recklessly dismisses. □

Hitler's *Mein Kampf*: day-dreams or foreign policy objectives?

Exercise Let us put Rich's criticism to the test. Please examine for yourself an excerpt from Hitler's *Mein Kampf* (document I.23(b) in *Documents 2*) and consider it as evidence of Hitler's ideas on foreign policy. ■

Discussion The passage is a clear, open rejection of the restoration of Germany's 1914 frontiers as a foreign policy objective. Revision of the frontiers laid down at Versailles would not be worth a war. Hitler rejects the 1914 frontiers as arbitrary, strategically weak and in any case inadequate. Not only would they still not include all Germans within the Reich (a *Grossdeutsch* aim), but they would not sufficiently enhance Germany's 'world power' status *vis-à-vis* Britain, America and France. The aim of Nazi foreign policy must by contrast be the forcible acquisition of *Lebensraum* – not as satellites or colonies but by outright annexation for resettlement by Germans, as a prerequisite to Germany's becoming a 'world power'. *Lebensraum* will involve war with France, but this will be a secondary war: its purpose will be to protect German gains in the east. *Lebensraum* is the only achievement that will justify war.

   The aim of *Lebensraum* represents a clean break both with the policy of the 1914 frontiers and with a *Grossdeutsch* policy. Explicitly it involves territorial conquest in Russia. □

Taylor on *Mein Kampf*

According to Taylor, far too much has been read into *Mein Kampf*. He points out that Hitler at the time he wrote the book, in 1924, was a nobody, an obscure failed street politician, who could not seriously expect ever to come to power. Writing *Mein Kampf* from his prison cell, Hitler was indulging in fantasy, regurgitating ideas about *Lebensraum* long current in right-wing circles. To Hitler, in Taylor's view, 'these were no more than day-dreams concocted in his spare time' (Course Reader, p.192). Hitler did not take them seriously and neither should historians. We should judge his foreign policy after 1933 in the light of circumstances at the time he directed it, and disconnect it from its supposed ideological origins in *Mein Kampf*. Just because after 1939 Hitler went on to attempt much of what he described as his aims in *Mein Kampf*, it does not follow that that was his intention all along. We should beware, says Taylor, of judging Hitler's pre-war policy with post-war hindsight, and extrapolating from *Mein Kampf* an illusory common origin, linking pre-war policy with policy in wartime. Before 1939, Taylor insists,

Hitler did no more in foreign policy than any other successful German statesman would have done, no matter what he may have written earlier. *Mein Kampf* and *Lebensraum* are red herrings.

However unlikely it was in 1924 that Hitler would be Chancellor nine years later, it does not follow either that he did not mean what he wrote in *Mein Kampf*, or that what he wrote bore no relation to his subsequent foreign policy. Repeatedly in the years after *Mein Kampf*, both before and, more significantly, after 1933, he reverted by implication and openly to the acquisition of *Lebensraum* as his principal ultimate objective. Evidence of this appears, for example: (a) in a speech to industrialists at Düsseldorf in January 1932 (Weinberg, *The Foreign Policy of Hitler's Germany*, vol.I, 1970, p.25); (b) in a speech to high-ranking generals and admirals, including the Commander-in-Chief of the army, in February 1933, immediately after becoming Chancellor, when he stated as the goal of his foreign policy the 'conquest of *Lebensraum* in the east and its ruthless Germanisation' (p.27); (c) in February 1934, when he told his new Commander-in-Chief and Chief of Staff to prepare for an eventual pre-emptive strike in the west, followed by an offensive war in the east, a strategy identical to that set out in *Mein Kampf* (p.178); (d) in March 1935, in conference with Goering, when he stressed that whatever interim stratagems he might adopt, his ultimate aim remained expansion eastward (p.226); (e) in August 1936, in a memorandum for a four-year plan, which defined his ultimate objective as *Lebensraum* (document I.14 in *Documents 2*).

If Hitler meant what he said in 1932, 1933, 1934, 1935 and 1936, why not in 1924? Taylor, though he does not refer to these later examples of evidence of Hitler's intentions, maintains that Hitler was merely day-dreaming or talking for effect. Paradoxically, however, as Rich points out, Taylor also agrees that 'the driving force in him [Hitler] was a terrifying literalism' (Course Reader, p.192). In other words, there were occasions when Hitler did mean what he said. The question, then, is did he mean what he said about *Lebensraum*? Taylor denies it, though his point that Hitler was merely repeating 'the conversation of any Austrian café or German beer-house' does not undermine but could corroborate his attribution to Hitler of 'a terrifying literalism'. While responding flexibly to circumstances in the successive international crises which he himself whipped up in order to destroy and reverse what was left of Versailles, Hitler kept his sights firmly set on the goals laid down in *Mein Kampf*. There seems therefore no valid reason to dissociate *Mein Kampf* from Hitler's subsequent pronouncements and actions: Hitler's book, as Rich says, provides 'an exposition of the ideas which he proposed to translate into action' (Course Reader, p.192).

The Hossbach Memorandum

Exercise   Please read document I.24 in *Documents 2*, an excerpt from the Hossbach Memorandum, 5 November 1937. What evidence does it suggest of Hitler's responsibility for World War II? ■

Discussion   It seems clear and cogent proof, consistent with *Mein Kampf* and Hitler's other pronouncements between 1932 and 1936, of his unabated determination to realize the goal of *Lebensraum* ('Germany's problem of space'). He posits the opposition of Britain and France to 'any further strengthening of Germany's position' in Europe by way of territorial expansion, concluding that such expansion 'could only be solved by means of force'. War was inevitable. The only questions were 'when and how'. Hitler stressed the need for a showdown by 1943/45 'at the latest', before German rearmament became obsolescent and while 'the rest of the world was still preparing its defences'. Expansion would begin with the 'elimination' of Austria and Czechoslovakia as independent states, the expulsion of their non-German inhabitants and their incorporation within Germany as a starting point for further action. □

Taylor on the Hossbach Memorandum

Taylor was at pains to deny the significance of this document, both in his book and in the Foreword which he added in 1963. In the Foreword he queried the memorandum's authenticity. He stressed that it was put in evidence after the war at Nuremberg, implying that this in itself makes it suspect ('those who believe the evidence in political trials may go on quoting the Hossbach Memorandum', p.22). In his book, describing the memorandum as 'this rambling disquisition' (p.170), he argued, as he did about *Mein Kampf*, that 'Hitler's exposition was in large part day-dreaming', and that in any case Hitler's point was that 'Germany would gain her aims without a great war; "force" apparently meant to him the threat of war, not necessarily war itself' (p.169). Taylor also produced the hypothesis that Hitler's address was designed as an internal political manoeuvre; and while he withdrew this suggestion in an article in 1965, he continued to dismiss the memorandum as another example of Hitler 'ranting in his usual fashion' (quoted in Robertson, ed., *The Origins of the Second World War*, 1971, p.136). Taylor insisted that no one took much notice of it at the time.

Most of Taylor's arguments seem to me perverse. It is one thing to question the memorandum's authenticity (as to which there is room for argument, the document being a copy of a copy); but to deny its evidential value simply on the grounds that it was accepted as proof by a tribunal of which Taylor disapproves is an argument *ad hominem*. Taylor offers nothing to support his suggestion that by 'force' Hitler only meant the threat of force. Hitler's own examples ('the campaigns of Frederick the Great for Silesia, and Bismarck's wars against Austria and France') are examples of war, not the threat of war; and, by the 'risks' attendant on 'the resort to force', Hitler surely meant defeat rather than war. Hitler himself speaks of 'the resort to force' (not 'the threat of force'), and of 'our attack' and 'take the offensive'.

As for its being a 'rambling disquisition', the memorandum is not a precise timetable, but it does restate a long-term objective of *Lebensraum*, interim aims regarding the conquest of Austria and Czechoslovakia, and the contingent questions of how and when to deal with Britain and France (who, Hitler rightly predicted, would not intervene in the event). As for not taking himself seriously, why should Hitler stress that the speech be regarded as 'his last will and testament' and summon his Foreign Minister, Minister of War and the three service chiefs to hear it, if he did not mean what he said? In fact, there is ample evidence both that he was in deadly earnest and that they took him seriously. Far from Taylor's assertion that none of those present 'gave it another thought' (p.171), later the same month Hitler told pupils at a Nazi training centre that his aim was *Lebensraum* in the east. In December 1937 the armed forces were ordered to prepare for a strategy of aggression against Austria and Czechoslovakia, even at the risk of intervention by Britain and France, with a view to realizing the explicit goal of *Lebensraum*. Goering gave orders to this effect to the *Luftwaffe* immediately after the 5 November meeting.

Early in 1938 Hitler dismissed the relatively cautious Blomberg and Fritsch, and replaced Neurath by Ribbentrop. He set Neurath (as 'Protector' of Bohemia–Moravia) the task of drawing up plans for the 'compulsory emigration of 2 million people from Czechoslovakia' (document I.24 in *Documents* 2). He abolished the Ministry of War, replacing it by a High Command of the Armed Forces (*Oberkommando der Wehrmacht*) responsible to himself as Supreme Commander. In March, he ordered his troops into Austria and prepared to invade Czechoslovakia.

Unbiased consideration of the evidence, direct and circumstantial, therefore, suggests that Taylor's basic thesis is untenable. As Rich complains, when it came to primary sources, the historian's basic raw material, Taylor ignored much of it 'and at the same time he cavalierly disregarded a great deal of other evidence which did not happen to fit with his own theories' (p.120). Instead of dismissing the Hossbach Memorandum because it did not match his interpretation of Hitler, he might tellingly have compared it with Wilhelminian plans for eastward expansion (for example, the War Council of 8 December 1912, see Book I, Unit 6, p.221) in support of his more disturbing thesis of an underlying continuity in German foreign policy. If war for *Lebensraum*, as Rich emphasizes (Course Reader, p.194), was 'the policy of a fanatic ideologue who ignored sober calculations of national interest in order to put his manic ideas into practice', how do we explain its ultimate acceptance by the military and Foreign Office if not in terms of at least *some* degree of continuity of aims?

Continuity and change in German foreign policy after 1933

Roberts, discussing Hitler's foreign policy aims (p.518), more or less follows Taylor. Hitler's demands 'did not seem very unusual': the destruction of Versailles, the recovery of 1914 *irredenta*, Germany's re-emergence as a great military power – '*Grossdeutsch* themes'. The policies outlined in *Mein Kampf* and the Hossbach Memorandum Roberts dismisses as 'only a vague dream of a racialist policy of *Lebensraum* in the east', rather than Hitler's ultimate objective and the mainspring of his foreign policy. Essentially, Roberts argues, Hitler's contribution to German diplomacy was 'not one of content, but of technique'. Even then, Roberts, like Taylor, sees Hitler's methods in terms only of 'great daring and dexterity', of opportunism and bluff.

Such a view of Nazi foreign policy fails to take account not only, as we have seen, of the qualitative leap from the foreign policy of Weimar (and even of Imperial Germany), but also of the radically different nature of Nazi *methods* in foreign policy. While Stresemann as Foreign Minister had been responsible to the Cabinet and to the *Reichstag*, Hitler was constitutionally accountable to nobody. In 1936, the year of his Rhineland *coup*, he summoned his Cabinet only four times. He conducted his own foreign policy, both in regard to long-term strategy and to immediate timing and method, in accordance with his own perceptions, unrestrained by institutional pressures, which he bypassed by submitting each successful *fait accompli* to the suffrage of a general election or plebiscite (or both simultaneously): on quitting the League of Nations, 1933 (plebiscite and *Reichstag* elections); on the reoccupation of the Rhineland, 1936 (election); on the *Anschluss* with Austria, April 1938 (plebiscite and election); on the incorporation of the Sudetenland, December 1938 (plebiscite and election). After Hindenburg's death in 1934, he made himself Head of State and Führer as well as Chancellor, and bound the armed forces to himself (rather than to the state) by exacting a personal oath of unconditional obedience.

Increasingly he distanced himself from the Foreign Office, whose cautious advice he despised. His Foreign Minister, Neurath, whom he inherited from Weimar, did not so much instigate policy as implement Hitler's directives. Hitler found in this conservative aristocrat a willing agent of accelerated revisionism, and retained him until 1938 to lend an air of respectability to each fresh *démarche*. Meanwhile the independent authority of the Foreign Office was increasingly downgraded. In March 1935, the Foreign Office learned only at the last moment of Hitler's decision to announce the reintroduction of conscription. The career diplomats of Imperial and Weimar Germany found their influence superseded by that of Nazi adventurers – 'men who, having taken an active part in the Nazi revolution, have a certain obduracy and a certain very characteristic preference for actions that might be interpreted as being rather defiant' (F. A. Voigt, *Manchester Guardian* correspondent, in a broadcast of March 1935, audio-cassette 3, item 7). Chief of these was Ribbentrop, formerly a travelling champagne salesman, after 1933 Hitler's chief foreign policy adviser and roving ambassador at large. By 1937 Ribbentrop's own organization of party contacts inside and outside Germany had greater influence on foreign policy than the Foreign Office. Convinced of Ribbentrop's superior expertise, especially in Anglo-German relations, Hitler in 1936 appointed him Ambassador in London (where he won the nickname 'Von Brickendrop'), and in 1938 Foreign Minister. Ribbentrop, a fanatical Nazi and a vain and dangerous amateur, persuaded Hitler that Britain was a 'hate-inspired antagonist' (document I.24), and egged him on in his increasingly reckless foreign policy.

The Weimar Foreign Office, despite its desire for frontier revision in the east, had not actively interfered in the internal affairs of neighbouring states. After 1933 a special Nazi Foreign Organization (*Auslandsorganisation*) was set up with the set purpose of fomenting dissent among German nationals abroad, particularly in Austria, Poland and Czechoslovakia (for example, through the Sudeten agitator, Henlein) and to destabilize the host countries. In 1937 this body was made part of the Foreign Office, but took its orders from Hitler's deputy, Hess.

The downgrading of the Foreign Office was compounded by the fact that most of the permanent officials, however much they feared Hitler's methods, applauded his revisionist achievements. Each foreign policy success, flouting their cautious fears, seemed to suggest that Hitler's instincts were surer than the judgements of the professional diplomats, and added to his prestige.

Exercise   What was new about Nazi foreign policy in action? ■

Discussion   Nazi methods exemplify what Karl Dietrich Bracher (*The German Dictatorship*, 1973, p.364) calls 'the change from traditional diplomacy to the strategy of surprise', freedom from traditional constraints, ruthlessness, speed, suddenness and the presentation of the *fait accompli* (often at the weekend) accompanied by expressions of peaceful intentions, all of which dazzled, disoriented and divided the other powers.

To take the main examples between 1933 and 1936:

1   October 1933: Germany ostentatiously withdraws not only from the Disarmament Conference (repeating a similar walk-out the year before) but also from the League of Nations, which it had joined only seven years earlier as a symbol of its international respectability.

2   January 1934: Germany signs a non-aggression pact with Poland. This *apparent* retreat from Weimar's intransigence over the eastern frontiers illustrates Hitler's flexibility and short-term opportunism: by this tactical *démarche*, designed to gain time for German rearmament, he postponed any threat of Franco-Polish co-operation in a preventive war against Germany, isolating both France and Poland until such time as it would suit him to settle accounts with each of them.

3   July 1934: assassination of the Austrian Chancellor, Dollfuss, in an attempted Nazi *coup*, to which (as Weinberg argues in *The Foreign Policy of Hitler's Germany*, vol.I, 1970, pp.102–4) Hitler was unquestionably privy, intended to lead to *Anschluss*.

4   March 1935: while Weimar Germany had rearmed in secret, Hitler publicly announces and triumphantly celebrates the reintroduction of conscription and the creation of the *Luftwaffe*, both in violation of Versailles. (Please see video-cassette 1, item 35, 'Germany asserts the right to re-arm', 21 March 1935. Note how the 'formidable demonstration of German armed discipline' is preceded by War Minister Blomberg's reassuring reference to 'a Germany at peace in a Europe appeased' and followed by the narrator's 'hope that Germany's aims are as pacific as her leaders' utterances declare them to be'.)

5   June 1935: Anglo-German naval agreement. While Weimar's pocket battle-ship, the *Deutschland*, was within the letter of Versailles, Hitler determined to build up German naval power in violation of Versailles and to pull off the diplomatic scoop of securing Britain's consent by undertaking, *for the time being*, to restrict the German navy to one-third of Britain's naval strength.

6   March 1936: German troops reoccupy the Rhineland, in violation both of Versailles and of Locarno. (Note the revealing newsreel title – video-cassette 1, item 36 – 'Hitler staggers Europe', 9 March 1936.)

Leaving aside the question of Hitler's ultimate objectives, then, Nazi *methods* in themselves introduced a disturbing new element to European relations: a new dynamism, characterized by open defiance not merely of the remnants of Versailles, but by implication of the existing European balance generally.

Nazi methods in foreign policy – 'a kind of *Blitzkrieg* diplomatic offensive' (Boyce and Robertson, *Paths to War*, 1989, p.6) – accentuated as never before the 'German problem', increased international tensions and made war more likely. □

3 *EUROPE AND THE RHINELAND CRISIS 1936*

Please read Roberts, pages 519–20.

Hitler's challenge

In March 1936, over-riding the fears of his War Minister and Foreign Minister, Blomberg and Neurath, Hitler ordered some 50,000 troops into the Rhineland zone – all that territory on the left bank of the Rhine and a fifty-kilometre-wide strip on the right bank which had been declared a permanent demilitarized zone at Versailles and Locarno.

The troops marched in on Saturday 7 March. As they did so Hitler addressed a broadcast speech to the *Reichstag*, repudiating the Treaty of Locarno as incompatible with the Franco-Soviet pact of 1935 and justifying the reoccupation of the Rhineland as a defensive measure to counter the danger to Germany of encirclement by France, Russia and Czechoslovakia. (The pretext of the Franco-Soviet pact was rightly derided in *Punch* as a 'cock-and-bear story'.)

At the same time, Hitler offered to negotiate a set of 'new agreements for the establishment of a system of European security' (document I.25 in *Documents 2*) and announced an immediate general election to approve the occupation.

The remilitarization of the Rhineland destroyed the basis of European security agreed at Locarno. Demilitarization was the key to strategic control of the 'German problem': with the gradual reassertion after 1919 of Germany's natural preponderance, the Rhineland zone blocked German military aggression. As long as the zone remained demilitarized, Germany could not invade France, Belgium or Holland; and since the zone left it open to invasion from the west, it could not attack in any other direction for fear of retaliation by France. The security of Austria, Czechoslovakia and Poland was thus directly linked with the maintenance of the zone.

Responsibility for enforcing Locarno lay with its other signatories: France, Britain, Italy and Belgium. Mussolini, rebuffed by Britain and France over Abyssinia, stood aside. Britain, France and Belgium took no counter-measures.

Nazi foreign policy techniques in the Rhineland crisis

1   *Timing*. While remilitarization in itself was not unexpected by the British and French governments, they had no contingency plans to counter it, and its timing took them by surprise, particularly since Hitler, Neurath and the German Foreign Office had given repeated assurances of loyalty to Locarno, including demilitarization. Hitler's orders were prepared with such secrecy that his own Cabinet did not know of them until the eve of the occupation. As with most of his foreign policy *coups* since 1933, Hitler enjoyed the psychological advantage of surprise, shock and the *fait accompli*. (See video-cassette 1, item 36, 'Hitler staggers Europe', for immediate British reaction. The narrator ends on a bewildered note: 'Where does it all lead? To a new war, or to a surer peace?')

2   *Presentation*. Hitler's speech to the *Reichstag* (part of which can be heard on audio-cassette 3, item 8) brings out his quite extraordinary effectiveness as a manipulator of opinion. In contrast to the fanatical quest for *Lebensraum* in *Mein Kampf*, he presented 'the motivating forces in the foreign policy of National Socialism' (quoted in F. J. Berber, ed., *Locarno*, 1936, p.204) as moderate and rational. He alternated themes that appealed to all shades of German opinion (contrasting the humiliation of Germany under Versailles with the recovery of German honour since 1933) with themes designed to conciliate foreign opinion. He made friendly references to Britain, France and Poland. He invoked the spirit of the Anglo-German Naval Pact of 1935 and the non-aggression pact of 1934 with Poland. He spoke of Germany as a bastion against Bolshevism and as a contributor to 'European culture and European civilization'. He posed, not as a rabid nationalist, but as a responsible and moderate statesman, who professedly did not even aim at Germany's 1914 frontiers, let alone at a *Grossdeutsch* policy, still less at *Lebensraum* – a good European, albeit a patriot, who sought to co-operate 'in lessening the strained tensions by means of a slow evolutionary development in

peaceful collaboration' (Berber, 1936, p.226). What better definition of 'appease-ment'? He denied hostile intentions against Poland or Czechoslovakia, dep-recated any idea of war, and while stating that he expected eventual colonial concessions, declared (not for the first or last time) that 'in Europe we have no territorial claims to put forward' (Berber, 1936, p.226).

Exercise   Please read document I.25 in *Documents 2*, which contains what Hitler called his 'concrete proposals' for peace. Summarize and assess them. ■

Discussion   To replace Locarno, Hitler proposed a bilateral demilitarized zone, non-aggression pacts with France and Belgium, guaranteed by Britain and Italy; an air pact with the Western powers, non-aggression pacts with the states to Germany's east, and Germany's re-entry to the League of Nations.

These offers were brilliantly designed in that: (a) they appeared to correspond with what Britain in particular had long been seeking; (b) they softened the sting of the occupation; (c) they gave Germany time to consolidate the occupation by sending in more troops, while Britain and France considered how to respond to the offers. □

But were they seriously meant?

1   Hitler can hardly have been serious about the bilateral demilitarized zone with France and Belgium. Such a zone would have rendered useless the Maginot Line which, as he knew, was built only for defence.

2   What could be the value of Hitler's commitment to a new Locarno, when he had just repudiated his obligations under the existing treaty?

3   When Britain and France attempted to follow up the proposals with detailed requests for clarification, they were fobbed off. The questions went unanswered. The proposals came to nothing. This surely suggests that they were never seriously intended except as a ruse.

Why did Britain not act?

Baldwin's Conservative government had been re-elected with a huge majority in November 1935. It was committed to rearmament on a limited scale and to 'collective security' through the League of Nations, at that time preoccupied with Italy's aggression against Abyssinia. Far from contemplating military action over the Rhineland, the government had agreed in 1935 that the zone was not a vital British interest, and had indeed hoped to 'trade' remilitarization in return for 'a new Locarno'.

After the *coup*, given Germany's enhanced 'power of mischief in Europe', Eden, the Foreign Secretary, told the Cabinet on 8 March, 'it is in our interest to conclude with her as far-reaching and enduring a settlement as possible while Herr Hitler is still in the mood to do so' (Haraszti, *The Invaders*, 1983, p.149).

British policy was rather to restrain France from taking any independent counter-measures against Germany which might drag Britain into war. The Chiefs of Staff warned that the country was in no condition to fight. Britain's dispositions in 1936 were directed against Italy, not Germany, with a possible Mediterranean conflict in mind, and never in the inter-war period was the United Kingdom more vulnerable. Its other naval and military resources were distracted by imperial commitments in India, Egypt and Palestine: the Empire, not Europe, remained central to defence planning between the wars. The most Britain could offer France was two divisions. Its naval and air forces at home were 'denuded to an extent almost unparalleled in the past', and Britain was 'perilously exposed in the air and completely open to attack by sea' (quoted in Emmerson, *The Rhineland Crisis*, 1977, p.136).

While Eden made it clear in the Commons on 9 March that a German attack on France or Belgium would be a *casus belli* for Britain, it was clear that Hitler had no intention of attacking east or west in 1936.

There was much expression of public sympathy for Germany, or at any rate of opposition to military action. Conservative backbenchers tended to be pro-German on the merits of the Rhineland case. The Labour opposition was adamant against action. 'Certainly the Labour Party', Dalton told the Commons, 'would not support the taking of military sanctions or even economic sanctions against Germany' (quoted in Lentin, *Guilt at Versailles*, 1985, p.149). For the Liberals, Sir Archibald Sinclair and even Lloyd George invited sympathetic understanding of German national feeling. While by no means sympathetic to Nazism as such, there were many on the Right who approved of Germany as a bastion against communism and favoured giving Hitler a free hand in Eastern Europe. Overt pro-Germans included a former Air Minister, Lord Londonderry, and Lord Lothian, formerly Philip Kerr, who, as secretary to Lloyd George, had penned some of the most vitriolic phrases of the Treaty of Versailles – see document I.21 in *Documents 2*. Lothian, a convert to the view that the current instability of Europe derived not from Hitler but from Versailles, summed up popular reaction to the reoccupation of the Rhineland: 'After all', he said, 'they are only going into their own back garden' (quoted in Lentin, 1985, p.147). 'The only way to peace', he told Lloyd George, 'is justice for Germany; and justice for Germany means dropping encirclement and letting Germany become the leading power in Central Europe' (quoted in Lentin, 1985, p.148).

The only British statesmen of influence to call for counter-measures were Austen Chamberlain (who distinguished between 'appeasement' of Weimar Germany and of Nazi Germany) and Churchill. Both were out of office.

Exercise　　Please read quickly through document I.26 in *Documents 2*, an editorial in *The Times*, 9 March 1936, and note briefly the writer's reaction. ■

Discussion　　While not denying that reoccupation of the Rhineland constituted a flagrant violation of Locarno, the writer (the deputy editor, Barrington-Ward) in effect extenuates and accepts it. He:

1　takes an even-handed attitude between France and Germany (Britain's official attitude since at least 1923);

2　criticizes Locarno as 'one-sided and unbalanced' (Hitler's argument);

3　stresses that Locarno was objectionable because 'it embodied the clauses of the Versailles Treaty which imposed demilitarization upon the German side only' (Hitler's argument);

4　argues that demilitarization could not last forever and that Germany was entitled to protect itself against the possibility of attack from France and Russia (Hitler's argument);

5　denies that German reoccupation of German territory constitutes 'aggression' (the 'back garden' argument);

6　urges Britain and France to accept the *fait accompli*, and to take up Hitler's offers. □

Exercise   Please read document I.27 in *Documents 2* (Eric Dunstan's commentary to *The Rhine*, 12 March 1936). How does Dunstan's message compare with Barrington-Ward's? ■

Discussion   Both commentators take a similarly passive view. Dunstan stresses the seriousness of the crisis in terms of the return of German troops and the repudiation of Locarno; at the same time he explains the event's symbolic significance for Germany and echoes Barrington-Ward's hopes of Hitler's offers of 'a new peace system on a surer foundation'. Note that neither even hints at the possibility of counter-measures. □

In this they are typical of the British press and media. The Labour *Daily Herald* said that the only alternatives were 'a new settlement' or war. 'Certainly the people of this country would not stand for such a war.' 'As to British opinion generally', wrote Barrington-Ward of the readers' letters to *The Times*, 'our difficulty has been to find enough letters stating what might be crudely called the anti-German view to balance the correspondence' (quoted in Lentin, 1985, p.149). (On *The Times* see Roberts, p.517, footnote 12.)

Documents I.26 and I.27 in *Documents 2* suggest little understanding in the media of the wider geopolitical and strategic significance of the *coup* in terms of a critical and fundamental disturbance to the balance of power. The objections are of a moralistic nature, noting the violation of Locarno, but offset by expressions of sympathy for German national sensibilities. From this viewpoint, German re-occupation of the Rhineland appeared venial compared to Italian aggression against Abyssinia. Thus public opinion reacted in inverse proportion to the gravity of the crises: Mussolini's aggression, however lamentable in itself, represented no immediate threat to European security; Hitler's action struck at its very root.

Why did France not act?

The remilitarization of the Rhineland was a far more direct threat to France and its alliance-system than to Britain. With the removal of the demilitarized buffer-zone, German troops now stood on the French frontier and began the work of fortification. Remilitarization of the Rhineland lost France the capacity to control Germany, to react to or to pre-empt German aggression by the threat of direct intervention on German soil without substantial risk of war. The limited security of Locarno was gone. The government and Foreign Office regarded it as essential to restore the *status quo ante*. This meant taking counter-measures to force a German withdrawal.

The Left–Centre Cabinet of Sarraut, which had been in office only a few weeks, was an interim administration awaiting an imminent general election, and already burdened with particularly heavy responsibilities – social, economic and financial. Not the least of these was to protect the franc from devaluation, a contingency likely to be sparked off by involvement in an international crisis.

Ever since the Ruhr debacle of 1923, it had been the cardinal principle of French foreign policy that no military action, however limited, against Germany could be contemplated without British support. Unlike their British counterparts, Sarraut, Flandin, his Foreign Minister, and Mandel, at once appreciated the significance of Hitler's challenge, and at first urged immediate independent military retaliation by France in the hope of subsequent British support. These initial reactions soon yielded to pessimistic counsels from the War Minister, Maurin, and the army Chief of Staff, General Gamelin.

Haunted by the experience of World War I, French strategic and tactical thinking was exclusively defensive. In the event of war with Germany, the French frontier and French troops would be protected by the Maginot Line, completed in 1936. No provision existed for operations east of the Maginot Line, there was not a single combat-unit ready for an emergency, and as far as the military were concerned, there could be no such thing as an expedition with the limited aim of driving the German troops out of the Rhineland. Gamelin informed the Chiefs of Staff on 8 March: 'By the fact of our entry into the zone, war would be unleashed' (*Documents diplomatiques français 1932–1939*, 2me série, vol.1, p.444).

Public opinion in France, to judge from the press, was uniformly against war or military action of any kind. From Right to Left, the message was the same, though for different reasons, which bring out the ideological cleavages in French society impeding the formation of a solid consensus on foreign policy. Thus while a majority of right-wing deputies approved the Franco-Russian pact of 1935 on grounds of *Realpolitik* as restoring the balance of power against Germany, the extreme Right was ideologically opposed to any alliance with international communism, held (like Hitler) that the pact itself had provoked the Rhineland crisis, and warned against involvement in war with Germany for the benefit of Russia.

The Rhineland crisis 1936: last chance to stop Hitler?

Exercise   Could Hitler have been stopped without war in 1936, as Churchill, among others, argued then and later? ■

Discussion   Hitler later said that had the French gone into the Rhineland, he would have had to order a German withdrawal. But this may have been mere boasting of his nerve and audacity at the time; and in any case a tactical withdrawal to a defensive line would have been perfectly consistent with armed resistance and with 'the *Wehrmacht*'s actual orders on 7 March to fall back, but not flee' (Nicole Jordan in Boyce and Robertson, eds, 1989, p.142). The language of his speech to the *Reichstag* on 7 March and of subsequent election speeches strongly suggests that Germany would have fought. The point is that no one dared to put it to the test. Baldwin told Flandin that because of the state of British defences, if the chance of war was only one in 100, he could not take it. Even if Germany were beaten, the British government asked, would war solve the 'German problem'? Harold Nicolson put the dilemma well:

> If we send an ultimatum to Germany, she ought in all reason to climb down. But then she will not climb down and we shall have war. Naturally we shall win and enter Berlin. But what is the good of that? It would only mean communism in Germany and France, and that is why the Russians are so keen on it. Moreover the people of this country absolutely refuse to have a war. We should be faced by a general strike if we even suggest such a thing. We shall therefore have to climb down ignominiously and Hitler will have scored. (Nicolson to Vita Sackville-West, 12 March 1936, *Diaries and Letters 1930–1939*, 1966, pp.249–50) □

Hitler's success dealt a death-blow to Versailles and Locarno. This was his first open challenge to the territorial settlement of 1919, even though it took place on German soil. Henceforth the balance of power and the diplomatic initiative shifted visibly from France and Britain to Germany. K. D. Bracher writes: 'the European peace order had collapsed, even though the façade continued to stand for another three years' (*The German Dictatorship*, 1973, p.375).

Popularity of Nazi foreign policy in Germany

Remilitarization had been contemplated in Weimar at least since the allied evacuation in 1930. But Hitler rightly took the credit for its implementation. His speeches to the *Reichstag* on 7 March and at German Remembrance Day ceremonies on 8 March were tremendous propaganda successes for Nazi foreign policy.

Exercise   Please listen to the recording of Hitler's peace offers from the broadcast speech (item 8 on audio-cassette 3), the script of which you have already examined. What evidence does it afford of opinion in the *Reichstag*? ■

Discussion   There is much loud cheering and applause following each of Hitler's proposals for peace. Since all political parties other than the Nazis had been banned in Germany since 1933, one would naturally expect the Nazi deputies to applaud what Hitler had to say. It may be that they would have cheered even if he had made a declaration of war, such, it may be argued, was his hold on his audience (which can certainly be felt in the recording). But the fact is that, whatever may have been Hitler's own lack of seriousness about a 'new Locarno', the only inference that can legitimately be drawn from the recording is that *prima facie* the *Reichstag* in 1936 expressed its overwhelming support for a policy of *peaceful* revisionism. □

Exercise   Please consider video-cassette 1, item 37, 'The Rhine' 12 March 1936 (the script of which you have already examined) as evidence of internal support for the remilitarization of the Rhineland. ■

Discussion   1   It is clear that the re-entry of troops into the Rhineland zone is popular with the local civilians. There is positive, active enthusiasm: waving of handkerchiefs and hats, offerings of flowers, cheering, taking of photographs. Note that few civilians give the Nazi salute: they welcome the event as Germans.

2   In the crowd scenes outside the temporary *Reichstag* and the chancellery in Berlin, by contrast, after Hitler's announcement of the remilitarization, nearly everyone is giving the Nazi salute. There is pleasure and excitement at the achievement *and* a mass expression of solidarity with the Nazi government which has brought it about. This identification of Nazi rule and the gratification of national feeling is further symbolized in the footage where the Berlin crowd both salutes and sings *Deutschland über Alles*.

3   In the Remembrance Day ceremonies in the Opera House (as in 1935 – see video-cassette 1, item 35), brilliantly stage-managed by Goebbels with dramatic use of lighting, music and symbol, the theme is of continuity of military tradition between Nazi and Imperial Germany. The solidarity of the army with the new regime (underlined in a fulsome speech from War Minister Blomberg on stage) is brought out by the lowering of the imperial banners and the joint singing of the national anthem and Nazi salutes. The theme of continuity and solidarity is personified in the presence of Hitler with Mackensen, veteran Field Marshal of the Great War on his right (and Neurath, Foreign Minister, on his left). Other ex-servicemen include Goering, head of the *Luftwaffe* (at the end of Hitler's box on

the right), Fritsch, the army chief, Raeder, the navy chief, and Seekt, creator of the *Reichswehr* under Weimar. ☐

Visual and aural evidence thus confirms overwhelming popular support, genuine and spontaneous, for Hitler's foreign policy in 1936, in so far as the remilitarization of the Rhineland was understood as the triumphant but peaceful vindication of national honour. Martin Broszat stresses that much of German society supported Hitler's active revisionism as long as it was accomplished without war. Hitler enjoyed 'support not only from the German middle class but also from the old political élite, from those sharing influence and power during the Nazi regime in the armed forces and the diplomatic and bureaucratic services, and even from most of the leading representatives of the Protestant and Catholic Churches' (Bull, *The Challenge of the Third Reich*, 1986, p.77).

The Rhineland *coup* consolidated Hitler's personal ascendancy. This was confirmed in the general election at the end of March, in which he invited the electorate (minus the now disenfranchised German Jews) to 'give their verdict as to my leadership' (quoted in Berber, *Locarno*, 1936, p.227): 98.9 per cent voted in his favour.

Remilitarization greatly enhanced his own confidence and the confidence of others in his judgement after what he privately admitted was the most nerve-racking crisis of his career. 'The world belongs to the man with guts!' he exclaimed after the *coup* (quoted in Fest, *Hitler*, 1977, p.683). He had taken the measure of Western statesmen and correctly foresaw that Britain and France would do nothing. Henceforth he would be still more daring and reckless in his defiance of the European *status quo*, advancing, as he boasted, 'with the assurance of a sleepwalker'. His standing rising far above that of the Foreign Office and General Staff, he succumbed increasingly to the extremist advice of Ribbentrop, Goebbels and Goering. In July 1936 he decided to intervene on Franco's side in the Spanish Civil War. In August he drew up a memorandum in which he insisted that the army and economy must be ready for general war by 1940 (see Unit 18, section 8); in November 1937 – the Hossbach Memorandum.

Britain and Appeasement

Britain after the Rhineland crisis was well set on the policy of 'Appeasement' which Chamberlain, on becoming Prime Minister in May 1937, was intent on carrying out more vigorously and consistently. British policy was not to stand by the 1919 settlement, but to take an active role in coming to agreed terms with German demands: to reach a lasting negotiated settlement on specific delimited issues instead of facing unilateral *faits accomplis*, like the Rhineland, involving dangerous and unpredictable international crises.

Britain's commitment to the *status quo* remained a limited liability. Even *The Times* agreed that the Rhineland crisis reconfirmed Britain's commitment to France and Belgium against attack. But as at Locarno, Britain took no responsibility for the 1919 frontiers in Central and Eastern Europe or for the integrity and independence of Austria, Czechoslovakia or Poland. Hitler was thus quite right to predict in 1937 that Britain (and therefore France) would do nothing to protect Austria or Czechoslovakia (the Hossbach Memorandum).

France

The Rhineland *coup* was a terrible rebuff to French policy and a revelation of chronic French impotence. France was forced to recognize what had been implicit since Locarno: that it was unable to uphold the settlement by force and that it lacked the military capacity to support armed action beyond its own frontiers.

France's ability even to defend itself was soon gravely and crucially compromised. In October 1936, Belgium, exposed by the remilitarization of the Rhineland to direct attack from Germany, repudiated its 1920 military alliance with France and withdrew into its pre-1914 neutrality. This completely undermined French defence strategy, since the Maginot Line stopped short at the Belgian frontier, leaving France open to invasion through Belgium, in 1940 as in 1914. Nor could France protect its Eastern allies, Poland and Czechoslovakia, or move to defend the independence of Austria, once the Rhineland was reoccupied, without out-and-out war with Germany.

The French government appreciated the German threat to the balance of power far more clearly than the British; but France had lost the will to oppose Hitler's challenge singlehanded and in 1936 in effect surrendered its foreign policy to Britain.

Italy

Hitler's success in 1936 was decisive in attracting Italy into the German orbit. Until then, Mussolini, despite much lip-service to fascist dynamism and for all his discontent with the 1919 settlement, had on the whole supported it. Italy had been a guarantor of Locarno. In 1934 Mussolini had prevented *Anschluss* after the assassination of Dollfuss by rushing Italian troops to the Brenner, in a bold stand against Hitler; and in 1935 he formed the 'Stresa Front' against Germany with Britain and France.

The invasion of Abyssinia, however, in 1935 signalled a switch to a policy of aggression, feebly (and in the case of France reluctantly) opposed by Britain and the League with economic sanctions, which antagonized Mussolini without saving Abyssinia.

The Rhineland *coup* increased Mussolini's contempt for French and British 'decadence'. Once assured that Hitler's pledge to re-enter the League was no more than a feint, he decided to align Fascist Italy with Nazi Germany and the Nationalists in Spain, intervening on Franco's side when the Civil War broke out in June. He appointed his pro-German son-in-law, Ciano, Foreign Minister, and in November openly joined the German camp, invoking a 'Rome–Berlin axis'.

The direct consequence of Italo-German *rapprochement* was the collapse of Austrian independence. Mussolini relinquished the role of protector of Austria as the price of German friendship. With his approval, Germany and Austria concluded a so-called 'gentleman's agreement' in July 1936, whereby Austria was declared to be a 'German state', whose foreign policy would comply with that of Germany. Provision was made for the entry into the government of pro-*Anschluss* Austrians. Meanwhile Hitler drew up plans for a military takeover of Austria, which he put into effect in 1938.

Russia

The revolutionary internationalism of the Comintern was by no means incompatible to Russia's rulers with a foreign policy based on *Realpolitik*. Lenin had shown this with his insistence on peace at any price at Brest-Litovsk and his view of Russia's treaties with Poland and the Baltic states as no more than temporary expedients. Ideological antipathy had not prevented good relations with Fascist Italy, or with Weimar Germany after Rapallo. Stalin, however, reacted quickly to the emerging threat of Nazism. As early as 1930 he appointed Litvinov as Foreign Commissar with a policy of co-operation with the West. While Russia in the 1920s had denounced Versailles and the League as instruments of capitalism, it changed its tune with the rise of Hitler, joining the League in 1934 and warning of the Nazi danger to Europe. Litvinov was an eloquent champion of 'collective security' during the Rhineland crisis, and whatever scepticism may be entertained about the duplicity of Soviet policy generally, the sincerity of Russian intentions about 'collective security' should not be dismissed as propaganda. The only state explicitly and repeatedly threatened with destruction by Germany, as Litvinov pointed out to the League with quotations from *Mein Kampf* and Hitler's speeches, was Russia. Narkomindel (the Soviet Foreign Ministry) believed that Hitler meant what he said about *Lebensraum*, and the Franco-Soviet pact of 1935 reflected this concern.

The Rhineland crisis, however, emphasized Russia's continued exclusion from European affairs as a result of British hostility. France desired Russian support as a counter-balance to Germany, but was discouraged by Britain from consolidating Franco-Russian ties. Encirclement of Germany was not compatible with the 'settlement' with it desired by Britain. In any case, Russia could not intervene militarily without the consent of the states of Eastern Europe, and, with the exception of Czechoslovakia, all were hostile. Russia was deliberately excluded from the Munich Conference in 1938 and continued to be discounted until 1939.

The United States

The Rhineland crisis emphasized the continued isolationism of the United States. The American Secretary of State, Cordell Hull, said that no appeal for American support had been received from any state and that 'he had no cause at all to concern himself with the Rhineland affair' (*Documents on German Foreign Policy 1918–1945*, series C, vol.V, p.66). Opinion in Congress was firmly isolationist. Problems in Europe made it more so. In 1937 Congress passed a permanent neutrality law, designed to outlaw foreign entanglements; and there was strong support for a resolution which would require a referendum before the United States could enter a war.

The League of Nations

The League of Nations as a peacekeeping organization lost all authority after the Abyssinian and Rhineland crises. 'Collective security' was dead. Europe reverted openly to power politics. The Rhineland, Nicolson lamented, 'does mean the final end of the League' (*Diaries and Letters*, 1966, p.250).

Exercise Please read Roberts on the League of Nations and its role in the 1920s and 1930s (pp.327, 346–50, 356–7, 511–15). Exemplify and account for the successes and failures of the League of Nations 1920–1936. ∎

Discussion The purpose of the League was to serve as the instrument of international conciliation that would prevent a recurrence of the catastrophe of world war and would oversee a general reduction in armaments. Member states undertook to submit their disputes to judicial settlement or arbitration, and the League Covenant provided for combined military action in case of aggression.

Roberts mentions the humanitarian work achieved by the League by way of famine relief, aid to refugees, and so on. He also lists, as political successes, the resolution of the Aaland Islands dispute (1921) and the delimitation of the German–Polish frontier in disputed Upper Silesia (1921).

However, in that it notoriously failed to prevent Italy's conquest of Abyssinia or to take measures to check Germany in 1936 (beyond formally declaring that Locarno had been violated – such gestures were compared by Dean Inge to 'resolutions by sheep in favour of vegetarianism'), or to prevent any subsequent aggression, the League must be accounted a failure as a peacekeeping organization. How are we to account for that failure?

Roberts explains the failure of the League by the absence of the United States (p.347), 'political rivalries' (p.347), lack of armed forces (p.349), lack of 'unreserved confidence . . . on the part of the great powers' (p.350). However, Roberts avoids the central question. The League was not in any real sense a 'supranational organization' (p.346). Sovereignty remained with the individual states.

The 'successes' of the League must be understood in terms of the *consensual* nature of international law. The reason why the measures taken by the League for the repatriation of prisoners-of-war, international control of the drug trade, control of epidemic disease in Eastern Europe, and so on, were complied with by most member states is that they were *willing* to comply with them; such measures were seen as in the interests of every state. Unanimity in authorizing these international activities did not make the League a 'supranational organization': it was simply the administrative and organizational channel through which agreed objectives could be realized. In this sense, the League was no more a supranational organization than the Conference of Ambassadors, the Red Cross, or the International Postal Union.

The same consensual basis explains the League's 'successes' in helping to settle such problems as the Upper Silesian frontier (Roberts, p.349). It was not the power or authority of the League which resolved the dispute, but the prior consent of the parties involved to submit the matter to the League. Germany in 1921 lacked the military power to enforce its claims. France strongly backed the Polish claim but, opposed by Britain, did not wish to take military action in support of it. Both sides therefore resorted to the League as an expedient method of resolving the problem. 'What Briand wanted was a way out which would justify his climbing down, and the League provides the solution' (Hankey to Balfour, 12 August 1921, British Library, Add MSS 49704/27). Conversely, in 1923, Poincaré decided on military action in the Ruhr rather than resort to the League, believing armed intervention to be more effective to counter Germany's breach of Versailles.

The use of force against aggression thus depended on the willingness of member states. In deciding this question, which was, after all, a question of war and peace, individual states were naturally concerned above all with calculations of self-interest. No state would risk war where it did not consider its own vital interests to be at stake. Still less would a state contemplate war where the outcome was doubtful. Thus, while members of the League were willing to apply economic sanctions against Italy in 1935, no state would contemplate war with Germany in 1936. 'The League "failed" because the British thought it was more dangerous to British security to use it than not to do so; the "failure" of the League was a consequence rather than a cause of British policy' (R. Parker in Mommsen and Kettenacker, eds, *The Fascist Challenge and the Policy of Appeasement*, 1983, pp.25–6). □

4 NEVILLE CHAMBERLAIN, 'APPEASEMENT' AND THE SLIDE TO WAR 1937–39

Exercise   Please read Roberts, pp.534–46, consulting Map 7 (Germany 1919–38) in the *Maps Booklet*, and document I.28 in *Documents 2*, Chamberlain's speech to the House of Commons, 24 March 1938, encapsulating his Appeasement policy.

What was Chamberlain's Appeasement policy, how new was it, and how successful was it in solving the 'German problem'? ∎

Discussion   Chamberlain's Appeasement policy was not new in itself. It had its origins at Locarno and even, in embryo, among the British delegation at Versailles (for example, Smuts). Ever since the Ruhr, British governments had sought, in some degree, to accommodate German national feeling by gradual, agreed revisions of Versailles.

As we have seen from British reactions to the Rhineland crisis, there was some sympathy with German grievances over Versailles and at any rate a desire to bring stability to Europe by coming to terms with them and adjusting to the fact of German predominance in Europe. Above all, there was abiding popular revulsion at the carnage and waste of 1914–18, and universal anxiety to avoid a repetition by reaching an 'understanding' with Germany.

What Chamberlain added was a sense of urgency and vigour, a conviction that he could 'do business' with Hitler direct. 'If we could sit with the Germans at the same table', he observed in June 1937, 'and, pencil in hand, run through all their complaints and claims, then this would to a significant extent facilitate a clearing of the atmosphere' (quoted in Haslam, *The Soviet Union and the Struggle for Collective Security in Europe 1933–39*, 1984, p.150). He spurned the League of Nations, which he saw as a time-wasting talkshop, which had alienated but not stopped Mussolini, whom Chamberlain continued, unsuccessfully, to try to isolate from Hitler. (Eden, who disagreed with Chamberlain's desire to appease Mussolini in February 1938 resigned, and was replaced by Halifax.)

Even if it could be organized, Chamberlain believed that 'collective security' against Germany, especially with Soviet participation, would be more likely to provoke than to deter war. Chamberlain wanted bilateral discussions, cut-and-dried solutions, and an end to drift, while rearmament, begun under Baldwin, continued apace. He felt that Britain had been in danger of sliding into war over the Rhineland.

Hence the British government's explicit refusal to be drawn into a commitment to Czechoslovakia, accompanied by expressions of British readiness to mediate between Berlin and Prague. Hence the visit to Hitler by Halifax, in November 1937, to find out, in effect, what Hitler wanted (and indeed to hint at specific concessions over Austria, Czechoslovakia and Poland). Appeasement under Baldwin had been largely a matter of responding to events, like the Rhineland.

Under Chamberlain, who dominated his Cabinet and personally directed foreign policy, it became a policy of actively seeking to pre-empt Hitler by offering Britain's good offices in settling his grievances and thus to prevent further unilateral *faits accomplis*. Changes in the 1919 settlement in the east, including the transfer of the Sudetenland from Czechoslovakia to Germany, were not objectionable to Chamberlain, provided that they were brought about peacefully and with the consent of the four Western European great powers (Britain, France, Germany and Italy).

Chamberlain was rightly alive to the danger of Britain's being dragged into war with Germany as a result of France's commitment to Czechoslovakia, where the crisis over the Sudeten German minority was accentuated by the *Anschluss* with Austria on 12 March 1938. Determined to forestall this danger, Chamberlain immediately formulated his policy, presented it to the Commons on 24 March (document I.28 in *Documents 2*), and followed it up with vigour, intervening directly in the Czech crisis.

● He pressed the Czech government to concede greater autonomy to the Sudeten Germans.

● He sent the Runciman mission to Prague in August to attempt to mediate over their grievances. (For the extent of Czech willingness to concede, listen to audio-cassette 3, item 12.)

● When mediation failed because Henlein (on Hitler's instructions) stepped up the Sudetenlanders' demands and asked for immediate incorporation within the Reich, Chamberlain flew to Germany himself, to see Hitler at Berchtesgaden, at Bad Godesberg and at Munich, where he agreed to Hitler's maximum demands for the immediate secession of the Sudetenland wherever there was a bare German majority.

The Munich Agreement (29 September 1938) achieved what Chamberlain sought:

1 a peaceful settlement of a European crisis by the four Western powers (Britain, France, Germany and Italy) and the exclusion of Russia;

2 the 'appeasement' of a German grievance by the revision of Czechoslovakia's 1919 frontiers in accordance with the principle of self-determination denied to the Sudeten Germans at Versailles.

The four powers promised to guarantee the rest of Czechoslovakia, once Polish and Hungarian claims had been met.

Appeasement postponed war, and gave Britain and France time to press on with rearmament (though it gave Germany time to do the same). But Chamberlain wanted permanent peace, not postponement of war; and that was what he thought Munich had brought, Hitler having assured him that 'this was the last of his territorial ambitions in Europe' (speech to the Commons, 28 September 1938). Chamberlain told the Cabinet 'he was satisfied that Herr Hitler would not go back on his word, once he had given it to him' (quoted in Middlemas, *Diplomacy of Illusion*, 1972, p.375). □

Some contemporaries and recent historians have asked: did Chamberlain have any effective choice of policy and did he not indeed make the best of a bad job? (See for example, Sir Patrick Donner, *Crusade*, 1984, pp.232–246; Roy Douglas, 'Chamberlain and Appeasement' in Mommsen and Kettenacker, eds, 1983, pp.79–88; Paul Kennedy, 'Appeasement' in Martel, ed., 1986, pp.140–61 and *The Realities behind Diplomacy*, 1985, pp.223–312; John Charmley, *Chamberlain and the Lost Peace*, 1989.)

1   Both France and Britain accepted that no military action could save Czecho-slovakia in the short term, and that to plunge Europe into war for the sake of preventing the Sudeten Germans from joining the Reich would not be understood or accepted by public opinion. It was certainly opposed by the Dominions. As over the Rhineland, France surrendered its foreign policy to Britain, in effect to Chamberlain.

2   Britain's military resources were limited. Its imperial commitments – regarded as paramount throughout the inter-war period – were over-extended. Overseas areas requiring a British presence included the Far East, the Middle East, and the Mediterranean. In December 1937 the Cabinet approved a policy document which listed strategic objectives in the following order of priority, reflecting the primacy of imperial defence:

(a)   protection of the United Kingdom against air attack;

(b)   protection of trade routes;

(c)   defence of British territories overseas;

(d)   co-operation in defending the territories of wartime allies. Chamberlain was warned by the Chiefs of Staff that Britain could not simultaneously take on Japan, Italy and Germany. It was accepted that Germany was the most dangerous.

3   British rearmament was not ready for war. Spitfires, Hurricanes, radar and anti-aircraft artillery were still only in production. The Committee of Imperial Defence advised Chamberlain that 'if war with Germany has to come, it would be better to fight her in say six to twelve months' time than to accept the present challenge' (quoted by Douglas, in Mommsen and Kettenacker, eds, 1983, p.86).

4   Economic decline had eroded Britain's capacity to rearm. As Chancellor of the Exchequer 1931–37, Chamberlain shared the Treasury's insistence on fiscal stability: the need to balance budgets in order to finance rearmament. As late as early 1939, the Treasury warned that continued high defence spending 'may well result in a situation in which the completion of our material preparations against attack is frustrated by a weakening of our economic stability, which renders us incapable of standing the strain of war' (P. Kennedy, 'Appeasement' in Martel, ed., 1986, p.152).

5   There was a clash between the Chiefs of Staff and the Treasury. The Chiefs of Staff believed that Britain's best hope of defeating Germany and Italy lay in a long war, in which the superior population and material resources of the Empire could be gradually deployed. The Treasury argued that given America's stated refusal to grant war loans on the pattern of World War I, Britain could only stand a year of war before its gold and dollar reserves ran out.

Exercise   Chamberlain's apologists thus argue that on the evidence then available, to go to war in 1938 would have courted bankruptcy and defeat in a bad cause. A. J. P. Taylor even asserts that 'the settlement at Munich was a triumph for British policy' (1964, p.234). Consider the counter-argument that Chamberlain's Appeasement policy was a contributory cause of World War II. (For a recent discussion see Sidney Aster, '"Guilty Men": the case of Neville Chamberlain' in Boyce and Robertson, eds, 1989, pp.233–68.) ∎

Discussion The argument against Appeasement is that Chamberlain blindly contributed to the re-establishment of German predominance without regard to the likely consequences for Europe (including Britain).

The cost of Munich was:

1 Disintegration of the remainder of Czechoslovakia, as Poland and Hungary followed Germany's example, and Germany stepped up its pressure on Prague. In March 1939 German troops marched into Prague, Bohemia and Moravia became a German 'protectorate' and Slovakia a German client-state. The only liberal and democratic state in Central Europe was finished off by fraud and brute force: Hitler summoned President Hacha to Berlin and threatened to bomb Prague unless he capitulated.

2 The further enormous disruption of the balance of power in Germany's favour, the accretion of Nazi prestige and a corresponding collapse of French and British standing with the abandonment of Czechoslovakia and its military and economic resources.

3 The lack of finality at Munich, despite Chamberlain's expectations. Far from satisfying Hitler and bringing stability and international *détente*, Munich was quickly followed by a rapid and dangerous increase in European tensions. We now know that Hitler, baulked of the *Blitzkrieg* against Czechoslovakia (which he had planned since at least the time of the Hossbach Memorandum), regarded Munich as a failure. At the same time, Munich increased Hitler's and Mussolini's contempt for the democracies ('little worms' was Hitler's description of Chamberlain and Daladier) and whetted their appetites for more. Hitler prepared for further aggression in Eastern Europe. Mussolini aimed at ousting Britain and France from the Mediterranean. In April he seized Albania. In May, Italy and Germany signed a 'Pact of Steel'.

Appeasement was based on the premise that Hitler had specific, limited objectives; that these were open to discussion, delineation and satisfaction; and that they related to the revision of Versailles along lines of national self-determination. But what if the cause of the Sudeten Germans was merely a pretext, Munich a stepping-stone to expansion against non-Germans, as *Mein Kampf* and the Hossbach Memorandum suggest, as the French, the Russians and the British Foreign Office warned, and as Hitler's subsequent take-over of Bohemia–Moravia demonstrated? What if Munich were simply a stage on the road to *Lebensraum*? Under these circumstances, appeasement as practised at Munich made eventual war more likely and the period after Munich no more than an armed truce.

Chamberlain seems to have ignored all these considerations, and, while he should not be criticized with benefit of hindsight, it is fair to blame him, as contemporary critics did, for failing to consider alternative arrangements if his perceptions turned out to be wrong. For all his good intentions (as Astor demonstrates), his perceptions of Hitler were consistently wrong while his confidence in his own judgement remained boundlessly optimistic. He does not seem to have shown any awareness of the risks he ran by Appeasement and which in fact materialized. And he rejected the logical alternatives of either giving Hitler a free hand in the east or of coming to terms with Russia in order to deter him, thus falling between two stools. □

Chamberlain discounted both America and Russia. America was wedded to neutrality, and would offer Britain 'all words and no action', he believed. This was a reasonable assumption in the light of American legislation of 1934 and 1937 prohibiting loans or arms exports to belligerents.

As for Russia, military opinion was sceptical as to its potential. Stalin in 1937 had liquidated two-thirds of the Red Army command. But more important, Chamberlain and his Cabinet were rigidly opposed to alliance with the USSR on ideological grounds. The policy of the USSR, as Chamberlain saw it, was to meddle in troubled waters, or to embroil Western Europe in war with Germany and then move in to take the pickings (a mirror-image, incidentally, of Russian perceptions of Chamberlain's policy). He was determined to keep Russia out of European affairs. On leaving to meet Hitler at Berchtesgaden, Chamberlain informed the King of his intention to attract Hitler by 'the prospect of Germany and England as the two pillars of European peace and buttresses against Communism' (quoted in Haslam, *The Soviet Union* . . . , 1984, p.182).

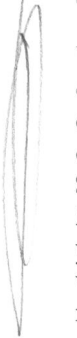

The immediate origins of World War II: Britain's diplomatic revolution 1939

World War II in its immediate origin was a quarrel between Germany and Poland over Danzig and the Polish Corridor, which erupted into a European war because of the intervention of Britain and France on Poland's side. Britain and France declared war on Germany, not the other way round. What Hitler wanted in September 1939 was a localized *Blitzkrieg* with Poland, not the general war for *Lebensraum* projected in the Hossbach Memorandum, for which Germany was not yet prepared. Ostensibly, as with the Sudetenland, the German case for revision was not implausible: the return of Danzig to Germany and a German road-and-rail link to East Prussia across the Corridor.

Exercise   Why did Britain extend a guarantee to Poland on 31 March 1939? Remember that this constituted a complete reversal of British policy since 1919, reasserted only the year before over Czechoslovakia. Britain had expressly avoided commitments in Eastern Europe; Austen Chamberlain had said that Danzig was not 'worth the bones of a single British grenadier'; the main point of Neville Chamberlain's Appeasement policy had been to avoid making the 1919 Eastern settlement a *casus foederis* (see document I.28 in *Documents 2*). Why the *volte-face* and abandonment of limited liability in 1939? ∎

Discussion    1   Public opinion in Britain, which had overwhelmingly supported Munich, was outraged by Germany's march into Prague. Before Prague, Hitler's demands had some appearance of legitimacy on the principle of national self-determination. Hitler himself had said that he had no more demands in Europe and wanted no Czechs in the Reich. Prague gave the lie to this, and Appeasement began to lose its lustre. Perhaps, too, as Churchill wrote (*The Second World War*, vol.I, 1964, p.304), 'Neville Chamberlain . . . did not like being cheated'.

2   The realization of the threat to Britain and France from the shifting (and now shifted) balance of power in favour of Germany. Unless swift diplomatic action was taken, other European states would draw their own conclusions from Anglo-French inactivity, and make their terms with Germany. Europe would fall under German domination unless action were taken to stiffen their resistance. As it was, a German attack on Poland was (wrongly) thought to be imminent. In April, guarantees were extended to Romania and Greece.

3   Munich had given both Britain and France time to bring rearmament up to a

state where both countries believed their armed forces at least capable of staving off defeat. □

Why no Anglo-Russian alliance in 1939?

Against the advice of the Chiefs of Staff, Chamberlain did nothing to conclude an alliance with Russia before offering the guarantee to Poland. Such an alliance might have convinced Hitler that Chamberlain was serious. As it was, Hitler did not believe that Britain and France would fight alone, and provided they were without Russian support, he was prepared to risk a general war. Preparations to attack Poland in late summer 1939 went ahead.

Litvinov was anxious after Prague and Hitler's seizure of Memel in March 1939 to come to rapid agreement with France and Britain. Germany was plainly about to strike eastward, and might ally with Japan – a Russo-Japanese border conflict raged from May to August. The French were anxious to over-rule their allies in Eastern Europe, since the reluctance of Poland and Romania to grant access to Russian troops was a stumbling block to agreement between Britain, France and Russia. Britain refused to treat these states as pawns in negotiations with Russia, thus appearing to let British foreign policy be decided by Warsaw and Bucharest. It was Russia, not Poland, that Chamberlain attempted to treat as a pawn, his tactic being 'to keep Russia in the background without antagonizing her' (29 April, quoted in Haslam, 1984, p.214), or, as the Russians complained, to treat Russia 'like suspicious characters with whom one has business and does not greet in the street' (quoted in Haslam, 1984, p.215).

This was indeed precisely the attitude of the government: Chamberlain had not renounced Appeasement: he was still hoping to arrange a resettlement of the Polish frontiers on the Munich model. The guarantee of 31 March affected Poland's 'independence', not its 'territorial integrity': Danzig and the Corridor remained negotiable. Thus Chamberlain hoped to avoid both fulfilling Britain's commitment to Poland and concluding an alliance with Russia. Such a wish was candidly put by the ex-Lord President of the Council, Lord Hailsham: 'I am more convinced than ever that the policy of guarantees in eastern Europe and its accompaniment of a Russian alliance is a mistake; if there is one thing that I could hate more than a Nazi hun it is a Bolshevik Communist, so that I am well out of the Government' (3 May 1939, quoted in R. F. V. Heuston, *Lives of the Lord Chancellors 1885–1940*, 1987, p.491). In truth, however, Hailsham's sentiments were those of the government.

Even when Litvinov was replaced by Molotov on 3 May as Commissar of Foreign Affairs, this did not signify that Russia had abandoned Litvinov's policy of alliance with Britain and France. It was at least as much of a reminder to Britain and France to treat Russian offers seriously, Molotov warning: 'the Western Powers must unambiguously state whether they agree to the clear and simple Russian proposals or not' (quoted in Haslam, 1984, p.215).

Exercise   How do you account for Chamberlain's failure to conclude an alliance with Russia? ∎

Discussion   Once Chamberlain had given the guarantee to Poland, the only realistic hope of deterring Hitler lay in alliance with Russia. Failure to clinch this lies with Chamberlain. His dilatoriness throughout the spring and summer of 1939 suggests that he authorized negotiations reluctantly and only under parliamentary pressure, and that he had no serious intention of coming to terms with Russia. He professed to believe that a statesman should never bluff. But brandishing the Russian card was surely a bluff: its aim – to deter Hitler by the spectre (though not the reality) of encirclement in order to force him to seek accommodation with Britain. As Taylor graphically puts it, Chamberlain was 'chalking a Red Bogey on the wall in the hope that Hitler would then run away' (*English History 1914–1945*, 1965, p.447). His policy was fundamentally unsound. In the first place, Russia suspected Chamberlain (rightly) not merely of playing a double game but (wrongly) of aiming to embroil Hitler in war with Russia, for which there is no evidence. On the contrary, the British government feared a repeat of Germany's victory over Russia in World War I, which would place European Russia under German control and enable Germany to turn on Britain and France. Second, and fatally, despite explicit warnings from the Chiefs of Staff of 'the very grave military dangers inherent in the possibility of any agreement between Germany and Russia', as late as the end of July Chamberlain refused to see that his policy would force Russia to come to terms with Germany. He 'could not bring himself to believe', he told the Cabinet on 27 July, 'that a real alliance between Russia and Germany was possible' (quoted in Haslam, 1984, p.213). A low-level British military mission, without plenipotentiary powers and with instructions to stall, was sent to Russia – by sea – at the beginning of August, and was unable to give assurances on the crucial question: would Poland, if attacked by Germany, allow Soviet forces on its territory, or if not, would Britain over-rule a Polish refusal?

Maisky, Russian Ambassador in London, told Harold Nicolson that 'he believes that Chamberlain hopes to get a compromise on the Danzig question, and that if he does that, he will allow the Russian negotiations to lapse. He says that he has a definite impression that the Government do not really want the negotiations to go through' (Nicolson, *Diaries and Letters 1930–1939*, 1966, p.406).

P. M. H. Bell argues (*The Origins of the Second World War in Europe*, 1986, pp.261–2) that even if Britain had acted with greater speed and conviction, Russia would still have closed with Hitler's offer of agreement – the Molotov–Ribbentrop pact, concluded on 23 August. Hitler had far more to offer: territorial advance to the Curzon line in Poland; a sphere of influence in Eastern Europe from Finland to Bessarabia and a non-aggression pact with Germany, that is, peace and expanding influence in return for mere neutrality. Britain and France could offer nothing except a possible military alliance, which might or might not deter Germany; if it did not, Russia would be drawn into war, in order, as Stalin put it, to pull the chestnuts out of the fire for Britain and France.

But in Moscow the Nazi–Soviet pact was considered a second-best, fall-back solution. Despite the immediate territorial gains which Russia seized once war began, Stalin was chiefly aware of the pact as a breathing-space, and that while alliance with Britain and France might have staved off the German threat, the greatest danger to Russia still came from Germany and Hitler's war for *Lebensraum*.

Bibliography

Adamthwaite, A. (1977) *France and the Coming of the Second World War 1936–1939*, Frank Cass.

Bell, P. M. H. (1986) *The Origins of the Second World War in Europe*, Longman.

Berber, F. J. (ed.) (1936) *Locarno*, Hodge.

Boyce, R. and Robertson, E. M. (eds) (1989) *Paths to War: New Essays on the Origins of the Second World War*, Macmillan.

Bracher, K. D. (1973) *The German Dictatorship. The Origins, Structure and Effects of National Socialism* (trans. J. Steinberg), Penguin.

Bull, H. (ed.) (1986) *The Challenge of the Third Reich*, Clarendon Press.

Carr, E. H. (1964) *The Twenty Years' Crisis 1919–1939. An Introduction to the Study of International Relations*, Harper Torchbook.

Charmley, J. (1989) *Chamberlain and the Lost Peace*, Hodder and Stoughton.

Churchill, W. S. (1964) *The Second World War, Volume I: The Gathering Storm*, Cassell.

Donner, P. (1984) *Crusade: a Life against the Calamitous Twentieth Century*, Sherwood Press.

Emmerson, J. T. (1977) *The Rhineland Crisis 7 March 1936. A Study in Multilateral Diplomacy*, Maurice Temple Smith.

Evans, R. J. (1987) 'The new nationalism and the old history: perspectives on the West German *Historikerstreit'*, *Journal of Modern History*, vol.59, no.4, December, pp.761–97.

Eyck, E. (1967) *A History of the Weimar Republic*, Vol.II, second edition, Harvard.

Fest, J. C. (1977) *Hitler*, Penguin.

Fink, C., Hull, I. V. and Knox, M. (eds) (1985) *German Nationalism and the European Response 1890–1945*, University of Oklahoma Press.

Fischer, F. (1986) *From Kaiserreich to Third Reich. Elements of Continuity in German History 1871–1945*, Allen and Unwin.

Grathwohl, R. (1973) 'Gustav Stresemann: reflections on his foreign policy', *Journal of Modern History*, vol.45, no.1, pp.52–70.

Haraszti, E. H. (1983) *The Invaders. Hitler Occupies the Rhineland*, Akadémiai Kiadó, Budapest.

Haslam, J. (1984) *The Soviet Union and the Struggle for Collective Security in Europe 1933–39*, Macmillan.

Heuston, R. F. V. (1987) *Lives of the Lord Chancellors 1885–1940*, Oxford University Press.

Hiden, J. (1988) *Germany and Europe 1919–1939*, Longman.

Hiden, J. and Farquharson, J. (1989) *Explaining Hitler's Germany. Historians and the Third Reich*, second edition, Batsford.

Hillgruber, A. (1981) *Germany and the Two World Wars* (trans. W. C. Kirby), Harvard University Press.

Kennedy, P. (1985) *The Realities behind Diplomacy. Background Influences on British External Policy 1865–1980*, Fontana.

Kitchen, M. (1988) *Europe Between the Wars. A Political History*, Longman.

Laffan, M. (ed.) (1988) *The Burden of German History 1919–45*, Methuen.

Lee, M. M. and Michalka, W. (1987) *German Foreign Policy 1917–1933. Continuity or Break?*, Berg.

Lentin, A. (1985) *Guilt at Versailles. Lloyd George and the Pre-History of Appeasement*, Methuen.

Lentin, A. (1990) *The Versailles Peace Settlement*, The Historical Association.

Margueritte, V. (1932) *Briand*, Flammarion.

Marks, S. (1976) *The Illusion of Peace. International Relations in Europe 1918–1933*, Macmillan.

Martel, G. (ed.) (1986) *The Origins of the Second World War Reconsidered. The A. J. P. Taylor Debate after Twenty-five Years*, Allen and Unwin.

Middlemas, K. (1972) *Diplomacy of Illusion. The British Government and Germany 1937–39*, Weidenfeld and Nicolson.

Mommsen, W. and Kettenacker, L. (eds) (1983) *The Fascist Challenge and the Policy of Appeasement*, George Allen and Unwin.

Nicolson, H. (1966) *Diaries and Letters 1930–1939*, Collins.

Post, G. (1973) *The Civil–Military Fabric of Weimar Foreign Policy*, Princeton University Press.

Robertson, E. M. (ed.) (1971) *The Origins of the Second World War. Historical Interpretations*, Macmillan.

Schmidt, G. (1986) *The Politics and Economics of Appeasement. British Foreign Policy in the 1930s* (trans. J. Bennett-Ruete), Berg.

Schuker, S. A. (1986) 'France and the remilitarization of the Rhineland 1936', *French Historical Studies*, vol.14, no.3, pp.299–338.

Sipols, V. (1982) *Diplomatic Battles before World War II* (trans. L. Bobrov), Progress Publishers, Moscow.

Stoakes, G. (1986) *Hitler and the Quest for World Domination*, Berg.

Taylor, A. J. P. (1961) *The Origins of the Second World War*, second edition, 1964, Penguin.

Taylor, A. J. P. (1965) *English History 1914–1945*, Clarendon Press.

Thorne, C. (1969) *The Approach of War 1938–1939*, Macmillan.

Weinberg, G. L. (1970) *The Foreign Policy of Hitler's Germany. Diplomatic Revolution in Europe 1933–1936*, Chicago University Press.

Weinberg, G. L. (1980) *The Foreign Policy of Hitler's Germany. Starting World War II 1937–1939*, Chicago University Press.

Wright, J. (1989) *Gustav Stresemann. A Political Biography*, Oxford.

INDEX